The Globalization of Cost-Benefit Analysis in Environmental Policy

The Globalization of Cost-Benefit Analysis in Environmental Policy

Edited by Michael A. Livermore and Richard L. Revesz

OXFORD
UNIVERSITY PRESS

OXFORD
UNIVERSITY PRESS

Oxford University Press is a department of the University of Oxford.
It furthers the University's objective of excellence in research, scholarship,
and education by publishing worldwide.

Oxford   New York
Auckland   Cape Town   Dar es Salaam   Hong Kong   Karachi
Kuala Lumpur   Madrid   Melbourne   Mexico City   Nairobi
New Delhi   Shanghai   Taipei   Toronto

With offices in
Argentina   Austria   Brazil   Chile   Czech Republic   France   Greece
Guatemala   Hungary   Italy   Japan   Poland   Portugal   Singapore
South Korea   Switzerland   Thailand   Turkey   Ukraine   Vietnam

Oxford is a registered trademark of Oxford University Press in the UK and in certain other
countries.

Published in the United States of America by
Oxford University Press
198 Madison Avenue, New York, NY 10016, United States of America

Library of Congress Cataloging-in-Publication Data

The globalization of cost-benefit analysis in environmental policy / edited by Michael A. Livermore,
Richard L. Revesz.
p. cm.
Includes bibliographical references and index.
ISBN 978-0-19-993438-6 (cloth : alk. paper)
1. Cost effectiveness.   2. Environmental policy—Developing countries.
3. Economic development—Developing countries.   I. Livermore, Michael A.
II. Revesz, Richard L., 1958-
HD47.4.C678 2013
333.709172'4—dc23
2012025648

ISBN 978-0-19-993438-6

CONTENTS

CONTRIBUTORS

Alberto Alemanno is Jean Monnet Professor at Ecole des Hautes Etudes Commerciales (HEC Paris), Adjunct Professor of Global Risk Regulation at Georgetown Law School, and Editor in Chief of the *European Journal of Risk Regulation*.

Miriam Allam works for the Middle East and North Africa Governance Programme at the Organisation for Economic Co-operation and Development.

Marcos Amend has been Executive Director of Conservação Estratégica since 2003.

Martha Macedo de Lima Barata is a professor and researcher at Oswaldo Cruz Foundation (Fiocruz), Brazil.

Wai-Mun Chia is Assistant Professor at the Division of Economics, Nanyang Technological University, and Associate Editor of the *Singapore Economic Review*.

Sarah Cordero is Costa Rican Center Director for the Institute for the International Education of Students (IES Abroad) and former dean of the Ulacit Business School in Costa Rica.

Maria Damon is Assistant Professor at New York University's Robert F. Wagner Graduate School of Public Service.

Jessica Donovan is Country Director for Conservation International in Liberia.

Georgina Echániz-Pellicer is an independent consultant on environmental law and education.

Leonardo Fleck is a program officer for the Andes-Amazon Initiative at the Gordon and Betty Moore Foundation in Palo Alto, California.

Verónica Garibay-Bravo is Director of Research on Air Quality at the National Institute of Ecology, Mexico.

A. J. Glusman is a legal fellow at the Institute for Policy Integrity at New York University School of Law.

James K. Hammitt is Professor of Economics and Decision Sciences at the Harvard School of Public Health, Director of the Harvard Center for Risk Analysis, and Visiting Professor at the Toulouse School of Economics.

Pawan Labhasetwar holds the positions of Scientist and Head, Water Technology and Management Division, CSIR-NEERI, Nagpur, India.

Keith Lawrence is Senior Director of Conservation International's Seascapes program.

Emilio Lèbre La Rovere is Associate Professor of the Energy Planning Program, Coordinator of the Environmental Sciences Laboratory, and Executive Coordinator of the Center for Integrated Studies on Climate Change and the Environment at the Institute of Postgraduate Studies and Research in Engineering, Federal University of Rio de Janeiro.

Anthony Leiman is Associate Professor of Economics at the University of Cape Town's School of Economics.

Michael A. Livermore is Executive Director of the Institute for Policy Integrity and an adjunct professor at New York University School of Law.

Kristina Mohlin is a PhD student in economics at the University of Gothenburg, Sweden.

Gonzalo Moyano is Visiting Professor at the School of Law of the University of Chile, Adjunct Fellow at the Institute for Policy Integrity, and Nonresident Fellow for the Climate Finance Project at the Frank J. Guarini Center on Environmental and Land Use Law at NYU Law.

Shahbaz Mushtaq is Principal Scientist and Deputy Director of Research at the Australian Centre for Sustainable Catchment, University of Southern Queensland.

Orapan Nabangchang is a faculty member of the School of Economics, Sukhothai Thammatirat Open University, in Thailand and Senior Economist at the Economy and Environment Program for Southeast Asia.

Christopher Neyor is a technical advisor to the President of Liberia on Energy and Climate Change.

Eduard Niesten directs Conservation International's Conservation Stewards Program.

Amaro Olimpio Pereira Jr. is an economist and Professor of Energy and Environmental Economics at Rio de Janeiro University.

Euston Quah is Professor and Head of Economics at the Nanyang Technological University in Singapore.

John Reid has worked in conservation since 1991, promoting the use of economics to address conservation challenges in the Amazon, Central America, and the Brazilian Atlantic Forest.

Richard L. Revesz is Dean and Lawrence King Professor of Law at New York University School of Law and Faculty Director of the Institute for Policy Integrity.

Lisa A. Robinson is an independent consultant who specializes in the economic analysis of environmental, health, and safety policies and regulations.

Leonora Rojas-Bracho is Director General for Research on Urban and Regional Pollution at the National Institute of Ecology, Mexico.

Jennifer S. Rosenberg is a graduate student at the Jackson Institute for Global Affairs at Yale University and former legal fellow at the Institute for Policy Integrity.

Thomas Sterner is Professor of Environmental Economics in Gothenburg, Sweden.

Gretchen A. Stevens is a technical officer at the World Health Organization in the Mortality and Burden of Disease team.

Jonathan B. Wiener is William R. and Thomas L. Perkins Professor of Law in the Law School, a professor of environmental policy in the Nicholas School, and a professor of public policy in the Sanford School at Duke University.

Eric Werker is Associate Professor and Marvin Bower Fellow in the Business, Government, and International Economy Unit at Harvard Business School.

Jiunn-rong Yeh is Professor of Law at National Taiwan University and Director of the Policy and Law Center for Environmental Sustainability.

PREFACE

While this book is about cost-benefit analysis around the world, our route to the global was deeply embedded in the local. In May 2008, we published *Retaking Rationality: How Cost-Benefit Analysis Can Better Protect the Environment and Our Health.* In that book, we argued that cost-benefit analysis as a tool of government decision making in the United States was here to stay and that, to be successful in promoting stronger environmental and public health regulation, advocacy groups should focus on mending, not ending, cost-benefit analysis.

The history of cost-benefit analysis is long; as Jonathan Wiener discusses later in this volume, it has roots in the foundations of modern government. But the recent history of cost-benefit analysis in the United States is very particular, and the perspectives of U.S. domestic political actors are deeply colored by this recent history. In brief, that history begins with the expansion of the regulatory state to cover areas like environmental quality and consumer protection in the 1960s and 1970s. As the power of administrative agencies increased, presidents took a series of steps to centralize regulatory authority in the White House and subject agency decision making to a rigorous analytic standard. Those efforts culminated in an executive order by President Ronald Reagan, adopted shortly after he took office in 1981, that vested the authority to review all newly proposed regulations in the Office of Information and Regulatory Affairs (OIRA) within the Office of Management and Budget in the White House. President Reagan selected cost-benefit analysis, a tool whose methodologies were grounded in neoclassical welfare economics, as the standard agencies should use to justify their rules to OIRA. For rules to move forward, the benefits of regulations, as defined by the standard economic measure of willingness to pay, needed to be greater than the costs that such regulations imposed.

Protection-oriented groups (such as environmentalists, labor unions, and consumer groups) were deeply distrustful of OIRA and cost-benefit analysis. In many ways, their fears were well founded: OIRA turned into a "black hole"—an utterly opaque office where regulations went in, but did not come out. Reagan had campaigned on an explicitly antiregulatory agenda, and used OIRA and cost-benefit analysis to implement his vision of smaller government. Protection-oriented groups' access to the White House was dwarfed by the ability of regulated industry to make its voice heard, and a series of battles between agency staff, Congress, and the White House helped cement the impression that cost-benefit analysis was anathema to strong environmental and public health protections.

In *Retaking Rationality*, we argued that protection-oriented groups overlearned the lessons of the 1980s, and, as a consequence, they have missed opportunities to improve the methodology of cost-benefit analysis and take advantage of ways in which the tool can be used to promote strong and smart government action. Especially during the Clinton years, groups continued to rail against cost-benefit analysis, even though OIRA's review of regulations using a cost-benefit standard began to attain the status of bipartisan consensus. In part because of this dynamic of regulated industries and antiregulatory ideological actors embracing cost-benefit analysis and protection-oriented groups opposing it, a set of biases and bad practices crept into the methodology. We argued that these biases and bad practices can be removed, and a new approach that is neither antiregulatory nor anti-cost-benefit analysis is possible, leading both to strong government protections where appropriate and to the use of cost-benefit analysis.

Our argument was entirely focused on the U.S. domestic context and was informed by our personal experiences. For Revesz, a turning point came when he was serving on the Science Advisory Board (SAB) Committee on Environmental Economics at the Environmental Protection Agency (EPA) during the Clinton administration, which was reviewing the agency's cost-benefit analysis practice. As a legal academic, Revesz had written a number of articles pointing out ways in which the practice of cost-benefit analysis was biased in an antiregulatory direction, and the SAB process was a way to help improve the methodology. But during those meetings, which touched on many of the most important questions in cost-benefit analysis, such as how agencies should value mortality risk reductions (the largest category of benefits for most EPA rules), industry was always well represented while environmental groups did not attend a single meeting. This was partly due to a lack of resources, but environmental groups are very adept at finding resources to participate in forums they believe are important. As we recount in *Retaking Rationality*, the deeper reason was that environmental groups had staked out a moral position that cost-benefit is wrong, "full stop." And when, in the words of fictional president Josiah Bartlet of *The West Wing*, "decisions are made by those who show up," environmental groups were left standing on the sidelines.

For Livermore, his time as an environmental advocate during and after his undergraduate education led him to the belief that to be successful, environmental groups need to learn how to present their arguments in economic terms. Over the course of several years, Livermore worked for the New York Public Interest Research Group, starting as a door-to-door canvasser and eventually running the organization's statewide campaign to refinance the bankrupt state toxic site cleanup program and create a new program to revitalize abandoned urban properties. During heated negotiations, in which pro-environment Republican governor George Pataki and a portion of the environmental community split with the Democratic State Assembly and other environmental groups, the regulated community consistently made economic arguments to which environmentalists were often at a loss to respond. Livermore saw that in the trenches where public policy is fought out, an inability or unwillingness to make economic arguments often placed environmental groups at a severe disadvantage.

Shortly after the publication of *Retaking Rationality*, we founded the Institute for Policy Integrity at New York University School of Law to promote and test some of the ideas we discussed in the book. At Policy Integrity, we work closely with nongovernmental organizations to help them use cost-benefit analysis in their advocacy, and we also participate directly in the regulatory process with the goal of promoting balanced economic analysis of administrative decisions. Since its founding, Policy Integrity has issued in-depth analysis on a range of pressing environmental issues, including control of mercury pollution from coal-fired power plants and regulation of greenhouse gases under the Clean Air Act. Policy Integrity has also worked with many of the most prominent national environmental groups, such as Earthjustice, the Environmental Defense Fund, the National Wildlife Federation, and the Natural Resources Defense Council, in addition to providing training and counseling to smaller environmental groups across the country.

Retaking Rationality and Policy Integrity have been warmly received in some quarters and criticized in others, but events subsequent to the publication of *Retaking Rationality* have vindicated many of our arguments. The administration of Barack Obama has moved forward with an aggressive regulatory agenda, while placing cost-benefit analysis even more firmly at the heart of the administrative process. With the appointment of Cass Sunstein, a longtime advocate of cost-benefit analysis and a friend of the president's from their time together on the faculty at the University of Chicago Law School, as director of OIRA, the president signaled that the bipartisan consensus on cost-benefit analysis would continue. At the same time, with strong new environmental rules on a range of issues, from automobile fuel efficiency to interstate air pollution from power plants, Obama has shown that cost-benefit analysis and strong protection can go hand in hand.

But it was the reception that our work received outside the United States that most surprised us. In the fall of 2008, an international student at NYU Law named Gonzalo Moyano approached us about organizing a conference on *Retaking Rationality* in his home country of Chile. We were skeptical that there would be much interest in our project outside the United States, but Gonzalo was persistent. At the same time, we recruited a law firm associate named Julissa Reynoso to serve as a part-time legal fellow at Policy Integrity, and she believed there would be interest in our work in the Dominican Republic, where she had both personal and professional ties. Despite initial skepticism on our part, she began outreach to the administration of President Leonel Fernández.

A few months later, after successful events in Santiago, Chile, and Santo Domingo in the Dominican Republic, we began to rethink our intuitions about the international relevance of our work. Of course, we were well aware that cost-benefit analysis is and has been practiced outside the United States for decades. But we began to see that the specific recent history of cost-benefit analysis in the United States could have useful lessons for government officials, advocates, and scholars operating in very different contexts.

In emerging economies all over the world, the rapid pace of growth is being matched by both increasing environmental risk and increasing environmental consciousness. This is likely more than mere correlation: growth in economic productivity is often accompanied by greater exploitation of natural resources and increased pollution, but it is also associated with the affluence that is a precursor to expanding societal concern with environmental quality. Emerging countries are faced with the dual challenges of continuing to foster economic growth while addressing very real local, regional, and global environmental threats.

In parts of the world where there is relatively little environmental regulation, huge gains in public health and environmental quality can be made with relatively small costs. In any policy context, the cheapest opportunities to achieve a social goal are likely to be utilized first. For example, the easy technological fixes with regard to water pollution were adopted first under the U.S. Clean Water Act, while the trickier problem of non-point source pollution from agriculture and storm-water runoff was put off for later. What this means is that for many emerging countries, which are at the beginning of the process of imposing environmental controls, cost-benefit analysis will show that environmental rules will be tremendously economically justified.

We directed our argument in *Retaking Rationality* to a skeptical audience: environmentalists and environmental law scholars who had rejected cost-benefit analysis, based on their experience with how it had been used in the United States. But for advocates, researchers, and government officials who were not burdened by that specific U.S. history, the utility of cost-benefit analysis for improving government decision making and, ultimately, environmental quality was clearer. This was particularly true for countries where development remained a key issue. In these contexts, a mechanism that can balance the need to expand prosperity with the imperative to control the negative effects of industrialization and resource exploitation is especially attractive. The link between cost-benefit analysis and a protection-oriented regulatory agenda was intuitive and obvious in a way that it has never been in the United States.

But if acceptance of cost-benefit analysis by civil society actors may be less of a problem, major roadblocks continue to prevent widespread adoption of this tool in many emerging economies. The expansion of cost-benefit analysis in some parts of the world has been limited by issues of capacity, the availability of data, and the absence of an administrative system capable of understanding and acting on sophisticated policy prescriptions. Also, experience with cost-benefit analysis of large-scale projects—like dams or roads—does not always translate easily into an examination of the effects of policies—like air quality standards or fuel standards.

As we continued to reach out to a global audience, with further workshops in Brazil and China, we also realized that the group of scholars, practitioners, and government officials who are carrying out cost-benefit analyses in emerging countries were often isolated from similar work happening elsewhere. Important efforts have been made by organizations like the Organisation for Economic Co-operation and Development, the Society for Risk Analysis, and the Economy and Environment Program for Southeast Asia to fill this gap. But there remains a somewhat fragmented discourse and set of practices around the globe as disparate international networks and isolated analysts attempt to adapt this tool to their needs. At the same time, these international networks and the accumulated work being conducted in domestic contexts all over the world point to a vast potential for cost-benefit analysis to serve as a genuine catalyst for environmental change on a global scale.

This book is meant to take a step toward realizing that potential. In October 2010, with the help of Gonzalo Moyano (then a legal fellow at the Institute for Policy Integrity), we convened a workshop in Abu Dhabi with the support of the NYU–Abu Dhabi Institute. Bringing scholars, practitioners, and government officials from around the world together for a two-day conference, we explored the ways in which cost-benefit analysis was already informing policymaking on a range of environmental issues in a variety of domestic contexts. We also discussed the barriers faced by developing countries that hampered the spread of cost-benefit analysis, and examined ways in which those barriers could be overcome. The papers presented at that workshop and the subsequent discussion form the basis for the chapters in this volume.

We are deeply indebted to many individuals who have helped make this project a reality. Several fellows at the Institute for Policy Integrity have made enormously important contributions. Gonzalo Moyano, now a professor of law at the University of Chile, was instrumental in building international interest for *Retaking Rationality*, identifying collaborators, and organizing the workshop in Abu Dhabi that served as the springboard for this book. Julissa Reynoso, who left Policy Integrity to serve as deputy assistant secretary of state and who has since been appointed by President Obama to serve as U.S. ambassador to Uruguay, was also an extremely important voice urging us to extend the reach of our work. Policy Integrity legal fellows A. J. Glusman, Jennifer Gomez, and Jennifer Rosenberg were extraordinarily helpful colleagues who worked closely with authors to ensure that the ideas in this book were clearly presented. Excellent research assistance was provided by Christopher Anderson and Razi Shaban. We are grateful to Policy Integrity's legal director, Jason Schwartz, and communications director, Edna Ishayik, for helpful comments and to Lia Norton for her editorial suggestions. Thanks are also due to Joseph K. Jackson, now at the University of Chicago Press, and to Terry Vaughn and the editorial team at Oxford University Press for their gracious and highly capable support.

Generous financial support for this project was provided by the NYU–Abu Dhabi Institute, Hewlett Foundation, Rockefeller Family Fund, members of the Board of Advisors for Policy Integrity, and former U.S. representative Frank J. Guarini. Many other individuals have provided important feedback and support for the project. In addition to the contributing authors for the volume, we would like to express our thanks to Leonel Fernández, former president of the Dominican Republic; Lan Hong, Associate Professor of Economics, School of Environment and Natural Resources, Renmin University, Beijing, China; Ricardo Katz, Associate Investigator, Centro de Estudios Publicos, Santiago, Chile; Philip Kennedy, Associate Professor of Middle Eastern and Islamic Studies and the former faculty director at the NYU–Abu Dhabi Institute; the logistics and operations team at NYU–Abu Dhabi (Maura McGurk and Sharon Hakakian Bergman in New York; Gila Waels, Nora Yousif, Tarek Chehab, and Antoine Jean El Khayat in Abu Dhabi); Al McGartland, Director, National Center for Environmental Economics,

U.S. EPA; Jorge Nogueira, Professor of Economics, University of Brasilia; and Mariët Westermann, former provost at NYU–Abu Dhabi and currently Vice President at the Andrew W. Mellon Foundation.

Some of the arguments in this chapter and elsewhere in this volume draw from our previous work: Richard L. Revesz and Michael A. Livermore, *Retaking Rationality: How Cost-Benefit Analysis Can Better Protect the Environment and Our Health* (Oxford University Press, 2008); Michael A. Livermore, "Can Cost-Benefit Analysis of Environmental Policy Go Global?" *New York University Environmental Law Journal* 19 (2011): 146–93; Michael A. Livermore and Richard L. Revesz, "*Retaking Rationality* Two Years Later," *Houston Law Review* 48 (2011): 1–41; Michael A. Livermore, "A Brief Comment on 'Humanizing Cost-Benefit Analysis,'" *European Journal of Risk Regulation* 2 (2011): 13–17; Nicholas Bagley and Richard L. Revesz, "Centralized Oversight of the Regulatory State," *Columbia Law Review* 106 (2006): 1260–1329; Laura J. Lowenstein and Richard L. Revesz, "Anti-Regulation Under the Guise of Rational Regulation: The Bush Administration's Approaches to Valuing Human Lives in Environmental Cost-Benefit Analyses," *Environmental Law Reporter* 34 (2004): 10,954–10,974; Samuel J. Rascoff and Richard L. Revesz, "The Biases of Risk Tradeoff Analysis: Towards Parity in Environmental and Health-and-Safety Regulation," *University of Chicago Law Review* 69 (2002): 1763–1836; and Richard L. Revesz, "Environmental Regulation, Cost-Benefit Analysis, and the Discounting of Human Lives," *Columbia Law Review* 99 (1999): 941–1017. We wish to thank all of the collaborators and supporters who helped make these projects and, therefore, this one, possible.

PART ONE

Introduction

1

Global Cost-Benefit Analysis

Michael A. Livermore, A. J. Glusman,
and Gonzalo Moyano

The application of cost-benefit analysis to environmental policy is widespread within advanced industrial economies. For thirty years, major environmental rules have been subjected to cost-benefit analysis in the United States, and the European Union has taken increasing steps to rely on formal and quantitative regulatory impact analysis that weighs costs against benefits. While cost-benefit analysis remains controversial as a tool to shape environmental policy (Ackerman and Heinzerling 2005), in developed countries the technique is likely "here to stay," and will continue to be a central instrument for evaluating and justifying regulatory decisions for the foreseeable future (Revesz and Livermore 2008, 11).

Cost-benefit analysis is no longer limited to these countries, however. Growing environmental and public health threats from industrialization have increased demand for stronger environmental policies around the globe, bringing the need for a systematic tool to compare costs to benefits. Many of the same questions that have arisen in the United States and Europe are becoming more common throughout the world: How clean is clean enough? What costs are we willing to impose to achieve environmental protection? How can we regulate to achieve optimal results? In answering these questions, countries are increasingly turning to cost-benefit analysis.

While cost-benefit analysis is not as prevalent in developing and emerging countries, the use of cost-benefit analysis as an aid to environmental decision making has expanded in recent years in countries throughout Latin America, Asia, and Africa.[1] In the context of developing and emerging economies, cost-benefit analysis has special potential to add quality, transparency, and efficiency to environmental, public health, and safety regulation. While there are important differences between regulating in a large, advanced economy like the United States and a small, rising economy like South Africa, appropriate use of cost-benefit analysis can help improve government decision making in a range of different circumstances around the world.

This book explores cost-benefit analysis of environmental policymaking at a particularly important moment: a new group of emerging powers, like Brazil, China, and India, have taken a more central place on the world stage, while economies in many places across Africa, Asia, Latin America, and the Middle East continue to experience rapid growth. Across the globe, expectations have been built for widespread improvements in living standards fueled by continued economic expansion. The situation presents obvious opportunities for tremendous advancements in human well-being, but also presents well-known local and global environmental challenges.

Balancing competing social goals is the heart of cost-benefit analysis. Defined variously as adoption of a "look before you leap" mentality,[2] as economic rationality, or, as described by Jonathan Wiener in this volume, "regulatory foresight," the core of cost-benefit analysis is the estimation and weighing of the positive and negative effects of government action. Recognizing that, in the real world of policymaking, difficult trade-offs must often be made, cost-benefit analysis attempts to render those trade-offs explicit, giving policymakers the clearest picture possible of the consequences of their actions. Cost-benefit analysis cannot always make these decisions easy, but it provides a way to aggregate the best available information about how policy choices will affect society.

This simple idea carries an enormous complexity both conceptually and in its practical application, especially as this tool is applied in a diverse set of policy contexts around the world. The chapters in this volume explore some of that complexity, attempting to bridge the sometimes-difficult gap between—in the words of Tony Leiman in this volume—"high theory" and "harsh reality." Starting with a set of chapters that examine cross-cutting issues posed by the application of cost-benefit analysis outside the most advanced economies, the book moves to a series of case studies located in very specific institutional, cultural, and political circumstances, and ends with a chapter drawing from both theory and practice to identify how our global experience to date lights a path forward for the development of cost-benefit analysis into a flexible tool with broad applicability. An overarching goal of this volume is to underscore the ways in which the practical application of cost-benefit analysis can challenge and improve the technique and our understanding of how it can be used.

The Advantages of Cost-Benefit Analysis in the Global Context

As the following chapters make clear, there are many challenges associated with the use of cost-benefit analysis in the developing and emerging world. But there are also reasons why cost-benefit analysis can provide special advantages in developing countries. Perhaps obviously, developing countries have less money to waste, and, therefore, mechanisms to ensure that regulations are delivering benefits that justify their costs are especially important. The economic problems within the United States and Europe that provided the political impetus for the adoption of cost-benefit analysis in past decades are small compared to the vastly larger economic challenges faced by many developing countries, where there is less social wealth to be spent generally, and on environmental, public health, and safety protections specifically. Given the more limited resources of developing countries, it is doubly important that regulations be able to achieve much with as little waste as possible.

At the same time, cost-benefit analysis will more easily justify regulatory expenditures, even in cases where governments face tight budget constraints, at the early stages of controlling environmental harm. Especially in countries where uncontrolled pollution or reckless resource extraction imposes large externalized costs on the public, substantial gains in environmental quality and public health can be achieved by relatively inexpensive investments. In the language of economics, improving environmental quality typically exhibits increasing marginal costs, meaning that the first steps are also the cheapest. Where there is low-hanging fruit in the form of a highly cost-effective intervention, cost-benefit analysis is perfectly suited to identifying it.

Cost-benefit analysis can also help improve regulatory systems that lack transparency, or in which special interest politics has become too dominant. Just as there is persistent concern within developed countries that regulatory agencies have been delegated too much power, there are similar questions about the exercise of state authority in many developing countries. Rules on transparency of government action, public participation, access to media, and judicial review are sometimes new, nonexistent, or poorly understood and enforced. Independent institutions that have power-checking functions in developed countries—like independent media, scholarly institutions, professional associations, and other civil society actors—can be weak, more subject to state control, or simply lacking the necessary information to bring government actors to account. More generally, democratic institutions can themselves be fragile, voters can be ill-informed about the day-to-day goings-on in government, and there may be ineffective oppositional forces to challenge ruling parties. While these same kinds of problems can affect even the most advanced developed countries, they are worse in many parts of the developing world.

Cost-benefit analysis improves transparency by making the decision-making process explicit, requiring decision makers to report their data, assumptions, and expectations, and subjecting analysis to outside scrutiny and criticism by experts. While the public may be ill-situated to evaluate cost-benefit analysis, scholars, political commentators, and civil society actors can review and criticize cost-benefit analysis in a way that is simply impossible when decisions are made behind closed doors. In this way, cost-benefit analysis can improve the ability of outside institutions to subject government actions to scrutiny. While cost-benefit analysis clearly cannot solve all of a society's transparency problems, forcing government actors to make both their choices and the information used to arrive at decisions more explicit can serve an extremely important transparency function.

A final important advantage of cost-benefit analysis is its ability to provide a neutral language with which to condemn unwise programs. The methodological limits of cost-benefit analysis create constraints on how far it can legitimately be stretched to justify wasteful programs that may be supported by political officials. At the same time, cost-benefit analysis casts criticism in a technocratic language that may be less threatening to powerful political actors. Cost-benefit analysis applies a neutral and universal standard, drawing attention to inefficient programs without resorting to inflammatory political or moral attacks.

Weighing Costs and Benefits

Cost-benefit analysis requires that the good things brought about by government policy—cleaner air and water, open space, biodiversity—be weighed against costs like capital investment, labor reallocation, and increased consumer prices. This requirement raises a host of valuation issues, which have formed an important part of the debate about how cost-benefit analysis should be conducted in both developed countries and in the development context. Perhaps the most controversial question is the dimension upon which costs and benefits are measured. In current practice, the standard measures are monetary representations of "willingness to pay" or "willingness to accept" (EPA 2010, xiv–xv). The compliance costs of regulation are weighed against how much individuals value the benefit that is produced by the regulation. Individual preferences, then, form the foundation for the practice of cost-benefit analysis, and give the results of analysis normative weight.[3]

Important questions have been raised about whether preference satisfaction is the appropriate dimension to weigh policy choices in the development context. Perhaps most prominently, economist and philosopher Amartya Sen has argued in favor of a "capabilities" approach to development, where standard criteria of development—like GDP per capita—are replaced with measures more finely tuned to identifying whether policies are providing people with the "ability to do valuable acts or reach valuable states of being" (Sen 1993, 30). The term "capability," which was developed by Sen, "represent[s] the alternative combinations of things a person is able to do or be—the various 'functionings' he or she can achieve."[4] Sen's ideas are not merely philosophical musings—they have been directly incorporated by the United Nations into its human development index, which helps structure a wide-ranging set of development decisions (UNDP 2010).

Happiness (or subjective well-being) has also been proposed as a more appropriate measure of progress than consumption or preference satisfaction. The country of Bhutan famously adopted "gross national happiness" to replace GDP as a measure of economic progress (Burns 2011), and even developed countries have questioned the relationship between economic growth and personal well-being (OMB 2011). Drawing especially on the work of Daniel Kahneman, Bronsteen, Buccafusco, and Masur (2010) argue that subjective well-being is the appropriate metric for conducting analysis of public policy.

The application of cost-benefit analysis in developing and emerging countries, then, raises numerous important challenges for how costs and benefits are weighed, even at the most basic level. This is the topic area addressed by the four chapters collected in Part II, "Valuation Issues." These chapters, which generally accept the standard economic framework of preference satisfaction as the dimension of policy analysis, explore different ways in which valuation in cost-benefit analysis can and should respond to the development context.

Euston Quah examines several market characteristics of developing economies that affect accurate valuation and explores how different valuation techniques hold up in light of the challenges of conducting cost-benefit analysis in a developing country. From disguised unemployment to financial systems charac-terized by firms exercising market power, there are important market distortions in many developing countries that can introduce error into the valuation pro-cess and that deserve careful attention by analysts. Surveying the standard tech-niques for assigning monetary values to nonmarket goods, Quah argues that the paired comparison approach, which is a relatively recent innovation in the design of surveys to elicit individual preferences, has important advantages in develop-ing countries over both traditional contingent valuation approaches and revealed preference studies.

In their chapter, Lisa Robinson and James Hammitt describe the use of benefit-transfer analysis to translate values derived in developed countries to the context of developing and emerging countries. Because of a relative dearth of data collected directly in developing countries, values are often transferred from studies done in developed countries. This practice raises a number of concerns, but, as the case studies in the volume will clearly demonstrate, practical realities often require its use. Robinson and Hammitt focus on the use of benefit-transfer to value air pollution–related mortality risks in sub-Saharan Africa, discussing best practices for the benefits-transfer approach and suggesting some innovations that appear particularly important when addressing low-income countries. The authors con-clude with the results and implications of their analysis.

Maria Damon, Kristina Mohlin, and Thomas Sterner discuss discounting of future costs and benefits, a factor that often dominates the analysis of long-term projects. The authors review some of the main issues that discounting presents and discuss some important recent debates over time-varying discount rates and the importance of relative prices when examining effects of public policy in the far future. The authors also collect and discuss the discount rates currently used by decision makers around the world, and explain how differences in level of devel-opment should and should not affect the discount rates used by analysts.

The final chapter in Part II, authored by Livermore and Jennifer Rosenberg, examines the role of distributional analysis as a complement to cost-benefit analy-sis and discusses ways in which the distribution of policy impacts could affect their valuations. For developing and emerging countries, many of which face extremely pressing issues of poverty and inequality, the distribution of costs and benefits can have important social impacts. Appropriately accounting for distribution is therefore a key concern. Surveying the options that are available to policymakers to account for distributional concerns, the authors conclude that certain types of distributional analysis are likely to lead to better decision making, but the wisdom of tailoring environmental protections to achieve redistributional goals cannot be determined in the abstract and depends heavily on a range of local factors.

Where Decisions Are Made

Institutions matter for cost-benefit analysis. In the United States, the practice of cost-benefit analysis of environmental decision making is intimately tied with the institutional context in which it arose. When President Ronald Reagan placed cost-benefit analysis at the heart of the administrative process in the United States in 1981, it was not merely as a substantive standard, but as the institutional reality of White House review of regulations that agencies, lawmakers, and interest groups were forced to recognize and respond to. The U.S. history of cost-benefit analysis is also the history of executive regulatory review, and it is impossible to understand one without an understanding of the other.

As the practice of cost-benefit analysis spreads around the globe, the institutional contexts where decisions are made and analyses are carried out will necessarily change. Different models of governance, market structures, and cultural, religious, political, and social practices will all affect how cost-benefit analysis is conducted, who it is consumed by, and how it is interpreted. Globally, the discourse around cost-benefit analysis within and among countries, and between domestic political actors and international institutions, will affect the types of analyses that are possible, both as a matter of imagination and as a matter of practical realities like funding and capacity.

The tremendous diversity of contexts where governance decisions are made in the twenty-first century raises many important questions for the theory and practice of cost-benefit analysis. The four chapters in Part III, "Institutional Matters," explore the way in which institutions shape cost-benefit analysis, from ways in which the decision-making institution influences how costs and benefits are measured and presented to how international institutions and networks have spread cost-benefit analysis methodology and capacity around the world.

In his chapter, Jiunn-rong Yeh discusses how changes in decision-making authorities precipitate changes in analysis, with a decision over casino gambling in Taiwan as a case in point. When cost-benefit analysis is prepared for executive oversight, it tends to include high levels of quantification and monetization; alternatively, when the general public becomes the decision-making authority, cost-benefit analysis has to be done in ways that are comprehensible to a broader audience. Yeh argues that when the general public will make the final decision, cost-benefit analysis must be done in a more dialectic way, engaging people with divergent concerns in discussions and presentations of their views. This dialectic process of cost-benefit analysis may help improve the quality of cost-benefit analysis as an effective tool for decision making and spur the development of different versions of cost-benefit analysis tailored to different decision-making contexts.

Alberto Alemanno explains that cost-benefit analysis, which is typically conducted from the point of view of the local country, tends to omit benefits and costs that are felt outside a jurisdiction. Through their cost-benefit analyses, countries assume that it is the right of the regulating state to act, irrespective of the external effects of such a regulation on other countries. But because of the broad interconnectivity of modern life, few regulations have purely domestic effects. Alemanno suggests that international regulatory cooperation, spurred by an interest in facilitating free trade, has the potential to promote and shape a different, expanded version of cost-benefit analysis. The trade effects of regulation provide a stepping-stone from purely domestic cost-benefit analysis to one that is more sensitive to global effects.

In his chapter, Jonathan Wiener discusses the international nature of cost-benefit analysis, tracing its roots to conversations between American and French intellectuals during the late eighteenth century and discussing the modern process of "hybridization" through which ideas about cost-benefit analysis, regulatory impact analysis, and review of the actions of administrative agencies have spread throughout the world. Rather than seeing a one-way flow of information from developed to developing countries, from North to South, or from the United States to the rest of the world, Wiener argues that the spread of cost-benefit analysis reflects a "modern reality of exchange of ideas across complex interconnected regulatory systems."

The final chapter in Part III, authored by Miriam Allam, discusses the role of the Organisation for Economic Co-operation and Development (OECD) in supporting the expansion of governance capabilities in Arab countries, focusing on the work of the Middle Eastern and North African (MENA)-OECD Governance Programme and its Working Group on Regulatory Reform. The Arab Spring has highlighted the urgency with which MENA governments must adopt ambitious and far-reaching reform plans. Allam argues that the extent to which regulatory policy tools such as regulatory impact assessments will help improve policymaking in the MENA region will depend on organizational capacities. She also argues that peer learning through the frank exchange of ideas and sharing of technical expertise can help pave the way toward the integration of evidence-based decision-making tools into regulatory management.

Harsh Reality

Every cost-benefit analysis of actual policymaking choices takes place under imperfect conditions. Data about the environmental and health effects of a policy are always incomplete, the possibility of corruption and noncompliance distorts predictions, and technological advances and innovation consistently defy expectations. Given that cost-benefit analysis is an exercise in predicting the future, it should not be surprising that the task is replete with practical difficulties and challenges. It is impossible to model the future accurately, with all of its complexity and randomness. But the alternative, of taking a blind guess without the benefit of the best information available, is unacceptable. So analysts must take advantage of the information that exists, leverage their intuitions and professional judgments, consult standard methodologies and assumptions, and give the clearest picture possible of what will always be a murky real-world situation.

The case studies that are presented in Part IV on pollution control and Part V on protection of natural resources demonstrate the determination of analysts to persevere under less-than-perfect conditions to help inform policymaking even in the face of great uncertainty. These chapters discuss studies examining the effects of everything from building irrigation ponds in China to electrification in South

Africa. Compared to the sophisticated cost-benefit analyses that are often carried out in developed countries—which can be multi-million-dollar undertakings carried out over the course of many years—many of the analyses that are discussed in these chapters are rudimentary, and all are limited by a lack of time, resources, and data. But the commitment demonstrated in each of these chapters to carry out balanced, forthright analysis of pressing environmental questions is truly inspirational. In the face of substantial challenges, the response demonstrated here is not resignation to failure but rather dedication to doing the best work possible in difficult circumstances.

The case studies were chosen to reflect the wide variety of circumstances where cost-benefit analysis is relevant, from evaluating gray-water recycling in rural schools in India to air quality control measures in Singapore. The countries in which these analyses were carried out are incredibly diverse, from relatively small countries like Panama and Liberia to large and populous nations like China, India, and Brazil. The world's major geographic regions are all represented, as are a wide range of economic circumstances, from countries that have arguably already "emerged" and could be properly considered among the developed nations of the world to those that continue to face highly pressing development issues. Our hope is that this diversity can help demonstrate the broad appeal of cost-benefit analysis in widely different contexts.

The collection of case studies in Part IV, "Case Studies in Pollution Control," begins in Mexico. In 2006, the Ministry of Environment and Natural Resources published a revised fuel quality standard in Mexico. To secure funding to produce low-sulfur fuels, the ministry was required to carry out a cost-benefit analysis of the health benefits and compliance costs. In their chapter, Leonora Rojas-Bracho, Verónica Garibay-Bravo, Gretchen A. Stevens, and Georgina Echániz-Pellicer describe the process that was undertaken and the challenges that the ministry faced in carrying out and obtaining approval of its analysis. The authors argue that, given the lack of thoughtful discourse among the agencies and the lack of a central oversight office, there is a risk that different agencies may take advantage of the lack of federal cost-benefit analysis methodology standards to manipulate results. They contend that a strong federal regulatory framework for cost-benefit analysis is needed.

Anthony Leiman poses the following question: How should governments in developing countries set about reducing the high external costs imposed by urban air pollution? The author suggests that cost-benefit analysis of proposed interventions provides one way forward and argues that South Africa has seen rising interest in the formal evaluation of air quality control interventions since the passage of the National Environment Management Air Quality Act No. 39 of 2004. Leiman discusses an analysis that he conducted of the economic costs and benefits of a suite of air pollution control measures, which found that the greatest benefit-to-cost ratio may exist in low-cost interventions that help curb the household emissions of those low-income households whose own members are the primary victims of poor air quality.

Euston Quah and Wai-Mun Chia assess the economic cost of air pollution on public health in 2009 in Singapore based on the newly revised air quality guidelines by the World Health Organization. Their analysis suggests that the health costs associated with a 15 μg/m^3 change in concentrations of particulate matter in the air are roughly $3.75 billion—about 2.04 percent of the total gross domestic product of Singapore in 2009.

Martha Macedo de Lima Barata, Emilio Lèbre La Rovere, and Amaro Olimpio Pereira Jr. address some methodological issues associated with estimating environmental mitigation costs in the Brazilian power sector within the framework of the voluntary targets for greenhouse gas emissions announced by the Brazilian government in 2009. Based on their analysis, the authors argue that the Brazilian experience has shown that tackling climate change early can be advantageous for technological innovation, the economy, and the social and environmental balance of the country.

Part V, "Case Studies in Protection of Natural Resources," focuses on cost-benefit analyses of projects to exploit, or protect, natural resources. Three of the chapters in Part V are drawn from the work of environmental organizations, using cost-benefit analysis directly in an advocacy context. The work of the Conservation Strategy Fund, an innovative nongovernmental organization working primarily in Latin America to train conservation groups in the use of economic arguments, is discussed in two chapters: one on the economic analysis of projects with forest impacts in Brazil, by Amend, Fleck, and Reid; and another on the distributional analysis of dam projects in Panama, by Cordero. Work undertaken in Liberia by Conservation International, an important conservation group with projects across the globe, is discussed in the chapter by Donovan, Lawrence, Neyor, Niesten, and Werker.

Because a substantial portion of Brazil is covered by the Amazon rain forest and because the rain forest is so valuable, environmental decision making in Brazil is closely linked with the Amazon. Marcos Amend, Leonardo Fleck, and John Reid canvass several case studies where researchers examined the costs and benefits of government-backed infrastructure projects with significant impacts on the Amazon. In all of these cases, the analyses conducted on behalf of the project were inadequate and failed to take into account a range of important considerations. The authors argue that the Brazilian experience shows that cost-benefit analysis can play an important role in shaping environmental policy in the context of an emerging economy. The authors conclude that cost-benefit analysis can add transparency to the decision-making process, force some degree of accountability for the effects of political decisions, and provide an important resource that can be utilized by civil society actors in their efforts to promote a more just and sustainable society.

Orapan Nabangchang explains that one of the most active debates in the field of conservation in Southeast Asia is whether local communities should be allowed to live on and use land and forest resources within protected areas. Policymakers are often deadlocked between conservation pressures to resettle local communities and equity considerations that favor allowing them to remain. Such debates are seldom informed by concrete evidence of the costs and benefits associated with resettlement. The author discusses cost-benefit analyses that were conducted for several policy options related to the resettlement of the village of Ban Pa Kluay, located in Ob Luang National Park in Chiang Mai Province in the Northern Region of Thailand. The analyses found that a compromise option, which did not involve resettlement, was preferable to either full resettlement or complete nonintervention by the national government. Based on this experience, Nabangchang argues that scholars and activists are likely to continue to look to cost-benefit analysis to improve the quality of policymaking, but for it to fulfill its promise, the usefulness of the technique will need to be more broadly recognized by the public and by political actors.

Shahbaz Mushtaq notes in his chapter that while parts of China suffer from water scarcity, this problem could be somewhat addressed in a cost-effective manner through small, multipurpose reservoirs. Cost-benefit analysis justifies this system because these reservoirs have contributed to the transfer of water from irrigation to higher-value uses by capturing rainfall and storing surplus water from other sources. The results of cost-benefit analysis show that reservoirs of all sizes are profitable. The author concludes that governments and investors should develop relatively large water conservation investment projects while limiting size so as to minimize the occurrence of serious environmental and social risks, and also concludes that more attention should be paid to conducting cost-benefit analysis of irrigation investments.

Pawan Labhasetwar observes that, because of widespread water scarcity, India has already invested a large amount of money in harnessing water resource projects. But these projects can have long gestation periods, massive cost overruns, resettlement issues, adverse environmental impact, costs and benefits that accrue outside the project site, and the potential for poor planning and execution as well as corruption. All of these factors introduce substantial uncertainty into large-scale water resource development. To answer questions about what types of water projects are justified, the government often uses cost-benefit analysis. In the past, large-scale dam projects have been particularly subject to cost-benefit analysis. For smaller-scale projects, the required scientific, engineering, and economic capacity to conduct such studies is sometimes lacking, but as knowledge of the technique grows, application of economic principles to small water projects has become more widespread. Labhasetwar discusses how cost-benefit analysis can be, and has been, used in the context of water resources in India, and concludes that, from small-scale projects like gray-water recycling at residential schools to analysis of the economic value of avoiding water-borne diseases, cost-benefit analysis can be used to inform decisions about how best to manage this precious commodity.

Sarah Cordero's chapter examines the importance of distributional analysis in understanding the equity consequences of government decisions, using as a case study the cost-benefit analyses of four hydroelectric projects contemplated by the Panamanian government in 2006. Detailed analysis showed that, while they may have some harmful effects, these projects were likely to generate net benefits. But the distribution of those benefits was highly skewed, with the Panamanian government and investors reaping most of the rewards, and local indigenous people and the environment incurring a large portion of the costs. Cordero suggests that distributional analysis can help inform policymaking to ensure that equity considerations are given appropriate consideration.

Jessica Donovan, Keith Lawrence, Christopher Neyor, Eduard Niesten, and Eric Werker describe Liberia's wealth of forests, and explain their cost-benefit analysis initiative and a plausible low-carbon policy process for Liberia. A low-carbon development strategy for Liberia would include a number of cost-beneficial policies, the most obvious being a transition to more efficient agriculture. Other beneficial policies include accelerating the establishment of protected areas; ensuring that tree crop plantations are located on degraded land rather than forest areas; and introducing energy-efficient stoves for charcoal and fuel wood. The authors conclude, however, that the net benefits of changes to forestry policies are less clear: reducing the number of timber sales contracts would be cost-beneficial, but replacing commercial timber with carbon concessions is more marginal.

The Future of Cost-Benefit Analysis

Like commerce, entertainment, trade, and communication, cost-benefit analysis has gone global. The question for policymakers, scholars, practitioners, and academics is how this reality will be reflected in the methodologies, institutional settings, and on-the-ground practices of cost-benefit analysis. This book provides no definitive answer to that question. Instead, it offers a window into how cost-benefit analysis is being practiced now and the types of conversations that we will likely continue to have as new contexts require this tool to adapt to new environments.

The final chapter of the book, by Michael A. Livermore, builds on the cross-cutting discussions in Parts II and III and the case studies in Parts IV and V to provide some insights into how developing and emerging countries have challenged, and may be challenged by, cost-benefit analysis. It discusses some of the recurring practical and theoretical issues in cost-benefit analysis in developing countries, such as the use of benefit-transfer, and how issues like employment can be incorporated into cost-benefit analysis using standard economic principles. Finally, the chapter discusses how cost-benefit analysis fits into the political process, drawing on more recent experience in the United States to offer a set of general observations about how politics is likely to affect the future of cost-benefit analysis.

Policymakers around the world face the task of making tough choices that can have significant impacts in their societies in the face of constraints on information and time. Cost-benefit analysis, properly reformed to take account of the circumstances of developing countries, can help in making these choices. While the technique will never be value-free or purely technical, it can help clarify value choices and ensure that policymakers are aware of the most efficient way to achieve their goals.

While cost-benefit analysis was developed in advanced countries as a political response to short-term economic downturns, it is a technique that has wide applicability throughout the world. Cost-benefit analysis serves the goal of rational decision making by aggregating available information, identifying goals, quantifying uncertainty, and helping political actors make choices that best achieve their social goals—maximizing the positive effects of public policy while minimizing its negative consequences.

Notes

1. The growing prevalence of cost-benefit analysis may make it a candidate for inclusion among those principles of national administrative procedure that countries are expected to respect, akin to other "global administrative law" norms such as the duty to disclose information and give notice of rules to affected parties (Cassese et al. 2008).

2. *Nomination of Cass R. Sunstein: Hearing Before the S. Comm. on Homeland Sec. and Gov't Affairs*, 111th Cong. 11 (2009) (statement of Cass R. Sunstein).

3. The welfare economics criteria underlying typical cost-benefit analysis is Kaldor-Hicks efficiency, or the potential compensation test, which derives its normative appeal from the fact that the outcome could be achieved through theoretical market transactions: "[The compensation] principle...simply amounts to saying that there is no interpersonal comparison of satisfactions involved in judging any policy designed to increase the sum total of wealth just because any such policy *could* be carried out in a way as to secure unanimous consent" (Kaldor 1939, note 1, 551). Criticism of this approach has been around for decades (Little 1957, 275; Chipman and Moore 1978). But what it may lack in terms of bulletproof conceptual support, it makes up for by offering analysts a tractable problem and a tool to process information.

4. Sen distinguishes the capabilities approach from ones that focus on "personal utility" (most akin to traditional welfare economics); "opulence" (presumably related to GDP, a common development index); purely freedom-based approaches (either negative freedom—i.e., libertarian—or positive freedom accounts); or "resource holdings as a basis of just equality" (distinguishing Dworkinian theories of distributive justice) (Sen 1993, 30). Nussbaum (1997, 287–88) identifies ten general areas where capabilities are important: life; bodily health; bodily integrity; senses, imagination, and thought; emotions; practical reason; affiliation; other species; play; and control over one's environment.

Bibliography

Ackerman, Frank, and Lisa Heinzerling. 2005. *Priceless: On Knowing the Price of Everything and the Value of Nothing.* New York: New Press.

Bronsteen, John, Christopher J. Buccafusco, and Jonathan S. Masur. 2010. "Welfare as Happiness." *Georgetown Law Journal* 98: 1583–1641.

Burns, George W. 2011. "Gross National Happiness: A Gift from Bhutan to the World." In *Positive Psychology as Social Change*, ed. Robert Biswas-Diener, 73–87. New York: Springer.

Cassese, Sabino, Bruno Carotti, Lorenzo Casini, Marco Macchia, Euan MacDonald, and Mario Savino, eds. 2008. *Global Administrative Law: Cases, Materials, Issues.* 2nd ed. 1–108. New York: Institute for International Law and Justice.

Chipman, John S., and James C. Moore. 1978. "The New Welfare Economics 1939–1974." *International Economic Review* 19 (3): 547–84.

Kaldor, Nicholas. 1939. "Welfare Propositions of Economics and Interpersonal Comparisons of Utility." *Economic Journal* 49 (195): 549–52.

Little, I. M. D. 1957. *A Critique of Welfare Economics.* 2nd. ed. Oxford: Clarendon Press.

Nussbaum, Martha C. 1997. "Capabilities and Human Rights." *Fordham Law Review* 66 (2): 273–300.

Revesz, Richard L., and Michael A. Livermore. 2008. *Retaking Rationality: How Cost Benefit Analysis Can Better Protect the Environment and Our Health.* New York: Oxford University Press.

Sen, Amartya. 1993. "Capability and Well-Being." In *The Quality of Life*, ed. Martha Nussbaum and Amartya Sen, 30–53. Oxford: Clarendon Press.

United Nations Development Programme (UNDP). 2010. *Human Development Report 2010. The Real Wealth of Nations: Pathways to Human Development.* New York: Palgrave Macmillan.

U.S. Environmental Protection Agency (EPA). 2010. *Guidelines for Preparing Economic Analyses.* Report EPA 240-R-10-001. Washington, D.C.: EPA.

U.S. Office of Management and Budget (OMB). 2011. *Report to Congress on the Benefits and Costs of Federal Regulations and Unfunded Mandates on State, Local, and Tribal Entities.* Washington, D.C.: OMB.

PART TWO

Valuation Issues

2

Cost-Benefit Analysis in Developing Countries

WHAT'S DIFFERENT?

Euston Quah

Nobel laureate and economist Simon Kuznets put forth the concept of gross domestic product (GDP) in response to a need for good data in public policy planning in the 1930s. Since then, policymakers have increasingly relied upon GDP and other national income indicators. Today, if only one macro indicator is available in any given country, chances are the indicator is the country's GDP. This demonstrates the extent to which national income has become the most important macroeconomic indicator.

However, as Kuznets himself and other critics of GDP have repeatedly pointed out, national income statistics are not ideal measures of welfare (Kuznets 1934). Of the many criticisms, two of the more prominent are the lack of consideration of equity and the fact that these statistics only measure economic activity and do not account for noneconomic costs of growth (Kuznets 1962).

The good news is that equity considerations are increasingly being accounted for by augmenting national accounts with measures of inequity (e.g., Gini coefficient). Unfortunately, no indicator for measuring the noneconomic costs of growth has been as successful as GDP in gaining wide acceptance; as a result, national income statistics continue to present only one side of the picture. The need for more data is clear—optimal policy formulation requires information on the trade-offs between choices.

The costs of economic growth are often nonmarket in nature, such as environmental harm or loss to psychological well-being. The list of nonmarket items is long; to properly account for the full costs of growth, all such items should be quantified, and any changes in their levels should be meticulously recorded. Additionally, to utilize the data to analyze trade-offs, it is necessary to assign monetary values to them. While this form of accounting may seem difficult to carry out, some semblance of it already exists in the form of what is popularly termed "green accounting."

Green accounting notwithstanding, maintaining a complete record of changes in the levels of all nonmarket goods is more of a grand vision than an achievable goal; the costs involved in such an endeavor are too high for most developing countries. Pragmatically, what these countries can do is account for these costs at the micro level by conducting cost-benefit analyses when considering public projects.

Why Cost-Benefit Analysis Is More Important to Developing Countries

Economic theory indicates that efficiency requires cost-benefit analysis. For developing countries there are three broad reasons why the need for cost-benefit analysis is especially pressing. First, to catch up to developed economies, developing economies need to grow even faster. The shorter the time frame for convergence, the faster developing countries need to grow. Based on the average growth rate over the last decade, it would take the least developed countries[1] approximately 190 years to catch up to the countries in the Organisation for Economic Co-operation and Development (OECD). The time required shrinks to around 130 years if the least developed countries instead grow at a rate just one percentage point faster.[2] Second, most of the world's natural resources are concentrated in developing countries. According to a United Nations report, the world's tropical forests are primarily located in developing nations (FAO 1997). For instance, the Amazon, the largest unbroken rain forest in the world, is largely located in Brazil and Peru. As a result, there is considerable international pressure on developing economies to take on greater responsibility for sustainable development. This was plainly illustrated during the Copenhagen Summit negotiations, when developed nations made it clear that they wanted developing nations to bear future responsibility in taking on the largest emissions reductions. Third, governments of developing countries face significantly greater budgetary constraints than their developed world counterparts. Taken together, the heightened urgency for development, the great international pressure for environmental conservation, and the relative lack of resources at governments' disposal mean that developing countries have to be extremely prudent about their choices of projects. In more popular terms, developing countries need more "bang for their buck." Since developing nations face the greatest need for optimal decision making, cost-benefit analysis becomes an important tool for estimating the net benefits of proposed projects.

A Brief Review of Cost-Benefit Analysis Principles

Given the clear differences in the circumstances faced by developed and developing economies, should cost-benefit analysis in developing countries differ? Answering this question requires a review of some fundamental principles of cost-benefit analysis (Mishan and Quah 2007). First, cost-benefit analysis must account for all benefits and costs of direct and indirect effects, including externalities. In addition, valuations must be as accurate as possible, reflecting the true social costs and benefits. This requires measuring use and non-use values, distortions in prices due to taxes or subsidies, and opportunity costs. Future benefits and costs must be discounted to allow a fair comparison in current dollars, and uncertainty must be accounted for through sensitivity analysis. Finally, double-counting must be avoided, and transfer payments should be ignored.

Clearly, the differing circumstances under which developed and developing economies operate have no bearing on the fundamental principles underlying cost-benefit analysis. However, in applying the principles, certain valuation techniques commonly used in developed countries are not appropriate for developing countries. To shed light on this, this chapter examines how labor, goods, and financial markets differ between developing and developed economies, and how these differences may result in erroneous cost-benefit analysis if certain valuation techniques are used. The chapter then discusses the relative advantages and disadvantages of employing various valuation techniques in conducting cost-benefit analysis in developing countries. Finally, the chapter looks at whether the limitations of cost-benefit analysis are more severe for developing nations.

Differences between Developing and Developed Nations and Implications for Cost-Benefit Analysis

LABOR MARKETS

There are three differences between developing and developed economies pertaining to labor markets that could significantly influence the results of cost-benefit analysis. The first is the higher level of disguised unemployment in developing economies; the second is the higher level of household production; and the third is the incompleteness of labor markets in developing nations.

Unlike in developed nations, the majority of the workforce in developing nations is employed in agriculture. In India, for example, 52 percent of the labor force is employed in the agricultural sector (CIA 2010). This in itself will not necessarily distort a cost-benefit analysis. However, a significant portion of these agricultural workers are actually employed in name only and paid a token wage despite making no marginal contribution to the production process. This practice is not uncommon in developing nations, where farm owners routinely hire family members and pay them a token wage, even when there are clearly no additional gains to be made from their employment apart from familial goodwill.

This phenomenon has serious implications for cost-benefit analysis, which requires that items be valued at their opportunity cost. The opportunity cost to reallocate a disguised unemployed laborer to a new position is zero. However, conventional cost-benefit analysis values the cost of labor using the wage rate. If a government project resulted in a laborer moving from disguised unemployment to a new, productive position paying the same wage, that new wage would count as a cost for a project. But, in reality, there is no opportunity cost associated with that laborer's prior position—the prior employer loses no productivity when the worker leaves, and just saves the wage.

The challenges posed by disguised unemployment are illustrated in the following scenario. Imagine a communal farm that currently produces $9,000 worth of output every year. The farm is co-owned by the whole village (population: thirty people), and all villagers who work on the farm receive an equal share of the total output's value ($300 per year). Because there are more than enough farmhands, ten of the workers do not actually contribute to the total farm output. That is, even if they stopped working, the farm output would remain exactly the same; therefore, the marginal output of the last ten farmhands working in the village is zero.

Now imagine that the government proposed to start a project in this particular village that would generate $1,000 in benefits. To carry out this project, the government will have to hire ten local workers, at a total cost of $3,000 (which is how much those ten villagers would have earned working at the farm for the year). A typical practice in cost-benefit analysis is to enter the prior wages of workers who switch jobs as a cost item, because it is assumed that their prior wages represent their productivity at their past jobs. Since the project reallocates their labor, the opportunity cost is the work they otherwise would have been doing.

Using this calculus, the hypothetical project yields net costs, because the wages of $3,000 are greater than the benefits of $1,000. However, in truth, the opportunity cost for the ten farmhands giving up their previous employment should be zero, since their marginal productivity was zero. When they quit working at the farm, it continues to generate $9,000 worth of output. The average output per farmhand increases to $450, because ten of the original workers no longer draw income from the farm. Those ten workers, in their new positions, together generate $1,000 worth of value. Adding together the farm and the new government project, the total productivity for the village is now $10,000. Indeed, the government could pay for the project by taxing the twenty villagers that remain as farmhands, and everyone could be made better off by the new project's additional benefits.

There is a caveat. Although hiring the disguised unemployed is said to carry zero opportunity costs based on productivity, this does not account for the value of forgone leisure or household production, including childcare and household work and maintenance. Such items may be significant if leisure is highly valued by individuals or if a large portion of the disguised unemployed are indeed actually employed in valuable household production.

This leads us to our next point: there are higher levels of household production in developing nations than in developed nations. Household production is defined as the production of goods and services by the members of a household for their own consumption, using their own capital and their own unpaid labor.[3] This value is difficult to measure. Valuation methods generally fall into two categories: the opportunity cost method, where household production is valued at the forgone wage rate, and the replacement cost method, where the value is the cost of employing other people to do the work (Quah 1993).

In developed economies, household production can be priced because labor markets are generally efficient and reflect opportunity costs, and because demand for hired help exists. The same cannot be said for developing economies, where labor markets are largely incomplete and households undertake most household production, as the name suggests. The households do not pay themselves for their household production, and, therefore, such production cannot be easily priced. The same problem can be seen in the production that occurs in the underground economy.

The valuation problem is twofold. First, there is the methodological issue that techniques that rely on market behavior to measure preferences will be inadequate because markets for hired help either do not exist or are significantly incomplete in developing countries. Second, the higher levels of production undertaken by households mean that cost-benefit analysis, which does not incorporate this production, is biased and inaccurate. While developed nations may sometimes face similar problems in conducting cost-benefit analysis, the scale of the impact is much smaller. Accordingly, the accuracy of the cost-benefit analysis is much higher because of the existence and relative efficiency of the market for hired help and the much lower levels of household production.

The third difference between labor markets in developing and developed economies is their relative incompleteness and, hence, inefficiency of the former when compared to the latter. This arises for a variety of reasons, including the extent of information failure and the ability of employers in developing countries to exercise monopsonistic (single buyer) power in the labor market.

The implication of the above differences is that wages in developing countries rarely reflect an individual's valuation of job attributes. In an efficient labor market, by contrast, undesirable job attributes are compensated with wage premiums, which may then be used to place a value on the job attributes. The wage premiums represent individuals' willingness to accept the disutility arising from the undesirable job attribute. The implication for cost-benefit analysis in developing countries is that intangible job characteristics, such as status and location, cannot be valued using hedonic pricing. A specific implication is the potential error in estimating the value of statistical life (VSL), which is conventionally calculated by studying the wage premiums associated with the increased level of risk of losing one's life on the job, and then extrapolating to estimate the theoretical amount required to compensate someone for the loss of life (Mishan and Quah 2007). Using wage premiums that do not accurately reflect the compensation required for the differing levels of risk results in an erroneous VSL. This has severe implications for all other cost-benefit analyses that will be used to evaluate projects that impact health and safety, since the values of many costs and benefits are derived from the VSL.

GOODS MARKETS

Another major difference between developing and developed economies is that the goods markets in developing economies are likely to be less efficient than those of developed economies because of information asymmetry. The disparity is even more apparent since the advent of the Internet, which has, by and large, been more accessible to and more effectively utilized by the developed world. This point is best illustrated by the growth of online shopping, which has driven down prices in the developed world but has not had the same impact in the developing world.

Additionally, unlike in developed economies, the goods markets of developing countries are more likely to be distorted by taxation, subsidies, or other forms of governmental intervention (Dinwiddy and Teal 1996).

The inefficiencies and distortions of the goods markets mean that in developing countries, prices may not reflect the true values of goods. Therefore, using prices to value input items, as is usually done in developed countries, would likely result in an inaccurate cost-benefit analysis in a developing country.

An indirect issue that arises from the inefficiencies and distortions of the goods markets is the valuation of intangibles and externalities. Typically, in developed economies where the goods markets are considered efficient, intangibles and externalities are valued in relation to consumption through a revealed preference approach. For example, in estimating the value of national parks and related recreation in the United States, the travel cost approach is commonly used. This approach obtains a demand curve by examining the price of recreation in a national park, which is the cost visitors are willing to pay to travel to visit the park (Fix and Loomis 1997; Beal 1995). However, the credibility of such revealed preferences breaks down when a goods market does not produce prices that reflect the true value of a good. In the example of the national park, if fuel were distributed through a rationing system, then the private cost of traveling would be very hard to determine, and the demand curve obtained through typical techniques would be inaccurate. Rations and other forms of price distortions are prevalent in many countries in the developing world. The consensus is that where there are market distortions, shadow prices should be used.[4]

The calculation of shadow prices is also subject to complications and much debate. Tradable goods in developing economies are an example of a class of goods for which it is difficult to obtain shadow prices. The problem arises due to the fact that exchange rates are required in the calculation of shadow prices for tradable goods. Unlike developed economies, the exchange rates of developing economies may fluctuate wildly and may not be reflective of the appropriate exchange rates. Cost-benefit analysis practitioners in developing countries must be mindful of the accuracy of their techniques in shadow price calculation.

FINANCIAL MARKETS

Like the labor and goods markets, the financial markets in developing economies are weaker than those in developed economies. Private banks in developing countries usually wield considerable monopolistic power, which they may exploit by charging interest rates above what a free market would produce (Yildirim and Philippatos 2007). This bears on the issue of discounting, as the social discount rate takes into account both the opportunity cost of capital and a society's time preference. In developed economies, the opportunity cost of capital is usually estimated by the market interest rate. This is reasonable because financial markets in developed economies are generally mature enough to generate sufficient competition to drive down the market interest rate so that it truly reflects the opportunity cost of capital. Thus, it is less contentious to use the market interest rate to represent the opportunity cost of capital in calculating the social discount rate in developed economies. Unfortunately, the same cannot be said for developing economies.

Interest rates in developing economies are likely to be higher than the true opportunity cost of capital, because of profiteering by private banks. If the social discount rate for developing economies is calculated using the market interest rate as the opportunity cost of capital, the result is a higher social discount rate than is appropriate. Consequently, both future benefits and costs are more heavily discounted, and cost-benefit analysis is biased in favor of projects that yield short-term benefits and long-term costs.

The market power exercised by private banks is different from the way that time preferences between developing and developed societies are influenced by other social and economic factors. Populations in developing economies have shorter life spans and lower incomes. Thus, these populations often have a higher preference for current, rather than future, consumption when compared to the preferences of populations in developed countries. Developing societies are likely to have shorter time preferences, and, all else being equal, their social discount rates will, therefore, be higher. This difference is not the result of some inefficiency in the market, but reflects genuine differences in individual preferences. However, where interest rates are inefficiently high because of the market power exercised by local banks, use of that market discount rate will bias results against projects with long-term benefits.

Overall, the nature of the labor, goods, and financial markets in developing economies clearly differs from those in developed economies. These differences can significantly affect the result and accuracy of a cost-benefit analysis if certain valuation or discounting techniques are used. These distinctions between developed and developing economies should be kept in mind by analysts seeking to develop accurate measures of the costs and benefits of social policies in developing countries.

Relative Advantages and Disadvantages of Various Valuation Techniques in Conducting Cost-Benefit Analysis in Developing Economies

Valuation techniques in cost-benefit analysis may be broadly classified into two categories: revealed preference approaches and stated preference approaches. Revealed preference approaches are indirect methods that attempt to discern the values of items by observing how people behave. To find out the value people attach to a particular view from a house (for example, a sea view), hedonic pricing— a revealed preference approach—may be employed. This involves comparing the prices of two houses that are similar in every aspect apart from the view. The price differential is then taken to be the value people attach to the view. Stated preference approaches are methods based on directly eliciting individuals' preferences. Going back to the example of valuing a view, a stated preference approach—called the contingent valuation method—could be used. It would entail a survey requiring people to state how much they would be willing to pay for a particular view

(Quah and Tan 1999). Hedonic pricing and the contingent valuation method are the prototypical examples of each approach.

Neither method is perfect. Most revealed preference approaches, including hedonic pricing and the travel cost method, require strong assumptions of rationality, perfect information, and perfect mobility to be valid (Quah and Ong 2009), while stated preference approaches, including the contingent valuation method, are susceptible to a large number of behavioral effects (Kahneman and Knetsch 1992; Carson et al. 2001) and methodological biases. In the context of a developing nation, such flaws may be magnified. We look at each approach in turn.

As illustrated in the previous section, incomplete accounting in the labor, goods, and financial markets in developing economies makes the assumptions required by revealed preference approaches untenable. Stated preference approaches may not be entirely suitable for developing economies either. The behavioral effects may be even more pronounced in developing economies because of the relative rarity of people's experiences in survey participation. Research (List 2003) shows that behavioral effects are, at least in part, brought about by a lack of experience with the decision-making circumstances. Therefore, the magnitude of behavioral biases in stated preference approaches is likely to be much more significant in developing nations. Methodological biases in stated preference approaches also tend to be larger in developing nations because of the lack of trained interviewers (Hanley and Barbier 2009). One common problem is the inability of both interviewers and interviewees to differentiate between willingness to pay and ability to pay. Such misunderstandings are further exacerbated by cultural and linguistic differences. Additionally, surveys typically carry significant costs that cash-strapped governments will be hard-pressed to cover.

A third valuation technique, the paired comparison approach, may prove to be the best solution, as it avoids the obvious flaws of the other two methodological classes (Quah et al., 2006). The paired comparison approach uses a survey to elicit individual preferences for public and environmental goods. Sets of elements are presented in pairs as discrete binary choices in a survey. The set may include gains, losses, activities, environmental resources, or anything else being scaled. Respondents choose the item that they feel is more important, in the sense that larger compensation should be paid for it than for the other (Rutherford et al. 1998). The variance stable rank method is then used to derive the ranking. This method takes the total number of times an element is selected by all respondents and divides it by the maximum number of times it could have been selected. Ordinal rankings are derived based on the results, with some degree of discretion allowed since some elements may have the same ranking.

Since a paired comparison uses surveys, like stated preference methods, it avoids the need for the strong assumptions required by revealed preference methods. It also overcomes the key behavioral effect that plagues contingent valuation methods, which is known as the endowment effect. The endowment effect uses willingness to pay, which is obtained from a buyer's point of view; by contrast, willingness to accept is obtained from a seller's perspective. These different reference points often result in different valuations (Knetsch and Sinden 1984). Paired comparisons offer a third reference point—that of the selector. As no real or perceived loss occurs in this case, behavioral effects like loss aversion, which can impact the results of a willingness to accept survey, are avoided (Kahneman, Ritov, and Schkade 1999).

Detractors claim that the paired comparison method has the severe drawback of not providing a measure of the net benefits derived from a project. While the method may indicate a society's priorities and may prove useful to policymakers in deciding which projects should take precedence over others, this method does not provide policymakers with information on how to get the maximum mileage out of their dollars. However, this concern can be addressed by including monetary items in the paired comparison choice set. Rankings of all items, both monetary and nonmarket, can then provide estimates of the upper and lower bounds of the monetary values of the nonmarket items.

While neither revealed nor stated preference approaches are entirely suitable for developing nations, a paired comparison approach may prove to be a valid and useful option. Nonetheless, in conducting cost-benefit analysis, governments of developing economies will have to exercise caution in choosing the most appropriate valuation method for their purposes in order to avoid distortions.

The Severity of the Limitations of Cost-Benefit Analysis for Developing Nations

A serious criticism of cost-benefit analysis is that it may result in foregoing equity in the pursuit of efficiency. In a typical cost-benefit analysis, the value of a dollar does not reflect who receives the benefits of a project or who pays its costs. Hence, it is conceivable that cost-benefit analysis could increase inequity by approving projects that yield net benefits even when most of the benefits accrue to the rich and most of the costs are borne by the poor. In a developed nation, this is not as big a problem, as there are usually governmental channels, such as progressive taxation and estate taxes, to redistribute wealth and prevent the income gap from widening too much or too quickly. Developing nations, however, tend to lack such channels. In fact, prevalent corruption—a chronic problem for most developing nations—specifically prevents the formation of such channels, because it is often in politicians' interests to line the pockets of their business-sector donors.

Additionally, income inequality is generally a larger problem for developing nations than for developed nations. When ranked by their Gini coefficients, the ten countries with the highest income inequalities are all developing nations, while the majority of the ten countries with the lowest income inequalities are developed nations (UNDP 2009).

Cost-benefit analysis need not completely ignore equity. One commonly proposed strategy is to apply weights to costs and benefits, to reflect the relative importance of monetary values to different social classes. For example, benefits or costs accruing to low-income groups may be multiplied so that the costs and benefits to them are magnified, and projects in their favor will have better chances of being approved.

While this principle is basically sound, the application of this weighting is highly problematic. First, there is the technical issue of determining what weights should be employed to adequately address inequity. While it is clear that the greater the importance attached to inequity issues, the larger the weights should be, the appropriate number is often difficult to calculate. One possible solution is to infer the implicit weights attached to different social groups by examining existing policies. However, this solution is problematic, as it can merely reinforce existing biases, which may be completely unjustified in the first place.

A second concern is the possibility of abuse. With equity weighting, cost-benefit analysis could be manipulated to produce any result desired simply by adjusting the weights attached to a particular group's welfare. In developing countries, the possibility of abuse is higher because of the relative lack of checks and balances on ruling powers. This further renders the usage of weights to address the inequity issue unsuitable for developing economies and, consequently, reduces the ability of cost-benefit analysis to take into account inequity issues in these economies.

Conclusion

As this discussion indicates, there are both similarities and differences between cost-benefit analyses conducted in developed and in developing countries. While the fundamental principles underlying cost-benefit analysis remain unchanged, the methodologies that are most appropriate in each context may differ. In fact, it is precisely in abiding by those principles that certain valuation techniques may become unsuitable. For example, it is specifically through the desire to achieve accurate valuations—a cardinal principle of cost-benefit analysis—that the incompleteness of the labor, goods, and financial markets in developing economies may render revealed preference approaches unsuitable and inferior to stated preference and paired comparison approaches.

In addition, the overall merits and limitations of cost-benefit analysis shift depending on the state of economic advancement. The need for cost-benefit analysis is indeed more pressing for developing economies, since they must contend with a number of conflicting and yet critically important goals, such as increasing economic growth while nonetheless conserving natural resources. However, cost-benefit analysis has severe limitations regarding equity concerns, which poses a pronounced challenge for developing economies utilizing the technique. The question then follows: should governments of developing economies employ cost-benefit analysis as a decision-making tool?

This analysis has argued that cost-benefit analysis can, and should, be used by the developing world. Cost-benefit analysis is a very useful tool for policymakers. Conducting the analysis requires asking important questions, including what costs and benefits should be measured and how to measure them; what communities will receive the benefits and pay the costs; how uncertainties and equity issues will be addressed; what the appropriate investment decision criteria are; and whether there are constraints on the results. Systematic decision making that uses consistent and transparent methodologies is valuable in formulating public policy in both developed and developing countries.

At the same time, cost-benefit analysis can only fulfill its potential if three important issues are taken into account. First, cost-benefit analysis is only meant to be a guide and should not be the final or only arbiter of project proposals. Second, in conducting cost-benefit analysis, the appropriate valuation techniques must be selected. Finally, potential equity issues must be independently considered and treated as an imperative complement to a robust cost-benefit analysis.

Notes

1. As defined by the United Nations Statistics division. The list of all forty-nine countries may be obtained from http://unstats.un.org/unsd/methods/m49/m49regin.htm#least.

2. The data involved in the calculation were obtained from the World Bank World Development Indicators Database.

3. For a more detailed definition, see Ironmonger (2001).

4. This issue is not a new one, and there is an abundance of literature dealing with the matter. Boardman et al. (2006) provide a good summary of the literature and methods.

Bibliography

Beal, Diana J. 1995. "A Travel Cost Analysis of the Value of Carnarvon Gorge National Park for Recreational Use." *Review of Marketing and Agricultural Economics* 63 (2): 292–303.

Boardman, Anthony, David Greenberg, Aidan Vining, and David Weimer. 2006. *Cost Benefit Analysis: Concepts and Practice.* 3rd ed. Upper Saddle River, N.J.: Prentice Hall.

Carson, Richard T., Nicholas E. Flores, and Norman F. Meade. 2001. "Contingent Valuation: Controversies and Evidence." *Environmental and Resource Economics* 19: 173–210.

Central Intelligence Agency (CIA). 2010. *The World Factbook: India.* Washington, D.C.: CIA.

Dinwiddy, Caroline L., and Francis J. Teal. 1996. *Principles of Cost-Benefit Analysis for Developing Countries.* Cambridge: Cambridge University Press.

Fix, Peter, and John Loomis. 1997. "The Economic Benefits of Mountain Biking at One of Its Meccas: An Application of the Travel Cost Method to Mountain Biking in Moab, Utah." *Journal of Leisure Research* 29 (3): 342–52.

Food and Agriculture Organization of the United Nations (FAO). 1997. *State of the World's Forests.* Rome: FAO.

Hanley, Nick, and Edward B. Barbier. 2009. *Pricing Nature: Cost-Benefit Analysis and Environmental Policy.* Northampton, Mass.: Edward Elgar.

Ironmonger, Duncan S. 2001. "Household Production." In *International Encyclopedia of the Social and Behavioral Sciences*, ed. Neil J. Smelser and Paul B. Baltes, vol. 20. 6934–39. Oxford: Pergamon.

Kahneman, Daniel, and Jack L. Knetsch. 1992. "Valuing Public Goods: The Purchase of Moral Satisfaction." *Journal of Environmental Economics and Management* 22 (1): 57–70.

Kahneman, Daniel, Ilana Ritov, and David A. Schkade. 1999. "Economic Preferences or Attitude Expressions?: An Analysis of Dollar Responses to Public Issues." *Journal of Risk and Uncertainty* 19 (1–3): 230–35.

Knetsch, Jack L., and J.A. Sinden. 1984. "Willingness to Pay and Compensation Demanded: Experimental Evidence of an Unexpected Disparity in Measures of Value." *The Quarterly Journal of Economics* 99 (3): 507–21.

Kuznets, Simon. 1934. "National Income, 1929–1932." *National Bureau of Economic Research* 49: 1–12.

Kuznets, Simon. 1962. "How to Judge Quality." *New Republic*, October 20, 1962.

List, John A. 2003. "Does Market Experience Eliminate Market Anomalies?" *The Quarterly Journal of Economics* 118 (1): 41–71.

Mishan, E. J., and Euston Quah. 2007. *Cost-Benefit Analysis*. New York: Routledge.

Quah, Euston. 1993. *Economics and Home Production*. Singapore: Ashgate.

Quah, Euston, and Khye Chong Tan. 1999. "Pricing a Scenic View: The Case of Singapore's East Coast Park." *Impact Assessment and Project Appraisal* 17 (4): 295–303.

Quah, Euston, Edward Choi, and Khye Chong Tan. 2006. "Use of Damage Schedules in Environmental Valuation: The Case of Urban Singapore." *Applied Economics* 38: 1501–1512.

Quah, Euston, and Qiyan Ong. 2009. "Cities and Happiness in Environmental Goods." In *World Cities: Achieving Liveability and Vibrancy*, ed. Ooi Giok Ling and Belinda Yuen, 277–98. Singapore: World Scientific.

Rutherford, Murray B., Jack L. Knetsch, and Thomas C. Brown. 1998. "Assessing Environmental Losses: Judgments of Importance and Damage Schedules." *Harvard Environmental Law Review* 22 (1): 51–101.

United Nations Development Programme (UNDP). 2009. *Human Development Report. Overcoming Barriers: Human Mobility and Development*. New York: Palgrave Macmillan.

3

The Benefit-Transfer Approach

VALUING HEALTH RISKS IN SUB-SAHARAN AFRICA

Lisa A. Robinson and James K. Hammitt

When faced with the health risks associated with air pollutants or other hazards, policymakers must decide whether to devote limited resources to abatement efforts, and thereby divert funds that individuals, firms, and government agencies might instead use to provide other desirable goods and services. Formal assessment of the costs and benefits of alternative policies provides useful information on whether the benefits of each action are likely to be commensurate with their costs and also identifies which action, if any, is most likely to maximize the net benefits to society.

To support this type of analysis, benefits must be measured in monetary terms. For health risk reductions (as well as other outcomes not directly bought and sold in markets), economists base these values on the willingness of the affected individuals to exchange income for their own changes in risk. This approach respects individuals' preferences for spending on risk reductions rather than on other goods and services. Individuals make decisions that reflect these preferences frequently: for example, by choosing more expensive housing in a less hazardous location, spending more for safer transportation, taking a safer job for less pay, or purchasing helmets or other protective equipment.

However, willingness to pay for health risk reductions has not been well studied in low-income countries. As a result, analysts often transfer values from studies conducted in much wealthier areas. This "benefit transfer" approach generally involves reviewing the quality and suitability of previous research to select the best available estimates, then adjusting the estimates to the extent possible to better fit the populations and risks of concern. While this approach is well established and widely used in policy analysis, applying it to populations with significantly different income levels is particularly challenging.

In this chapter, we describe the use of benefit-transfer to value air pollution-related mortality risks in sub-Saharan Africa within the traditional benefit-cost analysis framework. We first introduce alternative approaches for valuation and describe the benefit-transfer approach. We next apply this approach, suggesting some innovations that appear particularly important when addressing low-income countries, and finally we discuss the results and implications of our analysis.

Approaches for Valuing Health Risks

Economists and other social scientists have developed several alternative measures for valuing health risk reductions, which differ in the types of trade-offs they consider. These approaches include (1) willingness to pay, including the value per statistical life (VSL); (2) monetized health-adjusted life-years, including quality-adjusted life-years (QALYs) and disability-adjusted life-years (DALYs); and (3) averted costs, including the costs of illness and lost productivity (i.e., human capital). Relying on willingness to pay is most appropriate in the benefit-cost analysis framework.[1] However, policy analysts at times use the other measures as proxies, primarily because of gaps in the available research. Because willingness-to-pay estimates often address risks or populations that are dissimilar to those addressed by a policy, the benefit-transfer approach has been developed to provide a structured method for evaluating the available research and identifying suitable estimates.

WILLINGNESS TO PAY AND THE VALUE PER STATISTICAL LIFE

Willingness to pay is the maximum amount of income (or wealth) that an individual is willing to exchange for a beneficial outcome, reflecting the types of trade-offs inherent in policy decisions. Given constrained resources, decision makers must determine whether to increase expenditures on risk-reducing policies, which in turn decreases societal expenditures on other desired goods and services.

For health risk reductions and other outcomes not directly bought and sold in the marketplace, willingness to pay is usually estimated based on either revealed or stated preference methods. Revealed preference studies use data from market transactions or observed behavior to estimate the value of nonmarket goods or outcomes. Stated preference studies collect data through surveys or similar approaches. Each method has advantages and limitations.[2] For example, revealed preference studies rely on actual behavior, but often address scenarios that differ from those of concern in policy analysis. Stated-preference studies allow researchers to better tailor the survey scenario to the risks of concern, but the responses are hypothetical and less credible.

When used to value small changes in risks, these estimates are usually expressed as the value per statistical case for nonfatal risks and as the value per statistical life (VSL) for fatal risks. A "statistical case" or "statistical life" involves aggregating small changes in risks across many individuals. For example, a 1 in 10,000 risk reduction that affects 10,000 individuals can be expressed as a statistical case (1/10,000 risk reduction × 10,000 individuals = 1 statistical case). In particular, a policy that is expected to "save" a statistical life is one that is predicted to result in one less death throughout the affected population in a specified time period, where the individual whose life would be extended cannot be identified in advance.

Individual willingness to pay for small risk changes can be converted to a value per statistical case by dividing willingness to pay by the risk change. For example, if an individual is willing to pay $20 for a 1 in 10,000 reduction in his or her risk of dying in the current year, the equivalent VSL is $200,000

($20 ÷ 1/10,000 = $200,000). When applied in benefit-cost analysis, these values can be understood as aggregating individual willingness to pay for small risk reductions (within a defined time period) across a large population. For example, a $200,000 VSL will result if each member of a population of 10,000 were willing to pay $20 on average for a 1 in 10,000 annual risk reduction ($20 × 10,000 = $200,000).

While this approach is well established and frequently used, the name is misleading and the concept is often misunderstood (see Cameron 2010; Robinson and Hammitt 2011). The VSL measures the rate at which an individual would give up money that he or she could spend on other goods and services to reduce current mortality risk by a small amount (Hammitt 2000). It is neither the value of saving a particular individual's life with certainty nor an indicator of an individual's moral or intrinsic worth.

Because willingness to pay represents the preferences of the affected individuals, it provides information on how decision makers can best design policies (and allocate funding or other resources) to reflect these preferences. At times, policy goals reflect priorities that differ from those of the affected population, or policy choices are constrained in ways that prevent a desired allocation of resources. Thus the willingness-to pay-estimates, as well as the results of the overall benefit-cost analysis, are likely to be only some of the many factors considered in policy decisions.

MONETIZED HEALTH-ADJUSTED LIFE-YEARS

Health-adjusted life-years are nonmonetary measures, such as DALYs (disability adjusted life-years) and QALYs (quality adjusted life-years), frequently used in cost-effectiveness analyses and in assessing population health.[3] These measures weight each year of life by its quality, typically represented on a scale anchored at 0 and 1, often using surveys to develop the weights. Calculating QALY or DALY gains involves comparing individuals' expected health-related quality of life with and without exposure to a hazard, including mortality as well as morbidity during the survival period.

A key difference between these approaches and those based on willingness to pay is the type of trade-offs assessed. QALYs and DALYs reflect trade-offs between different health states and their duration, while willingness to pay reflects the trade-offs between spending on health or longevity versus on other goods and services (see Hammitt 2002). Willingness to pay is a broader measure and is more consistent with the trade-offs being considered when deciding how much to spend on risk-reducing policies.

However, when willingness-to-pay estimates are lacking, health-adjusted life-years are sometimes monetized for use as rough proxies in benefit-cost analysis (e.g., Lvovsky et al. 2000). Often, analysts assume that the value of a QALY or DALY is equal to the value per statistical life-year (VSLY) that is calculated by dividing the VSL by the discounted number of expected life-years remaining. This approach assumes that the VSLY is constant, which is not supported by theory and is contrary to the available empirical evidence (Hammitt 2007; Aldy and Viscusi 2007; Krupnick 2007). Hence the use of a constant VSLY has not been supported by expert panels (Morgan and Cropper 2007; NAS 2008). An Institute of Medicine expert panel also recommended against the use of monetized QALYs or DALYs in benefit-cost analysis because of inconsistencies in the types of trade-offs considered and the lack of evidence supporting a constant dollar value (Institute of Medicine 2006). Recent empirical research indicates that the value of a QALY is likely to vary depending on the severity and duration of the health effect (Haninger and Hammitt 2011).

AVOIDED COSTS (COST OF ILLNESS AND LOST PRODUCTION)

Avoided cost approaches consider the direct costs and indirect productivity losses associated with illness and premature death. Typically, direct costs include those for medical treatment; at times, other costs, such as those related to insurance administration or litigation, are also considered. Valuing lost productivity involves considering the effects of illness or death on paid and often unpaid work time—that is, on the human capital devoted to production.

Avoided costs often understate the value of risk reductions. Perhaps most importantly, they exclude the value of avoiding pain and suffering and other quality-of-life impacts. For example, when used to value mortality, human capital estimates are generally much smaller than the VSL.[4]

Avoided costs also address an outcome that differs from the outcome of most risk-reducing policies. For example, medical expenditures cover treatments that may not return an individual to his or her initial health state. In contrast, risk-reducing policies may allow an individual to completely evade the health condition. Costs paid by third parties (such as government programs or insurance companies) complicate this relationship. Subsidies may encourage individuals to seek medical treatments that they would not willingly finance themselves.[5]

Using the human capital approach involves estimating the decreased output of goods and services that may result when individuals work less because of illness or premature death. Analysts frequently assume that workers are paid the value of their marginal product and use compensation rates to estimate the value of these losses. A number of simplifying assumptions regarding individual behavior and the functioning of labor markets underlie this approach.

While avoided cost estimates appear straightforward and easy to calculate, there is little formal consensus or guidance on best practices. Hence, different studies can produce significantly different estimates (Bloom et al. 2001; Akobundu et al. 2006; Lipscomb et al. 2009). In addition, many cost-of-illness studies focus on average annual costs throughout a population, rather than on the lifetime costs per case that are needed to value risk reductions in policy analysis.

BENEFIT-TRANSFER

Policy analysis often involves taking values developed in one context (a primary research study) and applying them in a somewhat dissimilar context (the policy study). The benefit-transfer approach provides a framework for this type of analysis and is widely used to value risk reductions due to gaps in the research literature. It generally consists of five steps.

1. *Describe the Policy Scenario.* Determine the characteristics of the risks and populations to be addressed by the target study.
2. *Identify Potentially Relevant Existing Valuation Research.* Search the valuation literature for primary research studies that address similar populations and types of effects.
3. *Review Existing Studies for Quality and Applicability.* Assess the quality of the primary research studies by determining whether they follow generally accepted best practices in terms of the data and methods used. Assess applicability in terms of (*a*) the similarity of the health effects; (*b*) the similarity of the populations experiencing the effects; and (*c*) the ability to adjust for differences between the scenarios in the primary research study and in the target study.
4. *Transfer the Estimates.* Conduct the transfer, making any necessary adjustments to the primary research estimates and applying them to the target scenario. This transfer may be based on the results of a single study or several studies.
5. *Address Uncertainty.* Address uncertainties in the estimates both qualitatively and quantitatively; for example, by conducting sensitivity or probabilistic analysis as appropriate and discussing the implications of uncertainty for decision making.

The main advantage of benefit-transfer is that it is less expensive and time consuming than conducting new primary research. The quality of the resulting analysis depends heavily on the good judgment of the analyst, however. The estimates are likely to be less accurate than those that would result from a carefully designed and implemented study that directly addresses the population and effects of concern. The implications of related assumptions and uncertainties should be reported as part of the analytic results so that these factors are considered in related decision making.

Valuing Air Pollution Risks in Africa

In this section, we use the benefit-transfer framework to estimate the value of reducing mortality risks from air pollution exposure. Mortality risks dominate the quantified benefits estimates for most air pollution policies, often accounting for 90 percent or more of the total monetary value (e.g., EPA 2011). Below, we summarize our approach to each of the five steps in the benefit-transfer process, emphasizing how we constructed the resulting estimates.[6]

DESCRIBE THE POLICY SCENARIO

Our study addresses the value of reducing mortality risks associated with exposure to fine particles in ambient air in sub-Saharan Africa.[7] We assume that a separate risk assessment has been completed, which estimates the number of statistical cases of premature mortality averted by the policy.[8] Our goal is to estimate the average value of these statistical cases for each country in the region.

IDENTIFY POTENTIALLY RELEVANT EXISTING VALUATION RESEARCH

Sub-Saharan Africa includes many of the poorest countries in the world.[9] Our review of the English language literature suggests that mortality risks have not been previously valued in any of the countries in this region, nor in other countries with similarly low incomes. We did, however, identify several recent studies from middle-income countries. In addition, we reviewed the studies from high-income countries used in previous benefit-transfers.

REVIEW EXISTING STUDIES FOR QUALITY AND APPLICABILITY

Much of the VSL research considers the trade-off between wages and job-related fatality risks, controlling for other factors that affect wage levels (see Viscusi and Aldy 2003 for review). A number of studies instead use surveys or other stated-preference methods to elicit these values, addressing different types of risks (often traffic safety, occasionally air pollution) and, in some cases, subpopulations other than working-age adults (see Lindhjem et al. 2011 for review). Because most of the available research considers risks other than air pollution, benefit-transfer is typically used for valuation regardless of the country involved. The key question is whether the starting point for the transfer should be estimates from middle-income or from high-income countries. Our initial review focuses largely on the quality of the data and methods used; we later address the suitability of these estimates for application to air pollution risks in sub-Saharan Africa.[10]

Primary research from middle-income countries. Our search for primary research yielded seventeen studies from nine middle-income countries. These include eight wage-risk studies and nine stated-preference studies.[11] Our review suggests that the wage-risk studies each have deficiencies that result largely from the limited information available for the populations of concern. For example, some lack data on individual worker characteristics or on nonfatal risks, making it difficult to accurately estimate the relationship between wages and fatal risks. The stated-preference studies also have several limitations. For example, some find that reported willingness to pay is not sensitive to the size of the risk change, and some are based on small, nonrepresentative samples. Thus while these studies often provide interesting and useful information, their limitations suggest that they should not be the sole basis for extrapolating to lower-income countries.

Previous benefit-transfers. VSL has been well studied in high-income countries, particularly in the United States. For analysis of air pollution and other regulations, the U.S. Environmental Protection Agency (EPA) has long relied on estimates from a review that covers studies published through 1992 (Viscusi 1992; 1993), as summarized in its 2010 *Guidelines for Preparing Economic Analyses* (EPA

2010). These estimates are derived from twenty-six studies conducted in the United States and other high-income countries, twenty-one of which are wage-risk studies. When inflated to 2007 dollars, the central estimates from these studies range from $1.0 million to $21.4 million, with a mean of $7.6 million.[12] The EPA does not adjust these estimates for the age of those affected, but adjusts for real income growth over time and for the time lag between changes in exposure and changes in incidence.

Most analyses of air pollution policies in middle-income countries appear to begin with the same VSL estimates used in the EPA guidelines, although the source is not always reported.[13] These studies adjust the VSL estimates for income differences and occasionally also for the age of those affected.[14]

After the EPA estimates were developed, researchers completed several meta-analyses that combine the results from different studies. These analyses vary in the issues they explore and in how they report their results, but are largely based on studies conducted in high-income countries. The central estimates (in 2007 dollars) range from about $1.9 million to about $10.7 million (Cropper, Hammitt, and Robinson 2011). Although the VSL meta-analyses have been used for benefit-transfer, they have several limitations. Most are based on relatively old primary research, which means that the data and statistical techniques may be outdated. In addition, expert review (Morgan and Cropper 2007; Swackhamer and Kling 2011) indicates that they are in need of several methodological improvements.

More recent review (Robinson 2008; Robinson et al. 2010) suggests that it may be preferable to rely on newer individual studies. In particular, this review recommends applying the results from Viscusi (2004), a wage-risk study that uses improved data and analytic practices. If inflated to 2007 dollars and adjusted for real income growth, the preferred estimate from this study is a mean VSL of $6.3 million, with a 95 percent confidence interval of $4.9 million to $7.9 million. This adjusted mean is slightly below the mean from the 2010 EPA guidelines and in the middle of the range of mean estimates from the meta-analyses.

Based on this review, we select the Viscusi (2004) study as the starting point for valuing mortality risk reductions in sub-Saharan Africa. Like much of the VSL research, it is a wage-risk study conducted in a high-income country, so it addresses a population and a type of risk that differ in some respects from those of concern. However, it utilizes data of good quality and reflects recent advances in understanding how to best model the relationships between risks and wages. It provides a mean VSL similar to the EPA estimate used as a starting point for many previous studies.

TRANSFER THE ESTIMATE

Inspection of the extent to which the VSL varies with risk and population characteristics suggests that the income level of the population studied may be the most significant difference between the Viscusi (2004) study and the policy scenario. As discussed in Robinson and Hammitt (2009), population characteristics such as age and life expectancy, underlying health status, and total mortality risks may affect the VSL, but the appropriate adjustments are uncertain.[15] Differences between job-related risks and air pollution risks, such as latency, morbidity prior to death, and the extent to which the risk is viewed as controllable, voluntary, or dreaded, also affect these values.

Because review of the potential effects of these factors suggests that their impact is likely to be smaller than the effect of income, we focus on income adjustments in determining how to conduct the transfer. Our approach involves two steps. First, we estimate the change in the VSL associated with a change in income, based on the available empirical research. Because this research does not address low-income countries, we next examine the theoretical relationship of VSL to lifetime income and consumption, and use this relationship to adjust the results.

Income Elasticity

While it may seem obvious that wealthier individuals would be willing to pay more than poorer individuals for small risk reductions, the proportional change in the VSL associated with a change in income (i.e., its income elasticity) is uncertain and may be greater or less than one. Assuming the elasticity is constant, it can be used to estimate the VSL as follows:

$$VSL_B = VSL_A * (Income_B/Income_A)^{elasticity}.$$

In this formula, VSL_B is the result of extrapolating from VSL_A given the ratio of the income levels for groups A and B and the estimated elasticity.

The effects of different elasticity estimates are illustrated in table 3.1. The calculations begin with the U.S. VSL of $6.3 million derived from Viscusi (2004) and U.S. 2007 per capita GNI of $46,000. The VSL is then estimated based on the per capita GNI for sub-Saharan Africa ($1,900 in 2007, based on purchasing power parity) using different elasticity estimates.[16] The results indicate that applying different values for elasticity changes the extrapolated VSL by orders of magnitude. We then convert each VSL to individual willingness to pay for an illustrative risk change (1 in 10,000), so we can compare it to the income estimate. As a percentage of average income in sub-Saharan Africa, willingness to pay increases when lower elasticity values are used and decreases when higher elasticity values are used, suggesting that elasticity estimates larger than 1.0 might be plausible when extrapolating to very-low-income countries, given the limited resources available to fund more basic needs.

A number of empirical studies have explored the VSL income elasticity (Hammitt and Robinson 2011). Most studies conducted in high-income countries suggest that the VSL increases at about half the rate of income; in other words, its income elasticity is approximately 0.5. In contrast, cross-country comparisons (e.g., Hammitt and Ibarrarán 2006), studies that follow an economy longitudinally as it develops (Hammitt, Liu, and Liu 2000; Costa and Kahn 2004), and research that explores elasticity in different income subgroups (Evans and Schaur 2010; Kniesner, Viscusi, and Ziliak 2010) suggest that elasticity greater than 1.0 may be

TABLE 3.1

Effect of Income Elasticity on the Estimated VSL for Income of $1,900

	Extrapolated VSL[a]	Willingness to Pay for 1 in 10,000 Risk Reduction	Willingness to Pay as a Percentage of Income[b]
Elasticity = 0[c]	$6.3 million	$630	33 percent
Elasticity = 0.5	$1.3 million	$130	7 percent
Elasticity = 1.0	$260,000	$26	1.4 percent
Elasticity = 1.5	$52,900	$5.29	0.3 percent
Elasticity = 2.0	$10,700	$1.07	0.06 percent

[a] Extrapolated from U.S. VSL of $6.3 million and U.S. per capita GNI of $46,000.

[b] The U.S. VSL of $6.3 million is 1.4 percent of U.S. income if converted to willingness to pay for a 1 in 10,000 risk change.

[c] Elasticity estimates in exhibit are illustrative; see text for discussion of related research.

reasonable when extrapolating to poorer populations. The appropriate elasticity is uncertain, given both the diverse results of the available studies and the lack of research in very-low-income countries.

Thus our transfer involves developing a range of estimates, indicating related uncertainties. We first estimate the VSL for each country by extrapolation from the U.S. estimate of $6.3 million from Viscusi (2004). We apply three alternative income elasticity estimates (1.0, 1.5, 2.0) based on our review of related research, and use GNI per capita (based on purchasing power parity) as our income measure (World Bank 2008b). As discussed below, we then explore the relationship of the extrapolated VSL to other measures.

Lifetime Income and Consumption

One question that arises is whether it is possible to compare the VSL that results from the application of alternative elasticity values to other measures to determine its reasonableness. Theory suggests that the VSL will exceed the present value of future earnings (i.e., of human capital) and of future consumption (discounted to reflect time preferences), because it reflects the values that individuals place on the joy and satisfaction of living in addition to their productivity or consumption. Thus we explore whether our extrapolated VSLs fall below estimates of future earnings and consumption. Because the data available for low-income countries is limited, these comparisons involve several simplifying assumptions.

Our comparison requires first estimating remaining life expectancy. The average age in the data that underlie the Viscusi (2004) VSL estimate is about half of U.S. life expectancy at birth (thirty-nine years versus seventy-eight years). Because life expectancy varies significantly across high- and low-income countries, we also use half of the life expectancy at birth ("midpoint age") for each country as the assumed current age for the calculations in that country.[17] We then determine remaining life expectancy for an individual of that age in each country. We simplify the calculations by assuming that individuals will live for this time period with certainty, rather than calculating survival rates conditional on reaching each year of age.

For income, we rely on the same estimates of 2007 per capita GNI as used in our VSL calculations. For consumption, we rely on 2005 estimates developed as part of

TABLE 3.2

Examples of Extrapolated VSL Compared to Future Income and Consumption (2007 dollars, 3 percent discount rate, purchasing power parity)

Country	Future Income[a]	Future Consumption[a]	Extrapolated VSL[b]		
			Elasticity =1.0	Elasticity =1.5	Elasticity =2.0
United States	$1,124,183	$831,545	$6,300,000	$6,300,000	$6,300,000
South Africa	$203,050	$132,517	$1,313,600	$599,800	$273,900
Kenya	$35,410	$29,418	$211,600	$38,800	$7,100
Tanzania	$26,361	$19,024	$164,900	$26,700	$4,300
Uganda	$20,515	$19,311	$126,400	$17,900	$2,500
Ethiopia	$18,509	$11,998	$107,200	$14,000	$1,800
Mozambique	$15,041	$14,025	$94,800	$11,600	$1,400
Liberia	$6,773	$6,535	$39,800	$3,200	$300

Note: See text for information on data sources and calculations.

[a] Present value of future income or consumption, discounted at 3 percent.

[b] Shading indicates that future income exceeds VSL estimate, **shading and bold** indicates that future consumption also exceeds VSL estimate.

the World Bank's International Comparison program (World Bank 2008a), updated to 2007 using U.S. inflation rates for simplicity.[18] As expected, the consumption estimates are less than GNI (to varying degrees) because of the effects of taxes, saving decisions, and other factors. We assume that income and consumption are constant at each year of age, discounting to the midpoint age using a 3 percent rate.

In table 3.2, we illustrate the results for selected countries in sub-Saharan Africa, listed in order of per capita GNI.[19] We also include the U.S. estimates for comparison. The table illustrates the changing relationship between the extrapolated VSL and the estimates of future income and consumption. As indicated by the shaded and bolded cells, the larger elasticity values lead to VSL estimates that are less than future income and/or consumption in the poorer countries. In these cases, we recommend that analysts test the sensitivity of their results to replacing the extrapolated VSL with the larger income- or consumption-based estimates.

ADDRESS UNCERTAINTY

The results in table 3.2 emphasize the need to test the effect of using different elasticity values when extrapolating VSL estimates from high- to low-income countries in policy analysis. The order of magnitude differences in the results could significantly affect the relationship between benefits and costs for alternative policy options. While the estimates of future income and consumption are also uncertain, particularly given our simplifying assumptions, these uncertainties are not likely to lead to the same order-of-magnitude differences. These uncertainties should also be explored, especially if they affect the resulting policy recommendation. In addition, analysts may find it useful to calculate the "break-even" VSL: that is, the VSL at which the benefits of a policy equal its costs or at which the ranking of the different policy options changes.

Implications and Conclusions

Given that valuing mortality risks provides potentially useful information on the relative costs and benefits of alternative policies in countries where the VSL has not been well studied, we expect that policy analysts are likely to continue to value these risks by extrapolating from studies conducted in higher-income countries. However, our research suggests that analysts should avoid relying on a single VSL estimate and should instead examine how the application of a range of estimates affects their results.

Because uncertainty about the appropriate income elasticity leads to a very wide range of VSL estimates for sub-Saharan Africa, our benefit-transfer analysis indicates a pressing need to conduct more research on the value of health risk reductions in low-income countries. These values may also vary because of other differences between the scenarios most frequently studied (job-related risks among high-income populations) and the air pollution risks of concern. In addition, these values will be affected by other factors such as cultural attitudes toward risks and characteristics of the labor market and health care resources.

Notes

1. Willingness to accept compensation is also consistent with this framework, but is used less often in practice because of concerns about its measurement. For simplicity, we refer to willingness to pay throughout this chapter.

2. See, e.g., EPA (2010); OMB (2003) (providing guidance on how to evaluate such studies).

3. For more information on QALY measures and related best practices, see Gold et al. (1996) and Institute of Medicine (2006). See also World Health Organization (2008) (providing further information on DALYs). The DALY metric is currently being revised as part of an update to the Global Burden of Disease study (Salomon 2010).

4. For example, lost earnings under the human capital approach for a U.S. individual who dies in middle age would be about $1.2 million (at age forty using a 3 percent discount rate) (Grosse, Krueger, and Mvundura 2009). In contrast, a typical VSL would be $6.3 million (Viscusi 2004). (Both estimates are for the year 2007.)

5. If a willingness-to-pay study is carefully designed to exclude third-party costs, it may be appropriate to add these costs to the willingness-to-pay estimates to more fully capture the impact of risk reductions on social welfare.

6. See Robinson and Hammitt (2009) and Hammitt and Robinson (2011) for more detail.

7. Robinson and Hammitt (2009) also discuss the valuation of nonfatal cases of chronic bronchitis and asthma.

8. Estimates of mortality risks associated with particulate matter exposure are generally based on epidemiological studies conducted in high-income countries. Thus risk

assessors also must address issues related to appropriately transferring estimates across different populations. In the United States, an estimated 80 percent of all air pollution-related deaths occur among individuals over age sixty-five (EPA 1999). We are uncertain whether a similar pattern would hold in sub-Saharan Africa, given the differences in underlying health status, life expectancy, exposure levels, and other factors.

9. We use the World Bank classification system to categorize countries by income levels. The categories are based on gross national income (GNI) per capita, converted to U.S. dollars using 2007 exchange rates. As of 2007, the categories were as follows: low income, $935 or less; lower-middle income, $936 to $3,705; upper-middle income, $3,706 to $11,455; and high income, $11,456 or more (World Bank 2012). Of the forty-eight countries in the sub-Saharan region, only one (Equatorial Guinea) is categorized as high income; twenty-seven are low income. Of the remainder, thirteen are lower-middle income and seven are upper-middle income. Most of population resides in low-income countries; the regional per capita GNI average was $952 in 2007 and $1,254 in 2012.

10. See Cropper, Hammitt, and Robinson (2011) for a more detailed discussion of best practices for VSL research.

11. The wage-risk studies include Liu, Hammitt, and Liu (1997); Simon et al. (1999); Kim and Fishback (1999); Shanmugam (2000; 2001); Hammitt and Ibarrarán (2006); Giergiczny (2008); Guo and Hammitt (2009). The stated-preference studies are reported in Ortuzar, Cifuentes, and Williams (2000); Melhuish et al. (2005); Vassanadumrongdee and Matsuoka (2005); Hammitt and Zhou (2006); Wang and Mullahy (2006); Bhattacharya, Alberini, Cropper (2007); and Gibson et al. (2007) (two of these articles report the results of more than one study).

12. Unless otherwise noted, all estimates are reported in 2007 U.S. dollars, inflated using the U.S. Consumer Price Index—All Urban Consumers. Bureau of Labor Statistics, CPI-U.

13. E.g., Larson and Rosen (2002); World Bank (2002a; 2002b; 2006); Stevens, Wilson, and Hammitt (2005). Some of the studies address cities or regions with low incomes that are located within countries with higher average incomes.

14. E.g., Lvovsky et al. (2000); World Bank (2002c).

15. The effect of age on the VSL has been particularly contentious. Related research suggests that the VSL may decrease between the middle-aged workers often studied and the older ages at which air pollution-related deaths are more likely to occur. However, there is little agreement on the rate of decline or on the VSL that results. See Robinson (2007); Hammitt (2007); Aldy and Viscusi (2007); Krupnick (2007); Morgan and Cropper (2007); NAS (2008).

16. In this discussion, we use international dollars based on purchasing power parity rather than exchange rates. Purchasing power parity is particularly important for lower-income countries because it accounts for differences in the relative prices of goods and services, including those that may not be traded in markets. For developing countries, GNI based on purchasing power generally exceeds GNI based on exchange rates.

17. Life expectancy data for 2008 (WHO 2010).

18. In the United States, 2007 prices were 1.06 times greater than in 2005, based on the Consumer Price Index. http://www.bls.gov/data/inflation_calculator.htm.

19. The World Bank's categorization scheme is based on exchange rates rather than purchasing power parity. Because the latter increases the estimates for poorer countries,

countries in the World Bank's low-income category ($935 GNI per capita and below based on exchange rates) tend to have GNI per capita of about $1,700 and below when calculated using the purchasing power parity measures reflected in table 3.2.

Bibliography

Akobundu, Ebere, Jing Ju, Lisa Blatt, and Daniel C. Mullins. 2006. "Cost-of-Illness Studies: A Review of Current Methods." *PharmacoEconomics* 24 (9): 869–90.

Aldy, Joseph E., and W. Kip Viscusi. 2007. "Age Differences in the Value of Statistical Life: Revealed Preference Evidence." *Review of Environmental Economics and Policy* 1 (2): 241–60.

Bhattacharya, Soma, Anna Alberini, and Maureen L. Cropper. 2007. "The Value of Mortality Risk Reductions in Delhi, India." *Journal of Risk and Uncertainty* 34 (1): 21–47.

Bloom, Bernard S., Douglas J. Bruno, Daniel Y. Maman, and Ravi Jayadevappa. 2001. "Usefulness of U.S. Cost of Illness Studies in Healthcare Decision Making." *PharmacoEconomics* 19 (2): 207–13.

Cameron, Trudy Ann. 2010. "Euthanizing the Value of a Statistical Life." *Review of Environmental Economics and Policy* 4 (2): 161–78.

Costa, Dora L., and Matthew E. Kahn. 2004. "Changes in the Value of Life, 1940–1980." *Journal of Risk and Uncertainty* 29 (2): 159–80.

Cropper, Maureen L., James K. Hammitt, and Lisa A. Robinson. 2011. "Valuing Mortality Risk Reductions: Progress and Challenges." *Annual Review of Resource Economics* 3: 313–36.

Evans, Mary F., and Georg Schaur. 2010. "A Quantile Estimation Approach to Identify Income and Age Variation in the Value of a Statistical Life." *Journal of Environmental Economics and Management* 59 (3): 260–70.

Gibson, John, Sandra Barns, Michael Cameron, Steven Lim, Frank Scrimgeour, and John Tressler. 2007. "The Value of Statistical Life and the Economics of Landmine Clearance in Developing Countries." *World Development* 35 (3): 512–31.

Giergiczny, Marek. 2008. "Value of a Statistical Life—the Case of Poland." *Environmental and Resource Economics* 41 (2): 209–21.

Gold, Marthe R., Joanna E. Siegel, Louise B. Russell, and Milton C. Weinstein, eds. 1996. *Cost-Effectiveness in Health and Medicine*. New York: Oxford University Press.

Grosse, Scott D., Kurt V. Krueger, and Mercy Mvundura. 2009. "Economic Productivity by Age and Sex: 2007 Estimates for the United States." *Medical Care* 47 (7 Supplement 1): S94–S103.

Guo, Xiaoqi, and James K. Hammitt. 2009. "Compensating Wage Differentials with Unemployment: Evidence from China." *Environmental and Resource Economics* 42 (2): 187–209.

Hammitt, James K. 2007. "Valuing Changes in Mortality Risk: Lives Saved versus Life Years Saved." *Review of Environmental Economics and Policy* 1 (2): 228–40.

Hammitt, James K. 2002. "QALYs versus WTP." *Risk Analysis* 22 (5): 985–1001.

Hammitt, James K. 2000. "Valuing Mortality Risk: Theory and Practice." *Environmental Science and Technology* 34 (8): 1396–1400.

Hammitt, James K., and María E. Ibarrarán. 2006. "The Economic Value of Fatal and Non-fatal Occupational Risks in Mexico City using Actuarial- and Perceived-Risk Estimates." *Health Economics Letters* 15: 1329–35.

Hammitt, James K., Jin-Tan Liu, and Jin-Long Liu. 2000. "Survival Is a Luxury Good: The Increasing Value of a Statistical Life." Prepared for the NBER Summer Institute Workshop on Public Policy and the Environment, Cambridge, Mass.

Hammitt, James K., and Lisa A. Robinson. 2011. "The Income Elasticity of the Value per Statistical Life: Transferring Estimates between High and Low Income Populations." *Journal of Benefit-Cost Analysis* 2 (2): Article 1.

Hammitt, James K., and Ying Zhou. 2006. "The Economic Value of Air-Pollution-Related Health Risks in China: A Contingent Valuation Study." *Environmental and Resource Economics* 33 (3): 399–423.

Haninger, Kevin, and James K. Hammitt. 2011. "Diminishing Willingness to Pay per Quality-Adjusted Life Year: Valuing Acute Foodborne Illness." *Risk Analysis.* 31 (9): 1363–80.

Institute of Medicine. 2006. *Valuing Health for Regulatory Cost-Effectiveness Analysis.* Ed. Wilhelmine Miller, Lisa. A. Robinson, and Robert S. Lawrence. Washington, D.C.: National Academies Press.

Kim, Seung-Wook, and Price V. Fishback. 1999. "The Impact of Institutional Change on Compensating Wage Differentials for Accident Risk: South Korea, 1984–1990." *Journal of Risk and Uncertainty* 18 (3): 231–48.

Kniesner, Thomas J., W. Kip Viscusi, and James P. Ziliak. 2010. "Policy Relevant Heterogeneity in the Value of Statistical Life: New Evidence from Panel Data Quantile Regressions." *Journal of Risk and Uncertainty* 40 (1): 15–31.

Krupnick, Alan. 2007. "Mortality-Risk Valuation and Age: Stated Preference Evidence." *Review of Environmental Economics and Policy* 1 (2): 261–82.

Larson, Bruce A., and Sydney Rosen. 2002. "Understanding Household Demand for Indoor Air Pollution Control in Developing Countries." *Social Science & Medicine* 55 (4): 571–84.

Lindhjem, Henrik, Ståle Navrud, Nils Axel Braathen, and Vincent Biausque. 2011. "Valuing Mortality Risk Reductions from Environmental, Transport, and Health Policies: A Global Meta-analysis of Stated Preference Studies." *Risk Analysis* 31 (9): 1381–1407.

Lipscomb, Joseph, K. Robin Yabroff, Martin L. Brown, William Lawrence, and Paul G. Barnett, eds. 2009. "Health Care Costing: Data, Methods, Future Directions." *Medical Care* 47 (7): Supplement 1.

Liu, Jin-Tan, James K. Hammitt, and Jin-Long Liu. 1997. "Estimated Hedonic Wage Function and Value of Life in a Developing Country." *Economic Letters* 57 (3): 353–58.

Lvovsky, Kseniya, Gordon Hughes, David Maddison, Bart Ostro, and David Pearce. 2000. "Environmental Costs of Fossil Fuels: A Rapid Assessment Method with Application to Six Cities." World Bank Environment Department, Pollution Management Series, Paper Number 78.

Melhuish, C., A. Ross, M. Goodge, K. K. C. Mani, M. F. M. Yusoff, and R. Umar. 2005. *Accident Costing Report AC 5: Malaysia.* Asian Development Bank, Association of Southeast Asian Nations, Regional Road Safety Program.

Morgan, M. Granger, and Maureen L. Cropper. 2007. "SAB Advisory on EPA's Issues in Valuing Mortality Risk Reduction." Memorandum from the Chair, Science Advisory Board, and the Chair, Environmental Economics Advisory Committee, to EPA Administrator Stephen L. Johnson. EPA-SAB-08-001.

National Academy of Sciences (NAS). 2008. *Estimating Mortality Risk Reduction and Economic Benefits from Controlling Ozone Air Pollution.* Committee on Estimating Mortality Risk Reduction Benefits from Decreasing Tropospheric Ozone Exposure. Washington, D.C.: National Academies Press.

Office of Management and Budget (OMB)). 2003. *Office of Management and Budget Circular A-4, Regulatory Analysis.* Washington, D.C.: OMB.

Ortuzar, Juan Dios de, Luis A. Cifuentes, and Huw C. W. L. Williams. 2000. "Application of Willingness-to-Pay Methods to Value Transport Externalities in Less Developed Countries." *Environment and Planning A* 32 (11): 2007–18.

Robinson, Lisa A. 2008. *Valuing Mortality Risk Reductions in Homeland Security Regulatory Analyses.* Prepared for U.S. Customs and Border Protection, Department of Homeland Security, under subcontract to Industrial Economics.

Robinson, Lisa A. 2007. "How U.S. Government Agencies Value Mortality Risk Reductions." *Review of Environmental Economics and Policy* 1 (2): 283–99.

Robinson, Lisa A., and James K. Hammitt. 2011. "Valuing Health and Longevity in Regulatory Analysis: Current Issues and Challenges." In *Handbook of the Politics of Regulation*, ed. David Levi-Faur. Northampton, Mass.: Edward Elgar.

Robinson, Lisa A., and James K. Hammitt. 2009. *The Value of Reducing Air Pollution Risks in Sub-Saharan Africa.* Prepared for the World Bank under subcontract to ICF International.

Robinson, Lisa A., James K. Hammitt, Joseph E. Aldy, Alan Krupnick, and Jennifer Baxter. 2010. "Valuing the Risk of Death from Terrorist Attacks." *Journal of Homeland Security and Emergency Management* 7 (1): Article 14.

Salomon, Joshua A. 2010. "New Disability Weights for the Global Burden of Disease." *Bulletin of the World Health Organization* 88: 879.

Shanmugam, K. R. 2001. "Self Selection Bias in the Estimates of Compensating Differentials for Job Risks in India." *Journal of Risk and Uncertainty* 22 (3): 263–75.

Shanmugam, K. R. 2000. "Valuations of Life and Injury Risks." *Environmental and Resource Economics* 16 (4): 379–89.

Simon, Nathalie B., Maureen L. Cropper, Anna Alberini, and Seema Arora. 1999. "Valuing Mortality Reductions in India: A Study of Compensating Wage Differentials." *Policy Research Working Paper Series* Number 2078, World Bank.

Stevens, Gretchen, Andrew Wilson, and James K. Hammitt. 2005. "A Benefit-Cost Analysis of Retrofitting Diesel Vehicles with Particulate Filters in the Mexico City Metropolitan Area." *Risk Analysis* 25 (4): 883–99.

Swackhamer, Deborah L., and Catherine L. Kling. 2011. "Review of Valuing Mortality Risk Reductions for Environmental Policy: A White Paper (December 10, 2010)." Memorandum from the Chair, Science Advisory Board, and the Chair, Environmental Economics Advisory Committee, to EPA Administrator Lisa P. Jackson. EPA-SAB-11–001.

U.S. Environmental Protection Agency (EPA). 2011. *The Benefits and Costs of the Clean Air Act from 1990 to 2020.* Washington, D.C.: EPA.

U.S. Environmental Protection Agency (EPA). 2010. *Guidelines for Preparing Economic Analyses.* EPA 240-R-10–001. Washington, D.C.: EPA.

U.S. Environmental Protection Agency (EPA). 1999. *The Benefits and Costs of the Clean Air Act, 1990 to 2010.* EPA 410-R-99–001. Washington, D.C.: EPA.

Vassanadumrongdee, Sujitra, and Shunji Matsuoka. 2005. "Risk Perceptions and Value of a Statistical Life for Air Pollution and Traffic Accidents: Evidence from Bangkok, Thailand." *Journal of Risk and Uncertainty* 30 (3): 261–87.

Viscusi, W. Kip. 2004. "The Value of Life: Estimates with Risks by Occupation and Industry." *Economic Inquiry* 42 (1): 29–48.

Viscusi, W. Kip. 1993. "The Value of Risks to Life and Health." *Journal of Economic Literature* 31 (4): 1912–46.

Viscusi, W. Kip. 1992. *Fatal Trade-Offs: Public and Private Responsibilities for Risk.* New York: Oxford University Press.

Viscusi, W. Kip, and Joseph E. Aldy. 2003. "The Value of a Statistical Life: A Critical Review of Market Estimates throughout the World." *Journal of Risk and Uncertainty* 27 (1): 5–76.

Wang, Hong, and John Mullahy. 2006. "Willingness to Pay for Reducing Fatal Risk by Improving Air Quality: A Contingent Valuation Study in Chongqing, China." *Science of the Total Environment* 367 (1): 50–57.

World Bank. 2002a. "Improving Air Quality in Metropolitan Mexico City." Policy Research Working Paper 2785. Washington, D.C.: World Bank.

World Bank. 2002b. *Thailand Environment Monitor: Air Quality.* Working Paper. Washington, D.C.: World Bank.

World Bank. 2002c. *Philippines Environment Monitor: Air Quality.* Working Paper. Washington, D.C.: World Bank.

World Bank. 2006. *Pakistan Strategic Country Environmental Assessment.* Report 36946-PK. Washington, D.C.: World Bank.

World Bank. 2008a. *Global Purchasing Power Parities and Real Expenditures.* Washington, D.C.: World Bank.

World Bank. 2008b. *Gross National Income per Capita 2007, Atlas Method and PPP, World Development Indicators Database.* Washington, D.C.: World Bank.

World Bank. 2012. *Country Classification Table, World Bank List of Economies.* Washington, D.C.: The World Bank.

World Health Organization (WHO). 2008. *The Global Burden of Disease: 2004 Update.* Geneva: World Health Organization.

World Health Organization (WHO). 2010. *Global Health Observatory Database.* Geneva: WHO.

4

Putting a Price on the Future of Our Children and Grandchildren

Maria Damon, Kristina Mohlin,
and Thomas Sterner

Discounting has the dubious distinction of being the most controversial issue in social cost-benefit analysis. This is largely because choosing the discount rate will often dominate other choices a modeler makes. For example, consider how we might estimate future damages from greenhouse gas emissions. In spite of the multiple layers of uncertainty surrounding natural science issues, most of the controversy over Stern's *The Economics of Climate Change* concerned one number: the discount rate. This number so dominates the estimates of climate damages that even a small change in the rate can lead to dramatically different conclusions.

The prevailing approach for evaluating projects using cost-benefit analysis is to estimate all associated costs and benefits over the lifetime of a project in current dollar values, and then discount those values using a social discount rate to determine the net present value of the project with the standard exponential approach. Discounting builds on the simple fact that money earns interest (i.e., capital is productive). In a growing economy, an investment of 100 units can be expected to give a return so that the accumulated value of the capital plus dividends grows exponentially. With a real interest rate of 6 percent (disregarding inflation), the capital will have increased to 106 units after a year. For this reason, we consider that a cost of 106 units in one year's time *is equivalent to* 100 units today. This is what we mean when we say that the discounted cost is 100 units.

The rest is just arithmetic—but powerful nonetheless. The psychology of the discounting debate hinges on the fact that most of us find exponential growth hard to fathom. There is a well-known puzzle that lecturers sometimes ask to spellbind their audiences: if you could fold a piece of paper forty times, how thick would it be? Many students guess a meter or two, but the correct answer is all the way to the moon. Doubling it three times is eight layers of paper. Ten doublings gives you just over a thousand (1,024), twenty folds gives about a million, and forty doublings is more than a thousand billion.[1] In another example of exponential growth, consider the economic growth rate in China, which has been chugging along at 12 percent in recent years. This means a doubling of the economy every six years. If this growth continued for 240 years, the Chinese economy would become a thousand billion times bigger, suggesting that this growth rate is unsustainable in the very long run.

If we go back to our example of a 6 percent growth rate, capital doubles in twelve years and multiplies more than 300 times in a century. Discounting in its very simplest form can be thought of as the inverse[2] of this growth. Thus, the value of $1 billion in 500 years with 6 percent discounting would be approximately 0.02 cents today.[3] It is easy to see that this may be disturbing from an ethical standpoint. Moreover, there are some mind-boggling details, such as the apparent nonlinearity of the effects. If we had used a 5 percent discount, instead of 6 percent, the value of the $1 billion would be over two cents. The *difference in discounted value between 5 and 6 percent is a factor of 100*, and yet serious people will propose anything from 1 to 10 percent discounting despite the enormous jump in the order of magnitude between percentage points: clearly, this is an area where we need to be particularly careful.

The crux of the discounting dispute comes from the fact that discounting appears to suppress the concerns about the far future: for example, of environmentalists over future damages from widespread climate change caused by activities being carried out today. For some people, this motivates them to reject the concept of discounting or cost-benefit analysis in general. In our view, they are throwing the baby out with the bathwater. Nonetheless, the fact remains that applying standard discounting to long-term projects may produce conclusions that many people find ethically unacceptable. The power of compounding describes a hypothetical value of far-distant benefits in today's terms assuming constant growth throughout the period. For long enough periods this produces a negligible, and apparently derisory, present value. Consequently, much of the ongoing argument and academic literature has centered on developing alternative methods for discounting long-term cost and benefit streams.

In international and transnational issues, such as climate change, there is further pressure to agree on a single discounting structure common to all countries. As it currently stands, and as we demonstrate in the last section of this chapter, national practices differ widely.

Choosing a Social Discount Rate

The appropriate choice of a social discount rate has long been batted around among economists. The social discount rate can be discussed in terms of the social rate of time preference (SRTP) or the social opportunity cost of capital (SOC). The social rate of time preference reflects society's valuation of a unit of *consumption* in the future relative to a unit of consumption today. The social opportunity cost of capital reflects the future net benefit accruing to society of *investments* made today. They thus represent the consumption and production side respectively and may differ due to taxation, treatment of uncertainty, or for other reasons. Both the rate of time preference and cost of capital can also be defined at the level of the individual. In the abstract, simplified, world of perfect markets without externalities or public goods populated by infinitely lived agents with no issues of inequality and wealth distribution, the individual and social figures would all be the same. In the real world with multiple market failures and complexities, all these rates are generally different. This has produced an area of theoretical literature on what is the appropriate rate to use for social discounting.

The standard economic approach uses the Ramsey framework as a starting point. This framework incorporates two separate issues: individuals' "pure" time preferences and the idea that the marginal utility of consumption will be lower in the future because people will be wealthier. Schelling (1995, 395) summarized the state of the literature as having "a near consensus that the appropriate discount rate should be conceptualized as consisting of two components. . . . One is pure time preference and 'deals with the impatience of consumers.'. . . The second reflects the changing marginal utility of consumption with the passage of time, and is decomposed into a rate of growth of consumption per capita and an elasticity of utility with respect to consumption." In other words, as people become wealthier, the value of an additional dollar declines, and thus a positive economic growth rate implies a positive discount rate, in addition to pure impatience.

In the Ramsey framework, a social planner is faced with the problem of how to distribute consumption and investment over time in order to maximize social welfare. The decision rule, also known as the Ramsey rule, which maximizes social welfare over time, is

$$r = \rho + \eta g_c. \tag{4.1}$$

The left-hand side of equation (4.1) is the marginal social rate of return to investment, r. The right-hand side is the (negative) social rate of return to postponed consumption, also known as the social rate of time preference. The two terms on the right-hand side represent the two different reasons why the value of an additional unit of consumption decreases with time. ρ is the pure rate of time preference (PRTP) and is positive if well-being at present is valued higher than well-being in the future. The two components of the second term are the growth rate of per capita consumption, g_c, and the elasticity of marginal utility, η. The elasticity of marginal utility is a parameter that describes by how much (the rate at which) the value of an additional unit of consumption decreases as the level of consumption increases. A positive elasticity of marginal utility reflects a standard assumption in economics that the well-being derived from an additional dollar is higher for a poor person than for a rich person. It is convenient for simplicity—but is in no way necessary—that any numbers in equation (4.1) are constant over time.

The pure rate of time preference ρ is often said to reflect impatience, or how much more we value utility now rather than later. A number of philosophers have argued in favor of a zero utility discount rate, or PRTP. Ramsey (1928, 543) described discounting as "ethically indefensible," and Harrod (1948, 40) said rather strikingly that discounting is "a polite expression for rapacity." Many others since then have argued essentially that there is no compelling moral reason for a positive discount rate for distant costs or benefits because a given cost or benefit in the future is no less real than the corresponding cost or benefit today

(Parfit 1984). This is illustrated by the dramatic thought experiment in Cowen and Parfit (1992, 145) concluding that "you, having just reached your twenty-first birthday, must soon die of cancer because one evening Cleopatra wanted an extra helping of dessert."[4]

The Ramsey rule thus embodies two key concepts: a preference component related to how much people care about future consumers relative to today's (or caring about one's own welfare tomorrow relative to today) and a component involving the product of the economy's growth rate and the marginal utility of additional consumption. Some economists are uneasy discounting *utility* across generations and thus are uncomfortable assuming a positive pure rate of time preference ($\rho > 0$). But many also believe that the existence of the consumption interest rate (ηg_c) provides a rationale for using a positive discount rate in cost-benefit analyses because costs and benefits pertain directly or indirectly to consumption.

Dasgupta and Heal (1979) have focused on the argument that the world will one day come to an end as the least controversial way of motivating a nonzero rate of pure time preference. For individuals, the risk of dying at any particular time is fairly significant and would motivate some pure rate of time preference for them. For society, however, the risk of extinction of all human life can only motivate a very low rate of pure time preference at the social level. (Typically, this is an *external* risk of extinction, for example, extinction from a giant meteor hitting the earth, to avoid the circularity of using a high discount rate to motivate actions that speed up the destruction of the planet and then retrospectively saying that the high discount rate was justified.)

In the standard Ramsey model, there are no externalities or market failures, so the social rate of time preference, the private rate of return, and the social rate of return to investment are equalized along the optimal path. They all denote the rate at which discounting costs and benefits—at different points in time during a project—does not change the economy's overall path of consumption and investment.

In reality, of course, all three rates are likely to be different from each other. The rate of time preference will differ from the rate of return to investment because of income and corporate taxation and other factors. Externalities and imperfect competition will also cause the private and social rates to diverge (Groom et al. 2005). Issues of equity, distribution, and uncertainty add further complications. So, which of these rates of return is the appropriate discount rate for cost-benefit analysis? This is a long-standing debate among economists and encompasses many more challenges that we have not yet mentioned. For instance, all the factors that affect the marginal utility of income or consumption may be relevant.

The behavioral literature in the last decade has shown that numerous other factors, such as positional concerns and habit formation, may affect marginal utility of consumption and thus discount rates. There are also issues related to risk in various shapes and forms. One source of risk is due to variations in the growth rate. Gollier (2008; 2010), for example, showed that if the growth rate varies, then the discount rate in the Ramsey formula should be lowered by a factor that depends on the variance of the growth rate and a measure of prudence.

The social rate of time preference reflects the opportunity cost of delayed consumption. Therefore, some argue that SRTP is the appropriate discount rate if a project is entirely funded by consumption. Along the same line of reasoning, a project entirely funded by displaced investment should be discounted with the social rate of return to investment. Alternatively, an average of the two rates could be used, weighted by the shares of displaced consumption and investment in financing the project. The most sophisticated approach is to multiply costs that displace investment and benefits that are reinvested by the shadow price of capital. This way, all costs and benefits will be expressed in consumption equivalents and can be discounted by the social rate of time preference (Groom et al. 2005).

Estimating a Social Discount Rate

Of course, neither the social rate of time preference nor the social opportunity cost of capital is directly observable or revealed in the market. Two main approaches to estimating these parameter values are (1) the descriptive approach, which relies purely on empirical values, such as market rates; and (2) the prescriptive approach, where the values of these parameters are based on ethical arguments (Arrow et al. 1996). Obtaining correct empirical estimates of the parameters, of course, presents a number of challenges, and many questions naturally arise regarding how people discount future costs and benefits.

What is observable for the descriptive approach is a large set of different market returns. A lot of the variation in rates of return can be explained by differences in risk across investments. But it is generally agreed that the social opportunity cost of capital should reflect the risk-free rate of return to alternative investments. Therefore, one suggested measure of the SOC is the pre-tax rate of return to low-risk private investment (Zhuang et al. 2007). A weakness of this measure is that the private rate of return may be different from the social rate of return because of externalities and imperfect competition (Groom et al. 2005).

Similarly, the social rate of return is also sometimes assessed by the after-tax rate of return on government bonds, since this reflects a nearly risk-free rate of return on saving for consumers (Zhuang et al. 2007). However, individuals' preferences for investment in public goods, such as endowments to future generations, might very well differ from their preferences in their own individual consumption (Sen 1961). Proponents of this reasoning prefer to estimate SRTP by taking the Ramsey rule as a point of departure. This approach requires, in its simplest form, establishing a value for the pure rate of time preference and the elasticity of marginal utility of consumption, as well as the expected growth of per capita consumption. This approach is often called *prescriptive*, since it establishes what the discount rate should be from normative discussions on the ethically correct choice of the parameters in the Ramsey formula, instead of from observation of market interest rates. But the pure time preference parameter ρ is difficult to isolate empirically, and some economists argue it can be inferred given a market-based estimate for r and estimates for g. Many others, however, argue against this *descriptive* approach, saying that it makes no sense to use observed market rates because of the many factors already mentioned (externalities, private versus social rates, risk, uncertainty, psychological aspects, etc.). If market rates are accepted, then there is no need for the Ramsey approach, but if market rates are not accepted as a guide for socially optimal discount rates, then they cannot be used to deduce the value of ρ either.

Moreover, even when evaluating shorter-term projects, there are potential challenges stemming from the fact that individual time preferences themselves can be dynamic and, in some cases, may be directly associated with the very project that is being evaluated; thus, it may not be a useful measure for evaluation. For example, many researchers have suggested that high observed rates of time preference among the poor imply a higher social discount rate for social and economic policies in developing countries than for those in the United States and Europe (Poulos and Whittington 2000). But if the observed rates are related not just to wealth but also to other factors—such as market failures in the credit, insurance, banking, or labor markets; or to increased uncertainty in poor, rural, and disease-affected regions—this could fundamentally challenge the notion that it is appropriate to consider observed rates when evaluating policies. If, for example, increasing a household's ability to insure against risks would directly lower an individual's rate, then observed time preferences in the face of rampant uncertainty are perhaps not an appropriate parameter for use in policy evaluation, especially if the policy itself is designed to help with goals, such as poverty alleviation, risk, or health, or other factors that might be a determinant of time preferences.

Discounting the Very Long Term

Discounting gets particularly interesting over the long term, largely for numerical reasons, since interest rates are compounded. The difference between a 3 percent and a 5 percent discount rate in twenty years is a 50 percent increase in value, which certainly is significant. However, the same discount rate difference over 200 years will increase the value fifty times, which completely transforms the calculation. In this section, we first look at time-varying discount rates because they are growing in popularity and have been adopted in a couple of European countries with some interesting motivations based on uncertainty about growth and its future composition. Then we turn to a particular class of models, multi-sectoral models, because growth rates are likely to vary among different sectors in long-term development. This implies that there will be relative price movements among the sectors, much like having different discount rates in each sector. Again, the changing economic composition also means that the discount rates are nonconstant over time, so they will in fact vary both over time and among sectors.

TIME-VARYING SOCIAL DISCOUNT RATES

Common practice in cost-benefit analysis is to use a discount rate that is constant over time, irrespective of whether we use social opportunity cost or social rate of time preference to derive it. A constant positive social discount rate effectively results in ascribing a close-to-zero weight on costs and benefits for distant future generations. This is problematic for a number of reasons involving irreversibility and long time horizons. One possible solution lies in a discount rate that declines over time.

A time-invariant discount rate implies that the rate of return to investment or consumption is expected to be the same for all future time. Returning to the Ramsey rule and rewriting the variables with time subscript yields

$$r\,(t) = \rho + \eta g\,(t). \tag{4.2}$$

If ρ and η are constant over time t, it is clear from equation (4.2) that the social rate of time preference is also constant if the growth rate is unchanging over time. The dotted line in figure 4.2 displays the level of per capita consumption at different points in time with a constant growth rate of 3 percent. A constant growth rate means that per capita consumption will grow exponentially with time. This means that if ρ and η are assumed to be time-invariant, then the implicit assumption when using a constant discount rate is exponential growth in per capita consumption in the future.

Conversely, the social rate of time preference will change over time if the growth rate changes over time. The solid lines in figures 4.1 and 4.2 show an alternative path of per capita consumption, in which the rate of growth decreases with time. If $\rho = 0$ and $\eta = 1$, SRTP is simply equal to the growth rate displayed in figure 4.1. Figure 4.3 illustrates how the present value of a unit of consumption, the

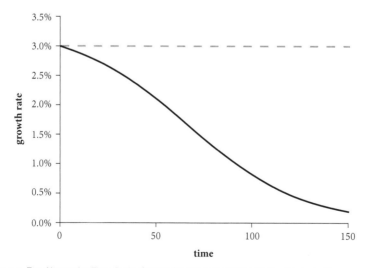

FIGURE 4.1 Two Alternative Time Paths for the Growth Rate of Per Capita Consumption

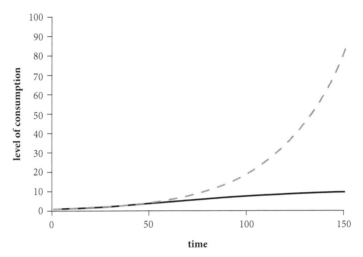

FIGURE 4.2 Future Per Capita Consumption with a Constant Positive Growth Rate (dotted line) and a Declining Positive Growth Rate (solid line)

discount factor, changes over time for the two growth paths under these assumptions. The present value, in this example where initial per capita consumption has been normalized to 1, is simply the inverse of the per capita consumption displayed in figure 4.2. It is clear from figure 4.3 that a constant discount rate will cause the discount factor to be close to zero in little more than one hundred years. This means that costs and benefits occurring further into the future will not significantly affect the net present value of public projects. With a declining discount

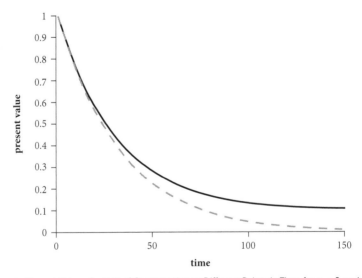

FIGURE 4.3 Present Value of a Unit of Consumption at Different Points in Time for $\rho = 0$ and $\eta = 1$, with a Constant Positive Growth Rate (dotted line) and Declining Positive Growth Rate (solid line)

rate, on the other hand, the discount factor remains significantly different from zero even centuries into the future.

Recent research on discounting in the context of long-term environmental problems has focused a great deal on declining rates, where costs and benefits more distant in time are discounted at lower rates than nearer ones. For one thing, empirical evidence supports the notion that people do not engage in standard exponential discounting when making decisions that involve trade-offs over time (Thaler 1981). Such "hyperbolic discounting," where discount rates are initially high (relative to the exponential discounting case) and then at some point fall substantially below the constant exponential discounting rate, appears empirically to more accurately reflect observed behavior (Laibson 1997). A problem with hyperbolic discounting is that it may introduce time inconsistencies. For example, a savings plan that appears beneficial at the present (time 0) may be abandoned if the owner computes its future value (at a later point time t): the low future discount rate at time t, which was projected at time 0, has in the present become inconsistent with the high initial discount rate. Time inconsistency is not, however, an inherent problem for declining social discount rates in general, although new information in the future may cause people to reverse previous choices. But if we return to the previously mentioned point that individuals' preferences for investment in public goods might very well differ from their preferences in their own individual consumption, it is not clear why individuals' seemingly hyperbolic discounting of their own personal consumption should inform the choice of social discount rate for projects extending over several generations. There are, however, several other theoretical justifications for a declining social discount rate (Groom et al. 2005).

Weitzman (1994) offered a clear justification for a declining discount rate grounded in environmental considerations. In his model, negative environmental externalities in production make the social rate of return to capital lower than the private rate of return. Weitzman assumed that some proportion of income must always be diverted to environmental improvement. He reasoned that this proportion is likely to increase with time and income because people can better afford to care about the environment at higher levels of income and because increased economic activity at higher incomes is likely to lead to more environmental damage. In essence, his point was that the social rate of return decreases with income and time because each extra unit of consumption is becoming less valuable relative to the environmental damage caused by the increased economic activity generating the extra income.[5]

Uncertainty naturally plays a significant role in problems with long time horizons and provides additional arguments for declining discount rates. Weitzman (1998) showed that when marginal projects are evaluated using the positive net present value criterion, uncertainty over future interest rates yields a declining certainty-equivalent discount rate, which approaches the lowest possible discount rate in the long run. Gollier (2008) used an extended Ramsey framework to explicitly analyze the effect of uncertainty on the growth rate of consumption. Gollier showed that if shocks to the growth rate have some permanent component and social preferences are in favor of precautionary saving, the certainty-equivalent discount rate declines over time.

DISCOUNTING IN MULTISECTORAL MODELS

The motivations discussed above for time-varying, or falling, discount rates range from the psychological to resource depletion and falling or uncertain growth rates. As mentioned earlier, there is some skepticism about both these motivations. Economists—who believe that we are not just bacteria in a dish or fish in a pond, multiplying endlessly—quite often counter the presumption that growth rates have to fall. They argue that the limits-to-growth argument only applies to physical growth—to objects that can be measured in tons. For instance, the *quantity* of oil, coal, or copper on earth must be limited. The limit may be high, but it exists. However, this says nothing about economic growth, which can include increases in *quality* in a good and can include growth in sectors that are not completely tangible, such as music or computer games.

If the "music" and "computer games" sectors were the only ones growing, their economic growth would impose little stress on the ecosystem. However, we also know that when people get more money they want cars and meat. This means that growth will require strict policies to ensure that it is sustainable, for instance, by steering consumption and production choices away from scarce goods and toward plentiful services. It also means that our modeling and discussions of discount rates should take changing sectoral composition of the economy into account.

Ultimately this touches on how we view our future, particularly our distant future. With 3 percent economic growth, we would be twice as rich in twenty-four years and almost twenty times as rich in a century. What does this mean? Would we really consume twenty times as much goods and services? Do we consume twenty times as much today as we did one hundred years ago? It is immediately clear that there are some exceptions, such as food: we do not eat twenty times as much food.[6] We do argue that there are many fundamental changes to our consumption, but that is far from the only exception. Take the example of domestic labor, such as housekeepers or gardeners: in spite of rapid economic growth, the demand for domestic labor has decreased significantly. It is not hard to see why: although incomes have risen, the relative price of housekeepers to other goods and services has gone up—precisely because salaries have gone up.

Thus, changes in relative prices are intimately tied to the same structural change that is created by the productivity that drives economic growth. This is a particularly useful setting for analyzing ecosystem services. Land, already in the writings of David Ricardo in the early nineteenth century, is characterized as a production factor that is in fixed supply. This fixedness need not apply literally to every resource (e.g., the land area of Holland has historically been increased), but the relative difficulty in producing such resources is still a fundamental characteristic of land and ecosystem services. We may be able to invest almost forever in man-made capital, but natural capital, such as fresh water, fish stocks, glaciers, and coral reefs, cannot be increased at will. Some of these stocks are fixed; some are subject to their own laws and may increase or decrease, depending on circumstances. However, we have to recognize that they are limited by nature. Quite a few will in fact decrease or be damaged as a result of current global changes, including climate change.

If discounting—and hence, growth—is essential for the valuation of future damage to environmental systems, and if this growth will be highly variable between sectors, then we should model it explicitly. Recent research has shown that, in a multisector model, the discount rates will depend on a weighted average of the different sectors' growth rates and thus vary over time as the composition of the economy changes. Actual full results are quite complicated and depend on a number of parameters, such as the elasticity of marginal utility and substitution among sectors, as well as the share of environmental sectors and growth rates. However, if we assume a situation where one production sector is growing and another ecosystem sector is not, then typically the discount rate will fall over time (Hoel and Sterner 2007; Guesnerie 2004; Gollier 2010).[7]

An ecosystem that does not grow is an interesting result here, since we arrive at nonconstant discount rates without making any unconventional assumptions. The reason is merely that we assume different growth rates, and thus the value share of the two sectors (production and ecosystem) changes over the trajectory. To calculate the future value of a change in environmental quality, we must consider both discounting and the change in the relative price (or valuation) of the environmental quality. This is akin to having separate discount rates for each sector—and thus typically lower discount rates for the ecosystem sector without growth. The difference in the discount rates is the equivalent of a change in relative price given in equation (4.3):

$$p = \frac{1}{\sigma}(g_C - g_E).$$

(4.3)

This price change depends on the development over time of the two sectors in the economy for conventional consumption goods (C) and ecosystem services (E). The price change is positive, provided the consumption sector grows faster than the environmental sector, and the relative price also depends on the elasticity of substitution between the two sectors. The elasticity of substitution is a parameter describing the ease with which we can substitute conventional consumption goods for ecosystem services. If, for example, the environmental quality is constant and consumption increases by 2.5 percent per year, and the elasticity of substitution is 0.5, then the relative price of ecosystem services will increase by an annual rate of as much as 5 percent.

The relative price effect normally counteracts the effect of discounting. The combined effect of discounting and the relative price increase of environmental goods are given by $r - p$. If both r and p are positive, then the sign of the combined effect is ambiguous. Limited substitutability and the increasing relative scarcity of environmental goods thus produce different discount rates for both environmental and conventional consumption that are nonconstant over time. Earlier, some economists intuited this result: Krutilla (1967) argued that in the future environmental goods would be more valuable, but the elegance of the latest modeling is that the relative price change comes from the same model and depends on the same set of factors as the discount rate itself.

Social Discount Rates in Selected Countries

The academic literature on social discounting has clearly presented government authorities with an overwhelming array of theoretical and empirical approaches for establishing a discount rate. The latest theory in practice is a declining discount rate. Table 4.1 presents social discount rates in selected countries around the world.[8] As we can see, the social discount rates applied in most countries are still time-invariant, but differ widely. In general, developing countries apply a higher rate than developed countries. Zhuang et al. (2007, 5) note in their excellent survey of social discounting practices that developed countries have generally favored lower discount rates in the past few decades, which reflects a trend toward the social rate of time preference approach. Notably, however, some developed countries, such as the United States, Canada, Australia, and New Zealand, still prefer estimates of the social opportunity cost of capital as the social discount rate.

India, the Philippines, and Pakistan also prefer the social opportunity cost of capital approach, while Chinese authorities instead use an average of the estimates of the social opportunity cost of capital and the social rate of time preference. The social opportunity cost of capital is assumed to be a marginal rate of return to investment of more than 11 percent in all four countries (Zhuang et al. 2007). While it seems reasonable to expect continued high rates of return in fast-growing economies, such as China and India, at least for quite some time in the future, high rates of return to investment appear less reasonable for low-growth economies, such as Pakistan and the Philippines. With standard estimates for the pure rate of time preference and risk aversion, the low gross domestic product per capita growth rates of Pakistan and the Philippines (at an average of 2 percent per year with high variability between 1996 and 2006) and the high SOC indicate a very large divergence between the social rate of return to investment and the SRTP. If such high marginal rates of return to investment really existed, they would have been exploited already and made to raise income growth. A possible motivation for unexploited high returns is credit constraints due to badly functioning credit markets. Perhaps a more reasonable explanation is that the high discount rates reflect the government cost of borrowing and investment risk in an uncertain institutional environment.

In the United Kingdom, the Treasury issues guidelines in the *Green Book* on appraisal and analysis in central government, to be applied consistently across government agencies. The *Green Book* recommends a 3.5 percent discount rate (HMT 2003). This is set using the SRTP approach with a pure rate of time preference of 1.5 percent, an elasticity of marginal utility of 1, and a long-term per capita GDP growth rate of 2 percent. In accordance with recent literature, the *Green Book*

TABLE 4.1

Real Social Discount Rates in Selected Countries

Country	Issuing agency or sector of application	Discount rate	Long-term rate	Theoretical approach	Reference
United Kingdom	HM Treasury	3.5%	Declining after 30 years	SRTP	HMT (2003)
France	Commissariat Général du Plan	4%	Declining after 30 years	SRTP	CGP (2005)
Italy	Central guidance to regional authorities	5%		SRTP	Zhuang et al. (2007)
Germany	Bundesministerium der Finanzen	3%		Federal refinancing rate	Zhuang et al. (2007)
Spain	Transportation	6%		SRTP	Zhuang et al. (2007)
	Water	4%		SRTP	Zhuang et al. (2007)
Netherlands		4%			Harrison (2010)
Sweden	SIKA[a]—transport	4%		SRTP	SIKA (2002)
	SEPA[b]—environment	4%		SRTP	Naturvårdsverket (2003)
Norway		3.5%		Government borrowing rate	Zhuang et al. (2007)
United States	Office of Management and Budget	7%	Sensitivity check, > 0%	SOC	OMB (2003)
	Environmental Protection Agency	2%–3%	Sensitivity check, 0.5%–3%	SRTP	EPA (2000)
Canada	Treasury Board	8%		SOC	Harrison (2010)
Australia	Office of Best Practice Regulation	7%		SOC	Harrison (2010)
New Zealand	Treasury	8%		SOC	Harrison (2010)
South Africa		8%		SOC	Harrison (2010)
China, People's Republic	NDRC[c]	8%[d]	Lower than 8%	Weighted average of SOC and SRTP	NDRC (2006)
India		12%		SOC	Zhuang et al. (2007)
Pakistan		12%		SOC	Zhuang et al. (2007)
Philippines		15%		SOC	Zhuang et al. (2007)
World Bank		10%–12%			Belli et al. (1998)
Asian Development Bank		10%–12%			Zhuang et al. (2007)

Note: SRTP = social rate of time preference; SOP = social opportunity cost of capital.

[a] SIKA = Statens Institut för Kommunikationsanalys.

[b] SEPA= Swedish Environmental Protection Agency.

[c] NDRC = National Development and Reform Commission and Ministry of Construction.

[d] However, NDRC also recommends different rates for different sectors, e.g., lower discount rates for water projects.

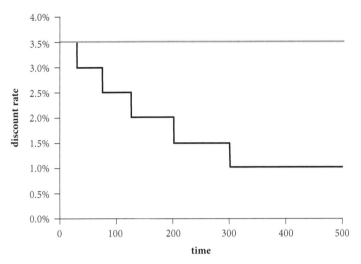

FIGURE 4.4 The Recommended Declining Social Discount Rate in the United Kingdom

also recommends a declining discount rate for long-term projects, and its main rationale for endorsing the declining discount rate is uncertainty about the future (HMT 2003, 98; Weitzman 1998; Gollier 2002).

The recommended rate declines in four discrete steps over a one-hundred-year time horizon, starting thirty years into the future. The resulting discount schedule is shown as a dark line in figure 4.4. Figure 4.5 presents the present value of one unit of consumption at different points in time for both the declining discount rate and a constant rate of 3.5 percent, with only minor difference. The discount factors drop to 0.05 within 100 years for the declining discount rate. After 200 years, the discount factor will be six times larger than with a constant rate and forty-three times

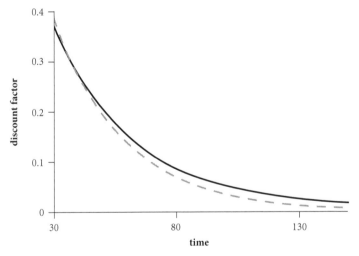

FIGURE 4.5 Discount Factors for a Constant Discount Rate of 3.5 Percent (dotted line) and the Declining Rate from Figure 4.4 (solid line)

larger after 300 years. However, after 300 years, the discount factor is less than 0.002 and keeps declining. It takes repeated large costs or benefits to significantly change the net present value of a project, even with this declining discount rate.

The *Green Book* also includes a section on the need for accounting for relative price movements. Environmental assets are mentioned as examples where scarcity, limited substitutability, and nonlinearities may contribute to relative price movements, in line with the multisector analysis described above. The recommendations also stress the importance of acknowledging distributional effects and suggest using equity weights in the evaluations.

In France, an expert group led by Daniel Lebègue revised the social discounting practices used by government authorities in 2005 (CGP 2005). The revision was partly motivated by concern that cost-benefit analyses favored a high number of transportation projects, despite long-term environmental costs, because of the previously recommended 8 percent discount rate. A commission looking into future prospects for nuclear power also chose to abandon the recommended 8 percent, which led the nuclear power commission to create a two-tiered discount schedule with a 6 percent discount rate for the initial period (2000–2030) and a 3 percent discount rate for subsequent years (Charpin et al. 2000). This sparked a debate over whether these discount rates should only apply to the energy sector or also be used in other sectors.

The Lebègue group recommended that the discount rate be lowered to 4 percent, marking a shift from an SOC to an SRTP approach and including a gradually declining rate, after thirty years, of 2 percent for the long term. The motivation for the declining rate was primarily uncertainty about the future growth rate of per capita income. The declining rate is based on a scenario in which the growth rate of per capita income can vary between two extremes: 2 percent with a two-thirds probability, and 0.5 percent with a one-third probability.

Figures 4.6 and 4.7 show the recommended discount rate and implied discount factors. The schedule is very similar to the UK recommendations, but is somewhat more conservative, since the discount rate is never allowed to be lower than 2 percent. Effectively, the difference from a constant rate is not great, but the move is a step away from the conservatism of constant rates in the past. The Lebègue group's revision also recognized that the relative value of environmental amenities is likely to appreciate over time and stressed the importance of recognizing this in long-term project evaluation.

Other French government authorities use a different, centrally recommended rate, but determine their own detailed methodology. The updated methodology for investments in infrastructure and transportation has a limited set of recommended relative prices for nonmarket goods related to transport, such as pollution, noise, and carbon emissions (METLTM 2004). These are generally assumed to increase at the same rate as per capita real income, except for the social cost of carbon, which is set to increase at 3 percent per year. Hence, the French Ministry of Infrastructure is an example where cost-benefit analysis guidelines set explicit recommendations on how the relative price of nonmarket goods should be assumed to develop over time.

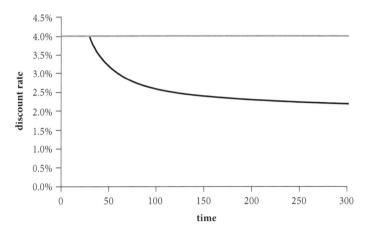

FIGURE 4.6 The Recommended Declining Social Discount Rate in France

In Sweden, the official recommendation is a 4 percent discount rate for public investments in infrastructure, based on a SRTP approach (SIKA 2002). Valuations of nonmarket goods are inflated by increases in real per capita income since the date of the valuation but not for future expected increases in real per capita income. The same recommendations also include a discussion of intergenerational discounting and suggest that a future review should include a sensitivity analysis with a 2 percent discount rate for the cost of carbon emissions. If a specific discount rate were applied only to the cost of carbon, it would correspond to an assumed annual relative price increase of 2 percent for the social cost of carbon emissions.

The Swedish Environmental Protection Agency also provides guidelines for cost-benefit analyses. It recommends a discount rate of 4 percent and a sensitivity

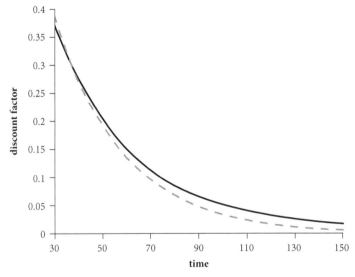

FIGURE 4.7 Discount Factors for a Constant Discount Rate of 4 Percent (dotted line) and the Declining Rate from Figure 4.6 (solid line)

analysis with a discount rate of 1 to 2 percent. Agency guidelines mention relative price increases on nonmarket goods, but discussion focuses on the already apparent difficulties in establishing current relative prices of nonmarket goods (Naturvårdsverket 2003).

In the United States, federal agencies must comply with federal guidelines for cost-benefit analyses, as outlined by the Office of Management and Budget (OMB). It recommends a 7 percent discount rate, which is derived from the average pretax rate of return to private capital (OMB 2003). However, it also includes a sensitivity analysis using an SRTP-based discount rate of 3 percent. For regulations with significant impact on future generations, OMB posits a further sensitivity analysis with a lower, but positive, discount rate.

The U.S. Environmental Protection Agency (EPA) favors an SRTP-based discount rate of 2 to 3 percent and the OMB-suggested 7 percent rate for sensitivity analysis (EPA 2000). EPA guidelines also ask for a presentation of the undiscounted flow of costs and benefits over time, which is also required for evaluating long-term policies with impacts on future generations. In such cases, the sensitivity analysis should include scenarios with discount rates of 0.5 to 3 percent and a discussion of the caveats of intergenerational discounting. EPA briefly mentions increases in the value of future benefits of environmental policy, especially for processes exhibiting nonlinearities.

China's National Development and Reform Commission (NDRC) and Ministry of Construction recommend a discount rate of 8 percent for short- and medium-term projects (NDRC 2006). These government institutions estimate a pure rate of time preference of 1 to 2 percent and an elasticity of marginal utility of 0.5 percent. Projected per capita growth rate is 7 to 8 percent, which yields an estimated SRTP of 4.5 to 6 percent. They project a rate of return to social capital of 9 to 11 percent and calculate the social discount rate of 8 percent as a weighted average of SRTP and SOC. However, the Chinese recommendations also state that different social discount rates should be used for different types of projects. For example, they may apply higher discount rates to transportation projects than hydraulic projects, or relatively low discount rates to certain special projects, such as those for environmental improvement and the exploitation and utilization of certain scarce resources. For some permanent projects or projects yielding benefits over a very long time period, they propose social discount rates lower than 8 percent. Social discount rates can also decline over different time periods in very long-term projects.

Chinese authorities have thus chosen to allow different discount rates across sectors, unlike most other countries. Spain, however, uses a higher discount rate in its transportation sector than in its hydropower sector. Using different discount rates in different sectors means that a dollar invested in one sector in ten years is valued higher than a dollar invested in another. The lower discount rate for some sectors like hydropower is presumably motivated by the long-run benefits of development, which would be nullified if the discount rates in other sectors were used. The difference in discount rates could perhaps be thought of as compensation for a systematic difference in externalities (negative in the case of transportation and negligible or perhaps positive in the case of hydropower). Of course, the present value of long-term costs of hydropower development will also be higher but is usually more difficult to quantify in monetary terms than the benefits. The higher discount rate for transportation also means that long-term or irreversible damages from infrastructure development will make little difference to the net present value of transportation projects. Although it is not clear how the Chinese guidelines are actually used in practice, the recommended discount rates should make projects in both sectors more easily pass the net present value criterion and in that sense are biased toward development.

The World Bank funds investment projects in many developing countries, which are evaluated according to the recommendations set out in the *Handbook on Economic Analysis of Investment Operations* (Belli et al. 1998). The *Handbook* notes that the discount rate should reflect not only the social opportunity cost but also the marginal rate at which individuals are willing to save in the country. Traditionally, however, the World Bank does not calculate a country-specific discount rate; instead, it uses a 10 to 12 percent discount rate that acts as a rationing device for its limited funds (World Bank 2008). It can also apply a different discount rate (other than 10 to 12 percent) if the World Bank's assistance strategy document for the individual country justifies it.

The World Bank also requires that project appraisals include an environmental assessment outlining costs and benefits. The guidelines on environmental assessment recommend that environmental costs and benefits use the standard social opportunity cost of capital (World Bank 2010). Long-term costs and benefits are not eligible for lower discount rate on the grounds that this could favor projects with adverse environmental consequences. The recommendations do ask that short- and long-term costs and benefits be estimated as carefully as possible and that a rigorous analysis of nonmonetary consequences, such as irreversible damages, supplement the standard cost-benefit analysis. Potential changes in nonmarket values over time are not explicitly discussed.

In the above discussion, we are particularly interested in the extent to which declining discount rates and changing relative prices of nonmarket goods are considered in actual policy evaluation. Detailed official cost-benefit analysis guidelines are not common or employed regularly by many countries, which makes a thorough investigation difficult (Pearce, Atkinson, and Mourato 2006). However, a brief survey of existing cost-benefit analysis guidelines in selected countries shows that the idea of declining discounting is slowly becoming accepted. Although it appears that only the United Kingdom and France have actual central guidelines for public policy analysis that include a declining social discount rate, other countries employ a lower flat discount rate for applications with long-term consequences. Also, in the EU's guidelines for appraising structural investment projects, the Directorate General for Regional Policy recommends a 5.5 percent rate for fast-growing countries, but 3.5 percent for mature member economies, thus formalizing a link between growth and discounting. The EU guidelines also state, in a footnote, that hyperbolic discounting merits fuller consideration (ECDGRP 2008, 208).

Although some countries' guidelines also acknowledge the significance of relative price movements for nonmarket goods, none of the guidelines reviewed above mention using different discount rates for environmental goods and services. Presumably, central authorities balk at the complexity of actually formalizing multiple or time-varying discount rates and prefer making explicit assumptions on changes in relative prices over time.

Conclusion

The choice of discount rate is one of the most critical factors in determining which policies pass a cost-benefit test, and it often dominates for long-term projects. Meanwhile, there are endless complexities involved in selecting an appropriate rate. Discounting behavior varies across individuals and commodities. Discount rates collected from revealed individual behavior appear to be consistent more with hyperbolic discounting than the standard exponential model with a constant rate, but the practical implications of applying rates that decline over time remain untested. Both economists and philosophers disagree over whether the approach should be prescriptive or descriptive.

Long-term environmental problems such as global climate change push the limits of discounting, but cost-benefit analysis is still needed to identify efficient projects. This chapter lays out many facets of the current thinking on choosing appropriate rates and surveys the current practices in a number of countries—all of which underlines the fact that a clear consensus has not yet emerged. However, the evidence in favor of questioning standard linear discounting is gaining momentum, and one thing is clear: applying a standard discounting approach in cost-benefit analysis of policies with long-term impacts severely reduces the value of costs or benefits in the distant future. There are a number of reasons to object to this. To address these concerns, an increasing number of countries are introducing a practice of using discount rates that fall over time.

Acknowledgments

Funding from FORMAS COMMONS is gratefully acknowledged.

Notes

1. The average distance to the moon is 384,000 km, so the story assumes the thickness of the paper is about one-third of a millimeter.

2. For the more technical reader, we assume a pure time preference of zero and logarithmic utility.

3. All monetary figures are U.S. dollars.

4. Broome (1994) and Arrow et al. (1995), as well as the papers in Lind (1982), have defended positive time preferences, whereas Cowen and Parfit (1992) and Parfit (1984)

have defended zero discounting. See also Harvey (1994) and Schelling (1995) for nuanced discussions of this issue.

5. Unlike most contributions to a long-term discount rate, Weitzman (1994) did not derive his discount rate as an equilibrium where the social rate of time preference is equal to the rate of return to investment, but rather focused on the latter. His lack of an explicit model of preferences and environmental goods has also been criticized (Groom et al. 2005).

6. Our consumption of meat, however, has risen, which means that the acreage appropriated for pastures, etc., has increased more than we might think.

7. See also Traeger (2007).

8. All numbers are real, unless otherwise stated.

Bibliography

Arrow, Kenneth J., W. R. Cline, K-G Maler, M. Munasinghe, R. Squitieri, and J. E. Stiglitz. 1996. "Intertemporal Equity, Discounting, and Economic Efficiency." In *Climate Change 1995: Economic and Social Dimensions of Climate Change* , ed. James P. Bruce, Hoesung Lee, and Erik F. Haites, 125–44, Cambridge: Cambridge University Press.

Belli, Pedro, Jock Anderson, Howard Barnum, John Dixon, and Jee-Peng Tan. 1998. *Handbook on Economic Analysis of Investment Operations*. Washington, D.C.: World Bank.

Broome, John. 1994. "Discounting and Welfare." *Philosophy and Public Affairs* 23 (2): 128–56.

Commissariat Général du Plan (CGP). 2005. *Révision du Taux d'Actualisation des Investissements Publics: Rapport du Groupe d'Experts Présidé par Daniel Lebègue*. Paris: CGP.

Charpin, Jean-Michel, Benjamin Dessus, and René Pellat. 2000. *Etude économique prospective de la filière nucléaire: rapport au Premier ministre*. Commissariat à l'énergie atomique et aux energies alternatives, Report No. 004001472. Paris: La documentation Française.

Cowen, Tyler, and Derek Parfit. 1992. "Against the Social Discount Rate." In *Justice between Age Groups and Generations*, ed. Peter Laslett and James S. Fishkin, 144–61. Philosophy, Politics, and Society. New Haven: Yale University Press.

Dasgupta, Partha S., and Geoffrey M. Heal. 1979. *Cambridge Economic Handbooks: Economic Theory and Exhaustible Resources*. Cambridge: Cambridge University Press.

European Commission, Directorate General Regional Policy (ECDGRP). 2008. *Guide to Cost-Benefit Analysis of Investment Projects*. Brussels: European Commission.

Gollier, Christian. 2010. "Ecological Discounting." *Journal of Economic Theory* 145 (2): 812–29.

Gollier, Christian. 2008. "Discounting with Fat-Tailed Economic Growth." *Journal of Risk and Uncertainty* 37 (2): 171–86.

Gollier, Christian. 2002. "Time Horizon and the Discount Rate." *Journal of Economic Theory* 107 (2): 463–73.

Groom, Ben, Cameron Hepburn, Phoebe Koundouri, and David Pearce. 2005. "Declining Discount Rates: The Long and the Short of It." *Environmental and Resource Economics* 32 (4): 445–93.

Guesnerie, Roger. 2004. "Calcul Economique et Développement Durable" [Economic calculation and sustainable development]." *Revue Economique* 55: 363–82.

Harvey, Charles M. 1994. "The Reasonableness of Non-constant Discounting." *Journal of Public Economics* 53 (1): 31–51.

Harrod, Roy Forbes. 1948. *Towards a Dynamic Economics*. London: Macmillan.

Her Majesty's Treasury (HMT). 2003. *The Greenbook: Appraisal and Evaluation in Central Government*. London: The Stationery Office.

Hoel, Michael, and Thomas Sterner. 2007. "Discounting and Relative Prices." *Climate Change* 84 (3–4): 265–80.

Krutilla, John V. 1967. "Conservation Reconsidered." *American Economic Review* 57 (4): 777–86.

Laibson, David. 1997. "Golden Eggs and Hyperbolic Discounting." *Quarterly Journal of Economics* 112 (2): 443–78.

Lind, Robert C. 1982. *Discounting for Time and Risk in Energy Policy*. Washington, D.C.: Resources for the Future.

Ministre de l'Équipement, des Transports, du Logement, du Tourisme et de la Mer (METLTM). 2003. *Instruction cadre relative aux méthodes d'évaluation économique des grands projets d'infrastructures de transport*. Paris: METLTM. Reference D04001752.

National Development and Reform Commission (NDRC). 2006. *The Economic Assessment Method and Parameters for Capital Construction Projects: Methods and Parameters*, 3rd edition (in Chinese). Beijing: NDRC.

Naturvårdsverket. 2003. *Konsekvensanalys steg för steg: Handledning i samhällsekonomisk konsekvensanalys för Naturvårdsverket*. Stockholm: Naturvårdsverket. ISBN 91-620-5314-0.

Office of Management and Budget (OMB). 2003. *Office of Management and Budget Circular A-4, Regulatory Analysis*. Washington, D.C.: OMB.

Parfit, Derek. 1984. *Reasons and Persons*. New York: Oxford University Press.

Pearce, David, Giles Atkinson, and Susana Mourato. 2006. *Cost-Benefit Analysis and the Environment: Recent Developments*. Paris: OECD.

Poulos, Christine, and Dale Whittington. 2000. "Time Preferences for Life-Saving Programs: Evidence from Six Less Developed Countries." *Environmental Science and Technology* 34 (8): 1445–55.

Ramsey, Frank P. 1928. "A Mathematical Theory of Savings." *Economic Journal* 38 (152): 543–59.

Schelling, Thomas. 1995. "Intergenerational Discounting." *Energy Policy* 23 (4–5): 395–401.

Sen, Amartya Kumar. 1961. "On Optimizing the Rate of Saving." *Economic Journal* 71 (283): 479–96.

Stern, Nicholas. 2006. *The Economics of Climate Change: The Stern Review*. Cambridge: Cambridge University Press.

Swedish Institute for Transport and Communications Analysis (SIKA). 2002. *Översyn av samhällsekonomiska metoder och kalkylvärden på transportområdet* (Review of socio-economic methods and recommended assessment parameters in the transport sector). SIKA report 2002:4.

Thaler, Richard. 1981. "Some Empirical Evidence on Dynamic Inconsistency." *Economics Letters* (3): 201–7.

Traeger, Christian P. 2007. "Theoretical Aspects of Long-Term Evaluation in Environmental Economics." Ph.D. diss., Alfred Weber Institute, University of Heidelberg.

U.S. Environmental Protection Agency (EPA). 2000. *Guidelines for Preparing Economic Analyses*. Report EPA 240-R-00-003. Washington, D.C.: EPA.

Weitzman, Martin L. 1994. "On the Environmental Discount Rate." *Journal of Environmental Economics and Management* 26 (2): 200–9.

Weitzman, Martin L. 1998. "Why the Far-Distant Future Should be Discounted at Its Lowest Possible Rate." *Journal of Environmental Economics and Management* 36: 201–8.

World Bank. 2010. *Environmental Assessment Sourcebook and Updates.* Washington, D.C.: World Bank.

World Bank. 2008. *World Development Indicators.* Washington, D.C.: World Bank.

Zhuang, Juzhong, Zhihong Liang, Tun Lin, and Franklin De Guzman. 2007. "Theory and Practice in the Choice of Social Discount Rate for Cost-Benefit Analysis: A Survey." *Economics and Research Department, Asian Development Bank*, Working Paper No. 94.

5

The Shape of Distributional Analysis

Michael A. Livermore and Jennifer S. Rosenberg

The sum of costs and benefits is a matter of economic efficiency. Who pays the costs and who receives the benefits is a question of distribution. While some efforts have been made by governments to account for how costs and benefits are distributed, for the most part these have been ad hoc and qualitative. Well-structured, rigorous, and consistent distributional analysis continues to elude even the most sophisticated government practitioners of cost-benefit analysis and has more often been the subject of scholarly debate than real-world implementation. This situation likely arises because distributional analysis, to truly inform the decision-making process, must not only present raw information about where benefits and burdens fall, but must also provide an evaluation of the relative importance of shifts in wealth from one group to another. In part because of the strongly normative and political connotations of such an evaluation, distributional analysis has remained a controversial subject that has not made its way into the mainstream practice of cost-benefit analysis.

As a larger number of developing and emerging countries incorporate cost-benefit analysis into their decision-making processes, however, distribution analysis may take a more prominent place. For countries with high levels of inequality or substantial populations living under conditions of dire poverty, the way that the costs and benefits of regulation are distributed can have profound implications for well-being. Policymakers are justifiably concerned about rules that impose costs on individuals subsisting at very low levels of consumption or that worsen the distribution of wealth. If distributional analysis becomes more widespread, it will continue to pose an important set of difficult methodological issues for developing countries.

This chapter looks at how the examination of distributional issues can complement standard cost-benefit tests of economic efficiency, especially in the context of developing countries, and discusses some of the most important challenges. Two basic arguments are developed. The first is that "value-neutral" distributional analysis, which simply prefers rules with flatter distributions of costs and benefits, cannot meaningfully be carried out for individual policies because the level of analysis (whether a policy is analyzed as a whole or in parts) can affect the outcome. System-wide value-free analysis, however, can be helpful in identifying whether biases exist within the regulatory process that disproportionally deny benefits or impose costs on certain groups, which would imply that policies that are efficient for all members of society are not being selected.

The second argument developed here concerns whether, and under what conditions, altering a regulation in light of distributional concerns can be justified. Kaplow and Shavell (1994; 2002) present a very powerful argument that using legal rules, such as environmental regulation, to achieve distributional goals imposes unnecessary efficiency costs because the same distributional result can be achieved at lower cost using the tax-and-transfer system. Real-world conditions in many developing countries, including the existence of a large informal economy or a lack of administrative capacity to effectually tax income and make transfers, however, can cut against the applicability of Kaplow and Shavell's argument. At least some of the time, therefore, regulation may be a superior redistributional tool.

Conducting Distributional Analysis

There are many ways that the distribution of regulatory costs and benefits may be, or may be perceived as, unfair. Perhaps most striking is when a particular subpopulation is shut out from enjoying the same regulatory benefits that many others enjoy. Residents of Qiugang, a village of 1,900 people in China's Anhui province, for years suffered from notoriously high levels of pollution emitted from nearby factories. The chemical plant runoff and other forms of pollution poisoned the local river and wafted toxic fumes into the air, posing serious health consequences for the village's residents and surrounding wildlife.[1] Fairness concerns arise when a particular group is systematically denied regulatory benefits that accrue to others, or disproportionately shoulders negative externalities without compensation. Likewise, a subpopulation could end up paying a disproportionate amount of regulatory costs. A measure that adds a small increment of increased safety to a large population but results in substantial economic losses for a small population—for instance, the loss of some otherwise productive asset—could raise distributional issues as well, although the regulation may nevertheless be justified. Finally, a regulation may produce an undesirable transfer of wealth from poorer to richer. Historic landmarks offer an illustrative example. If such landmarks are preserved, relatively affluent local landowners may benefit from increased property values, but less wealthy members of society may be harmed because future development is hindered, leading to fewer new housing opportunities.

In the United States, distributional analysis is required by executive order and a handful of other federal policies, although these requirements are not always met (Hahn and Dudley 2007; OIRA 2011). The European Union also includes distributional concerns within its regulatory framework (European Commission 2009). But even in these advanced systems, distributional analysis is not an easy endeavor (e.g., Schmitz and Schmitz 2010; Vining and Weimer 2010; Loomis 2011; Zerbe and Dively 1994).

The lack of distributional analysis may be explained in part by the fact that it is a deeply normative enterprise. Starting with the initial accounting, in which aggregate costs and benefits are broken down into a more detailed account that includes information on the parties that bear costs or receive benefits, value-laden decisions must be made. Analysts must decide, for example, which characteristics at what level of granularity are relevant to classifying parties or communities as being affected by the policy. Distribution can be measured according to geographic location, income, race, age, socioeconomic status, business size, industry, or any other of a potentially limitless set of characteristics that could be considered relevant for policymaking. The initial decision about the groups to be targeted for distributional analysis will form the bedrock of future decisions about how to weigh inequalities in the allocation of costs and benefits. Value choices affect the analysis from the start.

Normative considerations also arise in determining the comprehensiveness or technical complexity of the distributional analysis. Policies and projects can have a wide range of direct and indirect effects, creating a potentially limitless analytic task if all distributional effects must be identified and estimated. In standard cost-benefit analysis, the traditional decision-making rule calls for the analysis to stop at the point where the value of information generated by additional investigation is outweighed by the cost of further research, including costs associated with the delay. But distributional analysis does not admit of such a straightforward rule, and instead requires a normative decision about the value of distributional information.

IDENTIFYING WINNERS AND LOSERS

Distributional analysis also faces a number of technical challenges. The indirect effects of a policy can be difficult to anticipate, and it can be especially hard to foresee who will bear the consequences of those secondary effects. Take, for instance, a cap-and-trade scheme on an environmental pollutant. Such a policy is likely to increase production costs for some industrial processes, potentially leading to losses in shareholder value, job losses, or both. Whereas shareholder losses would presumably be felt by more well-off members of society, workers' losing their wages could be a regressive imposition of regulatory costs. Another secondary consequence might be a boon to an industry that sells a substitute good or that manages to comply with the regulation more efficiently. These benefits may increase the value of shareholders' stock or stimulate hiring. In addition, the regulation may spur an increase in consumer prices for basic necessities, like energy or food—a regressive effect. Alternatively, prices for luxury goods may increase—a progressive effect.[2]

Two additional factors complicate the task of identifying winners and losers. First, where possible, it is likely that the benefits of an environmental regulation will be incorporated into the market process, diffusing the benefit across market actors. For example, a land use ordinance restricting the construction of new buildings in a city's center is likely to raise the property value of existing buildings. Some building owners will seize the opportunity to sell into the market, capturing a windfall profit for themselves and producing a consumer surplus for the new buyers. Existing tenants, on the other hand, will experience disruption and transition costs if rental prices increase on account of the change in the market. In this scenario, standard cost-benefit analysis could simply identify increased property values as benefits of the regulation, which could then be compared to the costs associated with development that is forgone. Distributional analysis, however, requires a much deeper investigation of who benefits and who loses out as the effects of the price increase ripple throughout the economy.

Second, proper distributional analysis may require that relative valuations of benefits are taken into account in a way that standard cost-benefit analysis does not. Individual valuation of the benefits of an environmental policy can be expected to track wealth: the higher a person's income, the higher the value she will place on a given environmental benefit. Currently, valuations are based on averages, and are standard for all beneficiaries. For example, under its current practice, the U.S. Environmental Protection Agency (EPA) assigns the same value of statistical life for all residents of the United States, whether they are rich or poor. Distributional analysis, to be accurate, has to take into account the reality that wealthier people will be willing to pay more for an environmental amenity or a mortality risk reduction. As a result, analysts must collect more information, both about the characteristics of the people that are affected by the regulation, and, more generally, about how wealth and other factors affect willingness to pay.

Is Value-Neutral Distributional Analysis Possible?

The claim that more egalitarian distributions of wealth, ceteris paribus, improve social welfare is not controversial among welfare economists. However, the agreement largely stops there, and there are a host of questions about how policies should be designed in light of the effects of wealth distribution on aggregate well-being. And, of course, outside the field of welfare economics, there is open discourse about egalitarian moral obligations owed by governments to their people (Dworkin 1977; 1997), and whether there is even an appropriate role for government in effectuating redistribution (Nozick 1974). Given the difficult set of moral and political questions raised by distributional analysis, it is tempting to look for a value-neutral way to take distributional considerations into account in the regulatory process.

PROBLEMS WITH CASE-BY-CASE VALUE-NEUTRAL ANALYSIS

After learning basic information about how costs and benefits will be distributed and to whom, policymakers must determine how distributional concerns will be factored into decision making. One seemingly attractive possibility might be to try to avoid inequitable distributions by generally favoring policies that have flatter distributions of costs and benefits. One appeal of this approach is that it does not require policymakers to arrive at value judgments about whether certain groups are more worthy of receiving benefits or less deserving of having to bear regulatory costs. Value-laden distributional analysis would explicitly make those normative decisions about how much redistribution, and between what groups, is desirable.

The value-neutral approach runs into serious problems. Ordinarily, in situations where there are a large number of policies, the distributional effects of some policies will be canceled out by the distributional effects of others: groups that benefit from one regulation may be burdened by other regulations. In this way, over a large number of policy choices, distributional imbalances will tend to be self-correcting, absent some systematic bias (discussed below). However, if distributional corrections are made at the policy-by-policy level, then some distributional effects that would have been adjusted for over the normal course of decision making may instead be eliminated by altering the policies individually, presumably at the expense of overall efficiency. As Shavell observes, "if legal rules [are] chosen individually, on the basis of their particular effects on income distribution, needless social losses would result, especially because of the failure to take into account the offsetting effects of legal rules" (Shavell 2004, 657).

An example is illustrative. Imagine two independent regulatory policy regimes: Air and Water. For each choice, the policymaker can choose either an intervention that will influence Market Incentives or a Command-and-Control-type intervention. There are two populations that will be subject to both policies: East and West. Furthermore, it is known that the Market Incentive approaches will generate higher net benefits, but have very skewed distributions—East comes out the big winner when the intervention is used to regulate Air, but loses when it is applied to Water. The consequences for West are reversed. It is also known that the Command-and-Control approaches generate fewer net benefits, but have flatter distributions. Table 5.1 provides a numerical illustration.

If a preference for flatter distributional outcomes is implemented on a policy-by-policy level—first, in deciding between a Market Incentive or Command-and-Control intervention in the context of Air, and then in making the same decision in the context of Water—then the Command approaches will be selected so long as the preference for a flatter distribution is sufficiently high to outweigh the loss of net benefits. In this example, policymakers must be willing to pay more than $10 to achieve the flatter distribution.

However, if the analysis is carried out at a more aggregated level in which all of the policy options and their distributional consequences are considered together, then the Market Incentive approaches will be chosen, because the

TABLE 5.1
Distribution of Costs and Benefits

	East		West		
	Costs	Benefits	Costs	Benefits	Net Benefits
Air: Market	$0	$200	$100	$0	$100
Air: Command & Control	$55	$100	$55	$100	$90
Water: Market	$100	$0	$0	$200	$100
Water: Command & Control	$55	$100	$55	$100	$90

distributional imbalances will cancel each other out. Whereas net benefits under the Command-and-Control policies total $180, of which East and West each receive $90, net benefits under the Market Intervention total $200, of which East and West each receive $100.

To summarize, if the policy options for Air and Water are evaluated separately, then the Command-and-Control interventions that have fewer distributional consequences, but also deliver fewer net benefits, may be selected. The result over both regulations lowers overall net benefits without affecting the distribution of costs and benefits between regions. If we suppose further that both East and West share veto power over policymaking, cannot reach an enforceable agreement, and evaluate Air and Water separately, we would expect a noncooperative equilibrium to arise, where the higher overall benefits of the Market Incentive approach are forgone for the less efficient Command-and-Control interventions. At the policy-by-policy level, a simple preference in favor of neutral—or at least flatter—distribution of costs and benefits generates the same result.

AGGREGATE LEVEL VALUE-NEUTRAL ANALYSIS IS POSSIBLE AND USEFUL

An alternative to looking at the distributional consequences of individual environmental policies is to look at government actions as a whole and determine whether there are groups that systematically bear greater costs and receive fewer benefits. This type of aggregate level value-neutral distributional analysis does not run into the same problems as the analysis of individual policies. To the contrary, aggregate analysis can help improve overall efficiency in the regulatory system.

To achieve efficient outcomes, the regulatory process should fairly consider the interests of all affected parties. As a practical matter, there may be systematic biases that favor some groups over others; for example, well-organized industry versus relatively unorganized consumers. More pointedly, the environmental justice movement in the United States has argued that environmental policies tend to ignore the disproportionate costs—often in the form of pollution exposure—borne by urban, minority, and poor communities (Schlosberg 2007); this occurs, they argue, in part because of failures in the political process (Lazarus 2007).

If some groups are routinely favored by the regulatory system, the pattern suggests systematic bias in the decision-making process. Such bias suggests not only unfairness and discrimination—which are serious problems in their own rights—but also inefficiency. If, as a consequence of unequal access to regulators or some other governance failure, the regulatory process is systematically benefiting some groups more than others, the discrepancy suggests that the most welfare-enhancing regulations are not being adopted. This bias will interfere with the ultimate goal of maximizing net benefits.

Aggregate level analysis would involve assessing the distributional impacts of a sufficiently large number of (randomly chosen) rules. The goal would be to determine whether distributional imbalances generated by individual rules are, in effect, washed out when the rules are looked at collectively. If distributional analysis finds that the regulatory system, over a large number of rules, tends to burden certain groups, or deny others benefits, it raises concerns that the regulatory process is not being equally responsive to the needs of all affected parties.

If systemic bias is found in the regulatory process, there are various ways that decision makers could respond. For instance, efforts could be made to enfranchise underrepresented communities, strengthening their ability to influence agenda-setting using the democratic process. Other responses include increasing transparency in the decision-making process to bolster political accountability; professionalizing civil servants; allowing for judicial review or for review by independent tribunals; engaging in targeted community outreach; and fostering institutional cultures that value all populations equally.

Governments can get creative with crafting process-oriented solutions, developing projects or policies to suit the particular nature or source of a bias that has been identified. For instance, the EPA is very proactive in involving local communities in deliberation over agency efforts to clean up Superfund sites, which are sites that have been contaminated with hazardous substances. The EPA fosters community education and participation in the decision-making process in several ways: by funding communities to hire independent, outside technical advisors who can help community leaders interpret and understand technical information about their Superfund status; by providing direct technical expertise and training; and by naming agency liaisons to organize Community Advisory Groups in affected areas, which then serve as the focal point for exchanging information between community members and state and federal regulators. Community Advisory Groups are intended to represent a cross-section of community stakeholders over the long term; they hold public meetings to foster a consensus-based approach for decision making and are officially recognized as a negotiating party in negotiations over site cleanups.

These types of process solutions can help ensure that regulatory systems are identifying welfare-maximizing regulations. Increasing the amount of information available to decision makers by creating broad systems of participation that facilitate dialogue with all social groups can reduce the risk that any individual or set of interests is systematically favored or disfavored in the regulatory system. Aggregate level distributional analysis can help identify if there are groups that have been excluded, so that policymaking processes can be reformed to make them more open.

Redistribution through Regulation

Beyond using aggregate level distributional analysis to identify ways in which the regulatory system may fail to maximize net benefits, environmental regulation can also be used as a means of effectuating redistributional goals. There are two general ways that regulators can effectuate redistribution. First, the stringency of regulations can be adjusted, making them stronger or weaker. When distributional equity is factored into environmental rulemaking, it will favor stronger environmental protections where the beneficiaries of the rule are disproportionately poor and those burdened are well-off. When those who will benefit from a rule are disproportionately wealthy and those who will pay the costs are disproportionately poor, then the adjustment will be in the direction of a less stringent rule.

Second, the government can carry out on-the-spot redistributions. Under this approach, regulators identify points along the rulemaking process where the government can use its authority to effectuate small-scale redistributions. There are several precedents that exist for this approach. Certainly, when large-scale development projects dislocate communities, it is standard for governments to provide some form of resettlement assistance, and this is one of the criteria used by development banks for evaluating project proposals (e.g., World Bank 2004). The U.S. Constitution establishes such a spot-redistribution requirement with the Takings Clause of the Fifth Amendment, which states, "nor shall private property be taken for public use, without just compensation."[3] The federal environmental assessment process has also used "mitigation measures"[4] to require certain types of environmental compensation such as replacing native trees that had to be removed in the course of laying a pipeline.[5]

One question within the field of law and economics concerns whether it is ever appropriate for a legal or regulatory regime to be used to promote redistribution, or whether the tax-and-transfer system is always superior. After briefly sketching out the key theoretical arguments on both sides of the debate, this following discussion will turn to the practical considerations that could support the use of regulation to achieve redistributional goals, at least in some contexts. These considerations may have even greater salience in developing countries, many of which lack the capacity to administer sophisticated tax systems, and face certain challenges—most important, a large informal sector—that are largely unknown in the most advanced economies. Thus, even if redistribution through the tax-and-transfer scheme is, in principle, superior, practical considerations on the ground may tell a different story.

IS REGULATORY REDISTRIBUTION EVER JUSTIFIED?

Once a government has determined that some redistribution is socially desirable, a tool to accomplish these redistributional goals must be selected. Two options have received the most attention: the first is to use the income tax system to effectuate a transfer of wealth from rich to poor; the second is to enact legal rules—regulations—that will effectuate a similar transfer, albeit less explicitly and in a nonpecuniary manner. Over the past twenty years, a view has emerged among many law and economics thinkers that the former option is universally superior. This view is grounded in the now classic argument developed by Louis Kaplow and Steven Shavell (1994; 2002) that for every legal rule (or regulation) that is designed to achieve redistribution, there is an alternative legal rule (or regulation) that, in concert with a redistributive tax scheme, could achieve the same sought-after transfer with the added benefit of increasing overall wealth.[6] This is because any legal rule designed to achieve redistribution will inherently cause an efficiency loss in the activity being regulated. (In fact, it will cause two distinct efficiency losses, or "distortions" in the market, explained below.) Such inefficiencies shrink the size of the economic pie, thereby reducing the amount of tax revenue the government is able to collect. By contrast, regulations designed with economic efficiency as the exclusive goal will maximize the size of that pie. The larger the pie, the larger the government surplus, and ultimately the more money the government has to transfer to the poor or spend on public goods that improve everyone's welfare (Frank 2000; Kaplow and Shavell 1994; 2002).

Kaplow and Shavell (1994; 2002) also note that it is comparatively easier to administer taxes than legal rules, and to do so with accuracy. Legal rules are by nature blunt instruments whose efficacy depends on various factors, including their enforcement. Thus, whether a legal rule designed to achieve redistribution could actually serve that purpose would depend on a multitude of external variables. Tax schemes can therefore hold administrative advantage over regulation as a redistributive tool. For the above reasons, Kaplow and Shavell conclude that taxes are more efficient than legal rules. Accordingly, the government should craft environmental and public health policy to maximize wealth, while relying solely on a modified income tax and transfer payments system to achieve redistributive goals.

In making this case for why redistribution through the legal system will always be less efficient than the tax-and-transfer system, Kaplow and Shavell employ a line of reasoning that has since been referred to as their "double-distortion argument" (Sanchirico 2000; 2001). The first distortion, or inefficiency, arises from the fact that redistribution of any kind distorts work incentives: as economic actors receive less financial reward for their work, they become more inclined toward leisure. According to Kaplow and Shavell, the distortion to the labor/leisure choice is the same regardless of whether a government effectuates redistribution through its tax system or through regulation. It makes no difference whether an individual's income is reduced on account of an increase in the marginal tax rate[7] or on account of a stronger regulatory scheme: that person will anticipate both reductions in income in the same way and take them into account when choosing how much income to earn from labor or deciding whether it is worthwhile to invest capital in innovation and production. Yet redistribution through legal rules carries with it an additional, second distortion: it causes inefficiencies in the regulated market. In the regulatory scenario, this distortion can be understood most plainly as the difference between the net benefits created by the economically optimal rule and the net benefits created by the redistributional rule. For example, if distributional concerns counsel for greater air pollution reduction, the costs companies incur for pollution control technologies are greater than the willingness-to-pay of beneficiaries for the cleaner air at the margin. Instead of requiring pollution reduction with greater marginal costs than benefits (which, in effect, converts $1 worth of regulatory expenditures into less than $1 of benefits), the government could simply tax the company and transfer the revenues directly to the regulatory beneficiaries. It follows from Kaplow and Shavell's "double distortion" premise that a bifurcated approach to redistribution—with regulatory policy designed solely to maximize aggregate welfare, and a tax code adjusted to correct for unequal distributions of well-being—is optimal.

The double distortion effect is only important for rules that are altered on the basis of income. If a regulation is designed regardless of income—say, all polluters are fined a fixed amount of damages based exclusively on the amount of harm they have caused—then it will have no impact on the labor-leisure choice (Sanchirico 2000). In such cases, individuals and firms are not being incentivized to *produce* less; they are given financial reason to *pollute* less. This is an extremely important distinction. So long as the low-productivity, high-pollution firm pays the same costs as a high-productivity, high-pollution firm, then the regime does not distort incentives to work or invest.

Moreover, it is possible that in a scenario where taxes and legal rules are employed simultaneously, their respective distortions would balance each other out. This is a consequence of the second-best paradigm, which holds that a legal rule that would be optimal in the abstract may not be the most efficient in the real world, in light of other legal rules or conditions that cannot be changed (Lipsey and Lancaster 1956). In this case, the next-best solution involves enacting legal rules, or regulations, that have offsetting distortions. Ultimately, the view that favors redistribution through taxation comes down to an empirical question about whether a systematic effort to modify legal rules on the basis of income would indeed affect labor supply, the degree of that effect, and whether there are offsetting distortions that should be taken into account in a particular jurisdiction.

PRACTICAL CONSIDERATIONS

While there may be theoretical reasons to believe that a tax-and-transfer system will achieve distributional goals more effectively, this may not be true in practice, at least not in all circumstances. For one, redistribution that is otherwise desirable may not be achievable through the tax-and-transfer system for political or cultural reasons. Kaplow and Shavell remain agnostic on the appropriate response in these circumstances:

> An argument sometimes offered in favor of redistribution through legal rules is that the tax system falls short of optimal redistributive taxation—perhaps because of the balance of political power in the legislature. This argument raises questions that we do not seek to address about the function of courts [or regulators] in a democracy. (Kaplow and Shavell 1994, 675)

This problem of political intransigence is perhaps exacerbated in developing countries. Although excessive inequality is a justification for a more progressive tax policy, it may also result in a concentration of political power among a small and wealthy segment of the population, making passage of redistributional policy less likely. Many developing countries in fact remain far from achieving high levels of progressivity in their tax codes. A variety of public choice failures can hinder sound policymaking, especially in developing countries under authoritarian rule or during periods of democratic transition (Esty 1999). While such failures plague all governments to some degree, many developing countries contend with high concentrations of wealth and political power, corruption, weak democratic accountability, and nascent civil society institutions. Such governance challenges stymie policymakers' ability to address even the most basic of public needs, including urgent health and security risks (Rose-Ackerman 1999; Ostrom, Schroeder, and Wynne 1993; Nye 1967). They also cast serious doubt on the ability of government actors to achieve the task of forming the political consensus necessary to enact optimal tax-and-transfer rules. Local context is important. In any given country, certain decision-making bodies may be more or less subject to public choice failures. Those that are less so will be better at effectuating socially desirable redistributional goals. In some countries, regulatory agencies will be preferable; in others, legislatures or courts may have a greater potential for success or be more reliable or transparent.

Even if the will to redistribute through taxation did exist, some developing countries would face steep challenges in implementing such a system. To start, a substantial portion of the workforce in developing economies subsists on agricultural labor or participation in small, informal businesses. These workers receive unsteady streams of income, and their wages are often paid in cash, making it difficult to calculate their tax base, collect tax payments, and effectuate transfers. An informal economic sector is, by definition, an economy that is not taxed, nor is it included in measurements of gross domestic product or regulated by the state. It consists largely of unreported income from the production of goods and services or barter transactions, economic activities that would otherwise be taxable if they were reported to the government. Informal economies may also include illegal activities, such as trade with stolen goods, fraud, or smuggling (Lippert and Walker 1997).

Informal economic sectors have sprung up in the developing world, where citizens sometimes struggle to earn legitimate incomes, although tax burdens and regulations may also contribute to the prevalence of informal economies (Schneider and Buehn 2009). Recent estimates put the size of these "underground" or "shadow" economies—which may include legal as well as illegal enterprises—at, on average, 35.5 percent of a developing country's GDP (Schneider and Buehn 2009) and half of its entire labor force (Schneider 2011).[8] The informal economies in high-income countries, by contrast, are much lower, at around 15.5 percent of GDP (Schneider and Buehn 2009). And in the United States, which is the focal point for much of the discourse on optimal redistributive policy, the informal economy stands at only 8.1 percent of GDP, making it one of the smallest in the world (Schneider and Buehn 2009).

The existence of large informal sectors should not be ignored in discussions of how to best effectuate redistribution in developing countries. First and foremost, the size of these sectors drastically narrows the tax base. Even business taxes cannot be fully exploited, since big firms may have the opportunity to avoid using the financial sector and to rely on cash transactions wherever possible (Gordon and Li 2009). Second, tax reforms that may be efficient in developed economies might actually reduce aggregate welfare in emerging economies, in light of informal sectors, just as conventional preferences for consumption taxes over border tariffs may not hold in the developing context, since increasing the former could exacerbate intersectoral distortions between formal and informal sectors (Emran and

Stiglitz 2005). Thus, informal sectors have serious implications for the wisdom of keeping redistribution the exclusive province of the tax code.

The effect of the existence of a sizable informal sector on whether taxation or legal rules are better tools for achieving redistributional goals is ambiguous, and therefore context specific. While redistribution through legal rules always comes with the double distortion effect identified by Kaplow and Shavell, redistribution through taxation can create a similar multidistortional effect in countries with large informal economies. In such countries, new or renewed efforts by the state to enforce a progressive income tax could further disincentivize movement toward the formal sector. The imposition of taxes will instead incentivize investment in legal tax avoidance and illegal tax evasion, at best resulting in deadweight loss, and at worst undermining the formal economy. These distortions resonate more loudly in developing countries, where it is much easier to exit or evade the formal economy than it is in developed economies.[9]

On the other hand, the transfer portion of the tax-and-transfer approach incentivizes low-income workers to enter the formal economy. If the informal economy largely covers the poorest members of society, a negative income tax, for example, creates incentives for members of the informal economy to formalize their employment situations. Experience in the United States with the Earned Income Tax Credit shows that this effect exists, although there are still individuals who continue to participate only in the informal economy based on their misperceptions about the tax system (Schneider 2011; Slemrod 2006). In cases where redistributional concerns favor stricter levels of environmental regulation, there are also incentives to invest in detection avoidance, which may also encourage firms to exit the formal economy to avoid enforcement of regulatory standards.

In addition to the fact that substantial portions of their domestic economies are not covered by the tax system, many developing countries lack the capacity to administer personal income tax systems, even within formal sectors. They may not have the necessary critical mass of well-educated, well-trained, and well-paid civil service employees. Many countries are also without the computerized record-keeping systems vital for operationalizing a tax code. Taxpayers themselves may have limited means for tracking and processing taxable accounts on account of illiteracy or other limitations in capacity (Tanzi and Zee 2001; Newbery 1987). "As a result," Tanzi and Zee point out, "governments often take the path of least resistance, developing tax systems that allow them to exploit whatever options are available rather than establishing rational, modern, and efficient tax systems" (Tanzi and Lee 2001, 1). Whereas richer, industrialized countries raise most of their tax revenue through personal income taxes and consumption taxes, developing countries tend to yield most of their revenue through corporate income taxes and consumption taxes, with personal income taxes playing a very minor role (Gordon and Li 2009).

Fewer additional administrative resources may be needed to effectuate redistribution through the regulatory system. Many of the costs associated with administering a regulatory regime are not sensitive to the stringency of the regulation, so that changes to regulatory stringency to achieve redistribution will not place additional burdens on government. Once a government has invested in a system to establish and enforce environmental rules, slightly altering regulatory stringency is unlikely to result in large additional expenditures. In cases where redistribution favors less stringent requirements, the administrative burden for government may even decline.

Finally, in some extreme cases, the tax-and-transfer system may not be sufficiently responsive to ensure that individuals or groups are not severely harmed by a particular policy. In these situations, the payment of immediate and direct compensation to a particular group may be needed, and if that is not possible, changes to a policy to avoid severe negative consequences for the affected group may be necessary. For instance, development projects often result in the displacement of peoples whose homes stand in the way of roads, power plants, reservoirs, or other sizable construction projects. People who are involuntarily ousted from their homes are forced to bear large economic and other costs. Potential risks inherent in forced displacement include joblessness, homelessness, food insecurity, increased morbidity, and lost access to common property (Cernea 1999).[10] Simply relying on the tax-and-transfer system to compensate the displaced for their losses may be too time-consuming. If immediate compensation cannot be paid, alterations to the underlying policy may be required.

Conclusion

Distributional analysis is often an important component of sound regulatory impact analysis. It is not a subset of cost-benefit analysis; rather, it is a complement that describes who will reap the economic benefits of a particular program or policy and who will be forced to pay the economic costs. Distributional analysis of individual rules that attempts to be value-neutral (i.e., that does not take a normative stand on how much redistribution, from and to what groups, is desirable) is not useful. Value-neutral distributional analysis at the aggregate level, however, can be deployed to identify any systematic biases in the administrative apparatus that warrant governmental response, such as the patterned imposition of disproportionate costs upon minority communities.

There are two foundational mechanisms through which governments can effectuate wealth transfers: through adjustments to the tax system and through changes in legal rules or regulations. The choice between the two mechanisms gives rise to its own set of questions about the administrative costs associated with each option, as well as the degree to which each mechanism would cause distortions or efficiency losses in the market. The answer will depend on local factors, including administrative capacity and whether there are any complementary regulations in effect that may generate offsetting distortions.

As developing countries expand their use of cost-benefit analysis, greater attention is likely to be paid to the question of how to appropriately consider the distribution of regulatory costs and benefits. These questions are deeply normative and often depend on highly contingent local circumstances. They do not admit of simple solutions, and are likely to continue to raise important challenges for analysts and policymakers in the years to come.

Notes

1. After a protracted campaign by local residents and environmental groups, the Chinese government committed $30 million to clean up the river and institute pollution controls (Xinhua 2010).

2. Despite the difficulties of modeling the distributional effects of greenhouse gas controls, several analysts have made sophisticated attempts (e.g., Burtraw, Sweeney, and Walls 2009).

3. U.S. Const. amend. V.

4. National Environmental Protection Act of 1969, 40 C.F.R. § 1508.20 (1970).

5. At least one scholar has suggested that governments require the construction of wind power and other renewable energy projects as formal mitigation measures intended to "offset or even reverse the otherwise unavoidable negative impacts of carbon emissions from fossil-fuel power production" (Wickersham 2004, 345).

6. Prior to Kaplow and Shavell, Aanund Hylland and Richard Zeckhauser (1979) demonstrated that in instances where optimal taxation is available, the choice between alternative government projects should be made entirely on the basis of their respective net benefits, uninfluenced by distributive aims.

7. For a survey of the literature on how marginal tax rate schemes affect labor incentives, including a thoughtful discussion on James Mirrlees's pioneering work on optimal income taxation, see Tuomala (1990). See also Mirrlees (1971).

8. Informal workers in African shadow economies constitute, on average, 54.2 percent of the entire labor force; the average in the three largest Asian countries (China, India, and Indonesia) is 36.5 percent, and in Latin and South America the average is 49.6 percent (Schneider 2011, 38–42). In some regions of sub-Saharan Africa and South Asia, more than 80 percent of all nonagricultural jobs are informal (Schneider 2011).

9. Domestic tax evasion through informal economies costs developing countries an estimated $385 billion in revenue each year (Cobham 2005). Individuals' offshore asset-holding and corporate profit-shifting across borders contribute to an additional $100 billion in lost tax revenue across the developing world (Cobham 2005; see also Kar and Cartwright-Smith 2008). For instance, over 50 percent of the cash and listed securities of wealthy Latin Americans is believed to be havened offshore (Juniac et al. 2003).

10. This is not to mention other risks such as the inducement of psychological trauma, especially to children, and the loss of civil rights or violation of human rights, including being subjected to communal violence in resettlement areas or by security forces and the loss of property without fair compensation (Robinson 2003). UN guidelines prohibit involuntary displacement in cases of "large-scale development projects which are not justified by compelling and overriding public interests" (OCHA 2004, Principle 6).

Bibliography

Adler, Matthew D. 2011. *Well-Being and Fair Distribution: Beyond Cost-Benefit Analysis.* Oxford: Oxford University Press.

Burtraw, Dallas, Richard Sweeney, and Margaret Walls. 2009. "The Incidence of U.S. Climate Policy: Alternative Uses of Revenues from a Cap-and-Trade Auction." Discussion Paper, Resources for the Future, Washington, D.C.

Cernea, Michael. 1999. "Why Economic Analysis is Essential to Resettlement: A Sociologist's View." In *The Economics of Involuntary Resettlement: Questions and Challenges*, ed. Michael Cernea, 5–31. Washington, D.C.: World Bank.

Cobham, Alex. 2005. "Tax Evasion, Tax Avoidance and Development Finance." Working Paper Series No. 129, Finance and Trade Policy Research Centre at the University of Oxford, Queen Elizabeth House.

Dworkin, Ronald. 1977. *Taking Rights Seriously*. Cambridge: Harvard University Press.

Dworkin, Ronald. 1997. *Freedom's Law: The Moral Reading of the Constitution*. Cambridge: Harvard University Press.

Emran, M. Shahe, and Joseph E. Stiglitz. 2005. "On Selective Indirect Tax Reform in Developing Countries." *Journal of Public Economics* 89 (4): 599–623.

Esty, Daniel C. 1999. "Toward Optimal Environmental Governance." *New York University Law Review* 74: 1495–1574.

European Commission. 2009. *Impact Assessment Guidelines*. Brussels, European Commission. SEC (2009) 92.

Frank, Robert H. 2000. "Why is Cost-Benefit Analysis So Controversial?" *Journal of Legal Studies* 29 (S2): 913–30.

Gordon, Roger, and Wei Li. 2009. "Tax Structure in Developing Countries: Many Puzzles and a Possible Explanation." *Journal of Public Economics* 93 (7–8): 855–66.

Hahn, Robert W., and Patrick M. Dudley. 2007. "How Well Does the Government Do Cost-Benefit Analysis?" *Review of Environmental Economics and Policy* 1 (2): 192–211.

Hylland, Aanund, and Richard J. Zeckhauser. 1979. "Distributional Objectives Should Affect Taxes But Not Program Choice or Design." *Scandinavian Journal of Economics* 81 (2): 264–84.

Juniac, Christian de, Andrew Dyer, Bruce M. Holley, and Mathieu Menegaux. 2003. *Winning in a Challenging Market: Global Wealth 2003*. Boston: Boston Consulting Group.

Kaplow, Louis, and Steven Shavell. 2002. "On the Superiority of Corrective Taxes to Quantity Regulation." *American Law and Economics Review* 4 (1): 1–17.

Kaplow, Louis, and Steven Shavell. 1994. "Why the Legal System is Less Efficient than the Income Tax in Redistributing Income." *Journal of Legal Studies* 23 (2): 667–81.

Kar, Dev, and Devon Cartwright-Smith. 2008. *Illicit Financial Flows From Developing Countries: 2002–2006*. Global Financial Integrity Executive Report. Washington, D.C.: Global Financial Integrity.

Lazarus, Richard J. 2007. "Environmental Law After Katrina: Reforming Environmental Law by Reforming Environmental Lawmaking." *Tulane Law Review* 81 (4): 1019–58.

Lippert, Owen, and Michael Walker, eds. 1997. *The Underground Economy: Global Evidence of Its Size and Impact*. Vancouver, British Columbia, Canada: Fraser Institute.

Lipsey, Richard G., and Kelvin Lancaster. 1956. "The General Theory of Second Best." *Review of Economic Studies* 24 (1): 11–32.

Loomis, John. 2011. "Incorporating Distributional Issues into Benefit-Cost Analysis: Why, How, and Two Empirical Examples Using Non-Market Valuation." *Journal of Benefit-Cost Analysis* 2 (1): Art. 5.

Mirrlees, James A. 1971. "An Exploration in the Theory of Optimal Income Taxation." *Review of Economic Studies* 38 (2): 175–208.

Newbery, David. 1987. "Taxation and Development." In *The Theory of Taxation for Developing Countries*, ed. David Newbery and Nicholas Stern, 165–204. Oxford: Oxford University Press.

Nozick, Robert. 1974. *Anarchy, State, and Utopia*. New York: Basic Books.

Nye, Joseph S. 1967. "Corruption and Political Development: A Cost-Benefit Analysis." *American Political Science Review* 61 (2): 417–27.

Office of Information and Regulatory Affairs (OIRA). 2011. *Annual Report to Congress on the Benefits and Costs of Federal Regulations and Unfunded Mandates on State, Local, and Tribal Entities*. Washington, D.C.: OIRA.

Ostrom, Elinor, Larry Schroeder, and Susan Wynne. 1993. *Institutional Incentives and Sustainable Development: Infrastructure Policies in Perspective*. Boulder: Westview Press.

Robinson, W. Courtland. 2003. *Risks and Rights: The Causes, Consequences, and Challenges of Development-Induced Displacement*. Brookings Institution-SAIS Project on Internal Displacement. Washington, D.C.: Brookings Institution.

Rose-Ackerman, Susan. 1999. *Corruption and Government: Causes, Consequences, and Reform*. Cambridge: Cambridge University Press.

Sanchirico, Chris W. 2000. "Taxes versus Legal Rules as Instruments for Equity: A More Equitable View." *Journal of Legal Studies* 29 (2): 797–820.

Sanchirico, Chris W. 2001. "Deconstructing the New Efficiency Rationale." *Cornell Law Review* 86: 1003–89.

Schlosberg, David. 2007. *Defining Environmental Justice: Theories, Movements, and Nature*. Oxford: Oxford University Press.

Schmitz, Andrew, and Troy G. Schmitz. 2010. "Benefit-Cost Analysis: Distributional Considerations Under Production Quota Buyouts." *Journal of Benefit-Cost Analysis* 1 (1): Art. 2.

Schneider, Friedrich. 2011. "The Shadow Economy and Shadow Economy Labor Force: What Do We (Not) Know?" Institute for the Study of Labor (IZA), Discussion Paper No. 5769.

Schneider, Friedrich, and Andreas Buehn. 2009. "Shadow Economies And Corruption All Over the World: Revised Estimates for 120 Countries." *Economics: The Open-Access, Open-Assessment E-Journal* 1 (9): 1–66, doi: 10.5018/economics-ejournal.ja.2007-9.

Shavell, Steven. 2004. *Foundations of Economic Analysis of the Law*. Cambridge: Harvard University Press.

Slemrod, Joel. 2006. "The Role of Misconceptions in Support for Regressive Tax Reform." *National Tax Journal* 59 (1): 57–75.

Tanzi, Vito, and Howell Zee. 2001. "Tax Policy for Developing Countries." International Monetary Fund (IMF), Economic Issues Series No. 27.

Tuomala, Matti. 1990. *Optimal Income Tax and Redistribution*. Oxford: Clarendon Press.

United Nations Office for the Coordination of Humanitarian Affairs (OCHA). 2004. *Guiding Principles on Internal Displacement*, 2nd ed. Geneva: United Nations.

Vining, Aidan, and David L. Weimer. 2010. "An Assessment of Important Issues Concerning the Application of Benefit-Cost Analysis to Social Policy." *Journal of Benefit-Cost Analysis* 1 (1): Art. 5.

Wickersham, Jay. 2004. "Sacred Landscapes and Profane Structures: How Offshore Wind Power Challenges the Environmental Impact Review Process." *Boston College Environmental Affairs Law Review* 31 (2): 325–47.

World Bank. 2004. *Involuntary Resettlement Sourcebook: Planning and Implementation in Development Projects*. Washington, D.C.: World Bank.

Xinhua. 2011. "A Village's Fight for Environment." *China Daily*, March 9.

PART THREE

Institutional Matters

6

Changing Faces of Cost-Benefit Analysis
ALTERNATIVE INSTITUTIONAL SETTINGS AND VARIED
SOCIAL AND POLITICAL CONTEXTS

Jiunn-rong Yeh

Over the past thirty years, cost-benefit analysis has developed into a strong analytic instrument to facilitate rational decision-making in the modern regulatory state (Revesz and Livermore 2008). Similar to environmental impact assessment, cost-benefit analysis first became widespread in the United States but has spread to other jurisdictions, a phenomenon described as cost-benefit analysis " go[ing] global" (Livermore 2011, 149). In observing varied practices of cost-benefit analysis, scholars often take the U.S. model as the standard and assess other countries' practices in terms of how much they diverge from that benchmark.

One of the most salient features of the U.S. model is its institutional setting and use as a tool for executive oversight. Yet cost-benefit analysis often provides insights that can be leveraged outside of the executive branch, and developing countries may want to conceive of cost-benefit analysis more broadly, as a tool for informing policy choices in varied decision-making contexts. The various ways in which countries other than the United States have integrated cost-benefit analysis within their own policymaking structures suggest a range of institutional possibilities for developing and refining the technique.

The typical uses of cost-benefit analysis share a number of distinctive features. First, it is used by the executive branch of government to exercise regulatory oversight and design regulatory policy. Second, the methodology involves quantifying and monetizing policy impacts, so that alternative policy options may be compared in common units. Third, it is relatively institutionalized.

This standard version of cost-benefit analysis reflects the need for coordination among government agencies. Coordinated programs between agencies are often costly and, therefore, are subject to close scrutiny by the chief executive. The agencies' diverse mandates can undermine smooth and coherent policy implementation (Hemphill 2007). In the United States, the institution charged with executive oversight to help achieve coordination and reduce incoherence is the president's Office of Management and Budget (OMB), which is authorized to review the regulatory proposals of administrative agencies.

One possible departure from this standard would be a shift of focus away from the executive branch. Although many public programs are administered by regulatory agencies, some programs and public policies are devised by legislatures, courts, or even the general public in the form of referendum. In what ways could cost-benefit analysis inform decision making by the legislature or even the general public? What functions can cost-benefit analysis provide for these alternative authorities? How will the underlying techniques or methodologies need to be revised to meet the particular goals or procedures of these institutions?

Another departure from standard applications of cost-benefit analysis may occur when cost-benefit analysis is conducted in different political and social contexts, including a democratizing state, a developmental state, or even an authoritarian state. When cost-benefit analysis is conducted in a stable constitutional democracy such as the United States, quantification or monetization of costs and benefits can be expected to be conducted with a level of bureaucratic professionalism and public scrutiny. In the context of an authoritarian state or transitional democracy, however, elite-centered decision-making mechanisms such as highly quantified or monetized cost-benefit analysis may be seen as a device for governing elites to reduce public participation and obscure their exercise of power. Application of cost-benefit analysis in these social and political contexts may unexpectedly generate political controversies and lead to politicization. It is thus important to examine how cost-benefit analysis operates in these more dynamic and less stable social and political contexts in order to understand its useful roles as well as its constraints.

This chapter attempts to provide a broader picture of cost-benefit analysis by looking into diverse decision-making dynamics in its application, examining both institutional and contextual variations. With cost-benefit analysis going global, it can be expected to be embedded in different institutional configurations. The discussion is divided into three main sections. The first section discusses the basic features of cost-benefit analysis as they have been developed in the United States and offers possible alternative models that may be developed in other institutional settings and social or political contexts. The second section describes the Penghu casino referendum case in Taiwan to illustrate the applications of cost-benefit analysis in an alternative institutional setting. Changing the decision-making authority that is attempting to use cost-benefit analysis has the potential to fundamentally change the technique, its functions, and its qualitative and quantitative nature. Inspired by the intriguing social and political context of the Penghu casino case, the third section shifts the focus to more general contextual variations of cost-benefit analysis. The varied contexts in which cost-benefit analysis is adopted and put into place, such as a developmental state or transitional democracy, do make a difference. The roles of cost-benefit analysis in different social and political contexts may require the technique to evolve beyond its original expert-focused orientation. Based upon these nuanced developments of cost-benefit analysis in different institutional settings and social or political contexts, this chapter concludes by arguing that cost-benefit analysis should move toward a more dialectic mechanism for policymaking in modern regulatory states.

Changing Faces of Cost-Benefit Analysis: Formal Institutionalization and Beyond

Cost-benefit analysis is designed to improve decision making by evaluating the cost and benefit sides of proposed policies or government actions. Since its introduction in the United States, cost-benefit analysis has been adopted by many other states and deployed in a wide and evolving range of scopes and contents. Writing cost-benefit analysis into law or installing formal institutions and processes for its implementation is a typical method by which many states have adopted cost-benefit analysis as a decision-making mechanism. However, other subtler or more nuanced applications of cost-benefit analysis in the decision-making process that may not be readily observable in formal laws or institutions have also been put in place in many societies that strive for better allocation of resources.

THE INSTITUTIONALIZATION OF COST-BENEFIT ANALYSIS IN THE UNITED STATES

Cost-benefit analysis has been developed as a tool to guide decision making, particularly in regulatory agenda-setting and public construction. Institutionalized cost-benefit analysis originated in the United States with the enactment of the Flood Control Act of 1936, which authorized the Department of Agriculture to assess costs and benefits in formulating flood control plans (Fuguitt and Wilcox 1999). In 1939, the Bureau of Reclamation exercised cost-benefit analysis in assessing the economic values of river navigation and commercial fisheries in accordance with the Reclamation Project Act. At the time, however, cost-benefit analysis was not the dominant factor in the decision-making process (Fuguitt and Wilcox 1999). It was not until Ronald Reagan's Executive Order 12,291 in 1981 that cost-benefit analysis became the central decision-making mechanism in the modern regulatory state (Pildes and Sunstein 1995; Hahn and Sunstein 2002). Cost-benefit analysis—together with its extended version, regulatory impact analysis (RIA)—has become a pivotal regulatory tool for many administrations despite some lasting controversies (Revesz and Livermore 2008). It has been widely used in many policymaking and regulatory areas, such as education, scientific research, national defense, forestry, urban development, and transportation.

Based on the model institutionalized in the United States, cost-benefit analysis typically has three salient features. First, cost-benefit analysis helps facilitate executive oversight. Through OMB's reviews of the cost-benefit analyses conducted by agencies for major federal regulatory initiatives, the president stands in a firm position to direct as well as coordinate the allocation of government resources. Second, as an institutionalized review mechanism, cost-benefit analysis is highly quantitative and involves the monetization of both cost and benefits. Those who conduct and review cost-benefit analysis are technical experts, generally with an educational background in the field of economics. Third, the introduction and application of cost-benefit analysis often involves different institutional settings, including legislative enactment, executive requirements, operational procedures, and designated government units.

Despite its full-fledged development, however, the institutionalization of cost-benefit analysis has not been without criticism. There are continuous efforts to improve the formats and functions of cost-benefit analysis in response to the dynamics of regulatory decision making. Some scholars have sought to improve cost-benefit analysis by exploring different applications of the technique. These nuanced developments include qualitative cost-benefit analysis, modified cost-benefit analysis, cost-effectiveness analysis, and multigoals analysis (Weimer and Vining 2004). Others are more critical of cost-benefit analysis applications and argue that cost-benefit analysis suffers from intrinsic flaws that cannot be cured by fine-tuning (Ackerman and Heinzerling 2004; Kysar 2006). Some have identified inherent constraints or even fallacies in the application of cost-benefit analysis, but maintain that cost-benefit analysis could be improved through better understanding and application (Revesz and Livermore 2008).

COST-BENEFIT ANALYSIS IN ALTERNATIVE INSTITUTIONAL SETTINGS AND CHANGING SOCIAL AND POLITICAL CONTEXTS

The concept of cost-benefit analysis is not new. Decision making based on some level of calculation between costs and benefits was not completely foreign to even preindustrial societies. Variations of cost-benefit analysis can be—and, indeed, were—employed in other social and political contexts featuring different institutional settings, ideological focuses, and economic conditions. In the context of Asia, for example, one can wonder whether cost-benefit analysis can exist comfortably alongside Confucianism. So far as the ancient teachings are concerned, Confucianism does frequently embrace utilitarian calculus. A good example is that education has long been regarded in Confucian societies as a calculated investment for personal prosperity. In this broad sense, the concept of cost-benefit analysis was already prevalent in ancient Chinese governance. It should not be surprising that some form of cost-benefit calculus was done before launching major public projects. The differences between the ancient calculation and modern cost-benefit analysis lie only in their formats and applications, as well as, more importantly, the nature of decision making in their respective social and political contexts.

Decisions on public policies or government projects are made by dictatorships, authoritarian states, and democracies alike. These decisions are, however, made against very different backdrops and with divergent institutional settings. The applications of cost-benefit analysis will be, to varying degrees, affected by these institutional and contextual variations.

Take the institutionalization of environmental impact assessment, for example. In the United States, environmental impact assessments are used to bring environmental considerations into the whole picture of policy concerns. Environmental concerns do not always outweigh other policy considerations. In Taiwan, however, because the environmental impact assessment law was enacted at the apex of democratization, in which political parties were competing to respond to social demands for environmental justice, the law gave Taiwan's Environmental Protection Agency a veto power over proposed projects or government actions based upon the findings of environmental impact assessments (Yeh 1996). Given the difference in social and political contexts and the resulting institutional variations, the format and process of environmental impact assessment in the United States and Taiwan have departed from each other significantly.

These institutional and contextual variations are equally present in the application of cost-benefit analysis. To better understand cost-benefit analysis and its divergent applications, we must investigate further these institutional or contextual details: Which decision-making authority decides to conduct cost-benefit analysis, for what reasons, and in which contexts? Who actually refers to cost-benefit analysis in the decision-making process?

In modern constitutional democracies, decision-making authorities can be the head of the government (president or prime minister), the legislature, or even citizens at large through public referenda. Cost-benefit analysis can be a helpful device for evaluating information or disseminating it to different decision-making authorities. As decision-making authorities change, the process of cost-benefit analysis may concurrently be altered and employed with different levels of quantification, monetization, or institutionalization. Decision makers, processes of decision making, and decision-making methods are all connected and interrelated issues.

THREE COST-BENEFIT ANALYSIS MODELS AND DECISION-MAKING PROCESSES

Decision-making authorities are increasingly willing to accept cost-benefit analysis as a decision-making device or as a reference in the process of decision making (Boardman et al. 2001). Complaints that cost-benefit analysts pay too much attention to technical rationality, with an attendant focus on quantification and monetization, have increased as well (Hansson 2007). Indeed, there are persuasive reasons to place greater attention on the institutional settings and social and political contexts of cost-benefit analysis than on statistical and quantitative techniques.

For example, cost-benefit analysis can have a targeted function in relation to decision making. When cost-benefit analysis is primarily for executive oversight, it is the president or senior administration officials who use cost-benefit analysis in making decisions on major federal actions. In this context, cost-benefit analysis is employed for internal review within the executive branch. If cost-benefit analysis is employed for a different purpose in a different context, it should be done in ways that satisfy the needs of the different decision-making framework. In the executive model, the decision-making authority in need of cost-benefit analysis is the president, ministries, or agencies. In alternative settings, decision makers may be the legislature or even the general public. Based upon the difference in decision-making authority, we can describe three different cost-benefit analysis models.

The first cost-benefit analysis model is the executive model, which was developed in the United States and is practiced mainly within the executive branch, the oversight of which is vested within the OMB, an office of the president. Its main function is to provide the president with internal oversight. With the president's substantial authority over executive agencies, the president can use cost-benefit analysis as a mechanism for holistic oversight of regulatory efficiency. Cost-benefit analysis is conducted in the executive model primarily from one end of the government (an agency or a ministry) to the other end (president or prime minister) for dissemination and evaluation of information relevant to decision making.

With this intragovernmental purpose, cost-benefit analysis's application in the executive model tends to be formally institutionalized and professionalized, valuing quantitative statistics over qualitative itemization. Hence, despite the continuous use of cost-benefit analysis from the Reagan administration through the current Obama administration, critics maintain their skepticism of cost-benefit analysis's reliance on quantification. Opponents of cost-benefit analysis believe it is biased against invisible, unpredictable, or long-term values, such as social justice or environmental factors (Atkinson and Mourato 2008).

Cost-benefit analysis for legislative reference may be an alternative to the executive oversight model. The legislature makes policy decisions independent from the executive in the form of legislation, budgets, or resolutions. Being collective in nature, the legislature (at least theoretically) makes decisions through open deliberation and debate on competing proposals and interests. While legislative deliberation generally reflects a broad range of policy concerns instead of focusing on detailed items of calculated costs and benefits, these discussions may benefit from a credible cost-benefit analysis of legislative proposals.

Compared to the technical nature of cost-benefit analysis in the executive model, cost-benefit analysis in the legislative model may be more informal, flexible, and interactive. When cost-benefit analysis is conducted for legislative reference in decision making, it facilitates legislative debate about major policies reflecting competing interests. For this purpose, cost-benefit analysis serves as a reference for decision makers, not as a means of making decisions. Accordingly, cost-benefit analysis in the legislative model is not necessarily based on technicality and itemization. It only needs to include items that legislators with general policy concerns are confident and comfortable with, and it can generally deemphasize technical discussions in favor of those intangible concerns that are of the most interest to legislative deliberation.

In both of these models, cost-benefit analysis is no guarantee of effective public interest decision-making. Public choice theorists have contended that political leaders can achieve their policy preferences by manipulating cost-benefit analysis, resulting in sacrificing public interests for private interests, especially with respect to highly controversial policies. The use of cost-benefit analysis in the executive or legislative models thus cannot prevent political elites from abusing their power.

The third model of cost-benefit analysis is the public vote model, which goes beyond branches of the government. While the former two models are directed to the decision-making needs of political elites, the public vote model provides cost-benefit analysis for the voting citizenry. When citizens make decisions through referenda, they need relevant information to evaluate the options available and make their own judgment. Using cost-benefit analysis to inform deliberation about public initiatives prior to a public vote can help build capacity for the meaningful exercise of direct democracy. Once voting citizens use cost-benefit analysis in referenda, the formats, methods, and contents of cost-benefit analysis must be correspondingly adjusted to this new decision-making framework. To serve this function, cost-benefit analysis must become less technical and more accessible; the costs and benefits of any policy under consideration need to be presented in ways that speak directly to the general public rather than to political elites. To satisfy the needs of public deliberation, cost-benefit analysis should not be confined to a small set of limited choices. To be most helpful to citizens at large, in addition to tangible data about policy alternatives, all of the pros and cons should be presented in simple language.

Unlike the previous two elite models, the public vote model can admit more than one cost-benefit analysis in a single policy decision because citizen groups with conflicting interests may present competing analyses during the process of public deliberation. The function of cost-benefit analysis in this context goes beyond instrumental efficiency. Applications of cost-benefit analysis in the public vote model should place greater focus on transparency and participation. These applications may even change the decision-making process to better reflect the spirit of democratic politics by fostering a more open and public debate (Ackerman and Fishkin 2004).

Cost-Benefit Analysis in Alternative Institutional Settings: The Case of Penghu Casino

Public policies are often controversial in nature, reflecting competing priorities, social values, or even public moralities. While there are a large number of factors involved in policy formation, different government structures and decision-making processes may explain how similar policies end up being made differently in various societies.

In some Asian societies, a government's decision to open a casino establishment may be highly controversial because of moral concerns. Yet this policy decision may still be reached in different ways in different Asian societies because of those societies' different social and political contexts and diverse institutional settings. For instance, Macao has developed itself into a paradise for gambling, attracting investors and visitors from within the region and beyond. In recent years, Singapore has allowed the development of two large casino establishments, standing firm on the top of the Asian casino tourism club. Interestingly, the casino establishment attracted almost no debate in Macao but stirred some public discussions in Singapore.

No casino establishment in Asia has stirred public debate as fiercely as the one in Taiwan. On September 26, 2009, the proposal for a long-awaited casino establishment in Penghu, an offshore island of Taiwan, was voted down by a public referendum set up by a special law regarding casino establishment. The result came as a surprise to local elites as well as the local and national governments. During deliberation over the proposed casino, several cost-benefit analyses of the project were introduced. The following discussion uses this casino case to illustrate the aforementioned three models of cost-benefit analysis and how cost-benefit analysis can be applied in alternative institutional settings.

PENGHU AS A CANDIDATE FOR CASINO ESTABLISHMENT IN TAIWAN

Penghu is Taiwan's largest offshore archipelago, located off the western coast of the Taiwan Strait and consisting of sixty-four small isles covering an area of 127 square kilometers. It has plentiful resources for tourism, including amazing geological landscapes, exotic biological species, a clean marine environment, and over 700 years of cultural and historical heritage. Affected by the northwest monsoon climate, however, Penghu is windy and cold in the winter, a huge disadvantage for tourism. Similarly, the agriculture and fishery in Penghu is also vulnerable to seasonal changes, and farmers and fishermen often have substantial difficulties during the winter months (Huang et al. 2010).

In the 1990s, local elites in Penghu began to consider the option of a casino establishment as an important way to increase tourism (Kuo et al. 2006). They argued that geographical and climatic factors placed a curb on local development and that the casino industry would substantially promote local economic growth, particularly of related industries such as transportation, tourism, construction, manufacturing, and even securities (Kuo et al. 2006). But the general public and many citizen groups expressed concerns about the negative impacts of casinos on the human and natural environments. In particular, they were worried about potential deterioration of public morality due to pathological gambling as well as related social problems, including increased criminal activities (Cheng 2009). A few groups were critical of the casino establishment taking place specifically in Penghu and argued that it was a result of "not in my backyard" (NIMBY) attitudes in other places of Taiwan, interpreting the proposal as a case of discrimination against those living on the offshore islands (Huang 2008).

Because gambling was made illegal in Taiwan, Penghu's casino establishment required the enactment of a special law to provide for an approval from the national and local government. As a consequence, the decision-making authorities involved included not only the local government, but also the national government and the legislature.

THREE STAGES OF POLICY FORMATION: FROM ENCLOSED REGULATORY PLANNING, TO LEGISLATIVE DEBATE, TO PUBLIC REFERENDUM

Policy formation regarding the establishment of Penghu's casino can be divided into three stages: administrative investigation (1990–2000), legislative resolution (2000–2008), and public vote (2008–2009). Each had some alternative versions of cost-benefit analysis.

In the first stage, Taiwan was in its golden decade of democratic transition from an authoritarian developmental state to a democratic regulatory state (Yeh 2008). Political transformation notwithstanding, major policy formation was still in the

TABLE 6.1

The Developmental Contexts of Penghu and Macau

	Penghu	Macao
Location	Taiwan	China
Geography	Offshore island	Peninsula
Area (km²)	126.9	20.1
Population (in thousands)	9.4	41
Annual visitors (in thousands)	40	783.4
Tourist population source	From Taiwan mostly	From Hong Kong mostly (78%)

Source: http://gisapsrv01.cpami.gov.tw/cpis/cprpts/Ponghu/total/table/4-11.htm.

hands of political elites in the local and central governments. Against this political and social backdrop, the policy discussion of Penghu's casino establishment was conducted only within the government. Nevertheless, different agencies expressed divergent views, reflecting the flux of policy formation in transitional politics.

The Council for Economic Planning and Development, the cabinet planning agency for national economic development, decided to support the casino establishment. But the Ministry of the Interior, concerned with the potentially grave impacts on public security, openly opposed it.[1] Each ministry used some version of cost-benefit analysis to support its position. Here, cost-benefit analysis was treated as a policy tool for administrative investigation. Tables 6.1 and 6.2 show the data from Penghu's Comprehensive Development Plan (PCDP), evidencing how administrative-based cost-benefit analysis became synonymous with economic analysis. Both tables included only the direct economic factors of Penghu's casino establishment, such as the growth of tourism, economic profit, and tax gains. Intangible social costs such as environmental degradation and potential danger to public security were given short shrift.

The second stage of policy formation on Penghu's casino establishment coincided with an eight-year period of divided government. In 2000, the longtime

TABLE 6.2

Cost-Benefit Analysis of the Penghu Casino Planning

	Macao 1994	Penghu 1994	Penghu (2018, expected)
Population (in thousands)	41.0	9.3	18.8
Tourist population (in thousands)	783.4	40.0	136.0
Casino trips (annual in thousands)	79.9		32.0
Casino employment (in thousands)	6.8		2.7
Casino profit (million USD)	1,760		704
Casino tax (million USD)	528.0		21.1
Government expenditures (million USD)	1,292.0	15.9	516.7
Inflation rate	6.25%	3.68%	Higher than now
Crime rate	1.48%	0.58%	Higher than now

Source: http://gisapsrv01.cpami.gov.tw/cpis/cprpts/Ponghu/total/table/4-12.htm.

opposition party, the Democratic Progressive Party (DPP), won the presidential election by a thin margin but failed to capture the majority in the legislature. The first regime change after more than one decade of democratization in Taiwan thus came with a divided government, with one party controlling the executive and the other the legislature. This division continued up to 2008, as the 2004 elections did not break the deadlock. The competition for decision-making powers between the executive and the legislature was fierce. The administrative influence on the decision-making process was substantially undermined. Key policies were negotiated not only between the executive and the legislature, but also between the central and local governments. Facing moral, economic, and environmental arguments against the Penghu casino, the executive eventually chose to defer to the legislature for final resolution. The cabinet conceded to the legislature that if a parliamentary consensus could be reached to pass the Amendments to Offshore Islands Development Act that authorized establishment of the Penghu casino, it could move forward with full support from the national government.

In this second stage, then, decision-making authority shifted from the executive to the legislature. The legislature conducted its own cost-benefit analysis of the casino. In it, the legislature considered not only economic costs and benefits but also other social and environmental impacts as requested by environmental and other interest groups. A more balanced cost-benefit analysis of Penghu casino policy was presented, reflecting both positive (benefit) and negative (cost) effects on issues beyond economic developments (Kuo et al. 2006) (table 6.3).

The third stage began with the end of the divided government and the return to executive power of the majority party in the legislature, the Nationalist Party, also known as Kuomintang (KMT). In 2008, a second regime change occurred, after which the pro-development KMT controlled both the executive and the legislature. The Penghu casino lobbyists were presented with a golden opportunity by the ascendance of the pro-development KMT. However, the KMT-controlled legislature chose not to make a final decision. Instead of passing a law to allow the casino in Penghu, the legislature sidestepped the issue by writing into law a public referendum provision, which would authorize such an establishment only

TABLE 6.3
The Effects of Penghu's Casino Policy

Positive	Negative
Increase employment rate and local GDP; promote local economic growth	Compress the development of traditional industries
Encourage domestic travel and decrease foreign exchange payments	Increase liquid capital and the risk of inflation rate
Import foreign capitals to improve local social welfare and education quality	Harm to local ecological environment
Offer legal leisure activities and decrease illegal gambling	Overemphasize the importance of the casino economy and distort comprehensive development plan
Exclude the influence of geographical and climatic factors toward local industries	Worsen crime rate and disturb public order

upon the approval of voting residents in the county where the casino establish-ment would be built.

Given the distrust and almost hostile attitude held by the KMT toward refer-endum as a decision-making device, the cabinet's green light to the legislative deal was unusual. The KMT cabinet wanted to push forward the casino establishment in Penghu for economic reasons and as a source of local patronage. But it was the KMT legislature that directly confronted public pressures on public morality and security concerns. Deferring the decision to a referendum became an inevitable political deal. To facilitate success in the public vote, the KMT cabinet and legisla-ture deliberately lowered the minimum voter participation threshold requirement for the referendum to pass, compared to the standard as specified by the Public Referendum Act.[2] Despite this complication, the local government of Penghu and the pro-casino alliance accepted the deal, believing Penghu residents would eas-ily approve the casino in the referendum. Cost-benefit analysis for Penghu casino policy therefore entered the third stage.

PUBLIC VOTE AND COST-BENEFIT CALCULUS

To promote local development, the county government of Penghu opted for a casino establishment patterned after Macao and Singapore. The casino proposal attracted some interest from international casino developers and pushed real estate prices up. But the proposal also encountered fierce resistance from anti-casino alliances and stirred serious debates within the government and the legislature. As the public referendum resolution was being written into law, public deliberation on this issue entered into a new stage. Many interest groups were involved in this campaign as well as the national government, the local government, the ruling KMT party, the opposition DPP party, anti-casino NGOs, environmental groups, and the casino industry.

During the campaign, these groups presented their views on the policy. The benefit dimension of cost-benefit analysis was based primarily on the projected economic benefits of having a casino sited in the region. Some referred to other success stories, such as the revenues of casinos in Las Vegas (approximately $7 to $8 billion per year). Others stressed the roughly $0.5 to $2 billion in annual reve-nue to the government that would come from taxing the casino, which otherwise would be untaxed in the black market gambling sector (Liu 2008). Still others praised the project for potential improvements to the tourism industry and job creation.

On the cost side of the project, however, opponents argued that the casino might increase speculation in real estate values, which could lead to further exploi-tation of undeveloped land and environmental degradation. Moreover, opponents also contended that the casino would have adverse impacts on the quality of local life and social stability, that crime rates would increase, and that the project would promote expansion of the underground economy. They worried that the tranquility of local fishing villages would deteriorate and moral values would be undermined.

In 2009, the local Penghu government put the issue up for a referendum. To the surprise of many, a majority (56.44 percent) voted against the project, as shown in table 6.4. This result reflected the reality that most of Penghu's residents disapproved of the government's plan for the casino. The voters in Penghu calculated the aforementioned costs and benefits provided by all interested parties and eventually exercised their own judgment. The proposal was accordingly turned down.

The magic of this big surprise lies in the alteration of the decision-making authority and the resulting change of decision-making paradigm. Unlike an elite-centric cost-benefit analysis, the referendum opened up the possibility for members of the general public to discuss in their own language the costs and benefits of the casino. In this particular case, the analysis on costs and benefits was conducted for a group of very different decision makers, the Penghu residents. During the campaign, religious groups, homemaker coalitions, and other interest groups presented their views to these ordinary citizens. They analyzed, they talked, and they debated.

The cost-benefit analysis was done in a rather different way than cost-benefit analysis in the executive or legislative model. Pros and cons were presented in ways understandable to ordinary citizens rather than through the traditional format, which relies on itemization and monetization and is geared toward bureaucrats and political elites. Moral issues and other social and environmental concerns were also raised clearly. It was a free and open debate, and with the help of informal cost-benefit analysis, all discussions were indeed focused on the costs and benefits of a potential casino establishment in Penghu. Many observers commented that the exercise of this public referendum, together with the surrounding debates, presented a high degree of rational engagement of citizens and was a most successful example of Taiwan's potential for democratic governance.

TABLE 6.4
Result of the Referendum on Penghu's Casino Installation Policy

Areas	Population	Voters	Agreement	Disagreement	Valid	Invalid	No. of Ballots	Voting Rate %
Penghu	93,973	73,651	13,397 (43.56)	17,359 (56.44)	30,756	298	31,054	42.16
MaKung	55,474	42,340	7,882 (40.29)	11,683 (59.71)	19,565	164	19,729	46.60
Hushi	13,145	10,622	2,098 (44.56)	2,610 (55.44)	4,708	49	4,757	44.78
Paisha	9,227	7,466	1,557 (56.05)	1,221 (43.95)	2,778	26	2,804	37.56
Hsiyu	8,235	6,692	1,183 (50.51)	1,159 (49.49)	2,342	31	2,373	35.46
Wangan	4,522	3,780	215 (31.11)	476 (68.89)	691	15	706	18.68
Chimei	3,370	2,751	462 (68.75)	210 (31.25)	672	13	685	24.90

Source: Penghu County Government.

The Role of Cost-Benefit Analysis in Changing Social and Political Contexts

We tend to presume that the decision-making authority conducting the cost-benefit analysis is always the same kind of authority, in the same institutional settings, and against the same social and political backdrop. For any given policy proposal, however, decision-making authority may change, with dynamics of institutional settings and in divergent social and political contexts. The democratic transition of Taiwan in general, and the development of the Penghu casino establishment policy in particular, have provided examples of where the role and application of cost-benefit analysis may fundamentally alter, depending on institutional and contextual variations.

THE DEVELOPMENTAL STATE, DEMOCRATIC TRANSITION, AND COST-BENEFIT ANALYSIS

Many states have transformed from a developmental state to a regulatory state through the process of democratization (Yeh 2008). This transformation may change the role of cost-benefit analysis and its application to public governance.

A developmental state favors technocrats for public governance and finds rule of law unreceptive to the demands of expediency that developmental strategies may require. The primary goal of state policy in a developmental state is placed on economic development. Public construction and technology developments are favored over social welfare and equal distribution (Yeh 2008). Before democratization, Taiwan was a typical developmental state, placing economic development at the top of government agendas while maintaining iron-clad controls over every sector of the society, including technology, industry, media, education, and even civil organizations.

When Taiwan was still developing, the ruling elite used cost-benefit analysis to entrench its policy preferences and governing ideology. Costs and benefits of key policies were considered, but only according to the preferences of the ruling elite, without being subjected to any public scrutiny or deliberation. In the earlier period of development, decision-making authority was mainly exercised through the party and the cabinet, and the same group of political elites and technocrats occupied both. The party allocated much of the budget to visible physical projects at the expense of egalitarian wealth distributions and social justice. The government steered industries by providing incentives or assistance through policy instruments or developmental programs.

In the 1960s and 1970s, Taiwan carried out its major policies through policy statements and administrative regulations without any prior legislative authorization. Legislative functions were limited to the provision of tax incentives, subsidies, or human resources for industrial use. Civil society was by and large suppressed. Thus, if any cost-benefit analysis was conducted, it was not done for legislative purposes or public debate, but for the executive's use. Because there were almost no organizations capable of conducting independent public policy cost-benefit analysis that were also empowered to express their views freely, the government's cost-benefit analyses were often biased, if not entirely erroneous.

As democratization took place in the late 1980s, institutional changes began to provide substantive and procedural checks on the exercise of government power and regulatory authority. The voting public gained influence, which led to a decrease in legislation's instrumental functions and increased the pressure on government decision makers to justify their decisions with substantive and procedural rationality (Yeh 2008). Meanwhile, vibrant civic organizations, professional associations, and academic institutions sprang up, further empowering civil society. These institutional and contextual changes began molding the regulatory environment to be more transparent and participatory and encouraged deliberation. Under these circumstances, cost-benefit analysis increasingly informed public discussions and facilitated rational public engagement.

Many vibrant economies in Asia have democratized with varying success over the last two decades. To understand fully the use of cost-benefit analysis in these countries, it is necessary to consider their democratic transitions.

CHANGING DECISION-MAKING AUTHORITIES AND COST-BENEFIT ANALYSIS

Fundamental social and political transformations often bring about changes in the decision-making process, even changing the decision makers outright. When the decision is not made by high-level authorities, but by the concerned citizenry, there is greater transparency and a higher level of participation in the decision-making process. As exemplified by the Penghu casino case, the referendum was not decided purely by the naked preferences of a small number of individuals or hasty political mobilizations by interest groups. Rather, facilitated by a more informal cost-benefit analysis, interest groups were able to present their articulation of costs and benefits on the casino establishment to attempt to win the support of the general voting public. On the flip side, ordinary citizens were able to get access to easy-to-understand data on the costs and benefits of the proposed project before they cast their vote. The availability of cost-benefit information helped inform a debate that shifted public opinion from what had been recorded in previous opinion polls to the final public referendum about the Penghu casino establishment. The villagers were the decision makers, and, to some extent, their decision was aided by cost-benefit analysis, however unconventionally.

The case of Penghu's casino shows that public participation may substantially change how cost-benefit analysis is conducted and applied. In the early experience of Taiwan, under the authoritarian developmental state, political elites dominated the entire process of cost-benefit analysis and placed economic developments at the top of the government's agenda. In a more democratic, regulatory state, however, political elites can no longer dominate cost-benefit analysis applications and evaluations in the same way. They must accept multiple goals in the application of cost-benefit analysis, such as social justice, local participation, and environmental protection. Even though these intangible goals may not be analyzed by quantitative methods or monetization, the discussions of their potential costs and benefits cannot be excluded entirely.

Conclusion

The purpose of cost-benefit analysis is to inform rational decision making. For controversial policies, there may be different decision-making authorities in different stages of policy formation. Cost-benefit analysis may be used as a helpful tool for decision making despite a change in decision-making authorities. When cost-benefit analysis is prepared for executive oversight, it tends to be done in a more professional and expert-driven way, with high levels of quantification and monetization. Alternatively, when the general public becomes the decision-making authority, cost-benefit analysis has to be done in ways that are comprehensible to a broader audience. Policy analysts are often inclined to draw a clear bottom line for any proposed public policy, indicating absolute gains or losses. But most public policies are too complicated to draw a clear line. Particularly if the general public stands in a position to make a final decision, cost-benefit analysis must be done in a more dialectic way, engaging people with divergent concerns in discussions and presentations of their views—either with itemization or with general description. This dialectic process of cost-benefit analysis may largely improve the quality of cost-benefit analysis as an effective tool for decision making and help spur the development of different versions of cost-benefit analysis tailored to different decision-making contexts.

While the institutionalization of cost-benefit analysis is a recent occurrence, the core concept of cost-benefit analysis as rational analysis in decision making has long been in practice in many societies despite varied formats and processes. The challenge becomes how to present and apply cost-benefit analysis within institutional settings and divergent social and political contexts.

With the increased application of cost-benefit analysis in contemporary regulatory states, some problems concerning cost-benefit analysis have been observed.[3] Decision makers have been repeatedly warned about the limitations of scientific rationality inherent in the analysis. On the other hand, contemporary applications of cost-benefit analysis have centered on economic analytical methodology, which has remained relatively insensitive to social contexts and institutional settings. Historical legacy, governance patterns, or democratic transition in many Asian new democracies, for example, may present quite different needs and operational scenarios of cost-benefit analysis in their respective regulatory contexts.

Taiwan presents a peculiar model of cost-benefit analysis in its transitional context (Yeh 2002). Analyzing cost-benefit analysis institutionally against the backdrops of democratic transitions enables us to understand some of the contextual significance of cost-benefit analysis. In interest-based politics, cost-benefit analysis based on efficient allocations of resources can serve as a referee for competing interests in setting regulatory agendas. The flip side of the coin is selection by political elites of a preferred policy that is justified, post hoc, by cost-benefit analysis. In an authoritarian developmental state, cost-benefit analysis may be employed to justify public policies—which will reflect policy preferences or the governing ideology of the ruling elites—rather than the will of the general public. But as these institutional and social contexts change, so too can the role of cost-benefit analysis. In observing the phenomenon of cost-benefit analysis going global, it is important to keep in mind the diversity of the decision-making settings where cost-benefit analysis is likely to be used.

Notes

1. See "Life News," *Min-Sheng Newspaper*, March 4, 2003, at A21.

2. The Public Referendum Act requires that for a standard referendum to pass, half of the eligible voters must vote, and a half of those who voted must vote affirmatively. This time, however, the special law for Penghu casino establishment required only that a half of those who vote vote affirmatively. Article 10-2 of Taiwan's Offshore Islands Development Act provides: "Before an Offshore Island may be opened to the establishment of tourist casinos, a local referendum thereon must be held in accordance with the Referendum Act, and more than half of the valid votes cast in the referendum must be votes of approval. However, the validity of the referendum result shall not require votes to have been cast by at least half of the eligible voters in the county or city."

3. For example, some scholars argued that there were ten classes of philosophical problems that affect the practical performance of cost-benefit analysis, including topic selection, dependence on the decision perspective, dangers of super synopticism and undue centralization, prediction problems, the indeterminateness of our control over future decisions, the need to exclude certain consequences for moral reasons, bias in the delimitation of consequences, incommensurability of consequences, difficulties in defending the essential requirement of transferability across contexts, and the normatively questionable but equally essential assumption of interpersonal compensability (Hansson 2007).

Bibliography

Ackerman, Bruce A., and James S. Fishkin. 2004. *Deliberation Day*. New Haven: Yale University Press.

Ackerman, Frank, and Lisa Heinzerling. 2004. *Priceless: On Knowing the Price of Everything and the Value of Nothing*. New York: New Press.

Atkinson, Giles, and Susana Mourato. 2008. "Environmental Cost-Benefit Analysis." *Annual Review of Environment and Resources* 33: 317–44.

Boardman, Anthony E., David H. Greenberg, Aidan R. Vining, and David L. Weimer. 2001. *Cost-Benefit Analysis: Concepts and Practice*. Upper Saddle River, N.J.: Prentice Hall.

Cheng, Ya-Wei. 2009. "Public Health Impacts of Casinos and Legalized Gambling." *Taiwan Journal of Public Health* 28 (6): 455–58. Chinese Electronic Periodical Services (CEPS) No. 1879278.

Fuguitt, Diana, and Shanton J. Wilcox. 1999. *Cost-Benefit Analysis for Public Sector Decision Makers*. Westport, Conn.: Quorum Books.

Hahn, Robert W., and Cass R. Sunstein. 2002. "A New Executive Order for Improving Federal Regulation? Deeper and Wider Cost-Benefit Analysis." *University of Pennsylvania Law Review* 150 (5): 1489–1552.

Hansson, Sven O. 2007. "Philosophical Problems in Cost-Benefit Analysis." *Economics and Philosophy* 23 (2): 163–83.

Hemphill, Thomas. 2007. "Cost-Benefit Analysis: Regulatory Reform or Favoring the Regulated?" *Business Economics* 42 (1): 61–65.

Huang, Yueh-Wen. 2008. "An Analysis of Social Justice of Establishing Casino in Penghu: NIMBY's Perspective." *Journal of Island Tourism Research* 1 (1): 1–29. CEPS No. 1614889.

Huang, Yueh-Wen, Chin-Cheng Ni, and Lei-Jen Shang. 2010. "A Basic Conceptual Framework for the Planning and Implementing Alternative Tourism on Wangan Island, Penghu." *Journal of Island Tourism Research* 3 (4): 1–25. CEPS No. 2212315.

Kuo, Jui-Kun, Jeng-Neng Lay, and Ying-Shyan Liao. 2006. "The Study of Stakeholders' View on Penghu Casino Policy Impact." *Journal of Public Administration* 20: 33–68. CEPS No. 556013.

Kysar, Douglas A. 2006. "It Might Have Been: Risk, Precaution, and Opportunity Costs." *Journal of Land Use and Environmental Law* 22 (1): 1–58.

Liu, Day-Yang. 2008. *The Development of Casino Resort in Taiwan and its Strategic Planning.* Taipei, Taiwan: Council for Economic Planning and Development. http://www.cepd. gov.tw/m1.aspx?sNo=0011557.

Livermore, Michael A. 2011. "Can Cost-Benefit Analysis of Environmental Policy Go Global?" *New York University Environmental Law Journal* 19: 146–93.

Pildes, Richard H., and Cass R. Sunstein. 1995. "Reinventing the Regulatory State." *University of Chicago Law Review* 62 (1): 1–129.

Revesz, Richard L., and Michael A. Livermore. 2008. *Retaking Rationality: How Cost-Benefit Analysis Can Better Protect the Environment and our Health.* New York: Oxford University Press.

Weimer, David Leo. 2008. *Cost-Benefit Analysis and Public Policy.* New York: Wiley.

Weimer, David Leo, and Aidan R. Vining. 2004. *Policy Analysis: Concepts and Practice.* Upper Saddle River, N.J.: Prentice Hall.

Yeh, Jiunn-Rong. 1996. "Institutional Capacity-Building Towards Sustainable Development: Taiwan's Environmental Protection in the Climate of Economic Development and Political Liberalization." *Duke Journal of Comparative and International Law* 6 (2): 229–72.

Yeh, Jiunn-Rong. 2002. "Constitutional Reform and Democratization in Taiwan: 1945–2000." In *Taiwan's Modernization in Global Perspective*, ed. Peter C. Chow, 47–77. Westport, Conn.: Praeger.

Yeh, Jiunn-Rong. 2008. "Democracy-Driven Transformation to Regulatory State: The Case of Taiwan." *National Taiwan University Law Review* 3 (2): 31–59.

7

Is There a Role for Cost-Benefit Analysis beyond the Nation-State? Lessons from International Regulatory Cooperation

Alberto Alemanno

In recent decades, governments across the world have cooperated to harmonize and coordinate policies "behind the borders" through a variety of efforts at the multilateral, regional, and bilateral levels. These efforts have been dictated by the trade liberalization agenda, which sees domestic regulatory action as a factor impeding international trade. While the World Trade Organization (WTO) has been successful in removing barriers to trade at the border, it is proving less effective in the fight against nontariff barriers (NTBs), today's most prominent obstacles to trade exchanges.

Given the current inability of the WTO to effectively address such concerns, some countries seem willing to go beyond traditional international treaty-making to explore new avenues of cooperation. The emerging phenomenon of "horizontal regulatory cooperation," with cooperation on crosscutting issues such as risk assessment, impact assessment, and cost-benefit analysis, seems to offer a promising avenue for overcoming regulatory divergence. These efforts are based on the assumption that substantive regulatory convergence can be facilitated through broader agreement about the manner in which regulators approach standard-setting.

At a time of growing international interest in cost-benefit analysis, this chapter explores whether cost-benefit analysis could be used to promote rationality in regulatory decision making beyond the nation-state. In so doing, it draws upon recent experiences in international regulatory cooperation of some industrialized countries and examines the extent to which developing and emerging nations may be willing and able to participate in this collaborative exercise.

The Genesis and Rationale of International Regulatory Cooperation

The trend toward cooperation between regulators has become a feature of the international regulatory environment in recent years.[1] Regulators are becoming the new diplomats, as Anne-Marie Slaughter (2005, 63) puts it, "on the front lines of issues that were once the exclusive preserve of domestic policy, but that now cannot be resolved by national authorities alone." Indeed, while regulation has been by definition a state prerogative, in an increasingly interdependent world, many regulatory issues are addressed in international forums, which produce a wide array of "supra regulations" at both multilateral and regional levels (Mattli and Woods 2009). These regulations are then commonly transposed and implemented in various national and regional contexts, but only after numerous formal and informal processes requiring the participation of a large variety of governmental and nongovernmental actors.[2]

Historically, much of the drive toward international regulatory cooperation can be found in states' attempts at reducing barriers to trade.[3] Following the remarkable success achieved by the world trading system (notably, the General Agreement on Tariffs and Trade [GATT]) over the postwar years in removing barriers to trade at the border, the subsequent need to tackle a remaining, though not less significant, category of trade obstacles—the nontariff barriers (NTBs) to international trade—appeared.[4] NTBs consist of national regulatory measures that had previously not been subject to international scrutiny and that often aim at pursuing legitimate objectives, such as the protection of the environment and the health and safety of citizens.[5] When one country's regulatory standard is higher than that of another, it acts as an NTB by making the importation of products or services from the other country difficult. Worse yet, states may sometimes deliberately adopt standards for protectionist reasons, that is, to shield domestic industries from foreign imports.[6] Regardless of intent, the mere existence of those measures, by generating regulatory divergence, translates into barriers to trade.[7] In sum, regulatory divergence obstructs imports and exports, creates inefficiencies, and increases costs for international business, which in turn impedes international trade and, other things being equal, slows global prosperity. As stated by Farber and Hudec (1994, 1402), "[T]he modern regulatory state inevitably produces burdens on trade, if only because of the unavoidable lack of regulatory uniformity." Moreover, the relative significance of nontariff measures that occur "behind the border" has grown exponentially in the context of increasingly globalized markets. As the breadth and depth of the external impact of domestic regulation tends to be amplified in today's free markets (Scott 2007), a troubling gap is emerging between "regulatory jurisdiction" and "regulatory impact" (Keohane 2003).

The simplest, but also the least realistic, solution to overcome regulatory divergence and, thus, close this gap is to promote standard harmonization. Generally speaking, harmonization makes the regulatory requirements of different jurisdictions more similar, if not identical.[8] Although states may have incentives to cooperate toward full harmonization, this often implies relinquishing the sovereign power to promulgate regulations. This explains why states agreed, when addressing the challenge of regulatory diversity within the WTO, to be subject to mere "procedural harmonization" as opposed to "substantive harmonization" (Majone 2006). By defining the limits of legitimate diversity through a set of procedural requirements promoting harmonization of procedures and methodologies rather than substantive standards, the former is more respectful of national sovereignty, yet less effective in the fight against regulatory divergence.

Procedural harmonization relies on the assumption that it is possible to harmonize decisional outcomes without imposing a predefined set of policies to which all WTO members must subscribe by merely constraining the discretion exercised by states in the adoption of domestic technical measures. As a result, under the Sanitary and Phytosanitary Agreement (SPS) and the Technical Barriers to Trade Agreement (TBT), which were set up at the end of the Uruguay Round negotiations leading to the establishment of the WTO,[9] member states are required to base their measures "on international standards, guidelines or recommendations, where they exist."[10] When they do so, member countries benefit from a presumption of full compliance with WTO law.[11] If they do not follow international standards (because these do not exist or states want to follow a higher level of protection), states need to either provide for scientific justification[12] or prove the "necessity"[13] of the adopted measures.[14] Both requirements, scientific justification and necessity, serve as proxies to detect whether a WTO member is pursuing legitimate objectives and whether the adopted measure is the least trade restrictive to achieve such objectives. As exemplified by the large number of remaining NTBs and the loaded SPS/TBT dispute records, this "procedural harmonization" approach falls short in addressing intrinsic negative trade effects.

If NTBs are observed from a domestic perspective, it is surprising that nothing is said about the need for an ex-ante analysis of proposed regulation, nor on whether the benefits of the adopted measure should outweigh its costs. So long as a national measure is based on an international standard or on a risk assessment, the fact that the measure's costs exceed its net benefits does not amount to a breach of the WTO agreements.[15] At a time of growing international interest and policy diffusion of cost-benefit analysis[16] via the introduction of mandatory regulatory impact assessment (RIA),[17] the prospect of using cost-benefit analysis to promote rationality in regulatory decision making beyond the nation-state is extremely appealing. How should we think about this appeal? Should economic analysis of regulation be mandated at the international level? Should states turn their domestic regulatory reform instruments (such as cost-benefit analysis) into policy tools aimed at solving the old, yet pending, issue of regulatory divergence? Is it too great an intrusion on domestic policy prerogatives, or might it be an appropriate tool for international cooperation? What kind of cost-benefit analysis should be developed internationally? Should it be broadened to include extraterritorial impacts?

The following discussion addresses some of these questions by examining whether cost-benefit analysis could be used beyond the nation-state in order to promote regulatory convergence.

"Horizontal Regulatory Cooperation": Where International Regulatory Cooperation Meets Cost-Benefit Analysis

Given the inability of the WTO framework to effectively mitigate the negative trade effects stemming from regulatory divergence, states actively seek innovative solutions with their trade partners to maintain the gains achieved through the multilateral trade system and possibly obtain more. In so doing, states seem willing to go beyond traditional international treaty-making and to explore new possible avenues of cooperation. As a mechanism for solving regulatory problems of a cross-border nature, international regulatory cooperation is increasingly preferred to the traditional route of concluding a multilateral treaty. In particular, recent years have witnessed the emerging phenomenon of "horizontal regulatory cooperation"[18] involving regulatory cooperation on crosscutting issues such as risk assessment, impact assessment, and cost-benefit analysis.[19] This innovative form of international cooperation is "horizontal" because it refers to the general analytical basis of regulation as opposed to "sector-specific" regulatory cooperation.

The basic assumption behind horizontal cooperation is that substantive regulatory convergence can be facilitated by convergence of the general method in which regulators approach standard-setting.[20] Convergence around a set of methodological tools aimed at improving the quality and rationality of legislation might indeed offer a promising course of action to remove existing barriers and prevent new ones from arising. More ambitiously, by focusing on the "how's" of regulation instead of on the "what's," horizontal regulatory cooperation seems to offer an appropriate contribution to a global governance project "shaped and formed by an overarching cosmopolitan legal framework" (Held 2002, 33). As it was recently described, the horizontal dialogue is meant "to appease, to counter the 'negotiation mode' of sector-specific dialogues and to gloss over fundamental differences by presenting regulatory policy as a nice set of best practices that can be transplanted" (Meuwese 2011, 264).

The most promising "best practice" for achieving such a result seems to be offered by one of the foundational policy tools of the economic analysis of regulation: cost-benefit analysis.

In simplified terms, cost-benefit analysis is an ex ante evaluation tool that has its historical roots in the pursuit of economic efficiency.[21] It therefore focuses on whether the sum of all benefits of regulation, including both market and nonmarket benefits, exceeds the sum of all costs. Since the 1980s, cost-benefit analysis has been introduced in the United States in a number of regulatory contexts through executive orders with the aim of informing the regulatory process.[22] It has since spread to several other jurisdictions[23] and, as a result, it is increasingly perceived as a potential principle of "global administrative law" together with other procedural norms, such as information disclosure, participation, and notice-and-comment (Livermore, 2011, 148).

Although cost-benefit analysis has been adopted and used with a predominantly domestic focus, this policy tool, because of its inherent rationalistic and welfare-maximizing commitment, strives for comprehensiveness and has, by its own nature, a cosmopolitan vocation. In particular, as states are not required to conduct a cost-benefit analysis under WTO rules (they need not show that the benefits of a given national measure outweigh its costs),[24] the prospect of using cost-benefit analysis to promote rationality in regulatory decision-making is extremely tempting in the international trade context. It is not difficult to imagine why cost-benefit analysis might be a "first-best trade-off device from an economic standpoint" (Trachtman 1998, 40).[25] This point is indeed intuitively obvious. By forcing regulators to follow a rational process through the evaluation of the costs and benefits of alternative approaches, this policy tool might ensure optimization in regulatory decision making and aid in the search for the solution that results in maximum net gains of trade and regulation. In other words, cost-benefit analysis suggests, as a welfare-maximizing procedure, the promise of national regulations based on the insights of welfare economics. This, in the long term, by paving the way to indirect harmonization, might contribute to the fight against regulatory divergence.

This scenario, as typically demonstrated in past experiences in transatlantic regulatory cooperation, is not entirely farfetched and might soon become the next frontier of international regulatory cooperation. Already today an increasing proportion of regulatory reform programs reflect a growing awareness of the international context. For instance, U.S. Office of Management and Budget (OMB) *Circular A-4*, the Canadian *Cabinet Directive on Streamlining Regulation*, the EU *Impact Assessment Guidelines*, as well as the Australian *Best Practice Regulation Handbook*, although largely geared toward domestic impacts of regulations, encourage regulators to consider the international trade and investment effects of their respective regulations. They do so not *sua sponte* but within the framework of international regulatory cooperation agreements, concluded typically at the bilateral level among countries.[26] As a result, analytical methods such as regulatory impact assessments and cost-benefit analysis are no longer limited to the domestic impact of regulation, but they also include (some of) the international impacts.

At the same time, given the global nature of an increasing number of policy challenges, such as those raised by climate change, an increasing number of policymakers seem to agree that a global, as opposed to domestic, measure of the benefits from reducing domestic emissions is preferable.[27] For this purpose, a U.S. interagency process was recently initiated to offer a preliminary estimate of the monetized damages associated with an incremental increase in carbon emissions, referred to as the social cost of carbon (SCC).[28] Since most regulatory actions are expected to have small, or "marginal," impacts on cumulative global emissions, the use of a global, as opposed to domestic, measure for SCC seems especially appropriate.[29] A global measure allows the expected social benefits of regulatory action to be incorporated into cost-benefit analyses. As will be illustrated, this approach represents a departure from past practices, which tended to put greater emphasis on a domestic measure of the SCC (limited to impacts of climate change experienced within U.S. borders). Interestingly enough, this trend toward global measurement, having being initiated spontaneously, does not stem from an international cooperation effort, but it might soon spread to other countries.

Before speculating on the pros and cons of an international use of cost-benefit analysis, the next section illustrates the challenges of promoting cost-benefit analysis beyond the nation-state. It sketches how, then, cost-benefit analysis could be structured as a policy tool to be employed beyond domestic boundaries.

What Kind of Cost-Benefit Analysis Is Optimal for International Regulatory Cooperation?

Although its inherent optimization promise and cosmopolitan vocation seem to make cost-benefit analysis the preferred tool to promote regulatory convergence, the kind of cost-benefit analysis to be advanced beyond the nation-state differs from its domestic version. Cost-benefit analysis, being typically conducted from the point of view of the local country, tends to omit how the benefits and costs are felt (and distributed) across the border. In a nutshell, cost-benefit analysis, as it is currently applied in most jurisdictions, is extraterritorially blind. It normatively assumes that it is the right of the regulating state to act, irrespective of the external effects of such a regulation on other countries. Therefore, to be meaningful and appropriate to an international context, cost-benefit analysis needs to go beyond the analysis of the domestic effects of regulation and also include extraterritorial impacts. As shown by a growing number of domestic cost-benefit analysis guidelines, international regulatory cooperation has the potential to promote and shape a different, expanded version of cost-benefit analysis. Yet the question remains how to methodologically develop a cost-benefit analysis that might include international impacts, that is, impacts felt *extramuros*.

Once it is established that cost-benefit analysis should be broadened to the international context, it is crucial to determine what its extraterritorial scope may be. Domestic cost-benefit analysis seems primarily designed to answer the question, "Does the expenditure of resources on this particular program provide a net benefit to the domestic economy and the domestic public?" For cost-benefit analysis to move beyond its domestic origins, it must be able to answer new types of questions. Which questions, therefore, should international cost-benefit analysis address?

Separating the intraterritorial from the extraterritorial is not always an easy task. As stated in the international trade context, "law in this area has moved sometimes by intuition, sometimes by social convention, and rarely based on sound intellectual grounds" (Mavroidis 2007, 278). As a result, similar to what occurs in domestic cost-benefit analysis, the scope of an international cost-benefit analysis is prone to varying interpretations and is subject to political judgment. This is clearly illustrated by the recent trend toward a global, as opposed to a domestic, measurement of the SCC.

GLOBAL COST-BENEFIT ANALYSIS VERSUS INTERNATIONAL COST-BENEFIT ANALYSIS

Should the benefits of regulation be contrasted with the trade and other costs of regulation? Or should the focus be limited to the benefits of the regulation for insiders versus the harm it causes to outsiders? In other words, should the focus be on the overall economic efficiency of the regulation or, rather, on how its costs and benefits are spread across the border?

The answers to these questions depend on the overarching goal governments want to pursue through cost-benefit analysis beyond the nation-state. Do they want to promote efficient regulation aimed at maximizing net gains, or do they desire merely an indicator of the degree to which the effects of a domestic measure will be felt externally (i.e., as a proxy to detect discrimination)?

While the first kind of expanded cost-benefit analysis seems *global*, or universal, in scope (global cost-benefit analysis), the second is more limited as it acts as a mere proxy to detect externalization, that is, costs on outsiders, and may be called *international* cost-benefit analysis. To illustrate the differences between these two forms of cost-benefit analysis, let us assume a domestic regulation whose costs fall mostly on nonresidents. Under global cost-benefit analysis, such a regulation might still be justified by a net global efficiency criterion if the globally felt benefits outweigh the costs. Conversely, it could never be justified under international cost-benefit analysis.

The embryonic forms of expanded cost-benefit analysis that have developed thus far in the framework of international regulatory cooperation seem to have embraced international rather than global cost-benefit analysis. Indeed, they have been relatively narrow in scope and have not seemed to nurture any global vocation. Although it is not the product of any international regulatory initiative, the recently adopted U.S. approach vis-à-vis the social cost of carbon represents an interesting exception in this regard. When incorporating into cost-benefit analyses the economic damages associated with greenhouse gas emissions, U.S. agencies, apparently, do not limit their analyses to the impacts of climate change experienced within U.S. borders. Rather, they rely on global measurements (IWGSCC 2010).

A COMPARATIVE OVERVIEW OF INTERNATIONAL COST-BENEFIT ANALYSIS EXPERIENCES

Following the conclusions of international regulatory cooperation agreements, several industrialized countries have expanded the scope of their regulatory analyses. As a result, analyses are no longer limited to domestic impacts of regulation, but they also seek to include some international impacts.

In the United States, Executive Order 12,866 is silent on international impacts. Under *Circular A-4*, analysis of economically significant proposed and final regulations from the domestic perspective is required, while analysis from the international perspective is optional. In particular, *Circular A-4* seems to rule international impacts out when it states that a regulatory impact analysis "should focus on benefits and costs that accrue to citizens and residents of the United States" (OMB 2003). Nevertheless, the same document acknowledges that "new U.S. rules could act as non-tariff barriers to imported goods" and therefore recommends that these concerns be "evaluated carefully" (OMB 2003, 6), but it does not offer clear guidance on how to consider the international trade and investment effects of U.S. regulation. *Circular A-4* also adds, "Where you choose to evaluate a regulation that is likely to have effects beyond the borders of the United States, these effects should be reported separately" (OMB 2003, 15). In practice, the current U.S. approach is to have regulatory impact analyses take into account only those direct impacts on foreign entities that are passed on to the U.S. economy.[30] Thus, for instance, if a regulation raises the costs of importing a product, and domestic prices increase as a result, the costs to domestic consumers due to those price increases tend to be considered in the impact analysis.[31] This is clearly not global cost-benefit analysis as it was previously defined. Yet as illustrated by the development of a global measure for the SCC, U.S. agencies seem disposed to depart from past practices, which tended to emphasize domestic impacts of regulation (IWGSCC 2010).

In the European Union, the *Impact Assessment Guidelines* explicitly require that impacts on international (extra-EU) trade and on third countries be taken into account. This requires *inter alia* an assessment of whether a proposed policy places EU companies at an advantage or disadvantage vis-à-vis external competitors. In practice, as often emphasized by the Impact Assessment Board (IAB) (the EU's regulatory oversight body),[32] European Commission proposals often lack consideration of international impacts, and, even when they do look beyond their borders, the analysis is limited to the impact of regulation on the WTO obligations of the European Union.

The main focus of the 2007 *Canadian Cabinet Directive on Streamlining Regulation* is on the identification and assessment of "the potential positive and negative economic, environmental, and social impacts on Canadians, business, and government of the proposed regulation and its feasible alternatives."[33] Yet the *Canadian Cost-Benefit Analysis Guide*, which complements the Directive, requires regulators to consider "the international impacts of their regulations" (TBC 2007, 9). However, this duty not only lacks operational guidelines but also seems to be contradicted by the following statement: "It is the benefits and costs accruing to the individual residents of Canada that are totaled to generate the aggregate net benefit for the country in any period. If the benefits are accrued to non-residents or to third countries, those benefits are usually excluded from the total benefits for the implementation of the regulation in question" (TBC 2007, 12).

In Australia, the *Best Practice Regulation Handbook* explicitly requires a trade impact assessment where a "proposed regulation has a direct bearing on export performance."[34] The export market is the only international impact of regulation referenced in this document.

As clearly exemplified by the U.S. and Australian examples, the kind of expanded cost-benefit analysis that is promoted within an international regulatory cooperation framework tends to be limited to "domestic trade impacts," that is, those international, direct or indirect, impacts on domestic or foreign entities that are passed on to the domestic economy. Perhaps this is not a surprising outcome. States willing to cooperate on regulatory issues have no incentives to subject themselves to a "global" cost-benefit analysis aimed at determining the overall efficiency of their measures. Rather, they prefer to identify those trade impacts that may affect their closest trade partners and that may ultimately be felt by their own economies. International cost-benefit analysis is therefore designed to guarantee that the external costs of regulation are considered by the domestic legislator only insofar as they are borne by a trade partner or by the domestic economy. The drive behind international cost-benefit analysis is not global economic efficiency but merely the economic interests of the parties to the agreement. Needless to say, difficult normative, institutional, methodological, and legitimacy questions lie behind any effort aimed at developing a form of global cost-benefit analysis.

Notwithstanding their differences in the level of individual commitment to international cost-benefit analysis, these jurisdictions are cooperating to improve the way in which they can incorporate international trade impacts in their regulatory analysis. In particular, the European Union and the United States have been working together, although with limited success, to ensure that assessment of future regulations takes into account impacts on international trade.[35] Similarly, Canada, the United States, and Mexico have undertaken a commitment, within the 2005 Security and Prosperity Partnership of North America (SPP) Regulatory Cooperation Framework, to "identify, develop and conduct pilot project(s) in joint regulatory impact analysis, including cost-benefit analysis and/or risk assessment."[36]

The next sections aim at analyzing the main benefits and costs stemming from the implementation of cost-benefit analysis beyond the nation-state via regulatory cooperation mechanisms.

The Benefits of International Cost-Benefit Analysis

The spread of cost-benefit analysis via international regulatory cooperation could provide several important advantages and benefits. Although it is not a panacea, cost-benefit analysis is widely believed to play an important role in policymaking. It is often argued that domestic cost-benefit analysis has two virtues: (1) it enhances the evidence base, thus optimizing the decision-making process; and (2) it improves the representation of the public interest by promoting transparency. In particular, by quantifying the costs and benefits of regulation in economic terms, cost-benefit analysis is believed to favor a democratic, participatory, and deliberative decision-making process, in which all stakeholders (policymakers, experts, interest groups, and citizens at large) contribute collectively to the shaping of policies.[37] But to what extent may these virtues of cost-benefit analysis also be ascribed to a form of cost-benefit analysis that goes beyond the nation-state?

Although the scope of existing international cost-benefit analysis is limited, its benefits for the overall efficiency of regulatory outcomes seem promising. Similar to what occurs at the domestic level, international cost-benefit analysis may reveal trade-offs, foster transparency, and even promote participation and accountability.[38] In particular, it may

- provide information to help clarify trade-offs derived from trade liberalization and the limits of trade negotiation positions;
- prevent tunnel vision and biases toward certain regulatory options;
- foster participation by including in the decision-making process a greater number of stakeholders and foreign authorities;

- build an open process of consultation around trade policy, creating a basis for an informed discussion with a broad range of stakeholders;
- enhance transparency so that foreign governments, including developing countries, and the public can (more easily) monitor domestic decision making.

Moreover, because of its rationalistic and comprehensiveness commitments, international cost-benefit analysis may promote the exchange and pooling of expertise among countries facing similar methodological and substantive policy issues.

Even more significantly, it seems that the most valuable benefit of international cost-benefit analysis relates to its ability to address claims of an emerging gap between regulatory jurisdiction and regulatory impact, which is particularly significant when it comes to the actions of industrialized states. While the internal political process cannot legitimize the international effects of domestic law (since foreigners cannot participate), international cost-benefit analysis renders decision making somewhat more transparent to and inclusive of external constituencies. By having the charge to evaluate impacts on foreign individuals who are affected by domestic choices, cost-benefit analysis might, at least in principle, reduce that "external accountability gap" (Keohane 2003, 15).

Overall, it seems that international cost-benefit analysis might help diminish regulatory divergence because, as a result, the decision-making process becomes more open and transparent. International cost-benefit analysis can be seen as akin to the discovery process during litigation for proposed regulations. In particular, by increasing the share of information that states exchange, international cost-benefit analysis might ensure that cooperating states receive "early warnings" on forthcoming policies. In certain circumstances, as illustrated by the case of climate change, only a form of global or universal cost-benefit analysis can provide an in-depth assessment of all of the economic, social, and environmental effects of a new regulation. Yet this does not necessarily imply that a supranational entity should conduct cost-benefit analysis and on only that basis should governments regulate. Rather, it suggests that governments, when assessing the costs and benefits of the available regulatory options, should rely (insofar as possible) on global measurements instead of limiting their analyses to the impacts experienced within domestic borders.

The Costs of International Cost-Benefit Analysis

The promise of international cost-benefit analysis to promote rational decision making through regulatory cooperation is not without its own risks and costs. Taking reality into consideration, the most immediate obstacle to the use of cost-benefit analysis beyond the nation-state is the different levels of penetration, development, and implementation of cost-benefit analysis across countries (OECD 2008). If thirty-one out of the thirty-four Organisation for Economic Co-operation and Development (OECD) countries require RIA of regulatory proposals, only a few boast a full cost-benefit analysis system (OECD 2009b). Although some developing countries are beginning to apply some form of regulatory assessment, their methods are generally incomplete and not applied systematically across policy areas (Kirkpatrick and Zhang 2004; Kirkpatrick and Parker 2004). In any event, few studies have considered the potential for using RIA in developing countries (Livermore 2011, 159–61), the chapters in this volume notwithstanding.

Further, each domestic version of cost-benefit analysis conceals considerable latitude for heterogeneity, and including international impacts represents a further challenge. If cost-benefit analysis means different things to different stakeholders, international cost-benefit analysis adds an additional layer of complexity. Indeed, the objectives, design, and role of administrative processes differ considerably among countries and among regulatory policy areas. Moreover, even among industrialized countries, the "first generation" debate about cost-benefit analysis's normative desirability is ongoing, and questions concerning "second generation" issues related to how to implement cost-benefit analysis have not yet been fully addressed (Kysar 2010). This reminds us that an additional obstacle to the use of cost-benefit analysis beyond the nation-state might be represented by the debate on the inherent limits of the practice of cost-benefit analysis today. As a growing body of literature has illustrated in recent years, cost-benefit analysis is vulnerable to a significant number of philosophical and moral objections.[39] Regardless of where states stand on this debate, the incorporation of cost-benefit analysis for the purposes of international regulatory cooperation cannot transcend this debate at the domestic level.

An expanded use of cost-benefit analysis also has inherent methodological and institutional design complexities. Although the cosmopolitan vocation of cost-benefit analysis may seem to render this policy tool ideal for use outside the domestic boundaries of the nation-state, when translated into applied methodologies, it "must be deployed by policy makers who serve as agents for a particular, confined community" (Kysar 2010, 18). This partly explains the current struggle in developing and applying a common methodology to evaluate the extraterritorial impacts of policies. As predicted, this question "cannot be resolved from within the cost-benefit methodology itself" but requires a clear, resounding political commitment (Kysar 2010, 18).

In the case of developing countries, designing and implementing international cost-benefit analysis requires special consideration of a number of issues. First, without a credible and operational preexisting domestic cost-benefit analysis system, developing countries will not be given the chance to enter the international cost-benefit analysis regulatory cooperation experiment. Second, methodological and operational difficulties can easily arise in the decision-making processes of developing countries. Third, the use of regulatory tools, such as cost-benefit analysis, requires a high level of expertise and access to extensive resources and information. Most developing countries do not yet meet these preconditions. Finally, although developing countries could greatly benefit from the creation of international cost-benefit analysis frameworks, by gaining access to the developed world's internal decision-making processes, they might struggle in setting up their own domestic cost-benefit analysis first. Policymakers in these countries have to evaluate and assess the weight of the tools they have available, and determine how to best use and combine them to achieve concrete results.

Conclusion

Although cost-benefit analysis, following the successful diffusion of RIA, is statutorily required in an increasing number of countries throughout the world, it is not mandated at the international level. This should not come as a surprise since cost-benefit analysis has developed as a policy tool, the main concerns of which have essentially been the domestic, rather than international, impact of regulatory action. Yet there seems to be an emerging belief that, despite this policy tool's adoption and use domestically, it might—should it become part of the international regulatory cooperation agenda—help overcome regulatory divergence, thus leading to the greater efficiency and effectiveness of regulatory policy at both the domestic and international level (Livermore 2011). However, to be meaningful in an international cooperation context, cost-benefit analysis has to be broadened in scope so as to include extraterritorial impacts. As illustrated above, to define the exact scope of an international cost-benefit analysis is an eminently political decision that clearly faces methodological and institutional challenges. Overall, it seems that the use of cost-benefit analysis in the context of international regulatory cooperation might face a fate similar to that within the domestic context: although it might promote benefits across jurisdictional lines, cost-benefit analysis might also encounter vivid resistance and methodological conundrums.

On the positive side, the introduction and diffusion of international cost-benefit analysis through international regulatory cooperation may—in several regulatory realities—help reduce regulatory divergence, because the decision-making process is believed to become more open and transparent. In particular, by increasing the share of information that states exchange during the decision-making process, international cost-benefit analysis might ensure that states receive early warnings on forthcoming policies. This might contribute to a more inclusive and reflexive regulatory process, which might address the emerging gap between regulatory jurisdiction and the regulatory impact that accompanies the globalization of markets. On the negative side, there are clear limits to how far cost-benefit analysis might be developed and used beyond the nation-state. Although cost-benefit analysis seems potentially useful in checking the economic optimality of domestic trade-offs having extraterritorial effects, there are latent problems in turning this promise into reality. International cost-benefit analysis, as it is developing within the international regulatory cooperation framework, is not global in scope and is best used as a "fire alarm" for trade partners affected by proposed regulation. Yet the emergence of an increasing number of policy challenges of global scope, such as those raised by climate change, may provide incentives to policymakers to depart from past practices, which tended to limit analysis to domestic impacts, and to instead begin developing global measurements.[40]

The regulatory cooperation experience, which has developed around cost-benefit analysis during recent years, is still in its infancy and has brought about mixed results. It is part of a broader transnational dialogue on regulatory reform, whose declared goal is to develop shared substantive standards of impact assessment, but which thus far has not delivered on its promises. On the exact role that cost-benefit analysis may play beyond the nation-state, the jury is still out.

Notes

1. Networks of regulators have emerged at the global level, often under the umbrella of the Organisation for Economic Co-operation and Development (Jacobsson 2006; Barrett 2007). Allio and Jacobzone (2012) discuss the specific role of the OECD in promoting this phenomenon.

2. Raustiala (1997, 481). ("[R]egulatory cooperation...is marked by the degree to which this process of implementation relies upon and is shaped by existing domestic institutions and political structures.")

3. See Bermann, Herdegen, and Lindseth (2000, 1). ("[I]nternational regulatory cooperation comprises a highly differentiated bundle of techniques for reconciling the needs of international trade with the diversity of national regulatory environments and public demand.")

4. For a detailed history of the evolution of GATT rules on domestic regulations, see Sykes (1995) and Mavroidis (2007).

5. It has been observed that democracies more typically create NTBs. In particular, it has been argued that democracies induce politicians to replace transparent risk barriers with less transparent ones. See Kono (2006).

6. Surprisingly, international law lacks an operational definition of protectionism. Hence, as illustrated below, recourse to proxies is inevitable in the WTO (national treatment; scientific justification; necessity test; etc.).

7. Unlike regular trade barriers, NTBs' impact on trade is mainly indirect. It consists of both additional cost of compliance for manufacturers/traders and impact on production functions and consumption decisions.

8. There are two models of harmonization: the full harmonization model and the equivalence model. Under full harmonization, two or more countries agree to adopt the same identical standard. Under the equivalence model, one country agrees to accept another's divergent standard as being equivalent to its own, without equalizing the standard.

9. Since the 1979 Tokyo Round, some countries have feared that the lowering of border measures would be circumvented by disguised protectionist measures in the form of technical regulations, notably sanitary and phytosanitary regulations. For this reason, a Plurilateral Agreement was adopted on Technical Barriers to Trade, also called the "Standards Code." See Trebilcock and Howse (1999). See also Marceau and Trachtman (2002). The operation of the Standards Code is generally perceived as a failure; see Victor (2000).

10. WTO Agreement on the Application of Sanitary and Phytosanitary Measures, April 15, 1994, Marrakesh Agreement Establishing the World Trade Organization, Annex 1A, Legal Instruments—Results of the Uruguay Round, 33 I.L.M. 1165 (1994), Art. 3 (hereinafter SPS); and WTO Agreement on Technical Barriers to Trade Agreement (1994), Art. 2.4 (hereinafter TBT).

11. All international standards are presumed necessary to achieve a legitimate objective. See SPS, *supra* note 10, at Art. 3 and TBT, *supra* note 10, at Art. 2.5.

12. SPS, *supra* note 10.

13. Under the "necessity test," a measure can only be found "too restrictive to trade" when there is an alternative measure that is not only less trade restrictive but also achieves the same level of protection as the measure adopted. TBT, *supra* note 10, at Art. 2.3.

14. SPS, *supra* note 10, at Arts. 2.2, 5.1; TBT, *supra* note 10, at Arts. 2.2.

15. SPS, *supra* note 10, at Art. 5.3, seems to be the only WTO provision that hints at an economic assessment of an adopted measure. It requires the risk assessors to take into account "the cost-effectiveness of alternative approaches to limiting risks," but only "in assessing the risk to animal or plant life or health."

16. The OECD has largely promoted this process of policy diffusion in recent years. See, e.g., OECD (1995); followed by OECD (1997a); (1997b, 3) (recommending, since 1997, that governments "integrate regulatory impact analysis into the development, review, and reform of regulations"); OECD (2009a). On the diffusion of RIA in OECD countries, see OECD (2009b).

17. Although there is a conceptual distinction between cost-benefit analysis and regulatory impact assessment (i.e., cost-benefit analysis is one among many types of regulatory impact analyses), these two terms are very often used as synonyms. The OECD adopted the term "RIA" and argues that "[i]n practice many countries do not adopt the rigorous cost-benefit analysis due to the difficulty of quantifying costs and benefits, and so have adopted a more flexible impact analysis system" (OECD 2004, 2).

18. For an initial analysis of this phenomenon, see Meuwese (2011), and Allio and Jacobzone (2012).

19. These established principles are often referred to as "meta-regulation"; see, e.g., Morgan (2003) and Radaelli (2007).

20. Along these lines, see Alemanno (2011); Meuwese (2011); and Ahearn (2009, 8) ("Until the regulatory structures themselves become more convergent or aligned, the major divergences in regulatory policies are unlikely to disappear").

21. For a classic introduction to cost-benefit analysis, see Mishan (1976).

22. Executive Order 12,866 establishes a requirement of cost-benefit analysis. 3 CFR § 638 (1994).

23. For an overview of impact analysis systems around the world, see OECD (2009b, 63–71) and Livermore (2011, 154–59).

24. See, on this point, Chang (2004); Crawford-Brown, Pauwelyn, and Smith (2004).

25. See Levmore (1983, 574) (arguing for use of cost-benefit analysis in cases of "interferences," and invalidation in cases of "exploitations" under the U.S. commerce clause), as well as Dunoff (1992) (arguing for a cost-benefit balancing test).

26. See, e.g., Protocol between the Australian Office of Regulation Review and the New Zealand Regulatory Impact Analysis Unit (on Trans-Tasman issues) (2007); Security and Prosperity Partnership of North America Regulatory Cooperation Framework, U.S.–Canada–Mexico (2005); Canada-EU Framework for Regulatory Cooperation (2004); Policy Research Initiative, Canada-US Regulatory Cooperation, Charting a Map Forward (2004); and US-EU Guidelines on Regulatory Cooperation and Transparency (2002).

27. See, e.g., IWGSCC (2010); Commission of the European Communities (2005, 180); Clarkson and Deyes (2002). For an overview, see Watkiss (2006).

28. This process was initiated by the Council of Economic Advisers and the Office of Management and Budget, with regular input from other offices within the Executive Office of the President, including the Council on Environmental Quality, National Economic Council, Office of Energy and Climate Change, and Office of Science and Technology Policy. Agencies that actively participated included the Environmental Protection Agency as well as the Departments of Agriculture, Commerce, Energy, Transportation, and Treasury.

29. The SCC is usually estimated as the net present value of climate change impacts over the next one hundred years (or longer) of one additional ton of carbon emitted to the atmosphere today. It is intended to include (but is not limited to) changes in net agricultural productivity, human health, property damages from increased flood risk, and the value of ecosystem services (Yohe et al. 2007; IPCC 2007).

30. There are, however, some legislative texts expressly ruling out the possibility of broadening the analysis to extraterritorial effects. *See, e.g.*, Unfunded Mandates Reform Act of 1995, Pub. L. No. 104–4, 109 Stat. 48, §§ 202, 205 (excluding effects on foreign governments, and perhaps implicitly including only U.S. private sector effects).

31. Since an analysis of the direct costs on foreign entities is a useful proxy of the costs on the U.S. economy, many U.S. RIAs incorporate this approach in order not to underestimate the costs of rulemaking.

32. This board consists of an internal group of five high-level officials with IA experience acting in personal capacity under the authority of the Commission president and is chaired by the deputy secretary general of the European Commission. The IAB provides not only quality support but also reviews, independently from the author services, draft impact assessments in order to assess the quality of the analysis and the coverage of all relevant impacts. *See* Wiener and Alemanno (2010, 331–33).

33. The only explicit commitment regarding "international impact" relates to the duty to publish proposals for new or changed technical regulations, conformity assessment procedures, and sanitary and phytosanitary measures "that may affect international trade" for a comment period of at least seventy-five days and take into account the comments received. A similar commitment to the exchange of information exists in the Cooperation Agreement between Australia and New Zealand on Trans-Tasman issues, i.e., those that refer to commerce between these two countries. PROTOCOL BETWEEN THE AUSTRALIAN OFFICE OF REGULATION REVIEW AND THE NEW ZEALAND REGULATORY IMPACT ANALYSIS UNIT (ON TRANS-TASMAN ISSUES) (2007).

34. AUSTRALIAN GOVERNMENT, BEST PRACTICE REGULATORY HANDBOOK (2010), 76.

35. *See* OMB AND THE SECRETARIAT GENERAL OF THE EUROPEAN COMMISSION, REVIEW OF THE APPLICATION OF THE EU AND U.S. REGULATORY IMPACT ASSESSMENT GUIDELINES ON THE ANALYSIS OF IMPACTS ON INTERNATIONAL TRADE AND INVESTMENT: FINAL REPORT AND CONCLUSIONS (2008).

36. SECURITY AND PROSPERITY PARTNERSHIP OF NORTH AMERICA REGULATORY COOPERATION FRAMEWORK, U.S.–CANADA–MEXICO (2005), § 3.

37. *See, e.g.*, Revesz and Livermore (2008). For a critical view, *see*, e.g., Ackerman and Heinzerling (2004); and Wagner (2009).

38. Arrow et al. (1996) (suggesting that cost-benefit analysis can play an important role in helping to inform regulatory decision making if utilized appropriately), and Revesz and Livermore (2008).

39. Rather than delve into the general debate regarding the utility, desirability, and morality of cost-benefit analysis as a technique of policy analysis, the author simply refers to some of the concerns raised by others. For an analysis of "standard objections" to cost-benefit analysis, *see*, e.g., Adler and Posner (2006, 154). For a sample of the critical literature criticizing cost-benefit analysis, *see* Ackerman and Heinzerling (2004).

40. For a skeptical view on the possibility of using cost-benefit analysis in tackling global issues such as climate change, *see*, e.g., Rose-Ackerman (2011).

Bibliography

Ackerman, Frank, and Lisa Heinzerling. 2004. *Priceless: On Knowing the Price of Everything and the Value of Nothing.* New York: New Press.

Adler, Matthew, and Eric Posner. 2006. *New Foundations of Cost Benefit Analysis.* Cambridge: Harvard University Press.

Ahearn, Raymond J. 2009. *Transatlantic Regulatory Cooperation: Background and Analysis, Report for Congress.* Washington, D.C.: Congressional Research Service.

Alemanno, Alberto. 2011. "How to Get Out of the Transatlantic Regulatory Deadlock over GMOs? Time for Regulatory Cooperation." In Transatlantic Regulatory Cooperation: The Shifting Roles of the EU, the US and California, ed. David Vogel and Jo Swinnen, 200–228. Northampton, Mass.: Edward Elgar.

Allio, Lorenzo, and Stephane Jacobzone. 2012. "Regulatory Policy at the Crossroads: the Role of the OECD in Mapping an Agenda for the Future." In *Better Business Regulation in a Risk Society*, ed. Alberto Alemanno, Frank den Butter, André Nijsen, and Jacopo Torriti. New York: Springer.

Arrow, Kenneth J., Maureen L. Cropper, George C. Eads, Robert W. Hahn, Lester B. Lave, Roger G. Noll, Paul R. Portney, et al. 1996. "Is There a Role for Cost-Benefit Analysis in Environmental, Health, and Safety Regulation?" *Science* 272: 221–22.

Barrett, Scott. 2007. *Why Cooperate? The Incentive to Supply Global Public Goods.* New York: Oxford University Press.

Bermann, George A., Matthias Herdegen, and Peter L. Lindseth, eds. 2000. *Transatlantic Regulatory Cooperation: Legal Problems and Political Prospects.* New York: Oxford University Press.

Chang, Howard. 2004. "Risk Regulation, Endogenous Public Concerns, and the Hormones Dispute: Nothing to Fear but Fear Itself?" *Southern California Law Review* 77 (4): 743–76.

Clarkson, Richard, and Kathryn Deyes. 2002. "Estimating the Social Cost of Carbon Emissions." Government Economic Service Working Paper 140, HM Treasury.

Commission of the European Communities. 2005. Winning the Battle against Global Climate Change: Communication from the Commission to the Council, the European Parliament, the European Economic and Social Committee and the Committee of the Regions. Office for Official Publications of the European Communities.

Crawford-Brown, Douglas, Joost Pauwelyn, and Kelly Smith. 2004. "Environmental Risks, Precaution and Scientific Rationality in the Context of WTO/NAFTA Trade Rules." *Risk Analysis* 24 (2): 461–69.

Dunoff, Jeffrey L. 1992. "Reconciling International Trade with Preservation of the Global Commons: Can We Prosper and Protect?" *Washington and Lee Law Review* 49: 1407–54.

Farber, Daniel A., and Robert E. Hudec. 1994. "Free Trade and the Regulatory State: A GATT's-Eye View of the Dormant Commerce Clause." *Vanderbilt Law Review* 47: 1401–40.

Held, David. 2002. "Law of States, Law of Peoples: Three Models of Sovereignty." *Legal Theory* 8: 1–44.

Intergovernmental Panel on Climate Change (IPCC). 2007. "Climate Change 2007—Impacts, Adaptation and Vulnerability." In *IPCC Fourth Assessment Report*, ed. M. L. Parry, O. F. Canziani, J. P. Palutikof, P. J. van der Linden, and C. E. Hanson. *New York: Cambridge University Press*.

Interagency Working Group on Social Cost of Carbon (IWGSCC). 2010. *Technical Support Document: Social Cost of Carbon for Regulatory Impact Analysis under Executive Order 12866*. Washington, D.C.: IWGSCC.

Jacobsson, Bengt. 2006. "Regulated Regulators: Global Trends of State Transformation." In *Transnational Governance: Institutional Dynamics of Regulation*, ed. Marie Laurie Djelic and Kerstin Sahlin-Andersson, 205–24. New York: Cambridge University Press.

Keohane, Robert O. 2003. "Global Governance and Democratic Accountability." In *Taming Globalization: Frontiers of Governance*, ed. David Held and Mathias Koenig-Archibugi. Cambridge, Mass.: Polity Press.

Kirkpatrick, Colin, and David Parker. 2004. "Regulatory Impact Assessment and Regulatory Governance in Developing Countries." *Public Administration and Development* 24 (4): 333–44.

Kirkpatrick, Colin, and Yin-Fang Zhang. 2004. "Regulatory Impact Assessment in Developing and Transition Economies: A Survey of Current Practice." Centre on Regulation and Competition, Working Paper Series, No. 83, University of Manchester.

Kono, Daniel Y. 2006. "Optimal Obfuscation: Democracy and Trade Policy Transparency." *American Political Science Review* 100 (3): 369–84.

Kysar, Douglas A. 2010. *Regulating from Nowhere*. New Haven: Yale University Press.

Levmore, Saul. 1983. "Interstate Exploitation and Judicial Intervention." *Virginia Law Review* 69 (4): 563–631.

Livermore, Michael A. 2011. "Can Cost-Benefit Analysis of Environmental Policy Go Global?" *New York University Environmental Law Journal* 19 (1): 146–93.

Majone, Giandomenico. 2006. "The Internationalization of Regulation: Implications for Developing Countries." In *Regulatory Governance in Developing Countries*, ed. Martin Minogue and Ledivina Carino, 6 4–101. Northhampton, Mass.: Edward Elgar.

Marceau, Gabrielle, and Joel Trachtman. 2002. "The Technical Barriers to Trade Agreement, the Sanitary and Phytosanitary Measures Agreement, and the General Agreement on Tariff and Trade: A Map of the World Trade Organization Law of Domestic Regulation of Goods." *Journal of World Trade* 36 (5): 811–81.

Mattli, Walter, and Ngaire Woods. 2009. "In Whose Benefit? Explaining Regulatory Change." In *The Politics of Global Regulation*, ed. Walter Mattli and Ngaire Woods, 1–43. Princeton: Princeton University Press.

Mavroidis, Petros. 2007. *Trade in Goods*. New York: Oxford University Press.

Meuwese, Anne. 2011. "EU-US Horizontal Regulatory Cooperation: Mutual Recognition of Impact Assessment?" In *Transatlantic Regulatory Cooperation: The Shifting Roles of the*

EU, the US and California, ed. David Vogel and Johan Swinnen, 249–72. Northampton, Mass.: Edward Elgar.

Mishan, Edward J. 1976. *Cost-Benefit Analysis*. New York: Praeger.

Morgan, Bronwen. 2003. "The Economization of Politics: Meta-regulation as a Form of Nonjudicial Legality." *Social and Legal Studies*. 12 (4): 489–523.

Office of Management and Budget (OMB). 2003. *Office of Management and Budget Circular A-4, Regulatory Analysis*. Washington, D.C.: OMB.

Organisation for Economic Co-operation and Development (OECD). 1995. *Recommendation of the Council of the OECD on Improving the Quality of Government Regulation*. Paris: OECD.

Organisation for Economic Co-operation and Development (OECD). 1997a. *Report on Regulatory Reform: Synthesis*. Paris: OECD.

Organisation for Economic Co-operation and Development (OECD). 1997b. *Regulatory Impact Analysis: Best Practices in OECD Countries*. Paris: OECD.

Organisation for Economic Co-operation and Development (OECD). 2004. *OECD Regulatory Impact Analysis Inventory*. Paris: OECD.

Organisation for Economic Co-operation and Development (OECD). 2008. *Building an Institutional Framework for Regulatory Impact Analysis: Guidance for Policy-Makers*. Paris: OECD.

Organisation for Economic Co-operation and Development (OECD). 2009a. *Regulatory Impact Analysis: A Tool for Policy Coherence*. Paris: OECD.

Organisation for Economic Co-operation and Development (OECD). 2009b. *Indicators of Regulatory Management Systems*. Paris: OECD.

Radaelli, Claudio M. 2007. "Whither Better Regulation for the Lisbon Agenda?" *Journal of European Public Policy* 14 (2): 190–207.

Raustiala, Kal. 1997. "Domestic Institutions and International Regulatory Cooperation—Comparative Responses to the Convention on Biological Diversity." *World Politics* 49 (4): 482–509.

Revesz, Richard L., and Michael A. Livermore. 2008. *Retaking Rationality*. New York: Oxford University Press.

Rose-Ackerman, Susan. 2011. "Putting Cost-Benefit Analysis in Its Place: Rethinking Regulatory Review." *University of Miami Law Review* 65 (2): 335–56.

Scott, Joanne. 2007. *The WTO Agreement on Sanitary and Phytosanitary Measures: A Commentary*. New York: Oxford University Press.

Slaughter, Anne Marie. 2005. *A New World Order*. Princeton: Princeton University Press.

Sykes, Alan O. 1995. *Products Standards for Internationally Integrated Goods Markets*. Washington, D.C.: Brookings Institution.

Trachtman, Joel P. 1998. "Trade and…Problems, Cost-Benefit Analysis and Subsidiarity." *European Journal of International Law* 9: 32–85.

Treasury Board of Canada (TBC). 2007. *Canadian Cost-Benefit Analysis Guide: Regulatory Proposals*. Ottawa: TBC.

Trebilcock, Michael, and Robert Howse. 1999. *The Regulation of International Trade*. New York: Routledge.

Victor, David G. 2000. "The Sanitary and Phytosanitary Agreement of the World Trade Organization: An Assessment After Five Years." *New York University Journal of International Law and Policy* 32 (4): 865–937.

Wagner, Wendy. 2009. "The CAIR RIA: Advocacy Dressed Up as Policy Analysis." In *Reforming Regulatory Impact Analysis,* ed. Winston Harrington, Lisa Heinzerling, and Richard D. Morgenstern, 56–81. Washington, D.C.: Resources for the Future.

Watkiss, Paul. 2006. *The Social Costs of Carbon (SCC) Review—Methodological Approaches for Using SCC Estimates in Policy Assessment.* London: UK Department of Environment, Food and Rural Affairs.

Wiener, Jonathan B., and Alberto Alemanno. 2010. "Comparing Regulatory Oversight Bodies across the Atlantic: The Office of Information and Regulatory Affairs in the U.S. and the Impact Assessment Board in the EU." In *Comparative Administrative Law,* ed. Susan Rose-Ackerman, Henry R. Luce, and Peter L. Lindseth, 309–35. Northampton, Mass.: Edward Elgar.

Yohe, Gary W., Rodel D. Lasco, Qazi K. Ahmad, Nigel W. Arnell, Stewart J. Cohen, Chris Hope, Anthony C. Janetos, and Rosa T. Perez. 2007. "Perspectives on Climate Change and Sustainability." In *Climate Change 2007: Impacts, Adaptation and Vulnerability*, ed. Gary W. Yohe and Rodel D. Lasco, 811–41. Cambridge: Cambridge University Press.

8

The Diffusion of Regulatory Oversight
Jonathan B. Wiener

The idea of cost-benefit analysis has been spreading internationally for centuries—at least since an American named Benjamin Franklin wrote a letter in 1772 to his British friend, Joseph Priestley, recommending that Priestley weigh the pros and cons of a difficult decision in what Franklin dubbed a "moral or prudential algebra" (Franklin 1772) (more on this letter below). Several recent studies show that the use of benefit-cost analysis (BCA), for both public projects and public regulation of private activities, is now unfolding in countries on every habitable continent around the world (Livermore and Revesz 2013; Quah and Toh 2012; De Francesco 2012; Livermore 2011; Cordova-Novion and Jacobzone 2011). This global diffusion of BCA is intermingled with the global diffusion of regulatory capitalism, in which privatized market actors are supervised by expert regulatory agencies (Levi-Faur 2005; Simmons et al. 2008), and with the international spread of ex ante regulatory precautions to anticipate and prevent risks despite uncertainty (Wiener et al. 2011).

The spread of regulatory precautions to govern markets and risks, and the spread of BCA as an analytic method to evaluate public projects and regulatory policies, have led in turn to the global diffusion of institutional systems for regulatory oversight. This chapter addresses the diffusion of such regulatory oversight systems, which often employ BCA as a tool for policy evaluation (typically under the rubric of regulatory impact assessment, RIA).

The diffusion of regulatory oversight systems, closely following the diffusion of regulation and precaution, makes intuitive sense as a mechanism for accountability and guidance of regulatory power. But this pattern also challenges conventional claims. First, it shows that orthodox notions of discrete "national styles of regulation" (Vogel 1986) and early "legal origins" of modern regulation (La Porta et al. 2008) are belied or at least markedly eroded by the modern reality of the exchange of ideas across complex interconnected and increasingly hybrid regulatory systems. History matters, but it is not destiny; modern regulatory systems exist in global networks and evolve through learning, borrowing, and hybridization (Levi-Faur 2005; Wiener et al. 2011). Second, precaution and RIA/BCA, though often portrayed as antagonists, are better understood as complementary components of a deeper trend: the diffusion of regulatory foresight. Both precaution and RIA are efforts to forecast the future consequences of current choices.

Such regulatory foresight is increasingly demanded as societies prosper and, ironically, as they become safer.

Both hybridization and foresight are essential strategies for risk management in a changing world. To make the most of these strategies, this chapter suggests, we should consciously construct a global policy laboratory—which in turn involves a bit of regulatory hindsight.

Regulatory Oversight

Regulations can be necessary to correct market failures such as externalities (e.g., health, safety, and environmental risks), asymmetric information, and market power. Regulation can help solve such social problems, but it can also induce its own problems, including compliance costs, inhibition of innovation, ancillary risks, and rent-seeking. As a result, wherever states deploy regulation, demand arises for oversight of the regulatory system to reduce the costs and side effects of regulation, increase the benefits of regulation, and promote transparency and accountability.

Regulatory oversight systems go further than academic or episodic project-oriented BCA by creating institutions for broad application of RIA (typically using BCA) to evaluate all significant regulatory actions, with a body to review the RIAs prepared by regulatory agencies (OECD 2009a). The function of regulatory oversight may be located in the judiciary (judicial review of administrative agency action), the executive (center-of-government regulatory review, typically in the presidency or head of government, sometimes in an agency or a multiagency council), the legislature (an expert body assisting the legislature, or legislative review of administrative action), or an independent entity (such as a neutral review board, auditor, or ombudsman).

A "regulatory oversight body" (ROB) typically means a centralized government unit atop the executive hierarchy that uses expertise to supervise regulatory action by agencies (Lindseth, Aman, and Raul 2008; Wiener and Alemanno 2010; Cordova-Novion and Jacobzone 2011). ROBs provide both expertise (through expert staff and analytic methods) and political accountability (such as to the president or prime minister); these attributes may be mutually reinforcing but may pose tensions at times (Shapiro 2006).

ROBs may have a variety of functions and powers, including commenting on (and assisting in improving) the quality of an agency's RIA; constraining agency action when an RIA is deemed inadequate or when the benefits of an agency's proposed regulation do not justify the costs; calling on agencies to review existing regulations for their benefits and costs; prompting agency action when BCA identifies a socially promising regulation that agencies are not yet promulgating; and fostering transparency in the reporting of regulatory impacts. And ROBs' functions and powers may differ across polities, in part because ROBs may be located in different branches or units of different constitutional structures accorded different roles and powers, such as parliamentary versus presidential systems. A key point here is that the ROB's authority to guide regulatory decision making will depend on its institutional role among the branches or power centers of government (Wiener and Alemanno 2010). (For more detailed analyses of ROBs' legal bases, functions, powers, and constitutional structures, see Wiener and Alemanno 2010; Cordova-Novion and Jacobzone 2011).

For example, in the United States, the Office of Information and Regulatory Affairs (OIRA), created in 1980, located within the Office of Management and Budget (OMB) in the Executive Office of the President, performs all of these functions pursuant to a series of executive orders issued by several presidents of both political parties (notably Jimmy Carter's Executive Order 12,044 of 1978, preceding OIRA; Ronald Reagan's Executive Order 12,291 of 1981; and Bill Clinton's Executive Order 12,866 of 1993, which remains in force today and has been extended by Barack Obama's Executive Orders 13,563 and 13,579 of 2011, and 13,609 of May 2012). OIRA regularly exercises its authority to "return" agency regulatory proposals that do not meet the analytic and net benefits criteria set forth in the executive order, and OIRA has occasionally sent a "prompt" to agencies to pursue regulations that promise net benefits (Graham 2007; Revesz and Livermore 2008). BCA had been employed in the United States to assess public projects for decades before the creation of OIRA, including for flood control projects and military procurement (Quah and Toh 2012). Following the wave of regulatory legislation and the expansion of the administrative state during the 1960s and 1970s, the advent of RIA in the 1970s and OIRA review in the 1980s created an institutional structure for regulatory oversight—a system that has been reaffirmed in a bipartisan consensus across every subsequent presidential administration (Kagan 2001; Wiener and Alemanno 2010). Many of the U.S. member states have also adopted RIA systems (Schwartz 2010). But in the United States, RIAs and OIRA review are evaluations of agency rulemakings—agency actions to implement authority delegated by the legislature through statutes—not appraisals of the bills initially proposed in the legislature.

In the European Union, impact assessment was launched by the Better Regulation Initiative over 2001–2006 (Wiener 2006), and the EU Impact Assessment Board (IAB) was then created in 2006. The IAB, a five-member board, is located within the Secretariat General in the Presidency of the European Commission. It began as a commenter on RIA quality and has grown to play a wider role (Wiener and Alemanno 2010). Since 2010, the president of the European Commission has required new regulatory proposals to obtain a positive opinion from the IAB before going forward (European Commission 2010, 11–12), giving the IAB an authority more akin to OIRA's "return letter" than the IAB had previously had. Strikingly, while the IAB returned for "resubmission" only 9 percent of regulatory proposals in 2007, by 2010 it was returning 42 percent (and then 36 percent in 2011, perhaps indicating a plateau) (European Commission 2012, fig. 4). And in the EU, impact assessment and IAB review includes evaluations of proposals for legislation—that is, proposals by the Commission that will be forwarded to the European Parliament and Council. Similarly, in France, the new Organic Law of April 15, 2009 (Loi organique n° 2009–403 du 15 avril 2009 relative à l'application des articles 34–1, 39 et 44 de la Constitution) requires an impact analysis reviewed by the Conseil d'Etat before a bill can be proposed to the National Assembly.

Diffusion

Regulatory oversight is now being "diffused throughout the globe" (Radaelli and De Francesco 2008). Just as the number of regulatory agencies worldwide has grown, especially rapidly since about 1990 (Levi-Faur 2011, fig. 1.4), so the number of ROBs has also grown over that period. Institutions for regulatory oversight have spread from about half of the twenty-seven OECD members in 1998, to virtually all of the now thirty-one OECD members in 2010 (Cordova-Novion and Jacobzone 2011, fig. 3) and to virtually all EU members (De Francesco 2012). Mechanisms for regulatory oversight are also appearing in international organizations (see the chapter by Alberto Alemanno in this volume).

The creation in 2006 of the ROB at the EU level, the IAB, followed at least five years of development of an RIA system—starting with the EU's Better Regulation initiative and its impact assessment guidelines (Wiener 2006). Additional examples of ROBs in OECD member states include the Productivity Commission and the Office of Best Practice Regulation (OBPR) in Australia (where RIA has been employed since 1985); the Simplification and Better Regulation Unit in Denmark; the function of the Conseil d'Etat in supervising impact analyses pursuant to the Organic Law of April 15, 2009, in France; the Administrative Burdens Board in the Netherlands; the Better Regulation Unit in Germany; the Administrative Evaluation Bureau in Japan; the Comisión Federal de Mejora Regulatoria (COFEMER) in Mexico; the Regulatory Reform Committee (RRC) and Regulatory Reform Bureau in South Korea; and the Better Regulation Executive and associated regulatory committees in the United Kingdom (a survey is provided in Cordova-Novion and Jacobzone 2011). In South Korea, spurred by an economic crisis in the 1990s, the government enacted the Basic Act on Administrative Regulations in 1998, and the RRC then undertook an extensive review of existing regulations resulting in thousands of revisions and repeals, as well as RRC oversight of RIAs for newly proposed regulations (Truen 2011; Cordova-Novion and Jacobzone 2011). In Chile, the economic evaluation requirement for environmental regulations (pursuant to Law 19,300 of 1994) has been supplemented by an RIA process created in Law 20,416 of 2010, though it remains unclear whether a ROB will supervise this RIA process (OECD 2011). Related systems exist or are being developed in other OECD members, including New Zealand, Poland, Portugal, Sweden, and Turkey (Cordova-Novion and Jacobzone 2011).

We can expect the spread of ROBs using RIA, and the collaborative dialogue among those institutions, to continue. In March 2012, the OECD issued a major set of twelve recommendations to all governments, including on evaluating regulatory quality, using RIA for both ex ante (prospective) and ex post (retrospective) regulatory review, creating ROBs, and engaging in international regulatory cooperation (OECD 2012). In May 2012, President Obama issued Executive Order 13,609 to promote international regulatory cooperation.

The legal bases, constitutional structures, and powers of these ROBs differ across countries. Just more than half (so far) of the ROBs in the OECD member states are empowered to review agency RIAs (Cordova-Novion and Jacobzone 2011, fig. 3). Some, like US OIRA, review agencies' proposed regulations to implement statutes already enacted by the legislature; others, like the EU IAB, review initial proposals for legislation (usually within the branch of government that initiates such proposals); this difference in structure entails differences in interbranch (executive vs. legislative) relations over policymaking and power (Wiener and Alemanno 2010). The U.S. OIRA, the EU IAB, the OBPR in Australia, the RRC in Korea, and COFEMER in Mexico must generally give a positive opinion for a proposed regulation to proceed, or they have the power to return regulatory proposals (though there are exceptions in each system) (Cordova-Novion and Jacobzone 2011, table A.1). Many or all ROBs can request analytic improvements in a draft RIA. Japan's Administrative Evaluation Bureau, the Administrative Burdens board in the Netherlands, and Germany's Better Regulation Unit can review the quality of RIAs but do not return proposed regulations (Cordova-Novion and Jacobzone 2011, table A.1). Review of the existing stock of regulations (also known as ex post, retrospective, or "lookback" review) is being emphasized in the Australian regulatory oversight system (Australian Productivity Commission 2011) and in the United States (under Executive Order 13,563 issued in 2011).

RIA and ROBs are also beginning to spread beyond the OECD to developing countries (Truen 2011; World Bank Group 2010; Jacobs 2006; Kirkpatrick and Zhang 2004). In many countries, as was the case in the United States and EU, the development of BCA as an analytic exercise by academics and project-funding agencies has preceded the creation of governmental RIA systems and the establishment of ROBs to supervise regulation. Some developing countries are now moving to adopt formal systems of RIA and to establish ROBs.

Countries seeking to join the EU are adopting RIA: Serbia adopted Rules of Procedure requiring RIA for new legislation in 2005, after having established a Council for Regulatory Reform and Quality Control in 2003 (OECD 2009b, 245); and Croatia required RIA beginning in 2005 and in 2007 created an RIA Coordination Office (OECD 2009b, 210–11). But Bulgaria has hesitated to adopt RIA, despite internal support (Truen 2011). Turkey has adopted significant administrative reforms, partly in response to encouragement from the EU and partly for domestic reasons, but apparently has not yet instituted RIA (Sezen 2011).

Elsewhere, in Russia in 2008 and South Africa in 2009, the OECD held informational workshops on RIA. South Africa has moved ahead to develop a pilot RIA process supported by the Cabinet Office (Truen 2011). RIA was adopted for environmental regulations in Uganda in 2003 (UNEP 2005), and in Kenya in 2007 (World Bank Group 2010). In Brazil, the Secretariat of Economic Monitoring (SEAE) has recently adopted RIA for some sectors (OECD 2008), although some observers predict that a broader RIA process in Brazil may turn out to be significantly influenced by political forces (Peci and Sobral 2011). The use of BCA has also become widespread across numerous countries in Asia (Quah and Toh 2012, offering numerous case studies). BCA for both project evaluation and regulatory policy evaluation has been employed in China and India (Livermore 2011), although the development of an RIA process for China's regulatory agencies has lagged (Hu 2009). The Philippines has an RIA process supervised by its National Economic and Development Authority, and is considering establishing an Office of Best Regulatory Practice to provide expert oversight and advice on this RIA process (Bird, Plunkett, and Bosworth 2010). Vietnam adopted RIA in 2008–9, with support from its Administrative Procedure Control Agency, the German GTZ, and the USAID's Vietnam Competitiveness Initiative (PERQ 2011; Truen 2011); an RIA is now required in Vietnam before a bill may be presented to the National Assembly (Truen 2011).

This diffusion of RIA and ROBs is part of a broader pattern. Several key concepts in environmental law and risk regulation have experienced considerable diffusion and borrowing around the world, including BCA through RIA, environmental impact assessment (EIA), emissions trading (cap and trade), public participation and access to government information, and information disclosure requirements on industry (Busch and Jorgens 2005; Wiener and Richman 2010; Ellerman et al. 2010; Wiener et al. 2011; Sand 2011).

Diffusion is a multifaceted concept of the spread of ideas (Levi-Faur 2005). Ideas can spread across numerous nodes in complex networks, including among individuals, groups, civil society, business coalitions, political parties, regions, agencies, countries, and international organizations (Lazer 2005). And ideas may evolve as they spread and be employed differently in different institutional settings. The literature on the diffusion of policy ideas is large (see generally Rose 1993; Dolowitz and Marsh 2000; James and Lodge 2003; Elkins and Simmons 2005; Berry and Berry 2007). Closely related concepts of diffusion as an evolutionary process have been developed in sociology (Hagerstrand 1968), economics (Rogers 2003), law (Sand 1971; Watson 1993; Tushnet 1999), political science (Walker 1969; Lazer 2005; Weyland 2005; Simmons et al. 2008), biology (Arnold 1997; Grant 1999; Deakin 2002), and history of science (Galison 1997). Legal scholars have borrowed from biologists the notion of "memes" as the unit, and counterpart of genes, in the evolution of ideas (Dawkins 1976; Deakin 2002). In biology, evolution was first understood to occur through competition among individuals within a species; later, through field studies, biologists began to appreciate that evolution also occurs through the exchange of genetic material across species via interbreeding (called "hybridization") (Arnold 1997; Grant 1999). Likewise, in law, evolution was initially understood to occur through competition among individual rules within a legal system (Priest 1977; Elliott 1985; Farber 1994; but for doubts about the efficiency of such legal evolution, see Hadfield 1993; Roe 1996); later, through the equivalent of field studies, legal scholars came to appreciate that legal evolution also occurs through the exchange of legal concepts across legal systems via borrowing (Watson 1993; Elliott 1997; Wiener 2001; Deakin 2002; Wiener 2003), also called "hybridization" (Wiener 2003, 254–61; Wiener 2006; Wiener et al. 2011, 541–44; Delmas-Marty 2006, 101–12).

There are reasons to expect the diffusion of regulatory policy approaches to have increased in recent years. The reality of contemporary international relations and information technology is a world of interconnectedness: networks and the transnational diffusion of ideas. Slaughter (2009, 1) argues:

> We live in a networked world.... In this world, the measure of power is connectedness.... The twentieth-century world was, at least in terms of geopolitics, a billiard-ball world, described by the political scientist Arnold Wolfers as a system of self-contained states colliding with one another.... The emerging networked world of the twenty-first century, however, exists above the state, below the state, and through the state.

Interconnectedness enables the more fluid spread of ideas, and thereby offers increased opportunities to borrow and collaborate on policy solutions (Lazer 2005). Regulatory ideas are increasingly being borrowed across the Atlantic, and worldwide, in an evolving web of global administrative law (Kingsbury et al. 2005; Rose-Ackerman and Lindseth 2010). Levi-Faur (2005, 20) writes:

> [T]he new order [of regulatory capitalism] is diffused rather than reproduced independently as a discrete event in each country and sector. Diffusion is a reflection of an increasingly interdependent world. Beyond economic interdependencies, there is a growth of "horizontal" channels of diffusion and an increase in the export and import of institutions and knowledge.

But the fact that we observe similar legal rules, policies, or institutions arising in multiple places does not necessarily mean that the identical idea has been (or should be) adopted in every place. There may be variation in the content of the idea as it is adopted in different places. RIA adopted in one country may have a different institutional role and analytic content than RIA adopted in other countries (Radaelli 2005; Wiener and Alemanno 2010). Careful comparison of the elements of each RIA system and ROB will be helpful in distinguishing what precisely was borrowed from where. And even if the idea is essentially the same in each place we observe it arising, that does not necessarily mean that the idea was learned and eagerly borrowed by one place from another; it might, for example, have been imposed coercively by a colonial power (Elkins and Simmons 2005; Simmons et al. 2008), or imitated unthinkingly as a passing fad (Lazer 2005), or arisen independently in each place in response to similar but independent conditions (as in "convergent evolution" and related concepts in biology, see Losos 2011). Dobbin, Simmons, and Garrett (2007, 462–63) warn:

> One weakness of many of the studies in this arena is that they take simple diffusion to be evidence of learning, without looking at whether there was evidence of the efficacy of a policy innovation before second- and third- movers adopted it.... [R]ational learning theory implies a kind of cost-benefit analysis.... People may draw lessons by observing the effects of policies other countries adopt, and they may engage in Bayesian updating, in which they constantly add new bits of evidence to the existing knowledge

base…the overarching theme here is that countries learn to pursue effective policies.

A similar point is that successful legal borrowing involves a kind of cost-benefit calculus: an evaluation of policies and institutions in other jurisdictions and a decision to borrow or translate the version that appears most promising for one's own needs (Wiener 2001; Levi-Faur 2005; Stone 2012). This kind of calculus—essentially what Benjamin Franklin advised—may be applied in horizontal legal borrowing across countries and in vertical legal borrowing across local, national, and international levels of governance (Wiener 2001; Levi-Faur 2005; Ovodenko and Keohane 2012).

The borrowing calculus that drives the diffusion of RIA and ROBs is undoubtedly based on a combination of factors. One source appears to be a demand, at least among presidents, to manage the growing regulatory state. Consider the adoption of the U.S. Administrative Procedure Act in 1946 following the New Deal, and the executive orders on regulatory review in the 1970s and 1980s following the burst of regulatory legislation of the preceding decade. Similarly, in Europe, Better Regulation and the IAB arose after the growth of EU regulation in the 1990s. A similar pattern may be at work in other countries. The presidential impetus to manage the regulatory state through BCA, RIA, and ROBs can focus on reducing costs and cutting red tape, but it can also seek to increase social net benefits through promotion of desirable new regulations (Kagan 2001; Graham 2007; Revesz and Livermore 2008). In addition, economic crises and fears about economic competitiveness appear to spur regulatory reform efforts—for example, in the United States after the stagflation of the late 1970s, in Europe with the Lisbon Agenda of jobs and growth since 2000, and in Korea and Mexico after economic crises in the 1990s (Cordova-Novion and Jacobzone 2011, Truen 2011). Looking ahead, RIA and ROBs will be more likely to be adopted if their methods can be made less costly and more beneficial, especially in lower-income countries facing constraints on administrative capacity.

Evidence is accumulating that policy approaches to RIA and regulatory oversight have actually been borrowed, based on learning about efficacy, across countries. Research on the emergence of "global administrative law" reflects both hybridization and the role of purposive actors consciously borrowing ideas (Kingsbury et al. 2005). There is clearly an epistemic community of experts sharing experiences about RIA and ROBs across countries; examples include Radaelli (2005), Renda (2006), Jacobs (2006), Cordova-Novion and Jacobzone (2011), Quah and Toh (2012), Truen (2011), Wiener (2006), Wiener and Alemanno (2010), and this volume itself. The OECD has been a major supplier of information and encouragement on regulatory quality improvement not only in OECD member states but around the world, as have the overseas development agencies of key countries like the United States and Germany. Direct testimonial evidence is also available; consider this express account of borrowing in the EU Better Regulation initiative by the prime minister of Ireland (Ahern 2004):

> Better Regulation is a core theme of our EU Presidency and featured prominently at the recent Spring Economic Council….There is a long tradition in

American Public Administration of focusing on the quality and impact of regulation. Many of the policies, institutions, and tools that support Better Regulation have their origins in the U.S.A....There is much that we have learned from the United States in relation to regulatory management and, through occasions like this, much that we can continue to learn....We hope too that there will be shared learning. While we in the European Union are newer to the game, I hope that we have moved beyond our rookie season! The Union is making up ground quickly in respect of Better Regulation. This is as it should be. There is a deeper understanding within the European Institutions and Member States of the need for regulatory reform.

A further kind of evidence of diffusion and learning is statistical analysis of the timing and location of the adoption of RIA across countries. De Francesco (2012) tested the historical pattern for the influence of several plausible variables. He found that trade relations and the country's legal system family were not significant predictors of RIA adoption; prior adoption of other information access laws helped predict RIA adoption; the OECD was important more for its information-sharing facility than for its nudging efforts; and the most influential factor in adoption of RIA, in De Francesco's model, was a country's connection to transnational information networks offering knowledge about regulatory innovations.

From National Styles to Regulatory Evolution

This pattern of diffusion has important implications for the comparison and evolution of law. Comparative law has traditionally presumed that important differences across countries are explained by discrete "national styles of regulation" (Vogel 1986), "families" of legal systems (Zweigert and Kotz 1998), and early "legal origins" (La Porta et al. 2008). The economic analysis of "legal origins" (La Porta et al. 2008) draws broad generalizations about modern business rules by grouping countries into ancient legal families (English, French, German, etc.) (for critiques of the "legal origins" literature, *see* Roe 2006; Curran 2009; Michaels 2009). Comparative law scholars have long recognized the possibilities for legal borrowing (Watson 1993), though often these transplants are individual doctrines, which may take root in the other system, or wither, or act as irritants—rare grafts from one discrete legal system into another, whose reception in the second legal system is precarious.

But as Reimann (2001) pointed out, extensive diffusion of legal ideas can erode the traditional categories of comparative law that are based on discrete national legal systems. The reality of major reforms of regulatory systems around the world, through BCA, RIA and ROBs, suggests that the model of stable discrete national styles of regulation, or early legal origins determining modern regulation, needs substantial rethinking. De Francesco (2012) finds little or no evidence that national legal origin explains modern adoption of RIA. Vogel (2012) concedes that national regulatory systems are far more open to wholesale change than he had previously argued (Vogel 1986). Even the "legal origins" advocates allow (in passing) that "legal origins" may not account for regulations in what they label "new spheres of social control," nor for regulations adopted following crisis events (La Porta et al. 2008, 307, 326)—two of the leading characteristics of risk regulation and regulatory reform.

Diffusion and hybridization are powerful forces in regulatory evolution. Hybridization, in law as in biology, exchanges genes or memes, and thereby interpenetrates the boundaries of "species," "systems," "families," and "styles." Hybridization creates hybrid offspring that are neither convergent with nor divergent from the prior populations, but new; they do not always succeed and are often less fit, but they prosper when conditions change, opening niches for which the hybrids are well adapted. Undertaking both a dozen qualitative in-depth case studies and a quantitative analysis of a large-N sample of risks, Wiener et al. (2011) find that U.S. and European systems of risk regulation are undergoing substantial hybridization, exchanging ideas on many topics, including precaution, better regulation, impact assessment, regulatory oversight, economic incentive instruments, information disclosure, and other key elements. Risk regulation lives in an unfolding network society (Castells 2000; Slaughter 2004; De Francesco 2012). The result is that it becomes increasingly difficult to distinguish or generalize about separate regulatory systems with discrete characters. Countries and cultures caricatured as sharply different turn out to share a great deal (Baldwin 2009). Amid such hybridization, claims of discrete national legal systems or families become stereotypes of a bygone era (if it ever existed).

This does not mean that no comparisons can be made. (Such a claim would itself be a hasty generalization drawn from inadequate data.) The view that comparative law is impossible because legal systems are so intrinsically different from each other that rules cannot be compared—what Siems (2007, 1, 6) critiques as the "strong form" of the claim of the "end of comparative law"—is both self-negating (it depends on the very kind of sharp comparison that it purports to deny) and empirically unsupported (because the United States, Europe, and, increasingly, other countries are sharing legal ideas, not veering off on separate paths). As Hiram Chodosh has nicely shown, those who assert that "comparing apples and oranges" is impossible are committing three errors: first, people do in fact compare apples and oranges at the grocery store every day (in terms of taste, color, shape, price, and so on); second, using the phrase "apples and oranges" itself requires a comparison between the two fruits (to deem them so different); and third, such an assertion itself rests on a comparison between the degree of contrast between the two fruits and the degree of contrast between the other two items sought to be compared (Chodosh 1999). (This defense of comparison applies not only to comparative law but to critiques of BCA as well.) Comparisons can and must be made, but on the basis of much more systematic empirical study, rather than generalizing to "national styles" based on a small and biased sample. The real tableau is a complex and evolving landscape that defies easy generalization—the busy world depicted with evident affection by both Pieter Brueghel (a medieval European) and Richard Scarry (a more modern American). An improved understanding will involve comparison of rules and institutions as modules or memes that can be exchanged across interconnected legal systems, rather than of categorical generalizations about national legal systems or legal origins.

Regulatory Foresight

Many of the contemporary debates over BCA and RIA were foreseen, of course, by Benjamin Franklin. He wrote to his friend, the English scientist Joseph Priestley, about whether Priestley should accept a new job (Franklin 1772):

> In the Affair of so much Importance to you, wherein you ask my Advice, I cannot for want of sufficient Premises, advise you what to determine, but if you please I will tell you how. When those difficult Cases occur, they are difficult, chiefly because while we have them under Consideration, all the Reasons pro and con are not present to the Mind at the same time; but sometimes one Set present themselves, and at other times another, the first being out of Sight. Hence the various Purposes or Inclinations that alternately prevail, and the Uncertainty that perplexes us.
>
> To get over this, my Way is, to divide half a Sheet of Paper by a Line into two Columns; writing over the one Pro, and over the other Con. Then during three or four Days Consideration, I put down under the different heads short Hints of the different Motives, that at different Times occur to me, for or against the Measure. When I have thus got them all together in one View, I endeavour to estimate their respective Weights; and where I find two, one on each side, that seem equal, I strike them both out. If I find a Reason pro equal to some two Reasons con, I strike out the three. If I judge some two Reasons con, equal to some three Reasons pro, I strike out the five; and thus proceeding I find at length where the Ballance lies; and if after a Day or two of farther consideration, nothing new that is of Importance occurs on either side, I come to a Determination accordingly. And, tho' the Weight of Reasons cannot be taken with the Precision of Algebraic Quantities, yet, when each is thus considered, separately and comparatively, and the whole lies before me, I think I can judge better, and am less liable to make a rash Step; and in fact I have found great Advantage from this kind of Equation, in what may be called Moral or Prudential Algebra.

Franklin appears to have anticipated so many core aspects of BCA and RIA: the pitfalls of neglecting important impacts; the need for a structured approach to identifying and weighing the pros and cons; the inevitability of uncertainty; the need to "estimate their respective weights" but the inability to achieve mathematical precision (yet still an "Equation…Algebra"); the issue of commensurability (crossing out like items); the avowedly normative ("moral or prudential") exercise; the use of BCA as a tool to help us "judge better," not an arithmetic rule; the cognitive approach to BCA as a tool to get all key aspects ("the whole") to appear "present to the Mind at the same time"; the behavioral role of BCA as a tool to avoid "a rash Step."

The letter itself illustrates the transatlantic diffusion of BCA via epistemic communities. It also records the diffusion of BCA preceding the establishment of RIA and ROBs. Franklin wrote to Priestley, and Priestley was in communication with Jeremy Bentham, who later wrote that he learned key elements of utilitarianism from Priestley (Bentham 1843); at least one historian suggests that Bentham got the idea of dividing and weighing the pros and cons from Franklin (Viner 1949, 368), though it is difficult to find evidence that Franklin and Bentham communicated directly (perhaps through Priestley). An intriguing additional possibility, difficult to document, is that Franklin, Priestley, and Bentham influenced the French engineer-economist Jules Dupuit, who developed the mathematics of marginal BCA in the early 1800s (Ekelund and Hebert 1975). Among other possible connections to Dupuit are that Franklin and Bentham each spent considerable time in Paris (Franklin was the American ambassador to France from 1776 to 1785), and Bentham's work was published in French by Etienne Dumont in the early 1800s. (Franklin's algebra was also later employed by Charles Darwin, to decide whether to marry, in 1838; a possible link is that Franklin had known Darwin's grandfathers, Erasmus Darwin and Josiah Wedgwood.) Franklin also helped send French engineers to America to assist with the Revolutionary War—a role that soon after contributed to the formation of the U.S. Army Corps of Engineers, modeled on the French Corps des Ponts et Chaussées, the group that included Jules Dupuit. And much later, of course, BCA was apparently first applied in the U.S. government by the Army Corps of Engineers under the Flood Control Act of 1936 (Quah and Toh 2012; Hines 1973).

The foresight needed in regulation is not only Ben Franklin's foresight about how to do BCA, but foresight about risks and regulatory impacts. In order to weigh the pros and cons, we need ways to foresee those pros and cons. That is the function of risk assessment, and of RIA. Foresight is also the ambition of precaution. Although precaution and RIA are often portrayed as antagonists, they are better understood as complementary components of a deeper phenomenon: the diffusion of regulatory foresight. Both precaution and RIA are efforts to forecast the future consequences of current choices.

Humans have a capacity to envision future scenarios, but these scenarios tend to be constructed in the brain out of fragments of our memories, and so are partly rooted in what is mentally available (Gilbert and Wilson 2007; Schachter, Addis, and Buckner 2008). This property of bounded foresight helps explain the observation that public risk perceptions are often galvanized by "available" recent crisis events (Sunstein and Kuran 1999). Precaution is an effort to foresee and prevent such risks before they occur. On the other side of the same coin, RIA is an effort to foresee the impacts of risk regulatory policies and ensure they are desirable. Meanwhile, policy diffusion itself can be vulnerable to the availability heuristic if policymakers adopt what they happen to see rather than what careful study would recommend (Elkins and Simmons 2005).

Regulatory foresight is increasingly demanded as societies prosper and, ironically, as they become safer. Increased demand for regulation is spurred by factors including prosperity, impersonal commerce, advancing science, crisis events, and rising safety itself. Prosperity reduces immediate risks to survival and extends longevity. But prosperity also feeds a rising demand for amenities such as environmental quality and risk protection, enhances the scientific methods used to detect more subtle and latent risks, and brings new technologies that reduce some risks but may create new risks. These factors help explain the increasing demand for precautionary policies in prosperous, safer countries—a phenomenon criticized by Wildavsky (1979), but perhaps understandable if demand for risk protection increases with income. Lower risk and greater longevity might also shift the demand for risk protection toward greater emphasis on latent risks, because even though greater longevity reflects decreasing risks, longer life spans may also lead people to care more about risks that may arise farther into the future. And, in a decreasing-risk world, those risks that do occur may be seen as more unusual and more outrageous by the public, spurring greater demand for protective measures (Godard et al. 2002, 29).

But precautionary regulations to reduce those risks can impose their own costs and ancillary impacts (risk-risk trade-offs) (Wiener 2002). Hence the rising demand for RIA—a companion form of foresight. International diffusion of RIA and ROBs are manifestations of the demand for regulatory foresight.

As a society becomes even safer through the joint effects of prosperity, precaution, and better regulation, that society may come to confront even lower-probability, higher-consequence risks—extreme catastrophic risks that would otherwise escape attention but that could be highly worth preventing (Posner 2004; Sunstein 2007). Scientific detection capabilities improve with prosperity and continuing research. Longer life spans mean that extreme risks become more plausible within one's own lifetime and the lifetime of one's children and grandchildren. And the bequest value to the living of protecting future generations may increase with wealth, safety, and foresight. (Whereas the Environmental Kuznets Curve hypothesis suggests that pollution levels would rise and then fall as a society becomes ever wealthier, this risk-prosperity-foresight hypothesis suggests that risks would shift toward the tail of remote risks as a society prospers and reduces familiar risks.) But these extreme risks may nonetheless go neglected where they are so rare that no present or memorable incident triggers the "availability" heuristic (Weber 2006). Furthermore, catastrophic risks may be neglected where the losses would be so large that the public becomes numb to their magnitude (Slovic 2007), and where the catastrophe would wipe out the very institutions meant to provide remedies and ex post sanctions (thus weakening ex ante incentives for prevention). These are "tragedies of the uncommons" (Wiener 2005; Wiener 2011), and they pose the strongest case for precaution. Still, precaution against tragedies of the uncommons must confront the twin challenges of priority-setting (choosing which extreme scenario to address, even as such scenarios multiply when the probability worth worrying about becomes ever smaller) and risk-risk trade-offs (because measures to prevent one catastrophic risk might induce another). Thus, even in cases where precaution is strongly warranted against uncertain catastrophic risks, the full foresight of RIA remains crucial.

To succeed, societies must manage both emerging risks (through precaution) and the ancillary impacts of their own risk protection measures (through impact assessment). Both are forms of foresight. The international diffusion of these strategies enables more countries to take advantage of their benefits, and enables researchers to study variations across countries from which we can learn and improve such policies. Both hybridization and regulatory foresight are essential strategies for risk management in a changing world. But diffusion can go awry if policymakers are not good students or are not well informed about other policy measures and impacts (Elkins and Simmons 2005). To make the most of these strategies, we should consciously construct a global policy laboratory (Greenstone 2009; Wiener 2011)—which in turn involves a bit of regulatory hindsight. We will need ex post evaluation of regulatory policies and of the diffusion of regulatory oversight systems, in order to see what difference those policies and oversight systems actually make (Coglianese and Bennear 2005). These retrospective assessments will help us revise those policies and oversight systems, foster smarter diffusion, and improve our methods of ex ante prospective regulatory foresight and policy choice.

Acknowledgments

The author thanks Alberto Alemanno, Fabrizio Cafaggi, Michael A. Livermore, Richard L. Revesz, and Peter Sand for helpful discussion, and Rocío Perez and David Strifling for valuable research assistance.

Bibliography

Ahern, Bertie. 2004. Speech by the Taoiseach (head of government of Ireland), Bertie Ahern, at the IBEC Conference on EU-U.S. Perspectives on Regulation. April 19, Dublin. www.betterregulation.ie/index.asp?docID_57_ (accessed May 24, 2010).

Arnold, M. L. 1997. *Natural Hybridization and Evolution*. Oxford: Oxford University Press.

Australian Productivity Commission. 2011. *Identifying and Evaluating Regulation Reforms*. Research Report, Canberra, December.

Baldwin, Peter. 2009. *The Narcissism of Minor Differences: How America and Europe Are Alike*. Oxford: Oxford University Press.

Bentham, Jeremy. 1843. "Extracts from Bentham's Commonplace Book." In *The Works of Jeremy Bentham*, edited by William Tait, 10: 142. London: Simpkin, Marshall & Co.

Berkowitz, Daniel, Katharina Pistor, and Jean-Francois Richard. 2003. "Economic Development, Legality, and the Transplant Effect." *European Economic Review* 47: 165–95.

Berry, Frances Stokes, and William D. Berry. 2007. "Innovation and Diffusion Models in Policy Research." In *Theories of the Policy Process*, ed. Paul A. Sabatier, 223–60. Boulder: Westview Press.

Bird, Kelly, Herb Plunkett, and Malcolm Bosworth. 2010. *Philippines: Options for Establishing an Office of Best Regulatory Practice.* ADB Technical Assistance Consultant's Report, Project Number: 40538-01. Manila: Asian Development Bank.

Busch, Per-olof, and Helge Jorgens. 2005. "The International Sources of Policy Convergence: Explaining the Spread of Environmental Policy Innovations." *Journal of European Public Policy* 12: 860–84.

Castells, Manuel. 2000. *The Information Age: Economy, Society, and Culture.* 2nd ed. 3 vols. Oxford: Blackwell.

Chodosh, Hiram. 1999. "Comparing Comparisons: In Search of Methodology." *Iowa Law Review* 84: 1025–1131.

Coglianese, Cary, and Lori Snyder Bennear. 2005. "Program Evaluation of Environmental Policies: Toward Evidence-Based Decision Making." In *Social and Behavioral Science Research Priorities for Environmental Decision Making*, 246–73. Washington, D.C.: National Research Council, National Academies Press.

Cordova-Novion, Cesar, and Stephane Jacobzone. 2011. *"Strengthening the Institutional Setting for Regulatory Reform: The Experience from OECD Countries."* OECD Working Papers on Public Governance, No. 19.

Curran, Vivian G. 2009. "Comparative Law and the Legal Origins Thesis." *American Journal of Comparative Law* 57: 863–76.

Dawkins, Richard. 1976. *The Selfish Gene.* Oxford: Oxford University Press.

De Francesco, Fabrizio. 2012. "Diffusion of Regulatory Impact Analysis among OECD and EU Member States." *Comparative Political Studies.* http://cps.sagepub.com/content/early/2012/02/15/0010414011434297.

Deakin, Simon. 2002. "Evolution for Our Time: A Theory of Legal Memetics." *Current Legal Problems* 55: 1–42.

Delmas-Marty, Mirelle. 2006. *Le Pluralisme Ordonné.* Paris: Seuil.

Dobbin, Frank, Beth Simmons, and Geoffrey Garrett. 2007. "The Global Diffusion of Public Policies: Social Construction, Coercion, Competition, or Learning?" *Annual Review of Sociology* 33: 449–72.

Dolowitz, David, and David Marsh. 2000. "Learning from Abroad: The Role of Policy Transfer in Contemporary Policy Making." *Governance* 13 (1): 5–24.

Eeckhoudt, Louis R., and James K. Hammitt. 2001. "Background Risks and the Value of a Statistical Life." *Journal of Risk and Uncertainty* 23: 261–79.

Ekelund, Robert B., Jr., and Robert F. Hebert, 1975. "Dupuit and Marginal Utility: Context of the Discovery." *History of Political Economy* 8: 266–73.

Elkins, Zachary, and Beth Simmons. 2005. "On Waves, Clusters, and Diffusion: A Conceptual Framework." *Annals of the American Academy of Political and Social Science* 598: 33–51.

Ellerman, A. Denny, Frank Convery, and Christian de Perthuis. 2010. *Pricing Carbon: The European Union Emissions Trading Scheme.* Cambridge: Cambridge University Press.

Elliott, E. Donald. 1985. "The Evolutionary Tradition in Jurisprudence." *Columbia Law Review* 85: 38–94.

Elliott, E. Donald. 1997. "Law and Biology: The New Synthesis?" *St. Louis University Law Journal* 41: 595–624.

European Commission. 2010. *Communication from the President: The Working Methods of the Commission 2010-2014.* C(2010) 1100 (February 10). http://ec.europa.eu/commission_2010-2014/president/news/documents/pdf/c2010_1100_En.pdf.

European Commission. 2012. *Impact Assessment Board, Report for 2011*. SEC(2012) 101 Final (January 2). http://ec.europa.eu/governance/impact/key_docs/docs/sec_2012_0101_En.pdf.

Farber, Daniel A. 1994. "Environmental Protection as a Learning Experience." *Loyola of Los Angeles Law Review* 7: 791–807.

Franklin, Benjamin. 1772. "Letter to Joseph Priestley, September 19." Reprinted in *Benjamin Franklin: Representative Selections, with Introduction, Bibliography and Notes*, ed. Frank Luther Mott and Chester E. Jorgenson, 348–49. New York: American Book Company.

Galison, Peter. 1997. *Image and Logic: A Material Culture of Microphysics*. Chicago: University of Chicago Press.

Gilbert, Daniel T., and Timothy D. Wilson. 2007. "Prospection: Experiencing the Future." *Science* 317: 1351–54.

Godard, Olivier, Claude Henry, Patrick Lagadec, and Erwann Michel-Kerjan. 2002. *Traité des Nouveaux Risques: Précaution, Crise, Assurance*. Paris: Gallimard.

Graham, John D. 2007. "The Evolving Regulatory Role of the U.S. Office of Management and Budget." *Review of Environmental Economics and Policy* 1: 171–91.

Graham, John D., and Jonathan B. Wiener, eds. 1995. *Risk vs. Risk: Tradeoffs in Protecting Health and the Environment*. Cambridge: Harvard University Press.

Grant, Peter R. 1999. *Ecology and Evolution of Darwin's Finches*. Princeton: Princeton University Press.

Greenstone, Michael. 2009. "Toward a Culture of Persistent Regulatory Experimentation and Evaluation." In *New Perspectives on Regulation*, ed. David Moss and John Cisternino, 111–25. Cambridge: Tobin Project.

Hadfield, Gillian. 1993. "Bias in the Evolution of Legal Rules." *Georgetown Law Journal* 80: 583–616.

Hagerstrand, Torsten. 1968. "The Diffusion of Innovations." In *International Encyclopedia of the Social Sciences*, ed. David L. Sills, 4: 174–78. New York: Macmillan.

Hines, Lawrence G. 1973. "Precursors to Benefit-Cost Analysis in Early United States Public Investment Projects." *Land Economics* 49: 310–17.

Hu, Jiabin. 2009. "Assessing the Governance of the Independent Regulatory Agencies in China." PhD diss., University of Southern California.

Jacobs, Scott. 2006. Current Trends in Regulatory Impact Analysis: The Challenges of Mainstreaming RIA into Policy-Making. New York: Jacobs & Associates.

James, Oliver, and Martin Lodge. 2003. "The Limitations of 'Policy Transfer' and 'Lesson Drawing' for Public Policy Research." *Political Studies Review* 1: 179–93.

Kagan, Elena. 2001. "Presidential Administration." *Harvard Law Review* 114: 2245–2385.

Kingsbury, Benedict, Nico Krisch, and Richard B. Stewart. 2005. "The Emergence of Global Administrative Law." *Law and Contemporary Problems* 68 (3): 15–62.

Kirkpatrick, C., and Y. Zhang. 2004. "*Regulatory Impact Assessment in Developing and Transition Economies: A Survey of Current Practice*." Working Paper Series, No. 83, Centre on Regulation and Competition, Institute for Development Policy and Management, University of Manchester.

La Porta, Rafael, Florencio Lopez-de-Silanes, and Andrei Shleifer. 2008. "The Economic Consequences of Legal Origins." *Journal of Economic Literature* 46: 285–332.

Lazer, David. 2005. "Regulatory Capitalism as a Networked Order." *Annals of the American Academy of Political and Social Science* 598: 52–66.

Levi-Faur, David. 2005. "The Global Diffusion of Regulatory Capitalism." *Annals of the American Academy of Political and Social Science* 598: 12–32.

Levi-Faur, David. 2011. "Regulation and Regulatory Governance." In *Handbook on the Politics of Regulation*, ed. David Levi-Faur, 3–21. Cheltenham: Edward Elgar.

Lindseth, Peter L., Alfred C. Aman Jr., and Alan C. Raul. 2008. *Administrative Law of the European Union: Oversight.* Ed. George A. Bermann et al. Washington, D.C.: American Bar Association.

Livermore, Michael A. 2011. "Can Cost-Benefit Analysis of Environmental Policy Go Global?" *New York University Environmental Law Journal* 19: 146–93.

Livermore, Michael A., and Richard L. Revesz, eds. 2013. *The Globalization of Cost-Benefit Analysis in Environmental Policy.* New York: Oxford University Press.

Losos, Jonathan B. 2011. "Convergence, Adaptation, and Constraint." *Evolution* 65 (7): 1827–40.

Michaels, Ralf. 2009. "Comparative Law by Numbers? Legal Origins Thesis, Doing Business Reports, and the Silence of Traditional Comparative Law." *American Journal of Comparative Law* 57: 765–95.

Organisation for Economic Co-operation and Development (OECD). 2008. *Government Capacity to Assure High Quality Regulation in Brazil.* Paris: OECD.

Organisation for Economic Co-operation and Development (OECD). 2009a. *Regulatory Impact Analysis—Tool for Policy Coherence.* Paris: OECD.

Organisation for Economic Co-operation and Development (OECD). 2009b. *Part III: Profiles of the Western Balkan Countries and Kosovo under UNSCR 1244/99.* Paris: OECD.

Organisation for Economic Co-operation and Development (OECD). 2011. *Regulatory Management Indicators: Chile 2011.* Paris: OECD.

Organisation for Economic Co-operation and Development (OECD). 2012. Recommendation of the Council on Regulatory Policy and Governance (22 March), at http://www.oecd.org/document/33/0,3746,en_2649_34141_48081633_1_1_1_1,00.html.

Ovodenko, Alexander, and Robert O. Keohane. 2012. "Institutional Diffusion in International Environmental Affairs." *International Affairs* 88 (3): 523–41.

Peci, Alketa, and Felipe Sobral. 2011. "Regulatory Impact Assessment: How Political and Organizational Forces Influence Its Diffusion in a Developing Country." *Regulation & Governance* 5: 204–20.

Program for Enhancing Regulatory Quality (PERQ). 2011. *RIA Compliance Manual.* Hanoi: PERQ.

Posner, Richard A. 2004. *Catastrophe: Risk and Response.* Oxford: Oxford University Press.

Priest, George L. 1977. "The Common Law Process and the Selection of Efficient Rules." *Journal of Legal Studies* 6 (October): 65–82.

Quah, Euston, and Raymond Toh. 2012. *Cost-Benefit Analysis: Cases and Materials.* New York: Routledge.

Radaelli, Claudio M. 2005. "Diffusion without Convergence: How Political Context Shapes the Adoption of Regulatory Impact Assessment." *Journal of European Public Policy* 12: 924–43.

Radaelli, Claudio M., and Fabrizio De Francesco. 2008. "Regulatory Impact Assessment." In *The Oxford Handbook of Regulation*, ed. Martin Cave, Robert Baldwin, and Martin Lodge, 279–301. Oxford: Oxford University Press.

Reimann, Mathias. 2001. "Beyond National Systems: A Comparative Law for the International Age." *Tulane Law Review* 75: 1103–19.

Renda, Andrea. 2006. *Impact Assessment in the EU*. Brussels: Center for European Policy Studies.

Revesz, Richard L., and Michael A. Livermore. 2008. *Retaking Rationality: How Cost-Benefit Analysis Can Better Protect the Environment and Our Health*. New York: Oxford University Press.

Roe, Mark J. 1996. "Chaos and Evolution in Law and Economics." *Harvard Law Review* 109: 641–71.

Roe, Mark J. 2006. "Legal Origins, Politics, and Modern Stock Markets." *Harvard Law Review* 120: 460–527.

Rogers, M. Everett. 2003. *The Diffusion of Innovations*. 5th ed. (1st ed. 1963). New York: Free Press.

Rose, Richard. 1993. *Lesson-Drawing in Public Policy*. Chatham: Chatham House.

Rose-Ackerman, Susan, and Peter Lindseth, eds. 2010. *Comparative Administrative Law*. Northampton, Mass.: Edward Elgar.

Sand, Peter H. 1971. "Current Trends in African Legal Geography: The Interfusion of Legal Systems." *African Legal Studies* 5: 1–27.

Sand, Peter H. 2011. "Information Disclosure." In *The Reality of Precaution: Comparing Risk Regulation in the United States and Europe*, ed. Jonathan B. Wiener, Michael D. Rogers, James K. Hammitt, and Peter H. Sand, 323–360. Washington, D.C.: RFF Press/Earthscan.

Schachter, Daniel L., Donna Rose Addis, and Randy L. Buckner. 2008. "Episodic Simulation of Future Events: Concepts, Data, and Applications." *Annals of the New York Academy of Sciences* 1124: 39–60.

Schwartz, Jason. 2010. *52 Experiments with Regulatory Review: The Political and Economic Inputs into State Rulemaking*. NYU Institute for Policy Integrity, Report No. 6.

Sezen, Seriye. 2011. "International versus Domestic Explanations of Administrative Reforms: The Case of Turkey." *International Review of Administrative Sciences* 77: 322–46.

Shapiro, Stuart. 2006. "Politics and Regulatory Policy Analysis." *Regulation* 29 (2): 40–45.

Siems, Mathias M. 2007. "The End of Comparative Law." *Journal of Comparative Law* 2: 133–50.

Simmons, Beth A., Frank Dobbin, and Geoffrey Garrett, eds. 2008. *The Global Diffusion of Markets and Democracy*. Cambridge: Cambridge University Press.

Slaughter, Anne-Marie. 2004. *A New World Order*. Princeton: Princeton University Press.

Slaughter, Anne-Marie. 2009. "The Networked Century." *Foreign Affairs* 88 (January—February): 94–113.

Slovic, Paul. 2007. "If I Look at the Mass I Will Never Act: Psychic Numbing and Genocide." *Judgment and Decision Making* 2 (2): 79–95.

Stone, Diane. 2012. "Transfer and Translation of Policy." *Policy Studies* 33 (4): 1–17.

Sunstein, Cass R. 2007. *Worst-Case Scenarios*. Cambridge: Harvard University Press.

Sunstein, Cass R., and Timur Kuran. 1999. "Availability Cascades and Risk Regulation." *Stanford Law Review* 51: 683–768.

Truen, Sarah. 2011. *Regulatory Impact Assessment in SADC: Improving Regional Regulatory Outcomes*. Los Angeles: AECOM International Development for USAID/Southern Africa.

Tushnet, Mark. 1999. "Possibilities of Comparative Constitutional Law." *Yale Law Journal* 108: 1225–1309.

United Nations Environment Programme (UNEP). 2005. *Regulatory Impact Assessment and Cost-Benefit Analysis in Uganda.* Nairobi: UNEP.

Viner, Jacob. 1949. "Bentham and J.S. Mill: The Utilitarian Background." *American Economic Review* 39: 360–82.

Vogel, David. 1986. *National Styles of Regulation: Environmental Policy in Great Britain and the United States.* Ithaca: Cornell University Press.

Vogel, David. 2012. *The Politics of Precaution: Regulating Health, Safety and Environmental Risks in the United States and Europe.* Princeton: Princeton University Press.

Walker, Jack L. 1969. "The Diffusion of Innovation among the American States." *American Political Science Review* 63: 880–89.

Watson, Alan. 1993. *Legal Transplants: An Approach to Comparative Law.* 2nd ed. Athens: University of Georgia Press.

Weber, Elke U. 2006. "Experience-Based and Description-Based Perceptions of Long-Term Risk: Why Global Warming Does Not Scare Us (Yet)." *Climatic Change* 77: 103–20.

Weyland, Kurt. 2005. "Theories of Policy Diffusion." *World Politics* 57: 262–95.

Wiener, Jonathan B. 2001. "Something Borrowed for Something Blue: Legal Transplants and the Evolution of Global Environmental Law." *Ecology Law Quarterly* 27: 1295–1371.

Wiener, Jonathan B. 2002. "Precaution in a Multirisk World." In *Human and Ecological Risk Assessment: Theory and Practice,* ed. Dennis D. Paustenbach, 1509–31. New York: Wiley and Sons.

Wiener, Jonathan B. 2003. "Whose Precaution after All? A Comment on the Comparison and Evolution of Risk Regulatory Systems." *Duke Journal of International and Comparative Law* 13: 207–62.

Wiener, Jonathan B. 2005. "Reviews of Catastrophe by Richard Posner and Collapse by Jared Diamond." *Journal of Policy Analysis and Management* 24: 885–90.

Wiener, Jonathan B. 2006. "Better Regulation in Europe." *Current Legal Problems* 59: 447–518.

Wiener, Jonathan B. 2011. "The Real Pattern of Precaution." In *The Reality of Precaution: Comparing Risk Regulation in the United States and Europe,* ed. Jonathan B. Wiener, Michael D. Rogers, James K. Hammitt and Peter H. Sand, 519–65. Washington, D.C.: RFF Press/Earthscan.

Wiener, Jonathan B., and Alberto Alemanno. 2010. "Comparing Regulatory Oversight Bodies across the Atlantic: The Office of Information and Regulatory Affairs in the U.S. and the Impact Assessment Board in the EU." In *Comparative Administrative Law,* ed. Susan Rose-Ackerman and Peter Lindseth, 309–35. Northampton, Mass.: Edward Elgar.

Wiener, Jonathan B., and Barak D. Richman. 2010. "Mechanism Choice." In *Research Handbook on Public Choice and Public Law,* ed. Daniel Farber and Anne Joseph O'Connell, 363–96. Northampton, Mass.: Edward Elgar.

Wiener, Jonathan B., Michael D. Rogers, James K. Hammitt, and Peter H. Sand, eds. 2011. *The Reality of Precaution: Comparing Risk Regulation in the United States and Europe.* Washington, D.C.: RFF Press/Earthscan.

Wildavsky, Aaron. 1979. "No Risk is the Highest Risk of All." *American Scientist* 67: 32–37.

Investment Climate Advisory Services of the World Bank Group (World Bank Group). 2010. *Better Regulation for Growth: Institutions for Regulatory Governance.* Washington, D.C.: World Bank.

Zweigert, Konrad, and Hein Kotz. 1998. *An Introduction to Comparative Law.* 3rd ed. Trans. Tony Weir. Oxford: Oxford University Press.

9

The Role of the OECD in Capacity Building for Public Governance

INSIGHTS FROM THE MENA-OECD WORKING GROUP ON
REGULATORY REFORM

Miriam Allam

Unprecedented change in the Middle East and North Africa (MENA) region is
a direct response to civil uprisings, which started with the Jasmine Revolution
in Tunisia and the ousting of the Ben Ali regime in January 2011. The causes for
the Arab Spring run deep and are fueled by a mistrust in the ruling elite, growing
inequalities, endemic corruption, and frustration with the lack of political freedom
and democracy. The Arab Spring has underlined the need to redefine the social
contract between government and society, such that countries in the region shift
toward governance that enables broader participation by civil society, nongovernmental organizations (NGOs), and the private sector in the policymaking process.
The strengthening of government transparency, accountability, and participation,
and capacity building for public governance will be integral to achieving economic
growth with broad social benefits.

The MENA region is composed of countries with different levels of economic
and democratic development, ranging from those with some of the highest gross
domestic products per capita in the world to those with emerging market economies and authoritarian regimes with high income disparities across population
sectors. Certainly, the heterogeneity of the MENA region will require different
solutions to what appear to be common problems.[1] Thus, while countries may
share similar reform objectives, cross-border variations exist in approaches to
reform. These variations follow the logic of deeply embedded domestic differences, rooted in different starting conditions, different constellations of interests,
distinct national identities that have been shaped by history, and different institutional settings.

Despite these differences, there are a variety of cross-cutting issues that can
form the basis for information sharing and capacity building through facilitated
dialogue between governmental actors, NGOs, civil society, and international
experts. A recent qualitative and comparative case study on progress in public
management in Arab countries finds that the wave of policy reforms that has
swept across the region since the start of the millennium shared certain common

concerns, including recognition of the interrelationship between public and private sector performance and the need to meet citizen expectations (OECD 2010b). Fears of lagging behind and sending negative signals to financial markets and investors have further prompted governments to accelerate reforms and catch up with other emerging and developed economies.

The Arab Spring highlights the urgency with which MENA governments must adopt ambitious and far-reaching reform plans. This chapter discusses the role of the Organisation for Economic Co-operation and Development (OECD) in supporting the building of governance capabilities in Arab countries, focusing on the work of the MENA-OECD Governance Programme and its Working Group on Regulatory Reform. As an international institution with experience in a range of different government settings, the OECD can be a useful partner for governments seeking to engage in governance reform. The Working Group on Regulatory Reform organizes MENA-regional dialogue about facilitation of modern regulatory principles, including impact assessments and cost-benefit analysis. The immediate relevance of regulatory policy to economic development and social welfare places it at the center of foreign and domestic efforts to create jobs and to embrace open, inclusive government frameworks.

This chapter is divided into two substantive parts. The first part will focus on OECD practices, the role of peer-learning for policy adaptation, and the work of the MENA-OECD Governance Programme. The second part will introduce the MENA-OECD Working Group on Regulatory Reform and discuss its work on regulatory impact analysis and cost-benefit analysis.

The OECD and the MENA-OECD Governance Programme

The OECD is an intergovernmental organization that was established in 1961 and has since developed into a knowledge hub for advice on good practices for government officials, providing a platform for peer learning and benchmarking to help countries identify appropriate policy responses to economic and social challenges. The OECD has been praised as a "purveyor of ideas" and a "policy pathfinder" (Mahon and McBride 2008, 3; see also Alasuutari and Pal 2010) and as a global network with the goal of promoting policies that "improve the economic and social well-being of people around the world" (OECD 2011a, 8). Its core activities are knowledge production and dissemination, with an eye toward promoting suitable policy options for addressing today's most pressing economic and social challenges.

Critics, on the other hand, refer to the OECD as an "exclusive club of rich nations" with a biased agenda toward economic neoliberalism. While membership stagnated in the 1970s, the OECD has expanded its membership from originally twenty in 1961 to thirty-four in 2010. Scholars urge the OECD to further transform itself from a club to a more inclusive organization if it wants to fulfill its aspiration of being a central actor in world economic governance (cf. Clifton and Diaz-Fuentes 2011a). Indeed, since the late 1980s, the OECD has actively sought an integration of nonmember countries in its everyday activities: it works together with Brazil, China, India, Indonesia, and South Africa through the "enhanced engagement" program; has opened membership discussions with Russia, China, and Estonia; and has fostered its relationship with nonmembers in regional programmes throughout the developing world in Africa, Asia, and Latin America and through the MENA program—which is the subject of this chapter.

Related to the criticism of being biased toward a neoliberal agenda, critics usually lament that countries are pushed to pursue economic growth through liberalization strategies. This has been brought forward especially in the context of the OECD relations with nonmember countries. Certainly, there is no one-size-fits-all recipe for diverse economies and societies, and the OECD itself underlines that "there are more paths to development than the 'OECD way'" (Clifton and Diaz-Fuentes 2011a, 301; see also OECD 2003).

In contrast to other international organizations like the International Monetary Fund or the World Bank, the OECD does not work on a basis of conditionality, which means it has limited direct leverage for enforcing its recommendations. However, all OECD countries agree to provide access to compliance monitors who conduct peer reviews and report findings on practices. As Pal summarizes:

> The OECD's comparative advantage is that it can draw on the willing support of its members (and other states) to provide "inside" information about what governments are doing in specific fields. (PAL 2008, 72)

In the same vein, Carroll and Kellow argue that the "secret of the OECD's success" is related to its status as an intergovernmental organization:

> The "ownership" of the OECD by its member countries is what makes its work of much higher value, and the depth of engagement of members in subsidiary bodies and their peer reviews also undoubtedly embeds within them a much greater awareness of the lessons to be learnt. (Carroll and Kellow 2011, 5)

Given its limited enforcement capacity, the OECD must rely on so-called soft instruments to ensure compliance with its recommendations, as described below.

PRACTICES AND METHODS

For over fifty years, the OECD has earned a strong reputation as being a "relatively impartial observer of global events" (Coicaud and Zhang 2011, 314) and as an important source of "reliable and high-quality data" (Clifton and Diaz-Fuentes 2011b, 298). The OECD engages in knowledge production through comparative analysis, data collection, and indicators. The OECD develops this knowledge through its two core method practices: peer reviews and benchmarking.

The forums provided by the OECD enable policymakers and practitioners to meet their peers and engage in a policy dialogue. As Clifton and Diaz-Fuentes (2011a, 305) conclude:

From the policy makers' perspective, their [policy dialogues'] advantage is that policy makers can talk frankly and exchange ideas in private, without having to be seen to "win" any particular debate.

The analysis and policy dialogue help form the basis for the OECD's policy recommendations, guidelines, codes, standards, and principles. The OECD also distributes road maps that encourage governments to engage in targeted self-reflection and policy modification. While these are "soft instruments"—part of a normative framework, as opposed to "hard instruments" like formal laws or directives—they can nevertheless exert strong influence. In fact, while critics of the OECD have referred to the limited conditionality as a weakness, others have argued that the power of peer pressure can be more effective than coercive measures of enforcement. In fact, the OECD is a soft power by choice; the limited enforcement capacity is part of the organization's identity. As Mahon and McBride (2008, 280) conclude:

> The OECD is able to reach far into domestic policy areas precisely because its edicts and recommendations are non-binding on member states. It relies instead on instruments of soft regulation—the production and dissemination of knowledge, the publication of comparative data, and peer review.

Moreover, the unconditionality of the OECD's work allows the organization to be "a seeker of, not only knowledge, but 'truth'" (Noaksson and Jacobsson 2003, 42). As Carroll and Kellow (2011, 264) argue, "the largely voluntary nature of the measures that are the products of the OECD can be seen to be more effective because they can embody clarity and higher quality." Countries that submit to the OECD review process do so voluntarily because they want to pursue the reform in question.

The OECD's unique working methods create transnational networks that support the diffusion of ideas and norms. How these transnational networks exert their power therefore touches upon the question of why actors come to adopt new ideas and how these ideas eventually become translated into policy action.

POLICY LEARNING

The process of "policy learning" is essential if OECD practices are going to be adopted and implemented globally. Policy learning is the core instrument for policy adaptation, which requires the continuous adaption to new social and economic circumstances characteristic of a changing world. Learning from others' successes can lead to a redefinition of goals and new policy reforms (Goldstein 1989; Wendt 1999). Related to policy learning, Odell (1982) and Hirschman (1982) claim that the critical moment for new ideas to be adopted is found in a major failure of a past policy or disillusionment. Goldstein and Keohane (1993) argue that policy failure is one of the main reasons why a preexisting consensus can be destabilized and replaced by another. In addition, Hall (1989) identifies persuasiveness as another factor to explain changes in policy ideas. Ideas become persuasive if they provide a tool to solve economic and political problems (Hall 1989, 369–70; Hall 1993). As Sikkink (1991, 247) puts it: "[s]uccess and failure are interpreted in terms of what are perceived as the most pressing problems facing a country at a particular time." Thus, ideas are always interpreted within the political and economic context in which they have been inserted: it is a political and economic context at a particular time.

However, the mechanics by which policy knowledge becomes actual policy are neither random nor automatic. Because "ideas are a dime a dozen," the concept of epistemic communities is helpful when attempting to understand the role of the OECD and why some ideas come to prevail over others (Haas 1992; Hall 1997). Epistemic communities are defined by Haas as "a network of professionals with recognised expertise and competence in a particular domain and an authoritative claim to policy-relevant knowledge within that domain or issue area" (Haas 1992, 4). In an increasingly complex and interdependent world, decision makers require the advice of epistemic communities that are able to coalesce expectations, find consensus, interpret problems, and provide solutions. The learning process requires the sharing of practices. As Adler and Haas put it, the development of new policy depends on the "diffusion of cause-effect understandings from country to country. The importance of these understandings lies not merely in being true but also in being shared" (Adler and Haas 1992, 386).

An epistemic community is therefore largely understood as a transnational group that shares common values and beliefs about *cause-effect relationships* (Haas 1990). Indeed, epistemic communities exert their power by providing causal road maps and helping actors to choose among strategies to attain their goals. Therefore, as described above, epistemic communities are especially strong in times of uncertainty and in the absence of a unique equilibrium. Here they can serve as focal points that provide guidance to find cooperative solutions "or act as coalitional glue to facilitate the cohesion of particular groups" (Goldstein and Keohane 1993, 12).

The OECD and other international bodies can help establish transnational links and foster epistemic communities that exert concurrent pressure on governments. However, epistemic communities can by no means replace domestic decision making. The state "remains the authoritative source of policymaking" (Adler and Haas 1992, 389). Rather, policy innovation provided by the epistemic community helps governments to redefine their expectations and coordinate actions.

In short, "ideas do not float freely," in the OECD or elsewhere (Risse-Kappen 1994, 187). Previous experiences are very persuasive in shaping policy learning and charting the course of future change. The epistemic nature of the OECD is essential to its ability to influence policy and to produce guidelines that promote appropriate and context-specific policy options.

THE MENA-OECD GOVERNANCE PROGRAMME

Through its external relation program, the OECD engages with many nonmember states in the MENA region. The MENA-OECD Governance Programme was created in 2005 and builds on several long-standing practices of the OECD,[2] including a broad effort to make systematic use of peer learning and policy advice. To help ensure that the OECD's work in this area meets country-specific needs, the Programme is owned and led by MENA countries.

Through its working and focus groups, the Programme has created regional policy dialogues among experts and decision makers. The emphasis on dialogue and peer learning allows the countries to *mutually* learn from each other and for MENA officials to be treated as peers. The Programme's organizational structure consists of one steering group that assembles all of the Arab and OECD chairs; the remaining groups—four working groups and two focus groups—are each chaired by a MENA country and cochaired by OECD countries. Delegates to the working and focus groups include representatives from both the MENA region and OECD member states. In addition, every two years, the MENA-OECD Initiative organizes major conferences at the ministerial level. It cooperates closely with other international organizations, such as the United Nations Development Programme and World Bank, and coordinates in-country with donors.

The working and focus groups are divided into core topics of public governance. The regional dialogue is supported by peer reviews, benchmark reports, and joint-learning studies produced by the OECD Secretariat.[3] The OECD also engages in capacity building, by organizing in-country workshops or trainings held in regional centers.

The working group of greatest relevance to the use of cost-benefit analysis is entitled Working Group IV: Public Service Delivery, Public Private Partnerships, and Regulatory Reform. This group is currently chaired by Tunisia and cochaired by Canada, Italy, and France. Delegates to the group are mostly high-level public officials, although gradually the group has expanded its policy-learning network to include civil society representatives. In addition, delegates from MENA have, in the past, served as ad hoc observers to the OECD's standard Regulatory Policy Committee (RPC), which allows them to access OECD research directly.[4] The observership in the RPC has supported consensus-building on policy reforms and allowed for the following up on progress with peers from all OECD member countries and other observers.

The MENA-OECD Working Group on Regulatory Reform

Excessive and ill-devised regulations impose high costs on businesses and citizens in the MENA region. Poor-quality regulations raise unnecessary obstacles to competition and stifle innovation, growth, and social development. And although improvements in the regulatory arena have been made in recent years, many issues remain unresolved (World Bank 2010). The recent OECD *Progress in Public Management in the Middle East and North Africa: Case Studies on Policy Reform* underlines a variety of ongoing problems: trouble managing the stock of regulations, unstable institutional settings, lack of coordination between institutions, overall weak capacities, lack of systemic impact assessments, scarcity of training opportunities, and limited stakeholder participation in the regulatory process (OECD 2010b).

The Working Group on Regulatory Reform is tasked with addressing all of these challenges. The group takes an integrated, whole-of-government approach that acknowledges all of the horizontal and vertical links between regulations and national and regional economic sectors. The implementation strategies adopted are meant to support regulatory quality to build an enabling environment for the rule of law and to facilitate fair economic development. To this end, the working group has developed the following sub-bodies to help develop and disseminate policy recommendations for countries in the MENA region:

- *Regional Network:* The working group coordinates a regional network of regulatory professionals. The network serves as a forum for policy dialogue, linking practitioners, policymakers, and experts from MENA countries with their OECD counterparts to promote reforms. This dialogue helps cultivate a common understanding of reform priorities, the expansion of good practices, appreciation for peer-learning studies, and support for policy implementation. The working group meets at least twice per year, once in the chair country of Tunisia and once at a special session of the OECD Regulatory Policy Committee in Paris, where the MENA delegates can meet with their peers from all OECD countries.[5]

- *Regional Charter:* The epistemic nature of the working group facilitated the translation of key policy ideas on regulatory reform into a set of guidelines for dissemination to regional policy actors. Working Group IV has directed the first regional soft law of its kind, the Regional Charter for Regulatory Quality (see box 9.1), which was endorsed by countries participating in the MENA initiative during the 2009 Ministerial Conference in Marrakesh. The charter calls for political support at a high level and sets forth guidelines for the improvement of regulatory policy in Arab countries. The charter also looks to use regulation and regulatory enforcement to reinforce the rule of law and enhance legal security for citizens and businesses. The charter is consistent with key OECD quality standards, including the 2005 Guiding Principles for Regulatory Quality and Performance. Future implementation of the regional charter provides a framework for evaluating improvements in regulatory processes throughout the MENA region.

- *Regional Centre of Expertise for Regulatory Quality:* Launched in 2009 by the working group, the Tunis-based Regional Centre of Expertise for Regulatory Quality aims to improve the quality of regulation and regulatory oversight by encouraging the use of regulatory impact analysis (RIA) and other internationally recognized analytical tools. The regional center is hosted by the Centre for Legal and Judicial Studies in the Tunisian Ministry of Justice, where it carries out applied research analysis and organizes regular training courses.[6]

- *Task Force on Legal and Constitutional Reform:* The working group created this task force to support MENA countries that have announced decisive constitutional reform. The task force was launched in 2011 by Tunisia and Egypt but is open to other countries that embark on processes of democratic transition and constitutional drafting. The transition phase implies decisive legal reform, as seen in Spain, Portugal, Chile, South Korea, and several postcommunist countries at the end of the twentieth century: many of these countries are now members of the OECD. The task force supports MENA countries in transition through policy dialogue and workshops with OECD peers who share their experiences of democratic transition.[7]
- *Regional Peer Support to Country-Specific Projects:* Working Group IV reviews the country-specific projects of the MENA-OECD Governance Programme in the field of regulatory policy. For example, the Practitioners' Guide on Regulatory Consultation in the Palestinian Authority (OECD 2011b) and the Assessment Report of the Legislative Drafting Manuals of the Palestinian Authority (OECD 2011d) (both reports are part of the MENA-OECD Initiative to Support the Palestinian Authority) were presented and discussed at various working group meetings and the RPC. Based on the insights of the good practice advice of the OECD Practitioners' Guide for the Palestinian Authority, delegates of the working group have invited the OECD Secretariat to prepare a regional handbook on public consultation in the rulemaking process. The experience of country-specific projects is thus actively integrated into the activities of Working Group IV. At the same time, national delegates who are leading the implementation of the country projects benefit from the wealth of experience accumulated in the MENA-OECD policy dialogue.

Policy learning in the working group means not only the exchange of new information but also the drawing of linkages between causes and effects—an essential feature of an epistemic community. Consensus on what makes a good regulation has driven the working group to emphasize utilizing cost-benefit analysis and creating regulatory impact assessments to guide regulatory policy, as discussed below.

ENHANCING REGULATORY QUALITY THROUGH REGULATORY IMPACT ANALYSIS (RIA)

Regulation is a key lever of state power. It can play a critical role in facilitating economic growth, by creating a business-friendly environment that incentivizes investment and job creation. Regulation is also needed to protect the environment and public health, and to accomplish other social goals. But regulations are only tools to achieve the socioeconomic objectives of a country, rather than ends unto themselves. The correct regulatory approach is defined by context, and policymaking must rely

BOX 9.1
Regional Charter for Regulatory Quality

Preamble
To improve national economies and to strengthen the role of government in guiding economic and social development, we have drafted this charter on law drafting and regulatory quality.

We will draw on the 1995 OECD Recommendation on Improving the Quality of Government Regulation and the 2005 OECD Guiding Principles for Regulatory Quality and Performance when improving procedures to draft laws and regulations that are adapted to our institutions, cultures and potential for development.

Regulatory Policy: A Broad Programme with a Whole-of-Government perspective
We recognize that regulatory reform should be supported at the highest political level, to promote consideration of regulatory policy, tools and institutions as a whole, and to communicate strategies and benefits to the public. We will strengthen co-ordination mechanisms inside the administration to foster coherence across policy objectives and to clarify responsibilities and roles.

We recognize that good regulation should (i) serve clearly identified policy goals, and be effective in achieving those goals; (ii) have a sound legal and empirical basis; (iii) produce benefits that justify costs, considering the distribution of effects across society, and taking economic, environmental and social effects into account; (iv) minimise costs and market distortions; (v) promote innovation through market incentives and goal-based approaches; (vi) be clear, simple and practical for users; (vii) be consistent with other regulations and policies; and (viii) be compatible as far as possible with competition, trade and investment-facilitating principles at domestic and international levels.

Building Institutional Frameworks for Regulatory Reform
We will develop and publicize an explicit policy for regulatory policy based on sound principles of good governance which can be the responsibility of an oversight unit to monitor, so that problems and gaps can be identified, the benefits of regulation measured, and progress reported on a consistent and regular yearly basis to the government and to the public.

We will establish institutional arrangements for regulatory quality that are accountable and transparent, including measures that promote integrity. Regulatory institutions should ensure that the public interest is respected.

Use of Regulatory Tools to Increase Transparency in the Process
We affirm the importance of administrative procedures for consideration of new regulations and laws, which must be clearly stated. These procedures should promote transparency, administrative certainty and due process. Consultation should be broadly based and balanced amongst different interest groups, and consultation processes themselves must be transparent and responsive. Law-drafting procedures should be managed efficiently, to reduce delays that create uncertainty and confusion, as when implementation decrees are needed to make laws effective.

Sustaining the Path of Regulatory Reform
In pursuit of these goals, we will develop specific action plans: (i) staff units adequately to carry out assessments of regulations against the principles of good regulation and assure compliance with quality standards, and to consider alternatives to regulation where appropriate and possible, (ii) assess and improve rule-making procedures to carry out a review of both the legal basis and the economic impacts of existing or new legislation; (iii) update existing regulations, and review regulations where change will yield the highest and most visible benefits; (iv) develop electronically accessible Websites to make rulemaking information

accessible to the public, to receive public comment on regulatory matters, to make all laws available to the public, (v) assure clear and plain-language drafting, including in translations, and (vi) reduce administrative burdens and licensing and permit requirements, with particular attention whenever new regulations and laws are drafted, and measure administrative costs for citizens and business.

We recognize that regulatory reform calls for a dynamic approach, sustained over time. Capacity has to be developed in stages, incrementally. We commit to participate in regional networks and centers dedicated to administrative simplification, regulatory quality and policy, and public service delivery. We will report on progress made through annual reports or other forms as appropriate.

Annex
The steps undertaken by OECD and MENA countries, in a framework of regional co-operation, are to be welcomed, as with all regional initiatives for regulatory reform. To overcome the difficulties of implementation related to the diversity and specific nature of juridical systems, linguistic diversity, and juridical methods and institutional frameworks, the charter, training and drafting guides must take these into account as part of a regional, coherent and progressive process.

---

on a process that includes an impact analysis based on a social discourse between the public and the government. The crux lies in developing "regulations that make sense and meet a high degree of compliance with minimal coercive enforcement" (OECD 2011c, 55). The issue need not be the law itself. If the legal reform process does not include a systematic impact analysis and participation of stakeholders, the process, rather than the substantive outcome, can cause concerns.

The risks related to political instability and social unrest will only increase if job creation and economic growth are not forthcoming. There are good reasons to believe that regulatory reform leads to better policy coordination, enhanced long-term productivity, and resilience, contributing to sustainable growth (Jacobzone et al. 2010; OECD 2010c). Sound regulatory policy is therefore a prerequisite for MENA countries in transition. And these risks have been exacerbated by the current global financial crisis, which has deeply affected MENA countries (OECD 2010b). In this context, regulatory reform has an even more important role to play.

To help promote impact assessments that can inform policymaking in a variety of government contexts, the OECD developed recommendations and a checklist for regulatory decision making that offers guidance on how to improve the quality of regulations (box 9.2; see also OECD 2012).

This checklist depicts a regulatory quality framework that requires the use of RIAs and stakeholder participation. Indeed, the RIA is an essential policy tool for regulatory quality—it provides a process for informing political decision-makers on whether and how to regulate to achieve public policy goals. RIA helps governments target the most relevant regulations. As Peci and Sobral (2011, 207) summarize: "The logic underlying the adoption of RIA is based on desires for a rational decisionmaking process, improved economic outcomes, and stronger democratic governance."

The use of RIAs has expanded rapidly throughout OECD countries in the last decade, as displayed in figure 9.1.

RIAs measure the likely benefits and costs of proposed regulations, using a consistent analytical method. The comparative impacts of alternative policies are

BOX 9.2
The OECD Reference Checklist for Regulatory Decision-Making

1. Is the problem correctly defined?
The problem to be solved should be precisely stated, giving evidence of its nature and magnitude, and explaining why it has arisen (identifying the incentives of affected entities).

2. Is government action justified?
Government intervention should be based on explicit evidence that government action is justified, given the nature of the problem, the likely benefits and costs of action (based on a realistic assessment of government effectiveness), and alternative mechanisms for addressing the problem.

3. Is regulation the best form of government action?
Regulators should carry out, early in the regulatory process, an informed comparison of a variety of regulatory and non-regulatory policy instruments, considering relevant issues such as costs, benefits, distributional effects and administrative requirements.

4. Is there a legal basis for regulation?
Regulatory processes should be structured so that all regulatory decisions rigorously respect the "rule of law"; that is, responsibility should be explicit for ensuring that all regulations are authorised by higher-level regulations and consistent with treaty obligations, and comply with relevant legal principles such as certainty, proportionality and applicable procedural requirements.

5. What is the appropriate level (or levels) of government for this action?
Regulators should choose the most appropriate level of government to take action, or if multiple levels are involved, should design effective systems of co-ordination between levels of government.

6. Do the benefits of regulation justify the costs?
Regulators should estimate the total expected costs and benefits of each regulatory proposal and of feasible alternatives, and should make the estimates available in accessible format to decisionmakers. The costs of government action should be justified by its benefits before action is taken.

7. Is the distribution of effects across society transparent?
To the extent that distributive and equity values are affected by government intervention, regulators should make transparent the distribution of regulatory costs and benefits across social groups.

8. Is the regulation clear, consistent, comprehensible and accessible to users?
Regulators should assess whether rules will be understood by likely users, and to that end should take steps to ensure that the text and structure of rules are as clear as possible.

9. Have all interested parties had the opportunity to present their views?
Regulations should be developed in an open and transparent fashion, with appropriate procedures for effective and timely input from interested parties such as affected businesses and trade unions, other interest groups, or other levels of government.

10. How will compliance be achieved?
Regulators should assess the incentives and institutions through which the regulation will take effect, and should design responsive implementation strategies that make the best use of them.

Source: OECD (1995). For the recently approved 2012 recommendation of the Council, see OECD (2012).

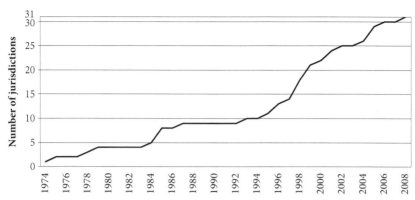

FIGURE 9.1 Trend in RIA Adoption by Central Governments across OECD Jurisdiction, 1974–2008

presented alongside one another, so policymakers can make more informed decisions about the desirability of different options. A strong consultation process, including meetings with key stakeholders, is crucial to ensuring the quality of an RIA.

The OECD has provided guidance in developing comprehensive RIA systems: the RIA process starts with the definition of the policy objective and the policy's legal, political, and social contexts. Related to the policy objective is the choice of the instrument: what is the proposed regulation supposed to achieve, and are there alternative policy tools that may be applied? The definition of the problem here and the impact analysis should always include the *no policy change* option as a benchmark for comparison. The RIA should also discuss possible alternatives to regulation (e.g., taxes and subsidies), alternative forms of regulation (e.g., self-regulation and co-regulation), and alternative implementation options.

Cost-benefit analysis included in the RIA can also be expanded to include a distributional analysis that explans which parties are likely to pay the costs of proposed regulation and which parties are likely to enjoy its benefits. However, to thoroughly understand the consequences of a regulation, one must look beyond purely financial effects and analyze a range of other impacts, such as the following:

- Impacts on market competiveness
- Impacts on consumers
- Impacts on socially excluded and vulnerable groups
- Impacts on citizens' rights
- Compliance and enforcement costs
- Social impacts
- Environmental costs and benefits

Certainly, it might be very difficult or even impossible to quantify every impact of a regulation, and the amount of resources spent on producing a thorough analysis should always stand in relation to the magnitude of the regulation's likely impact. Commentators have criticized cost-benefit analysis on the ground that it often assigns monetary values to normative considerations (Peci and Sobral 2011). However, this is not an insurmountable barrier because analysts can always include tangible as well as intangible costs and benefits for each option, and they can note in qualitative terms who will bear the costs or reap the benefits. There are several different catego-ries of costs and benefits—including tangible and intangible; direct and indirect; and pecuniary and non-pecuniary. Table 9.1 summarises the different types that should be considered when carrying out an RIA, using an irrigation project as an example.

Thus, conducting an RIA is not a purely quantitative exercise that expresses impacts in solely monetary terms, but should also include a stakeholder process to identify and distill qualitative factors, including impacts on socially excluded and vulnerable groups, the environment, and commercial activities (OECD 2010a). In this respect, public consultation is essential for various reasons. At the technical level, the consultations are pivotal for collecting empirical information, measuring expectations, assessing costs and benefits, and identifying alternative policy options. At the policy level, stakeholder involvement enables a transparent policymaking process and increases the level of social acceptance of decisions (OECD 2011b).

Certainly, public consultation is not a panacea that automatically improves the quality of regulation, nor is there a simple one-size-fits-all solution. Public partici-pation is a demanding and time-intensive process that requires institutional support and political will. However, the costs of consultations are best viewed as invest-ments in better long-term policies. Public participation enhances transparency and strengthens democracy by opening up new means for government watchdogs to monitor and act as a check against government incompetence and corruption. Of course, voice is not the same thing as political power, which is retained by govern-ment authorities, and public consultation is not equivalent to a referendum (OECD 2011b). Public consultation as part of an RIA process is rather a way to promote debate, collect information, and improve evidence-based policymaking (OECD 2011b). Moreover, since opposing groups are able to voice their opinions in the context of informing an RIA, these processes have the potential to play an impor-tant role in reconciling competing interests and parties; this collaborative culture may go a long way toward sustaining the legitimacy of government actions in tran-sitioning environments when trust in government has been badly shaken.[8]

Public consultation in RIA processes is a thematic priority of Working Group IV of the MENA-OECD Governance Programme. A practitioner's guide on

TABLE 9.1
Irrigation Project

Real		Benefits	Costs
Direct	Tangible	Increased farm output	Cost of pipes
	Intangible	Beautification of an area	Loss of wilderness
Indirect	Tangible	Reduced soil erosion	Diversion of water
	Intangible	Preservation of rural society	Destruction of wildlife
Pecuniary		Relative improvement in farm equipment industry	

Source: Mulreany (2002).

stakeholder involvement in the rulemaking process has been prepared and peer reviewed by the delegates of the working group (OECD 2011b). Based on good practices, this manual issues guidance to policymakers as to why, who, how, and when to consult on regulations. In fact, public consultation in the rulemaking process is a recent concept in the MENA region. Only a handful of Arab countries have started to engage the public in developing regulations. The Palestinian Authority is one such example, organizing regulatory consultations in the form of hearings and workshops. Stakeholders can participate in these forums upon invitation only, and the entire process is somewhat informal, since public consultation is not mandatory and not governed by official rules of procedure. By and large, when public consultations do occur in MENA countries, they are organized ad hoc and not as part of a comprehensive RIA process. This means, unfortunately, that the consultation process tends to have little influence on how cost-benefit analysis is conducted.

While evidence-based policymaking tools in regulatory management are not yet systematically applied in MENA countries, there is a growing demand to adopt formal mechanisms for conducting RIAs. This is a general trend throughout emerging market economies and developing countries (Kirkpatrick and Zhang 2004). Certainly, RIA processes must be adapted to country-specific contexts if the results are going to be meaningful. Individual countries are poised to begin implementing self-styled RIA procedures. The Egyptian Government Initiative ERRADA (Egyptian Regulatory Reform and Development Activity) launched an RIA effort, and Tunisia has put in motion a pilot program for conducting comprehensive RIAs. The pilot project in Tunisia is being carried out in conjunction with the MENA-OECD Working Group on Regulatory Reform, and thus the results will be reviewed and vetted by the working group's delegates. Lessons learned will form the basis for regional guidelines and provide a model for other countries in the region looking to incorporate cost-benefit analysis into their policymaking.

Conclusion

The working methods of the MENA-OECD Governance Programme establish good practices, standards, and benchmarks against which MENA countries can situate themselves and measure progress over time. The issuing of recommendations and other soft instruments such as the Regional Charter for Regulatory Quality are cases in point for the ability of the working group to translate ideas into guidance for policy action. Clearly, reform is context-dependent, and translating international good practice advice is an active process during which the embedded policy ideas are constantly shaped and implemented differently into the domestic contexts. Working Group IV of the MENA-OECD Governance Programme works precisely to support the framing of regulatory policy issues in the context of MENA countries.

Ultimately, the extent to which regulatory policy tools such as RIAs will help improve policymaking in the MENA region will depend upon organizational capacities. Previous studies in emerging market economies have demonstrated that the poor quality of available information, lack of stakeholder involvement, and misunderstandings about cost-benefit analysis obstruct the path toward RIA-based decisionmaking. The MENA-OECD Governance Programme levers the power of epistemic communities to build capacities. Peer learning through the frank exchange of ideas and sharing of technical expertise will help pave the way toward the integration of evidence-based decision-making tools in regulatory management.

Acknowledgments

The views expressed in this chapter are those of the author and do not represent the position of the OECD or its member countries. The author would like to thank Alessandro Bellantoni, Carlos Conde, and Josef Konvitz for their comments.

Notes

1. According to the World Bank, "of the 355 million people of MENA, 85% live in Middle Income Countries, 8% in High Income Countries, and 7% in Low Income Countries" See World Bank (2011, 1).

2. The MENA-OECD Governance Programme is part of the OECD Initiative on Governance and Investment for Development in the Middle East and North Africa. This initiative consists of two pillars: the MENA-OECD Governance Programme and the MENA-OECD Investment Programme.

3. The OECD Joint Learning Studies (JLS) is a methodology developed by the MENA-OECD Governance Programme that combines the traditional OECD analysis with peer-to-peer policy dialogue among MENA and OECD countries, complemented by capacity-building activities. For further information on the methodology and examples of JLS, see OECD Directorate for Public Governance and Territorial Development, OECD Joint Learning Studies.

4. Egypt and Tunisia are currently ad hoc observers to the Regulatory Policy Committee (RPC). The RPC assists OECD members and nonmembers in building and strengthening capacity for regulatory quality and regulatory reform. See generally OECD (2010c).

5. For the documentation of the annual working group meetings in Tunis and the special sessions of the OECD Regulatory Policy Committee in Paris, see the MENA-OECD Working Group on Public Service Delivery, PPPs and Regulatory Reform website.

6. For example, "Capacity Building Seminar: Using the Regional Charter for Regulatory Quality Effectively" was organized by the Regional Centre of Expertise for Regulatory Quality in Tunis, June 12, 2010.

7. In a first series of policy dialogue, the task force brought together key actors from Egypt, Tunisian, and Morocco with OECD peers from former transition countries to discuss processes of engaging the civil society and communicating legal and constitutional reforms to stakeholders and the wider public. See generally Working Group IV on Regulatory Reform, MENA-OECD Governance Programme website.

8. For example, a recent study points to the potential of public consultation in the Palestinian Authority to reduce the vacuum created by the absence of the Palestinian Legislative Council (OECD 2011b).

Bibliography

Adler, Emanuel, and Peter M. Haas. 1992. "Conclusion: Epistemic Communities, World Order, and the Creation of a Reflective Research Programme." *International Organization* 46 (1): 367–90.

Alasuutari, Pertti, and Leslie A. Pal. 2010. *The OECD as an International Referent in National Policy Debates: Comparing Canada and Finland.* Presented at the Eighteenth Network of Institutes and Schools of Public Administration in Central and Eastern Europe Annual Conference on May 12–14, 2010.

Carroll, Peter, and Aynsley Kellow. 2011. *The OECD: A Study of Organisational Adaption.* Cheltenham: Edward Elgar.

Clifton, Judith, and Daniel D íaz-Fuentes. 2011a. "From 'Club of the Rich' to 'Globalisation à la carte'? Evaluating Reform at the OECD." *Global Policy* 2 (3): 300–311.

Clifton, Judith, and Daniel D íaz-Fuentes. 2011b. "The Organisation for Economic Cooperation and Development 1961–2011: Challenges for the Next 50 Years." *Global Policy* 2 (3): 297–99.

Coicaud, Jean-Marc, and Jin Zhang. 2011. "The OECD as a Global Data Collection and Policy Analysis Organization: Some Strengths and Weaknesses." *Global Policy* 2 (3): 312–17.

Goldstein, Judith. 1989. "The Impact of Ideas on Trade Policy: The Origins of U.S. Agricultural and Manufacturing Policies." *International Organization* 43 (1): 31–71.

Goldstein, Judith, and Robert O. Keohane, eds. 1993. *Ideas and Foreign Policy: Beliefs, Institutions and Political Change.* Ithaca: Cornell University Press.

Haas, Ernst B. 1990. *When Knowledge Is Power: Three Models of Change in International Organizations.* Berkeley: University of California Press.

Haas, Peter M. 1992. "Introduction: Epistemic Communities and International Policy Coordination." *International Organization* 46 (1): 1–35.

Hall, Peter A. 1997. "The Role of Interests, Institutions and Ideas in the Comparative Political Economy of the Advanced Industrial States." In *Comparative Politics: Rationality, Culture and Structure,* ed. Mark Irving Lichbach and Alan S. Zuckerman, 174–207. Cambridge: Cambridge University Press.

Hall, Peter A. 1993. "Policy Paradigms, Social Learning, and the State: The Case of Economic Policymaking in Britain." *Comparative Politics* 25 (3): 275–96.

Hall, Peter A., ed. 1989. *The Political Power of Economic Ideas: Keynesianism across Nations.* Princeton: Princeton University Press.

Hirschman, Albert O. 1982. *Shifting Involvements: Private Interest and Public Action.* Princeton: Princeton University Press.

Jacobzone, Stephane, Faye Steiner, Erika L. Ponton, and Emmanuel Job. 2010. "Assessing the Impact of Regulatory Management Systems: Preliminary Statistical and Econometric Estimates." Working Papers on Public Governance, No. 17, OECD.

Kirkpatrick, Colin, David Parker, and Yin-Fang Zhang. 2004. "Regulatory Impact Assessment in Developing and Transition Economies: A Survey of Current Practices." *Public Money and Management* 24 (5): 291–96.

Mahon, Rianne, and Stephen McBride, eds. 2008. *The OECD and Transnational Governance.* Vancouver: University of British Columbia Press.

Noaksson, Niklas, and Kerstin Jacobsson. 2003. "The Production of Ideas and Expert Knowledge in OECD: The OECD Jobs Strategy in Contrast with the EU Employment

Strategy." Score Rapportserie 2003:7, Stockholm Centre for Organizational Research.

Odell, John S. 1982. *U.S. International Monetary Policy: Markets, Power, and Ideas as Sources of Change*. Princeton: Princeton University Press.

Organisation for Economic Co-operation and Development (OECD). 1995. *The OECD Reference Checklist for Regulatory Decision-Making*. Paris: OECD.

Organisation for Economic Co-operation and Development (OECD). 2003. *The Transition Economies: The OECD's Experience*. Paris: OECD.

Organisation for Economic Co-operation and Development (OECD). 2009. *Recent Trends in RIA Implementation*. Paris: OECD.

Organisation for Economic Co-operation and Development (OECD). 2010a. *A New Agenda for the Regulatory Policy Committee: Issues for the Next Three Years, 2010–12*. Paris: OECD.

Organisation for Economic Co-operation and Development (OECD). 2010b. *Progress in Public Management in the Middle East and North Africa: Case Studies on Policy Reform*. Paris: OECD.

Organisation for Economic Co-operation and Development (OECD). 2010c. *Regulatory Reform for Recovery: Lessons from Implementation during Crises*. Paris: OECD.

Organisation for Economic Co-operation and Development (OECD). 2011a. *Better Policies for Better Lives: The OECD at 50 and Beyond*. Paris: OECD.

Organisation for Economic Co-operation and Development (OECD). 2011b. *Regulatory Consultation in the Palestinian Authority: A Practitioners' Guide for Engaging Stakeholders in Democratic Deliberation*. Paris: OECD.

Organisation for Economic Co-operation and Development (OECD). 2011c. *Regulatory Policy and Governance: Supporting Economic Growth and Serving the Public Interest*. Paris: OECD.

Organisation for Economic Co-operation and Development (OECD). 2011d. *The Legislative Drafting Manuals of the Palestinian Authority: Assessment Report*. Paris: OECD.

Organisation for Economic Co-operation and Development (OECD). 2012. *Recommendation of the Council on Regulatory Policy and Governance*. Paris: OECD.

Pal, Leslie A. 2008. "Inversions without End: The OECD and Global Public Management Reform." In *The OECD and Transnational Governance*, ed. Rianne Mahon and Stephen McBride, 60–76. Vancouver: University of British Columbia Press.

Peci, Alketa, and Filipe Sobral. 2011. "Regulatory Impact Assessment: How Political and Organizational Forces Influence Its Diffusion in a Developing Country." *Regulation and Governance* 5 (2): 204–20.

Risse-Kappen, Thomas. 1994. "Ideas Do Not Float Freely: Transnational Coalitions, Domestic Structures, and the End of the Cold War." *International Organization* 48 (2): 185–214.

Sikkink, Kathryn. 1991. *Ideas and Institutions: Developmentalism in Brazil and Argentina*. Ithaca: Cornell University Press.

Wendt, Alexander. 1999. *Social Theory of International Politics*. Cambridge: Cambridge University Press.

World Bank. 2010. *Doing Business Report 2010: Reforming through Difficult Times*. Washington, D.C.: World Bank.

World Bank. 2011. *Middle East and North Africa: Regional Brief*. Washington, D.C.: World Bank.

PART FOUR

Case Studies in Pollution Control

10

Environmental Fuel Quality
Improvements in Mexico

A CASE STUDY OF THE ROLE OF COST-BENEFIT ANALYSIS IN
THE DECISION-MAKING PROCESS

Leonora Rojas-Bracho, Verónica Garibay-Bravo,
Gretchen A. Stevens, and Georgina
Echániz-Pellicer

Poor air quality is estimated to cause more than 7,000 deaths per year in Mexico (Stevens et al. 2008).[1] After past efforts to clean up factories and refineries, especially those located in densely populated areas such as Mexico City, private vehicles and trucks remain the main source of pollutants that are most harmful to health (SMADF 2010). To reduce mobile source emissions, fuel quality and vehicular emission standards must be improved together, given that, for instance, sulfur must be reduced in fuels so that advanced emissions control technologies may function.

In 2006, the Ministry of Environment and Natural Resources (SEMARNAT) published a revised fuel quality standard in Mexico. The new standard sought to require the best possible targets and rates of reduction of sulfur levels in gasoline and diesel, so that advanced emissions control technologies could be introduced in new vehicles. To secure funding to produce low-sulfur fuels, SEMARNAT, in coordination with PEMEX (a state-owned fuel producer), was required to carry out a cost-benefit analysis for the first time. In this chapter, we describe the process that was undertaken and the challenges that the ministry faced in carrying out and obtaining approval of its analysis.

Cost-Benefit Analysis in the Mexican Public Policy Arena

In Mexico, two agencies are required to conduct cost-benefit analyses: first, the Ministry of Economy must carry out cost-benefit analyses in support of regulations and standards; second, the Ministry of Finance must complete a cost-benefit analysis when making a decision about federal funding of a major investment project.

In the late 1990s, the Organisation for Economic Co-operation and Development (OECD) recommended that member countries adopt regulatory impact assessments (RIAs) for the systematic analysis of potential social impacts of regulations. Mexico responded by launching a program to improve governmental regulatory processes. To institutionalize these efforts, the Federal Commission for Regulatory Improvement (COFEMER) was created in 2000. COFEMER is a part of the Ministry of Economy and is charged with ensuring that public regulations are developed and implemented rationally and transparently (COFEMER 2010a). COFEMER's mission includes reviewing all federal laws, rules, regulations, and standards, and guaranteeing that the social benefits of regulations exceed their costs before they become official. This requires that all regulatory proposals be accompanied with an RIA that includes a cost-benefit analysis.

Depending on the regulatory instrument, the level of detail in the RIA varies, but it generally comprises a portrayal of the policy problem and alternative policy options; an analysis of the impacts of those policies, including their costs and benefits; and supporting information. Regulations deemed "high impact" require a detailed cost-benefit analysis. For all other regulations, the sponsoring agency is only required to answer a few questions about the quantifiable and nonquantifiable costs and benefits of the proposed regulation (COFEMER 2005). COFEMER can waive the RIA requirement if the sponsoring agency contends that a regulation does not entail additional costs for private stakeholders. Whether a regulation imposes additional costs may depend on whether it creates, modifies, or affects legal obligations, or whether it reduces, restricts, or affects rights or benefits. For every scenario described, the proposed regulation, with its corresponding RIA, must be sent to COFEMER, where it goes through a process for public comments and evaluation by the commission. If the regulation is approved by COFEMER, the sponsoring agency then publishes the regulation in the Mexican federal registry (COFEMER 2010b).

In addition, since 1993 the Ministry of Finance has reviewed and approved investment projects that require federal funding, such as projects relating to roads, hospitals, schools, refining facilities, and electricity generation units.[2] In 2001, to promote the use of cost-benefit analysis in evaluating investment decisions, the authorities in charge of each project were required to carry out a cost-benefit analysis. To that end, the ministry created specific guidelines for conducting cost-benefit anlaysis (García 2002). According to the current guidelines issued in 2008 by the ministry, a detailed cost-benefit analysis is required for major projects (that is, all investments over $12 million, or approximately 150 million pesos), as well as for other investment projects at the ministry's discretion.[3] The cost-benefit analysis must include a detailed description of the status quo; a thorough account of the proposed project; an evaluation of the costs and benefits and the financial viability of the project (that is, the net present value and internal rate of return), including a sensitivity analysis; and an explanation of the risks associated with the project (COFEMER 2005, 53; SHCP 2005b; 2008).

The case study below illustrates how these requirements were fulfilled by SEMARNAT in evaluating a project to improve air quality in Mexico.

The Problem: High Sulfur Content in Mexican Fuels

In the late 1980s and early 1990s air quality in the Mexico City Metropolitan Area (Mexico City) was the worst in its history, and lead, sulfur dioxide, carbon monoxide, ozone, and particulate concentrations far exceeded national air quality standards.[4] To combat the problem, authorities from federal government ministries, PEMEX, local governments, scientists, and academics, worked jointly to develop the Integrated Program for Air Pollution Control (PICCA).[5] This program incorporated standards to improve fuel quality and reduce emissions from private and public transportation vehicles. Even though PICCA aimed at improving air quality in Mexico City, its analyses of strategies to control pollutant emissions led to the creation of nationwide standards. Environmental authorities from the Ministry of Urban Development and Environment (SEDUE) subsequently published the first fuel quality standard (NOM-086-ECOL-1994), as well as revised emissions standards for light- and heavy-duty new vehicles (NOM-042-SEMARNAT-1993; NOM-044-SEMARNAT-1993).

Under the fuel quality standard, lead was phased out nationwide, both because of the direct public health consequences and also to allow for catalytic converters in new vehicles.[6] By late 1990, deleaded gasoline had become available in the metropolitan area surrounding Mexico City,[7] and by 1993, federal environmental authorities from SEDUE negotiated a nationwide phase-out with PEMEX. Unleaded fuels became available nationally by 1997.

The 1994 standard established additional fuel specifications, including sulfur content reductions in gasoline, diesel, and fuel oil. The insight to reduce sulfur levels came from international experience. Sulfur in fuels was first regulated together with emission controls in the 1970s in developed countries. The benefits were reductions in sulfur-based emissions, such as sulfur dioxide (SO_2), which had been shown to acidify rain, soil, and lakes, and to act as precursors to secondary particulates, contributing to urban air pollution and affecting public health. In Mexico, by the turn of the century, Magna gasoline contained 1,000 parts per million (ppm) of sulfur throughout the country, except in the three major metropolitan areas of Mexico City, Guadalajara, and Monterrey, where levels were 500 ppm. In contrast, Premium gasoline, marketed as a superior quality fuel, was mostly imported and had lower sulfur levels nationwide, with average and maximum concentrations of 250 ppm and 300 ppm respectively.[8] Diesel for vehicular use had a maximum sulfur level of 500 ppm.[9]

Policy Strategy: Update the Fuel Quality Standard and Develop an Investment Fuel Quality Project

In 2000, federal authorities from the Ministries of Environment and Energy worked with PEMEX and the Mexican Association of Automobile Industry (AMIA) to revise the 1994 fuel quality standard.[10] AMIA drafted a proposal to harmonize vehicular fuel quality in accordance with the Worldwide Fuel Charter

(WWFCH) recommendations.[11] The main objective was to lower sulfur requirements to allow for the introduction and efficient performance of more advanced,
cleaner technologies in light- and heavy-duty vehicles. The preliminary proposal
reached a standstill in early 2001, when PEMEX insited on redefining the timeline
of reductions in sulfur concentrations. In 2002, the process was reinitiated under
the lead of SEMARNAT.

Most representatives of the environmental sector and AMIA advocated a
rapid transition to ultra-low-sulfur fuels, and the former also aimed at having
more stringent vehicular emissions standards. This would have required PEMEX
to supply gasoline with 30/80 ppm sulfur levels and diesel with a maximum sulfur content of 15 ppm. For vehicles, the goal was to issue standards that would
be equivalent to light- and heavy-duty standards currently in place in the United
States and Europe. The combination of fuel and vehicular standards would generate significant reductions in emissions of fine particulate matter, sulfur and nitrogen oxides, and hydrocarbons. Sulfur and nitrogen oxides, which are precursors
to particulate matter, and hydrocarbons, which contribute to ground level ozone,
have substantial effects on health, including premature mortality.[12] As it stood,
the air quality standards for these pollutants were already frequently exceeded in
major metropolitan areas, harming close to thirty million urban dwellers.

The revision process entailed working on two tracks simultaneously. First, as
set forth above, the regulatory procedures that governed standard-setting and federal investment projects demanded an RIA be conducted, including a cost-benefit
analysis. The second track was the actual development of a proposal outlining how
PEMEX would undertake the costly investments that would be needed to revamp
existing refineries.

THE STANDARD REVIEW PROCESS AND INVESTMENT
PROJECT DEVELOPMENT

The Ministry of Environment and Natural Resources (SEMARNAT) convened a
formal working group of over twenty-five representatives from public and private
institutions, including PEMEX, in 2002.[13] This group met regularly to develop the
new standards and design the investment project, since the final versions of the
new standards would be needed to carry out the cost-benefit analysis required by
the Ministries of Finance and Federal Commission for Regulatory Improvement
(COFEMER).

In November 2003, the working group presented a proposal of the revised
standard to COMARNAT, SEMARNAT's legally endowed committee for the
review and approval of environmental standards. The proposal included a timetable that aimed at rapidly producing ultra-low-sulfur fuels in the near term:
sulfur levels in all fuels would be reduced by 2008. PEMEX estimated that such
improvements in fuel quality would entail upgrades to the refining infrastructure with associated costs of $2 billion. Accordingly, the investment project would
require formal authorization from the Ministry of Finance and, subsequently,
from Congress. Additional issues included effects on the federal budget through

proposed modifications to the gasoline imports program, and potential increases in the price of fuels. Given the potential for budgetary and consumer effects, the President's Office of Public Policy was called upon to oversee the approval process. COMARNAT then decided to delay the publication of the draft proposal for the required sixty-day period of public comments until it was clear that the Secretariat of Finance and Public Credit (SHCP) would approve the project.

For two years, SEMARNAT and the Ministry of Energy (SENER) worked closely with PEMEX to devise a compliance calendar that would be feasible for PEMEX and that would allow for the rapid introduction of low-sulfur fuels. The high sulfur content of Mexican crude oil, high investment costs, administrative budget constraints, and the failure to define the basic engineering that would be required to revamp the refineries were the reasons behind PEMEX's resistance to finalizing the standards. After intense negotiations, PEMEX put forth a new proposal that SEMARNAT and SENER agreed to in September 2005, referred to as the "Fuel Quality Project."

In the new proposal, PEMEX's cost estimates increased to $2.7 billion. PEMEX was expected to apply for federal financial support, with close to $2.5 billion coming from a financial scheme established by the government in the early 1990s to finance public infrastructure projects; these investments, which were jointly funded by the government and private investors, were known as Proyectos de Infraestructura Productiva de Largo Plazo con Registro Diferido en el Gasto (PIDIREGAS).[14] PEMEX's new proposal also included a tiered approach to the introduction of ultra-low-sulfur fuels countrywide. Premium gasoline would be available throughout the country by October 2006. Lower sulfur Magna gasoline would be introduced in major metropolitan areas by October 2008, and the rest of the country would follow a few months later during the beginning of 2009. Diesel would be delivered first throughout the Mexico-U.S. border region, in January 2007, followed by major metropolitan areas in early 2009, and the rest of the country by mid-2009. The logic behind prioritizing the supply of low-sulfur diesel in the northern border region was a response to pressure from the United States. The United States had introduced advanced diesel emissions control in 2007, and U.S. authorities argued that in light of the intensive commercial activity in the region— heavy-duty trucks circulating between the United States and Mexico—a supply of ultra-low-sulfur diesel was needed to guarantee equipment durability and efficient functioning of vehicles equipped with advanced emissions control technologies.

The working group adopted PEMEX's Fuel Quality Project, and SEMARNAT presented the draft standard to COFEMER along with a request for a waiver of the RIA requirement. COFEMER replied immediately, granting the waiver on the ground that there was "no cost" to outside stakeholders since PEMEX was to be the only stakeholder tasked with carrying out activities (production and importation of fuels) required by the new standard. SEMARNAT then published the proposal in late September 2005 for a sixty-day public comment period.[15]

Meanwhile, PEMEX sought support from the President's Office of Public Policy and the Ministry of Finance to include the Fuel Quality Project in the official federal budget and to approve a multiannual investment project with PIDIREGAS funding. Projects to be considered under the PIDIREGAS scheme needed to generate sufficient revenues, by means of sales of goods and services, in order to cover their financial obligations, which included paying interest on funding provided by private investors. As mentioned above, all investment projects carried out with federal funds were required by law to include an economic feasibility analysis demonstrating their potential profitability, in economic as well as social terms.[16] As a result, the Ministry of Finance decided to require a cost-benefit analysis of the project to determine whether it would generate net benefits to society prior to approving the budget (SHCP 2005a).

COST-BENEFIT ANALYSIS FOR THE FUEL QUALITY STANDARD AND FOR THE FUEL QUALITY PROJECT

The National Institute of Ecology (INE), the research arm of the Ministry of Environment,[17] was asked to complete the cost-benefit analysis, and the authors of this chapter carried out the analysis in collaboration with other INE staff. First, INE calculated the benefits of reducing sulfur in gasoline and diesel, assuming that strict vehicle emissions standards would immediately follow sulfur reductions. When considering the benefits, the team of analysts focused on similar analyses conducted for the United States, where improvements in health (specifically, reductions in mortality) comprise the majority of benefits of policies that improve air quality.

The team estimated the reduction in direct emissions of particulate matter from vehicles, as well as reductions in pollutants that form particulate matter in the atmosphere. We then modeled changes in exposure to particulate matter, and its effects on health, including reductions in mortality. We assigned a monetary value to the reduction in mortality using the value of a statistical life (VSL) methodology, which estimates individuals' willingness to pay to reduce their risk of death. Perhaps most controversially, we estimated a VSL for Mexico based on various factors: an accepted value used in the United States, the ratio of gross national income per capita in the two countries, and an estimate of how much people were willing to pay for health increases according to their income. We assessed costs based on the investment costs calculated and provided by PEMEX, excluding the additional costs of manufacturing vehicles with advanced emissions control technologies. Both benefits and costs were calculated for the time period 2005 through 2030, and we estimated the net present value of benefits using a discount rate of 12 percent, as required by the Ministry of Finance. We also carried out our calculations under a variety of assumptions, to test the sensitivity of the results to our analytic decisions (figure 10.1).

This was the first time that an economic evaluation of a major investment project within the government would include a calculation of environmental externalities. Since there was no oversight office and little familiarity with cost-benefit analysis, INE formed an ad hoc scientific panel with leading Mexican and international scientists.[18] Members of the panel reviewed our methods, commented on needed improvements when required, and wrote letters of support noting their

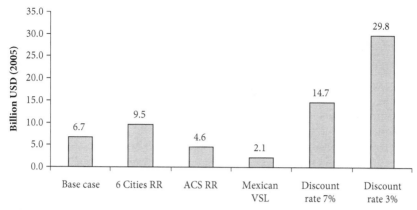

FIGURE 10.1 Present Net Benefits of Reducing Sulfur in Gasoline and Diesel under Alternate Assumptions. "Base case" uses relative risks (RR) for adult mortality from the American Cancer Society (ACS) study; uncertainty around the RR was characterized by calculating a lognormal uncertainty distribution with the ACS RR as the 50th percentile, and the 6 Cities RR as the 95th percentile. "6 Cities RR" uses the results of the Six Cities study to estimate health benefits. "ACS RR" uses the results of the ACS study to estimate health benefits and standard errors as they were reported in the study. "Mexican VSL" uses the results of a Mexican study to estimate willingness to pay. Discount rates of 7 percent and 3 percent were used to estimate the present value of net benefits according to U.S. guidelines.

suitability. Nevertheless, the Ministry of Finance, the President's Office of Public Policy, and SENER raised several concerns about the methods that we employed for the cost-benefit analysis. On the benefits part of the equation, the most relevant discussions were related to limitations on how to choose epidemiological evidence of health effects associated with exposures to air pollution, the methods and the actual figures used for assigning an economic value to health benefits, and the discount rate to be applied.

Representatives of the Ministry of Finance and the President's Office of Public Policy were initially concerned about how epidemiological evidence was used to calculate the difference in numbers of deaths and other outcomes from the esti-mated pollution levels in the low-sulfur fuels and business-as-usual scenarios. There are estimates of the effects of poor air quality on mortality from studies carried out in Mexico City, but these time-series studies only captured short-term effects because of their design. Therefore, we decided to use estimates from cohort studies of the general U.S. population, because the latter captured both long- and short-term impacts of air pollutants on mortality (Künzli et al. 2001). Hence, rela-tive risks from U.S. cohort studies provided a more complete estimate of the total health burden attributable to air pollution (Stevens et al. 2008). In spite of the initial resistance to use U.S. rather than Mexican information, the aforementioned approach was finally accepted by PEMEX and the Ministry of Finance.

Methods for placing an economic value on the health benefits of the policy were more contentious. Much of the discussion centered on the potential impli-cations for future policy decisions of using the VSL approach. At first, the VSL concept was not easily accepted, and the specific value used was considered to be inappropriate. Once we clarified that using VSL was more comprehensive than considering only direct costs, which was the preferred method for part of our audience, our approach gained greater acceptance. There was only one study on willingness to pay for mortality risks associated with air pollution exposures in Mexico (Hammitt and Ibarrarán 2006). These authors used the approach of hedonic wages to estimate the VSL, which compares average wages in dangerous jobs to those with safer jobs to determine individuals' trade-off between income and safety. For adults, this method resulted in a VSL of $300,000. They also carried out a contingent valuation survey, in which individuals are asked how much they would pay for a reduction in children's mortality risk, and found a VSL of $1.3 million for children. Since there was only one Mexican study at hand and because VSL estimates in the United States varied by more than an order of magnitude from one study to another, we used values from a meta-analysis of studies conducted in the United States. These were adjusted for Mexican incomes (year 2000 dollars), using an estimate of how much willingness to pay for health increases with rising income.

Our estimate of the VSL for premature mortality (cardiopulmonary, lung cancer, infant mortality for respiratory causes, and sudden infant death syndrome) was $660,000. This estimate was questioned, with some arguing that it was too high, and others believing it was too low. It was much lower than the VSL used for U.S. populations: at the time, the U.S. Environmental Protection Agency (EPA) was using a VSL of $6.3 million. Representatives of SENER and the President's Office of Public Policy interpreted this to mean that a Mexican was "worth much less" than an American. However, in spite of this initial misinterpretation, the prospect of increasing this figure was not welcomed. Representatives of the Ministry of Finance and the President's Office of Public Policy were concerned that in future cost-benefit analyses conducted for social investment projects, such as construction of health care facilities, a higher VSL figure would "artificially" increase the benefits, forcing the Ministry of Finance to approve costly investments. All parties ultimately agreed to use the VSL calculated by INE.

Although INE was making sound methodological decisions to estimate the most accurate value possible, there was general agreement that a better approach would have derived a VSL for Mexican populations using results obtained from more than one study conducted in Mexico. Official guidelines on what figure to use would have been very helpful. In the alternative, an edict from a central oversight office regarding the appropriate valuation would have lent legitimacy to the analytic decision.

In the United States, a social discount rate of between 3 and 7 percent is recommended for cost-benefit analysis (OMB 2003). Some authors argue that it should be lower (1.4 percent) when it is used to value the well-being of future generations (Broome 2008). On the other hand, some research indicates that social discount rates should be higher in developing countries (Poulos and Whittington 2000). Following the U.S. recommendations for social discount rates, INE requested the use of a lower discount rate than the one recommended by the Ministry of Finance (12 percent) for PIDIREGAS analysis. The Ministry of Finance, however, claimed that 12 percent was the appropriate discount rate and rejected this request. It had arrived at this percentage by taking a market-based approach that asserted that the social cost of capital for public funds is determined by the source of the underlying investment funds, which in this case were private funds (Cervini 2004).

As part of our analysis, we carried out extensive uncertainty and sensitivity analyses, some of which are shown in figure 10.1. Yet we chose not to present our uncertainty analysis to the Ministry of Finance or the President's Office of Public Policy because we anticipated that obtaining approval for our analysis would be difficult enough without the added complexity of accurately communicating uncertainty. Perhaps because they were not familiar with the methodology, none of the agencies involved ever requested a formal uncertainty analysis.

An important challenge we faced in carrying out the cost-benefit analysis was an exposure assessment—that is, the question of how to translate changes in vehicle emissions to changes in human exposure to harmful pollutants such as fine particulate matter and ozone. Rather than using the gold-standard method (namely, an atmospheric dispersion model, for which we had neither the required meteorological data nor the technical capacity to run), we adapted estimates from the United States based on differences in population density between the United States and Mexico. Neither the Ministry of Finance nor the President's Office of Public Policy ever discussed this highly uncertain and influential parameter, again perhaps because of their lack of familiarity with environmental cost-benefit analysis.

Policy Outcome: Is Mexico on the Way to Producing the Low-Sulfur Fuels It Needs?

THE STANDARD AND THE INVESTMENT PROJECT FOR A FUEL QUALITY UPGRADE: TARGETS AND TIMELINE

Despite uncertainty about funding for the project, the final standard (NOM-086-SEMARNAT-SENER-SCFI-2005) was published in the official federal government journal on January 20, 2006. It stated that low-sulfur fuels would be introduced in Mexico based on the timetable that PEMEX had presented in 2005, conditioned on Congress's approval of the investment project.[19]

After the standard was published, INE and PEMEX were able to finalize the cost-benefit analysis and submit the report to the Ministry of Finance in March 2006. Soon thereafter, Congress granted its approval of the project. Officially, the investment project was included in the 2006 budget, with funds for the initial engineering development coming from the 2006 federal budget, and all other funds from PIDIREGAS.

SULFUR FUEL QUALITY PROJECT: PROGRESS ACHIEVED

In July 2006 federal elections took place, and in December the new president, Felipe Calderón, took office. One year later, new authorities from the Ministry of Energy and PEMEX shared the following news with their new counterparts from the Ministry of Finance and SEMARNAT regarding the implementation of the Fuel Quality Project.

Since the initial plan was proposed in 2005, PEMEX had made some progress in providing ultra-low-sulfur fuels in Mexico: ultra-low-sulfur Premium gasoline was available throughout the country as of October 2006, and starting in January 2007, ultra-low-sulfur diesel was available in the Mexico-U.S. border region. However, compliance proved to be more costly than anticipated, since 100 percent of the internal market of ultra-low-sulfur fuels was met by imports (Secretaría de Energía 2007). In fact, there had been zero progress on the technical engineering plans to revamp the refineries to produce ultra-low-sulfur diesel. In addition, PEMEX informed its counterparts that ultra-low-sulfur Magna, which was slated to be sold in three major metropolitan areas by October 2008, would be delayed by over three years. The timetable for ultra-low-sulfur diesel availability would ultimately lag behind its proposed timeline by approximately four years.

At this point, PEMEX proposed a significant increase in the project's budget and a delay in its implementation. The investment still needed for the completion of the low-sulfur Magna gasoline portion of the project was close to $1.8 billion. For diesel, the increase was dramatic and amounted to almost $3.4 billion, more than double the initial estimate. PEMEX's new total budget was estimated at approximately $5.9 billion, including interest payments (close to $280 million) and direct funding from the federal budget ($420 million). This was a significant increase vis-à-vis the approximately $3 billion estimated in 2005.

These changes demanded a significant amount of additional funding, and thus required an updated cost-benefit analysis. Again, PEMEX and INE worked together on this task. In early 2008 the new cost-benefit analysis was finalized. Even though some of the benefits were lost with the delay in compliance, the cost-benefit analysis showed net benefits from the project despite higher costs estimated by PEMEX, and the inclusion of higher manufacturing costs for new lower-emissions vehicles. This was partly because INE had improved its analysis of human exposure to vehicular emissions since conducting its previous cost-benefit analyses, which resulted in a substantial increase in estimated net benefits (Stevens 2008).

This time around, there were no discussions of the methodologies used to determine the value of projected benefits. This was likely the result of INE having dealt with the issues in the previous analysis; moreover, a very thorough effort to explain the methodology to ministry representatives had already taken place, when the new administration had taken office. Also, at this point, the most pressing matter in terms of public policy was for PEMEX to explain the dramatic changes to the project, including its revised timetable and cost estimates.

Fuel Quality in Mexico: Current Status, Institutional Context, and Lessons Learned

Both cost-benefit analyses—the first one using the initial timetable and its corresponding budget, and the second one with its delayed timetable and respective budget—showed that the benefits of the project would outweigh its costs (INE 2006; 2008). These results were crucial in establishing the favorable atmosphere that led the Ministry of Finance to approve the necessary funding. Since then, the project has resulted in a better quality of fuels nationwide: by 2011, ultra-low-sulfur Premium gasoline was available countrywide; ultra-low-sulfur Magna was sold in the three main metropolitan areas; and ultra-low-sulfur diesel was being distributed in the northern border region and the three main metropolitan areas (UNEP 2012). Unfortunately, distribution of ultra-low-sulfur Magna and diesel in the rest of the country will be delayed, probably until 2013 or 2014. These new dates must be incorporated into a revised regulation. Since the Ministry of Finance will have to authorize additional resources for the revised project, it is likely that a new cost-benefit analysis will be required.

COST-BENEFIT ANALYSIS IN THE PUBLIC POLICY ARENA

Cost-benefit analysis has been legally required by both COFEMER (for new federal regulations) and by the Ministry of Finance (for federal investment projects) since at least 2000. COFEMER and the Ministry of Finance share the same objective in requiring cost-benefit analysis: to better evaluate the social costs and benefits of public policy decisions. Nevertheless, as a tool, cost-benefit analysis can be used even more effectively. At present, each agency has produced its own set of methodological guidelines (COFEMER 2010b; SHCP 2005a). These guidelines differ, even though there are fundamental similarities and assumptions that should be shared between them. The need to develop a common framework for conducting cost-benefit analysis was evident in the case of the fuel quality standard. Whereas COFEMER had readily issued a waiver from the analytical requirement (pursuant to the argument that the regulation would result in "no cost to private stakeholders"), the Ministry of Finance insisted the analysis be conducted, ultimately helping to legitimate the project by showing that even though it entailed significant costs (both for PEMEX and consumers), the benefits outweighed those costs.

Environmental policymaking in Mexico still does not include a great deal of cost-benefit analysis. The value of cost-benefit analysis would increase if analysts had specific guidelines on how to perform it when assessing investment projects with environmental effects. Since environmental authorities in Mexico have not traditionally included monetized health benefits in their analysis, in the case of the fuel standards, analysts spend substantial time and resources communicating to government officials the usefulness of conducting cost-benefit analysis and educating them about the appropriate methodologies.

COFEMER's 2005 guidelines for the RIA utilized quantified benefit estimates and included examples that seem to have been drawn from our previous reports.[20] This parallel shows that a learning process permeated the agency. In addition, the Ministry of Energy has since incorporated the calculation of environmental externalities into its authorization process for new electric generating units, although this requirement is currently constrained to greenhouse gas emissions. Furthermore, the Ministry of Finance has incorporated the estimation of externalities, in terms of health effects from pollutants, in its procedures for authorizing federal funding of power generation projects. And recently, our team has been asked to collaborate with both ministries in harmonizing their respective guidelines.

VSL AND DISCOUNT RATES

Appropriate VSL and discount rates are especially critical for conducting cost-benefit analysis properly. In general, concepts like VSL are largely unknown or misunderstood in Mexico. As for discount rates, these obviously have significant impacts on the results of a cost-benefit analysis whose benefits extend into the future, as our sensitivity analysis showed. Nonetheless, a one-size-fits-all discount value of 12 percent is currently recommended by the Ministry of Finance for social projects. For reasons stated above, this remains problematic.

Conclusion

Moving forward on the analytical decision-making path will require much more work. Cost-benefit analysis for large investment projects and regulatory impact assessments need to be consistent in terms of concepts and tools to ensure that they accurately evaluate policy impacts. There is a pressing need to develop one set of guidelines for cost-benefit analysis in Mexico. Specifically, a well-researched VSL for Mexican populations must be developed, rather than importing and adjusting figures from another country. To date, guidelines produced by the two agencies that require cost-benefit analysis in Mexico do not include methods for placing a monetary value on health or other intangible environmental benefits. In addition, an appropriate social discount rate should be developed. Working with federal authorities to lower the discount rate would allow us to value future generations as much as we value our own.

In Mexico, the capacity to carry out and evaluate cost-benefit analysis must be improved in all government ministries. Our experience demonstrates that we had substantial leeway in analytic decisions, and we endeavored to base our choices on the best available methods and information. However, given the lack of thoughtful discourse among the agencies and the lack of a central oversight office, there is a risk that different agencies may take advantage of the absence of federal standards to manipulate results. The inconsistent application of cost-benefit analysis methods could also reduce the legitimacy of the tool in the eyes of primary decision-makers and the public.

Our experience shows that a strong regulatory framework for cost-benefit analysis, including technical oversight by a federal office, is needed. Technical guidelines on discount rates and monetary values for intangible benefits should be developed in a transparent manner. Continuous educational efforts on best global practices for conducting cost-benefit analysis are also in demand. We believe that within such a framework, cost-benefit analysis could become a much more powerful tool for environmental regulators in Mexico, and it could help the regulators better negotiate with industries and other stakeholders.

Notes

1. In Mexico there are fewer deaths caused by urban air pollution than in the United States, given differences in population size and average ages. In Mexico, teenagers and young adults are dominant in the population. In addition, the population is about three times smaller. Therefore, deaths from diseases that strike the elderly, and illnesses that are associated with air pollution, such as cardiopulmonary diseases, are an order of magnitude smaller in Mexico than in the United States. The young average age of the population in Mexico also means that a larger proportion of deaths caused by air pollution are infant deaths, estimated to be 1,000 annually (13 percent of deaths caused by air pollution).

2. To our knowledge, these were the first efforts to request the analysis of potential impacts derived from investment projects to feed into the decision-making process of federal resource allocation.

3. Unless stated otherwise, all figures are in U.S. dollars.

4. Cámara de Diputados del H. Congreso de la Unión, Ley Federal de Presupuesto y Responsabilidad Hacendaria, in *Diario Oficial de la Federación* (2006).

5. Un compromiso común (PICCA), *Programa Integral Contra la Contaminación Atmoférica 75 (1990). Comisión Ambiental Metropolitana, Gobierno del Distrito Federal, Gobierno del Estado de México, and Secretaría de Medio Ambiente y Recursos Naturales y Secretaría de Salud, Programa para Mejorar la Calidad del Aire de la Zona Metropolitana del Valle de México 2002–2010* (Mexico City: Gobierno del Distrito Federal, 2002). PICCA was developed by the Intergovernmental Technical Secretariat, which was integrated by representatives from the ministries of environment, energy, finance, commerce, transportation, and health, among others, as well as from authorities from the government of Mexico City and from the State of Mexico. This Secretariat also worked with experts from Japan, the United Kingdom, Germany, Canada, and the United States.

6. See Walsh (2007); Cámara de Diputados del H. Congreso de la Unión, Ley Federal de Presupuesto y Responsabilidad Hacendaria, in *Diario Oficial de la Federación* (2006).

7. Un compromiso común (PICCA), *Programa Integral Contra la Contaminación Atmoférica* (1990, 75).

8. SEMARNAT-SENER-SECOFI, Acuerdo de Modificación de la Norma Oficial Mexicana NOM-086-SEMARNAT-SENER-SCFI-2005, Especificaciones de los Combustibles Fósiles para la Protección Ambiental, 2006, *Diario Oficial de la Federación: México*, 3.

9. SEMARNAT-SENER-SECOFI, Norma Oficial Mexicana NOM-086-SEMARNAT-SENER-SCFI-2005, Especificaciones de los Combustibles Fósiles para la Protección Ambiental in NOM-086-SEMARNAT-SENER-SCFI-2005, 2006, *Diario Oficial de la Federación: México*, 18.

10. SEMARNAT, *Minuta de la séptima reunión del Subcomité II: Energía y Actividades Extractivas,para la Revisión de la NOM-086-ECOL-1994*, Dirección General de Energía y Actividades Extractivas, Editor 2002: México D.F.

11. International Organization of Motor Vehicle Manufacturers, Worldwide Fuel Charter (2006). The WWFCH includes representatives from the most important automobile and engine manufacturers' associations from around the world. In fact, the Charter was

established in 1998 to harmonize fuel quality worldwide in accordance with the engine and vehicle needs of different markets around the world.

12. See WHO (2006); Bell et al. (2005); Anderson et al. (2004); Pope et al. (2002); Borja-Aburto et al. (1997); Dockery and Schwartz (1995); Dockery et al. (1993).

13. By law each ministry has a standard revision committee with specific operational rules. COMARNAT, which is the committee responsible for reviewing and approving environmental standards, has within its operational rules a procedure for officially integrating working groups. To meet these standards, the working group included officials from ministries that exercise power over fuels, such as the Ministry of Energy (with PEMEX) and the Ministry of Economy; representatives from local governments with air pollution problems, such as Mexico City and the State of Mexico; members of industrial chambers and associations; those affiliated with automotive distributors; and light- and heavy-duty vehicle manufacturers.

14. See Reyes-Tépach (2008); SHCP (2005b). The 1995 economic crisis restricted the government's capacity to fund investment projects that were required for the development of petroleum resources, but the Mexican constitution states that only the Mexican people can profit from oil extraction. To solve these financial constraints, the Mexican Congress modified two laws (Ley de Presupuesto, Contabilidad y Gasto Público Federal; Ley General de Deuda Pública). Under this revised legal framework, private investors can provide funding for infrastructure projects in the oil and electric public enterprises, although reforms adopted in 2008 limited the availability of private funds for PEMEX. These loans are then paid back by the government from the revenues generated from the long-term operations of the projects. Such long-term investment schemes are called PIDIREGAS (Proyectos de Infraestructura Productiva de Largo Plazo). PIDIREGAS projects are controversial because the federal government transfers public resources, sharing the oil rent with the private sector through the payment of the interests generated by the financial investments. In this particular case, the payment would come from an increase in fuel prices.

15. Comisión Federal de Mejora Regulatoria. 2005. *Respuesta a la solicitud de exención de la MIR por No Costos para el anteproyecto de Proyecto de Norma Oficial Mexicana PROY-NOM-086-SEMARNAT-2005.- Especificaciones de los Combustibles Fósiles para la Protección Ambiental*: México DF; SEMARNAT-SENER-SECOFI, *Proyecto de Norma Oficial Mexicana PROY NOM-086-SEMARNAT-SENER-SCFI-2005, Especificaciones de los Combustibles Fósiles para la Protección Ambiental* SEMARNAT, Editor 2005, Diario Oficial de la Federación 17.

16. Cámara de Diputados del H. Congreso de la Unión. 2006. Ley Federal de Presupuesto y Responsabilidad Hacendaria, Congreso de la Unión, Editor, *Diario Oficial de la Federación*.

17. In 2000, INE went through a transformation of its mission and main responsibilities, shifting from its managerial and regulatory powers, to instead a mission of conducting research.

18. This panel included (in alphabetical order): Stephano M. Bertozzi, executive director of the Center of Research and Evaluation of Surveys, National Institute of Public Health, Mexico; John Evans, Department of Environmental Health Sciences, Harvard School of Public Health; Javier Gala, Center of Studies for the Preparation and Evaluation of Socioeconomic Projects (CEPEP), Mexico; James Hammitt, director of the Harvard Center for Risk Analysis; Mauricio Hernández, general director, National Institute of Public Health,

Mexico; and Mario Molina, Nobel laureate and director general, Mario Molina Center for Studies on Health and Environment.

19. SEMARNAT-SENER-SECOFI. 2006. Norma Oficial Mexicana NOM-086-SEMARNAT-SENER-SCFI-2005, Especificaciones de los Combustibles Fósiles para la Protección Ambiental in NOM-086-SEMARNAT-SENER-SCFI-2005, *Diario Oficial de la Federación* 18.

20. COFEMER guidelines do not include a list of references. Therefore, it is not possible to confirm whether the examples were drawn from our analysis.

Bibliography

Anderson, H. Ross, Richard W. Atkinson, Janet L. Peacock, Louise Marston, and Kostas Konstantinou. 2004. *Meta-Analysis of Time-Series Studies and Panel Studies of Particulate Matter and Ozone*. Copenhagen: World Health Organization.

Bell, Michell L., Francesca Dominici, and Jonathan M. Samet. 2005. "A Meta-analysis of Time-Series Studies of Ozone and Mortality with Comparison to the National Morbidity, Mortality, and Air Pollution Study." *Epidemiology* 16 (4): 436–45.

Borja-Aburto, Victor H., Dana P. Loomis, Shnkant I. Bangdiwala, Carl M. Shy, and Ramon A. Rascon-Pacheco. 1997. "Ozone, Suspended Particulates, and Daily Mortality in Mexico City." *American Journal of Epidemiology* 145 (3): 258–68.

Broome, John. 2008. "The Ethics of Climate Change." *Scientific American*, June, 69–73.

Cervini, Héctor. 2004. "El Costo de Oportunidad Social de los Fondos Públicos y la Tasa Social de Descuento en México 1970–2001." Working paper, El Centro de Estudios para la Preparación y Evaluación Socioeconómica de Proyectos (CEPEP).

Comisión Federal de Mejora Regulatoria (COFEMER). 2005. *Sistema De Elaboración De Manifestaciones De Impacto Regulatorio y Remisión De Anteproyectos A La COFEMER A Través Del Portal*. Mexico City: COFEMER.

Comisión Federal de Mejora Regulatoria (COFEMER). 2010a. "Antecedentes." Last modified September 22, 2010. http://www.cofemer.gob.mx/contenido.aspx?contenido=86.

Comisión Federal de Mejora Regulatoria (COFEMER). 2010b. "Manual de la Manifestacion de Impacto Regulatorio." In *Diario Oficial de la Federación*. Mexico City: COFEMER.

Dockery, Douglas W., C. Arden Pope, Xiping Xu, John D. Spengler, James H. Ware, Martha E. Fay, Benjamin G. Ferris, Jr., et al. 1993. "An Association between Air Pollution and Mortality in Six U.S. Cities." *New England Journal of Medicine* 329 (24): 1753–59.

Dockery, Douglas W., and Joel Schwartz. 1995. "Particulate Air Pollution and Mortality: More Than the Philadelphia Story." *Epidemiology* 6 (6): 629–32.

García, Hector Saavedra. 2002. "Sesión IV: México—Un Nuevo Sistema Para Mejorar la Asignación del Gasto de Inversión." In *CEPAL—SERIE Seminarios y Conferencias*, No. 18, 47–73. Santiago de Chile: Comisión Económica para América Latina y el Caribe (CEPAL).

Hammitt, James K., and Maria Eugenia Ibarrar án. 2006. "The Economic Value of Reducing Fatal and Non-fatal Occupational Risks in Mexico City Using Actuarial- and Perceived-Risk Estimates." *Health Economics Letters* 15 (12): 1329–35.

Instituto Nacional de Ecología (INE). 2006. *Estudio de Evaluación Socioeconómica del Proyecto Integral de Calidad de Combustibles: Reducción de Azufre en Gasolinas y Diesel*. Mexico City: INE/Semarnat/Pemex Refinación.

Instituto Nacional de Ecología (INE). 2008. *Estudio de Evaluación Socioeconómica de la Reducción del Contenido de Azufre en Gasolina Magna y Diesel.* Mexico City: INE/Semarnat/Pemex Refinación.

Künzli, Nino, Ramon Suárez Medina, Reinhard Kaiser, Philippe Quénel, F. Horak Jr., and M. Studnicka. 2001. "Assessment of Deaths Attributable to Air Pollution: Should We Use Risk Estimates Based on Time Series or on Cohort Studies?" *American Journal of Epidemiology* 153 (11): 1050–55.

Office of Management and Budget (OMB). 2003. *Office of Management and Budget Circular A-4, Regulatory Analysis.* Washington, D.C.: OMB.

Pope, C. Arden, III, Richard T. Burnett, Michael J. Thun, Eugenia E. Calle, Daniel Krewski, Kazuhiko Ito, and George D. Thurston. 2002. "Lung Cancer, Cardiopulmonary Mortality, and Long-Term Exposure to Fine Particulate Air Pollution." *Journal of the American Medical Association* 287 (9): 1132–41.

Poulos, Christine, and Dale Whittington. 2000. "Time Preferences for Life-Saving Programs: Evidence from Six Less Developed Countries." *Environmental Science & Technology* 34 (8): 1445–55.

Reyes-Tépach, M. en E. 2008. *La Construcción de la Infraestructura Productiva en PEMEX a Través de la Inversión Pública Presupuestaria y los Proyectos PIDIREGAS.* Cámara de Diputados, Servicios de Investigación y Análisis, Subdirección de Economía, SE-ISS-13-08. Mexico City: Cámara de Diputados.

Secretaría de Energ ía. 2007. *Prospectiva de Petrolíferos 2007–2016.* Dirección General de Planeación Energética. Mexico City: Secretaría de Energía.

Secretaría de Hacienda y Crédito Público (SHCP). 2005a. *Lineamientos para la Elaboración y Presentación de los Análisis Costo y Beneficio de los Programas y Proyectos de Inversión de la Administración Pública Federal.* Unidad de Inversiones, Subsecretaría de Egresos, Oficio Circular No. 400.1.410.05.035, July 18. Mexico City: SHCP.

Secretaría de Hacienda y Crédito Público (SHCP). 2005b. *Norma para el Tratamiento Contable de las Inversiones en Proyectos de Infraestructura Productiva de Largo Plazo (NIF-009 B).* Subsecretaria de Egresos, Unidad de Contabilidad Gubernamental e Informes Sobre la Gestion Publica. Mexico City: SHCP.

Secretaría de Hacienda y Crédito Público (SHCP). 2008. "Lineamientos para la Elaboración y Presentación de los Análisis Costo y Beneficio de los Programas y Proyectos de Inversión." In *Diario Oficial de la Federación* (March 18, 2008): 2–13. Mexico City: SHCP.

Secretaría de Medio Ambiente del Distrito Federal (SMADF). 2010. *Inventario de Emisiones de Contaminantes Criterio de la ZMVM—2008.* Mexico City: SMADF.

Stevens, Gretchen A., Miriam Zuk, L. Rojas, and James K. Hammitt. 2008. "The Benefits and Costs of Reducing Sulfur in Mexican Diesel Fuels." In "Environment and Health in Transition in Mexico: Risk Assessment and Economic Evaluation." Doctoral thesis, Harvard University.

Stevens, Gretchen A., Rodrigo H. Dias, and Majid Ezzati. 2008. "The Effects of 3 Environmental Risks on Mortality Disparities across Mexican Communities." *Proceedings of the National Academy of Sciences of the United States of America* 105 (44): 16860–65.

United Nations Environment Programme (UNEP). 2012. "Status of Fuel Quality and Vehicle Emission Standards: Latin America and the Caribbean." Partnership for Clean Fuels and Vehicles, UNEP, Nairobi, Kenya.

Walsh, Michael P. 2007. "The Global Experience with Lead in Gasoline and the Lessons We Should Apply to the Use of MMT." *American Journal of Industrial Medicine* 50 (11): 853–60.

World Health Organization (WHO). 2006. *WHO Air Quality Guidelines for Particulate Matter, Ozone, Nitrogen Dioxide and Sulfur Dioxide. Global Update 2005*. Geneva: WHO.

11

Health Care Costs of Urban Air Pollution in South Africa

Anthony Leiman

Spare a thought for Odysseus as he navigated the straits of Messina: on his left the high yapping menace of Scylla; on his right the yawning reality of Charybdis. The policymaker—addressing pollution problems in any third-world country—is in a similar position: on one side, and regularly making itself heard, lurks high theory; on the other, harsh reality. The elegant world of tradable permits, Pigouvian taxes, and Coasian bargaining confronts a reality in which monitoring is expensive and unreliable, and in which firms are often unaware of their own wasteful spending. How then should governments set about reducing the high external costs imposed by urban air pollution? Cost-benefit analysis of proposed interventions provides one way forward.[1]

Since the passage of the National Environment Management Air Quality Act No. 39 of 2004, South Africa has seen rising interest in the formal evaluation of air quality control interventions. The act was designed to increase the efficiency of such interventions by providing a base set of emissions standards at the national level. These can be made more stringent by provincial governments, and municipal authorities can strengthen them further. The rationale was straightforward: most of South Africa has low population densities, and airborne pollutants in such areas engender few if any anthropocentric impacts. Rigorous standards in such areas would merely tax rural enterprises. Since the external cost imposed by a given emission is primarily a function of the number of potential victims, optimality requires that urban centers with high population densities should face more stringent regulations than rural areas. Policymakers should also consider the local landscape, particularly features such as temperature inversions that are tied to local topography and climate. Some of South Africa's population centers have proven particularly vulnerable in this regard. Simple technologies can also be relevant: where temperature inversions are a common feature, the impact of a given air pollutant declines with the height of the smokestack through which it is emitted.

The determinants of the externalities associated with emissions being so variable, the act's key feature was the facility to increase regulatory stringency where population densities are high and where topology and climate tend to trap pollutants at low levels above ground. The central Highveld—the area around Johannesburg Witbank (Malahleni), Krugersdorp, and Vereeniging—is an especially high-risk zone in this regard.

Municipalities that wish to improve consistently poor air quality clearly have an incentive to identify cost-efficient interventions. Policymakers initially focused on dirty fuels and on mitigating pollution by improving combustion technologies.

Like any regulation, pollution abatement standards would affect each sector of the South African society differently. Polluters will tend to criticize standards as placing them at a competitive disadvantage. However, as long as mobility is easy and entry/exit costs are low, cleaner producers, or firms in areas with less severe regulations, will pick up the slack left by penalized firms. In other words, so long as the product being manufactured is not traded on international markets, the domestic economy as a whole should not lose. This free market response is a variant of the Tiebout Effect (Baumol and Oates 1988), in which firms locate within domestic jurisdictions to minimize costs.[2] Another consequence might be a change in the price of property. In areas with poor air quality, the value of property will drop, and those prepared to tolerate lower air quality would benefit by electing to buy or rent there. Despite the appeal of this notion, it has to be recognized that for South Africa's urban poor there is no such choice. This distributional aspect is of particular concern as air quality is typically poor in low-income residential areas all around the country.

Policy Analysis

To inform state decision making on air quality, the National Economic Development and Labor Council (NEDLAC)[3] commissioned a series of studies, one of which was a wide-scale cost-benefit analysis of thirty-two potential interventions. In selecting interventions there were two clear concerns. The first was that although the new legislation had been particularly well thought out, the country's monitoring and enforcement mechanisms are weak. The second was a need to identify the existing major sources of air pollutants. An indication of these sources is provided in table 11.1.

TABLE 11.1

Source Contributions to Total Annual Emissions from Fuel-Burning Activities in Major Metropolitan Centers (Pretoria, Johannesburg, Ekurhuleni, Mpumalanga Highveld, Vaal Triangle, Durban, and Cape Town)

	Sulfur Dioxide	Nitrogen Oxides	Total Particulates
Electricity generation	70.5%	54.9%	36.0%
Industrial fuel-burning	26.5%	23.0%	44.1%
Motor vehicles	2.0%	21.3%	4.7%
Domestic fuel-burning	0.8%	0.2%	8.8%
Shipping & aircraft	0.1%	0.4%	0.1%
Biomass burning (wildfires)		0.3%	6.2%

Source: Scorgie et al. (2004a).

Footnote to "Motor Vehicles": Scorgie et al. (2004b) noted that, after inhalable coarse particulates (PM10, associated with coal-fired power stations and domestic fuel-burning), the most important pollutants in urban areas were nitrogen dioxide and aromatic hydrocarbons, e.g. benzene (all associated with vehicles and therefore expected to increase with vehicle numbers).

According to table 11.1, the state should focus on electricity generation and on industrial fuel-burning, and indeed this was the premise on which policymakers based new air quality legislation. A closer analysis, however, suggests that this logic can be challenged. A series of studies by Howells and Laitner (2003; 2005) and Howells et al. (2003) showed profligate waste of energy in the industrial and power generation sectors, which are both technically and economically inefficient. These studies suggest that it is primarily widespread inertia that causes firms to ignore Pareto-improving energy savings that would enhance air quality. Despite this, the state's limited monitoring capacity suggests that nonindustrial interventions might make greater financial sense.

Domestic fuel-burning offers one possibility. While contributing relatively little to total emissions, its contribution is typically either indoors or at ground level in areas of high population density. The health impacts of domestic fuels are also made disproportionately high by timing: household emissions peak in the early morning and early evening, times when temperature inversions are common and families are at home.

Of the thirty-two proposed interventions (table 11.2), seven focus on using domestic fuel more efficiently. Four of the interventions relate to improved housing insulation that would reduce or remove the need for heating. Nine look at processing fuels to reduce potential emissions. Four interventions examine technology to cut emissions from given fuels. Three involve electrification: since the bulk of South Africa's electricity is generated at coal-fired thermal power stations, electrification means using the same fuel, but more efficiently, with a higher smokestack, and in a location more distant from urban areas. Finally, five interventions aim at substituting away from problematic fuels.

This spread of potential interventions and approaches makes implausible the classic textbook approach of identifying an optimal emissions level at which marginal abatement cost equals marginal external cost. However, the theory remains relevant. Because the interventions are not mutually exclusive, assembling measures in rank order of their benefit-to-cost ratios yields an approximate marginal net benefit function. Marginal net benefits of abatement fall as the more efficient options (i.e., those with high benefit-cost ratios) are exhausted and marginal costs move closer to marginal benefits. The limit of efficiency is attained when the benefit-to-cost ratio reaches 1. All subsequent interventions are economically inefficient.[4]

A spreadsheet model was developed with two main components: the first assessed each measure individually while the second considered their combined impacts. The model's layered format allowed for the sequential consideration of direct *financial* costs and benefits, direct *economic* costs and benefits (adjusted for distortions), and indirect economic impacts. It also allowed for distributional effects—the impacts of the measures on different stakeholders, including government, firms, and households.

The model's prime concern was with health costs: rural impacts of acid rain from nitrogen oxides (NOx) and sulfur oxides (SOx) were disregarded. Eskom, the national electricity generator, monitors rain for sulfates, nitrates, and acidity. Its records show that sulfate and nitrate levels at its industrial monitoring site

TABLE 11.2
Proposed Interventions

	Proposed Interventions
Using Domestic Fuel More Efficiently	
Intervention 1	The Basa Njengo Magogo project, if implemented *only in Johannesburg and the Mpumalanga Highveld*. It educates the public about the health and efficiency benefits of the efficient stacking and top-down ignition of coal stoves as opposed to the more common practice of bottom-up ignition.
Intervention 2	The Basa Njengo Magogo project extended to *all* South African cities.
Intervention 9	Coal stove maintenance and parts replacement for 5 percent of all urban households.
Intervention 10	Coal stove maintenance and parts replacement for 20 percent of all urban households.
Intervention 26	Requiring *new* passenger vehicles to comply with Euro 2 standards.
Intervention 27	Requiring *new* passenger vehicles to comply with Euro 4 standards.
Intervention 29	Making *all* petrol vehicles Euro 2 compliant.
Improving Housing Insulation	
Intervention 4	Requiring insulation for 5 percent of households heated by fuel-burning *in Johannesburg and the Mpumalanga Highveld*.
Intervention 5	Requiring insulation for 20 percent of households heated by fuel-burning *in Johannesburg and the Mpumalanga Highveld*.
Intervention 6	Requiring insulation for 5 percent of *all* the country's fuel-burning urban households.
Intervention 7	Requiring insulation for 20 percent of *all* the country's fuel-burning urban households.
Processing Fuels	
Intervention 3	Developing low-smoke fuels. This entails the production (and distribution) of coal-treated fuels to reduce the health impacts of its combustion.
Interventions 19–25	Reducing the sulfur, benzene, and aromatics contents of petrol and diesel respectively, and removing lead (#23).
Cutting Emissions through Technology	
Intervention 11	The desulfurization of all power station emissions; sulfur oxides from thermal power stations are a significant source of air pollution.
Intervention 15	Reducing particulates emitted from coal-fired boilers.
Intervention 16	Reducing emissions from steel refinery coking ovens.
Intervention 18	The desulfurization of Sasol-Secunda's power station emissions.
Electrification	
Intervention 8	The electrification of coal-using households. Electrification would improve air pollution levels as consumers switch away from coal stoves.
Intervention 32	The electrification of paraffin-burning households.

(continued)

TABLE 11.2 *(Continued)*

	Proposed Interventions
Intervention 12	Decommissioning an old technology power station to the west of Pretoria, a densely populated area.
Substituting Problematic Fuels	
Interventions 13–14	Implementing wind-generated energy technology through financial incentives (10,000 and 37,000 GWhr block respectively).
Intervention 17	Replacing coal with natural gas/carbon monoxide while upgrading Highveld Steel & Vanadium's smelter.
Interventions 30	Converting 10 percent of petrol vehicles to LPG.
Intervention 31	Converting 20 percent of petrol vehicles to LPG.

were as high as those in the northeastern United States and central Europe. Rain in the area had average pH of 4.35, but most of the acidity was neutralized by base cations in the soil. Since dose-response functions for airborne pollutants are widely available, and studies typically ascribe over three-quarters of the benefit from air quality improvements to reductions in premature mortality (e.g., Burtraw et al. 1997; Blackman et al. 2000), impacts on statistical life and disability-adjusted life-years seemed obvious routes forward.

Converting such physiological estimates of impacts into pecuniary ones is always problematic. Here, the benefit-transfer methodology provides estimates of value of statistical life. In assessing the benefits of the U.S. Clean Air Act, analysts covered twenty-six values of statistical life (VSL) estimates found in the literature (EPA 1999a). The majority clustered between $3 million and $7 million, with a central estimate of $5 million in 1990 terms (EPA 1999b). However, most of these estimates were generated by wage-risk models. Five of the twenty-six used contingent valuation, and the average VSL among these was a lower $2.88 million. This estimate was further reduced by 50 percent, to $1.44 million, in line with the later finding of Krupnick et al. (2000) that the EPA estimates were overstated by this percentage. This value was then converted to South African rands and adjusted to South African income levels. Following Pearce and Howarth (2000):

$$V_{sa} = V_{us}(Y_{sa}/Y_{us})^{\text{elasticity}}. \tag{11.1}$$

Where V_{sa} is the value in South Africa, V_{us} the value from the United States, Y_{sa} is the average income level in South Africa, Y_{us} the income level in the United States, and elasticity is the income elasticity of demand. Clearly the income elasticity chosen can crucially affect the outcome of the transfer. While the income elasticity of demand for health-related goods and services is not known in South Africa, it seems likely, a priori, that the demand for them will rise with disposable income. Pearce and Howarth cite a set of observations of income elasticities between 0.3 and 1.1 for goods that could reduce risk to life, most being in the region of 0.3 (Pearce and Howarth 2000). This is consistent with the general finding that health care is a necessary good. Nonetheless, to ensure conservative benefit estimates we assumed an income elasticity of 1.5, on the grounds that willingness to spend incremental income on health services will be far higher in countries with poor public health care systems than in richer, developed countries with established and easily accessed health services. At the lowest levels of consumption, health care is a somewhat less necessary expense than food and basic shelter, so that once those absolute necessities are taken care of, a large proportion of additional income may be allocated to health care expenses to help ensure that breadwinners stay healthy.

It is important to note that the income elasticity estimate applies to statistical life for the average person and thus runs the risk of being an under- or overestimate if applied uniformly to people of all ages. It is open to debate whether older people attach a lower value to reduced risk than do younger people, though many researchers suspect this to be the case. Various techniques exist to capture this effect. One of the simpler and potentially less biased approaches is to apply a single age-adjustment based on whether an individual is likely to be over seventy or not at the time of death (EPA 2002). This is consistent with observations by Jones-Lee (1989), and Jones-Lee et al. (1985; 1993) and more recent findings by Krupnick et al. (2000) that the only significant difference in willingness to pay (WTP) is between those under and those over seventy. To correct for this effect, an adjustment factor is applied to those over seventy defined as the ratio of the seventy-year-old individual's WTP to a forty-year-old, which is 0.63 based on Jones-Lee (1989) and 0.92 based on Jones-Lee et al. (1993). To show the maximum impact of the age adjustment, 0.63 was used here, though this needed further adjustment since South African mortality data is divided into "persons under 65" and "over 65."

A lower bound on the value of mortality and morbidity reduction benefits was obtained using a human capital approach. This reflected the value of labor time lost because of poor health. It also introduced an income constraint to estimates, something not evident on transferred estimates of willingness to pay.

A brief theoretical aside may be useful at this point. Cost-benefit analysis ordinarily ignores transfers and pecuniary externalities. The reason is that while a technological externality can shift the physical production boundary of an economy, a transfer or a pecuniary externality merely indicates a change in the distribution of wealth or relative prices. The efficient allocation of resources in a free market is based on such shifting prices, and cost-benefit theory consequently dictates that they be ignored. They may, nevertheless, be politically significant and can have profound local welfare effects for specific subgroups of the population. Think of the motorcar's impact on the incomes of farriers and harness-makers. While such impacts will not influence the NPV or benefit-cost ratio of a proposed policy intervention, they may still be of real interest to decision makers. A "stakeholder analysis" can be used on top of the conventional cost-benefit evaluation to capture such impacts.

If this requires further rationalization, it is worth considering the implications of unemployment. The conventional analysis presupposes full employment: the economy is presumed to be on its production-possibility boundary. Anything that shifts the boundary is therefore relevant, but anything that merely changes one's location on the boundary is not. When an economy has high unemployment (South Africa's has been variously estimated at between 25 percent and 40 percent) a change in relative prices could have profound implications for employment levels. Since the market mechanism has shown itself unable to bring the economy to full employment, such issues have real political and economic relevance.

In this study a standard set of results was generated for each measure for reporting purposes. This included a conventional cost-benefit treatment encompassing the following:

- Overall annual costs and benefits and net present value (NPV), performed from both a financial and an economic perspective
- The financial and economic benefit to cost ratios

It also included a stakeholder analysis that showed the following:

- NPVs of impacts on stakeholders
- Employment impacts over time

The project requirements described by NEDLAC included an analysis of each intervention's "multiplier effects"—that is, the rounds of spending in the circular flow of income that follow from a project. Cost-benefit analysis correctly ignores these effects, but the demand for a multiplier analysis therefore provided justification for some kind of analysis of distributional impacts on local stakeholders.

The approach taken was as follows: the analysis first used each option's direct costs and benefits, which provided a primary measure of economic desirability. Any measure that did not pass the cost-benefit test was not considered further, regardless of potential subsequent stakeholder impacts.

Importantly, the stakeholder analysis only measured the distribution and impacts of changes in expenditure in the first round and ignored the impacts on affected stakeholders during subsequent rounds of the circular flow. For example, in the first round of expenditure changes, Basa Njengo Magogo would decrease spending on coal and medical services. This is recorded as a decrease in turnover by these firms. However, if one looks at subsequent rounds of expenditure, the reduced spending on coal and medical treatment could be redirected to other firms, or else saved. While coal and pharmaceutical producers may suffer, other sectors could gain. The point is that while resources could be redirected away from what can be seen as problematic or unproductive spending—on coal (a dirty fuel) and associated health costs—it is not clear what expenditure items (or savings options) would replace these items. It is important to stress that these estimates of sectoral losses and gains do not reflect the efficiency of a measure, but merely the distributional impacts of its adoption.

In the stakeholder analysis, the coal-retailing and health care sectors are repeatedly impacted by the interventions. The majority of the interventions in the household sector are aimed at reducing coal consumption. The impact on the sector, however, would *not* be significant. The household coal market is currently between 1.5 and 2 million tons per annum, a small fraction of South Africa's total production of approximately 250 million tons per annum. Moreover, the local market is characterized by a fairly severe shortage of coal for industrial use, particularly for small industries that use coal in boilers. Retail coal merchants currently outbid small industrial users seeking additional coal. Any reduction in household coal use would thus be beneficial for these industries and would not result in lower coal production or job losses at mines.

Each intervention's implications for sectoral employment were estimated using input/output tables and the national social accounting matrices. Such an analysis is clearly static, though attempts were made to make forward-looking projections. The limits of such static analysis are well known.

Each intervention was analyzed first in terms of simple financial costs and benefits. These were then adjusted for missing markets, value-added tax, tariffs/quotas, indirect taxes and subsidies, and exchange rate and factor market distortions. Shadow price adjustments were performed for unskilled labor, petrol and diesel, electricity, and exchange rates where relevant, using shadow prices provided in the current South African cost-benefit analysis guidelines (Mullins et al. 2002).

The Policy Outcome

Three of the most promising interventions, according to the analysis, are discussed further below.

INTERVENTION NO. 1: BASA NJENGO MAGOGO

The Basa Njengo Magogo project addresses public education about the benefits of the stacking and top-down ignition of coal stoves as opposed to the more common practice of bottom-up ignition.

The project is cost-benefit justified. The estimated financial net present value (NPV) was R756.3 million (US$100.52 million) with an economic NPV of R653.7 million (US$86.88 million) and a benefit-to-cost ratio of 177.

The stakeholder analysis focuses on politically relevant transfers and pecuniary externalities, both of which are issues that cost-benefit analysis ordinarily ignores. The analysis indicated that government and households enjoyed net gains with present values of R414 million (US$55 million) and R173 million (US$22.99 million) respectively. Because of the increased efficiency of coal fires lit from above, however, sales of coal would fall and firms selling it would suffer a drop in earnings with a present value of R76 million (US$10.1 million). The resulting net gains indicate the extremely low costs of rolling out the program. The financial costs and benefits would be incurred by each stakeholder group annually. The costs and benefits for each stakeholder group were treated as constant over time, with the government experiencing the highest net gains, households experiencing less than half the net gains the government did, and firms incurring the greatest losses.

Domestic coal retailers absorb all of the first-round costs with a present value of R150 million (US$19.94 million). The four largest coal producers, as well as Eskom (classified as implementing firms), would fund the project and expect costs with an economic present value of R2.8 million (US$0.37 million). These costs would be balanced in part by improved labor productivity (NPV R106 million, or US$14.09 million). Benefits to households would be a mix of efficiency gains (R150 million, or US$19.94 million, worth of reduced coal expenditure) and transfers (R1.8 million, or US$0.24 million, in wages for employees of the program).

The improved air quality emerging from this project yields benefits to households with a present value of R48 million (US$6.38 million). These improvements naturally also affect the health care industry, though the impacts are ordinarily omitted from analysis. The initial projections suggested income losses to health care employees with a present value of R59 million (US$7.84 million) as a result of decreased demand for their services and the loss of forty-four jobs for health care workers. However, current shortages in health care provision mean such a drop is unlikely.

Table 11.3 shows the assumptions that were used in the generation of results in figure 11.1.

INTERVENTION NO. 7: HOUSING INSULATION, AFFECTING 20 PERCENT OF ALL FUEL-BURNING HOUSEHOLDS

A far larger project than the Basa Njengo Magogo project was the proposed insulation of 20 percent of all fuel-burning households. This was estimated to offer a financial NPV of R1.704 billion (US$0.23 billion), and an economic NPV of R1.407 billion (US$0.19 billion) and a benefit-to-cost ratio of 7.9. The stakeholder analysis indicates that the government and households would gain R873 million (US$116 million) and R538 million (US$71.51 million) respectively, while firms would lose R131 million (US$17.4 million). These stakeholder losses include a first-round drop in coal sales (present value of R462 million (US$61.4 million)) as demand for coal falls, though firms installing insulation would enjoy gains with a present value of R209 million (US$27.8 million). Health effects would improve labor productivity and result in a benefit to firms with a present value of R161 million (US$21.4 million).

Among the real benefits of the program would be savings on heating fuel (present value of R472.4 million [US$62.79 million]) and mortality reductions with a

TABLE 11.3
Assumption Chart

Public sector as % of total health costs	82.5%
Number of households approached	271,940
Uptake: % households approached	50.0%
Number of households affected	135,970
Average annual coal saving per household	US$20.00
Capex cost per household	US$4.93
Proportion of cost for wages	50%
VAT percentage (if included)	14.0%
Company tax rate (if included)	0.0%

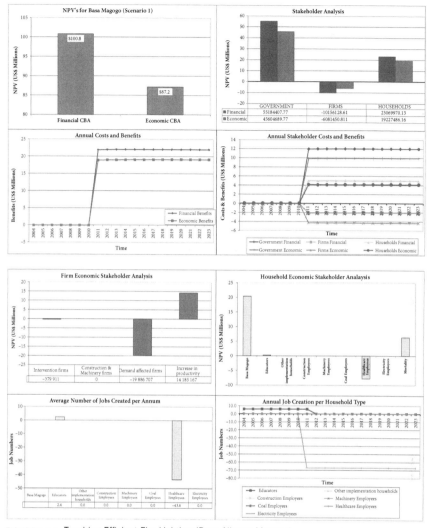

FIGURE 11.1 Teaching Efficient Fire Lighting (Basa Njengo Magogo)

present value of R98 million (US$12.77 million). Transfers (which appear in the stakeholder analysis but not in the cost-benefit analysis) are less clear-cut: households that contain employees implementing the program would receive wage payments (present value of R22.8 million [US$3.03 million]), though households that contain health care employees could incur income reductions with a present value of R159.7 million (US$21.23 million) as demand for their services drop (though again this is likely to be mitigated by the current shortfall in qualified health care workers). The annual effects will remain steady over time.

The financial rewards amount to a little over R400 million (US$53.16 million), and the economic ones to almost R350 million (US$46.52 million). More specifically, the government stands to achieve almost R250 million (US$33.23

TABLE 11.4
Assumption Chart

Public sector as % of total health costs	82.5%
Number of fuel-burning households	1,453,679
Uptake: % households approached	20.0%
Number of households affected	290,736
Percentage coal burning amongst households	53.1%
Reduction in fuel use	40.0%
Installation cost per household	US$173.33
Coal use per household (per annum)	US$100
Wood use per household (per annum)	US$0
VAT percentage (if included)	14.0%
Company tax rate (if included)	3.3%

million) and R200 million (US$26.6 million) in financial and economic rewards respectively per year. Households would experience financial and economic returns of almost R90 million (US$12 million) and R70 million (US$9.3 million) respectively per year, and firms would incur financial and economic costs of over R50 million (US$6.65 million) and R80 million (US$10.63 million) respectively per year. Health care employees potentially suffer the greatest number of jobs lost, though this impact is unlikely, while employment in other sectors is unaffected.

Table 11.4 shows the assumptions made in this analysis, the results of which are reported in figure 11.2.

INTERVENTION NO. 8: ELECTRIFICATION

Township electrification has an estimated financial NPV of R1.044 billion (US$0.14 billion) and an economic NPV of R790 million (US$105 million), but a benefit-to-cost ratio of only 1.2. This apparently surprising outcome is largely due to the increased likelihood of accidental electrocution—a frequent cause of death in townships where electricity is commonly tapped illegally.

The stakeholder analysis shows the present value of government and firms gaining R2.382 billion (US$0.32 billion) and R2.180 billion (US$0.29 billion) respectively, but households incurring costs of R1.549 billion (US$0.21 billion) (largely a result of electrical accidents). Additionally, the stakeholder returns to government assume that there is no theft of electricity. To the degree that this is incorrect, government (here largely local government) gains are overstated.

The basic real benefit would be improved worker health from improved air quality. While this is a real and measurable benefit to the worker, it is also a benefit to firms (NPV of R347 million [US$46.12 million]). From the perspective of conventional cost-benefit analysis, inclusion of both would be double-counting. It is important, however, in the context of stakeholder analysis. Firms selling coal would incur first-round drops in net sale revenues (present value of R196 million [US$26.05 million]), while those involved in implementation would enjoy

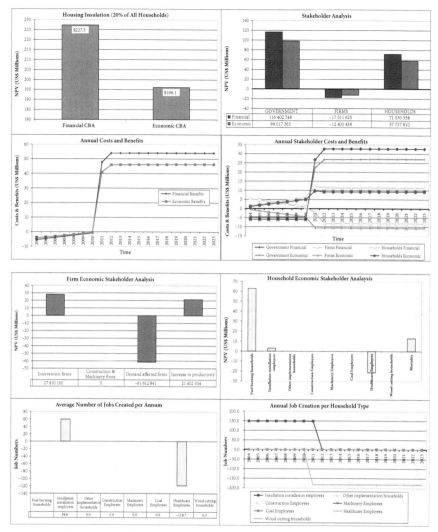

FIGURE 11.2 Housing Insulation

revenue increases (present value of R955 million [US$126.93 million]) with a further R719 million (US$96 million) for construction and machinery firms.

Households affected by the program would spend R495 million (US$66 million) in the purchase of home appliances (such as stoves, refrigerators, and microwaves) and in payments toward capital costs. Wages with a present value of R223 million (US$30 million), R38 million (US$5 million), R38 million (US$5 million), and R48 million (US$6.4 million) respectively would accrue to employees in the electricity manufacturing, construction, machinery, and home appliance sectors. Health care employees could lose R447 million (US$59.4 million) should demand for their services drop. Although improved air quality would reduce mortality (present value of R183 million [US$24.3 million]), this would be offset by the R1.175 billion (US$0.16 billion) expected impact of accidental electrocutions.

South Africa is a country with a chronic unemployment problem; indeed, the issue of "jobless growth" has dominated local economic policy debates for the past two decades. Recent estimates for the cost of creating a new job in the economy have fallen between R100,000 (US$13,291) and R500,000 (US$66,455). Incremental employment could, therefore, be incorporated into the cost-benefit calculus, though it was set aside in this analysis. Our projections suggested that under this program, about 750 new jobs in electricity manufacturing, over 600 new jobs in domestic appliance manufacturing, over 400 new jobs in machinery, and a little over 200 new jobs in construction would be created per year, while over 270 jobs in the health care industry could be at risk.

While the positive NPV of electrification is clear, the stakeholder analysis suggests an unexpected distribution of costs and benefits. Unlike the previous two scenarios, electrification induces increased financial expenditures by households, which spend over R400 million (US$53.16 million) more per year. Unsurprisingly, private sector firms enjoy financial benefits of almost R200 million (US$26.6 million) per year, with economic costs of about R20 million (US$2.66 million). The government should experience financial and economic benefits of about R450 million (US$59.8 million) and R375 million (US$49.8 million) per year.

The estimates were based on the assumptions shown in table 11.5; figures 11.3 and 11.4 report results.

Theoretically, the optimal level of intervention per emission is attained when the marginal private benefit provided by the emission (or the use of the dirty fuel) just matches the marginal abatement cost of the intervention being used to reduce it (as outlined in the body of the report). The mere reduction of a specific emission is not the ultimate goal of these interventions. The goal is to maximize net benefits for the South African public. To achieve this, a slightly different approach is useful. One begins by ranking technically feasible interventions by their benefit-to-cost

TABLE 11.5
Assumption Chart

Public sector as % of total health costs	82.5%
Number of households burning coal	691,598
Uptake: % households approached	55.0%
Therefore, number of households affected	380,379
Average annual coal saving per household	US$50.00
Capex cost per household	US$400.00
Construction costs as a percentage of capex costs for electricity	56.0%
Machinery costs as a percentage of capex costs for mines	44.0%
Construction costs as % of capex costs for others	10.0%
Machinery costs as % of capex costs for others	90.0%
VAT percentage (if included)	14.0%
Company tax rate (if included)	3.3%

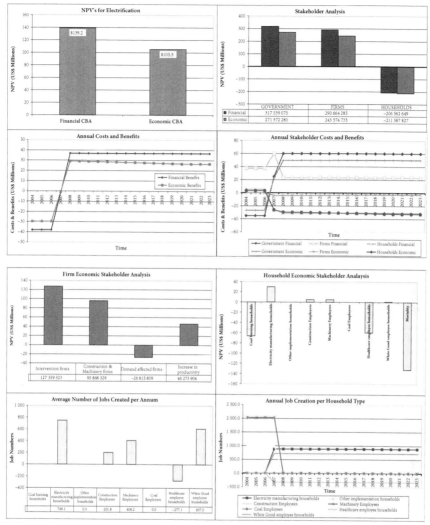

FIGURE 11.3 Electrification

ratios, and then establishing which are clearly and robustly justifiable. Of these, some will offer large and immediate benefits, while others will have smaller benefits. From a policy perspective, one would like to see the larger, strongly positive interventions pushed forward first. A graphical approach that uses both benefit-to-cost ratios and NPVs illustrates this (figure 11.5).

Table 11.6 summarizes the findings of the study. Interventions highlighted were dropped from the final analysis because they had been set in place before the completion of the study.

In terms of a net present value, the most valuable interventions were numbers 7 (housing insulation for 20 percent of *all* the country's fuel-burning urban households), 8 (electrification of coal-using households), 10 (coal stove maintenance

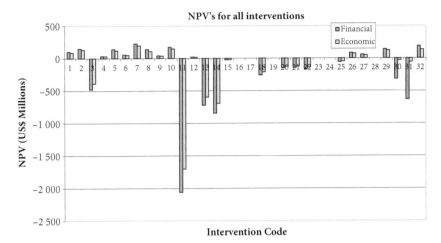

FIGURE 11.4 NPVs for All Interventions

and parts replacement for 20 percent of urban households), and 32 (electrification of paraffin-using households). However, from a benefit-cost perspective the most valuable interventions were numbers 1 and 2 (the education of households through the Basa Njengo Magogo project), followed by interventions 9 and 10 (maintenance of coal stoves, first of 5 percent and then 20 percent of stoves), and thereafter interventions 6, 7, 5, and 4—all involving the provision of housing insulation. Projects 8 and 32, the extensive electrification of households, despite relatively low benefit-to-cost ratios, achieved high net present values simply because of their magnitudes. Too strong a focus on NPV can be misleading, especially if financial resources are scarce, projects are not mutually exclusive, and large projects are "lumpy" (i.e., nonmodular and therefore coming online with significant excess capacity).

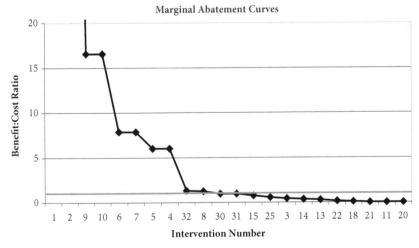

FIGURE 11.5 NPVs and Benefit-Cost Ratios of Interventions

TABLE 11.6

Net Present Values for All Interventions

	Net Present Values for All Interventions		
	Net Present Value s (US$ thousands)		Economic BC Ratio
Int	Financial	Economic	
1	Top-down ignition—plateau roll out	101	87	177.0
2	Top-down ignition—all conurbations	150	129	120.1
3	Low-smoke fuels	−479	−389	0.4
4	Housing insulation—5 percent of plateau fuel-burning households	35	30	6.0
5	Housing insulation—20 percent of plateau fuel-burning households	140	121	6.0
6	Housing insulation—5 percent of all fuel-burning households	57	49	7.9
7	Housing insulation—20 percent of all fuel-burning households	227	196	7.9
8	Electrification of households	139	105	1.2
9	Stove maintenance and replacement—5 percent of all households	43	37	16.5
10	Stove maintenance and replacement—20 percent of all households	173	148	16.5
11	Desulfurization of all power station emissions	−2,059	−1,703	0.0
12	Decommissioning of Pretoria West power station	21	18	20.8
13	Renewable wind energy (10,000 GWh block)	−724	−598	0.3
14	Renewable wind energy (37,000 GWh block)	−845	−695	0.3
15	Emission reductions for coal fired boilers	−25	−23	0.8
16	Iscor coke oven gas cleaning project			
17	Highveld Steel & Vanadium replace coal with CO			
18	Desulfurization of Sasol Secunda power station emissions	−258	−212	0.1
19	DME strategy to reduce sulfur content of petrol to 500ppm			
20	DME strategy to reduce sulfur content of petrol to 50ppm	−149	−126	0.0
21	DME strategy to reduce benzine content of petrol to 1 percent	−146	−124	0.0
22	DME strategy to reduce aromatics content of petrol to 35 percent	−165	−140	0.1
23	DME strategy to phase out leaded petrol	0	0	1.0
24	DME strategy to reduce sulfur content of diesel to <500ppm			
25	DME strategy to reduce sulfur content of diesel to 50ppm	−59	−49	0.5
26	DME strategy for all new vehicles to comply with Euro 2 standards	84	72	
27	DME strategy for all new vehicles to comply with Euro 4 standards	56	48	
28	Taxi Recapitalisation Programme			
29	DME strategy for all petrol vehicles to be Euro 2 compliant	141	121	
30	Conversion of 10 percent of petrol vehicles to LPG	−318	−30	1.0
31	Conversion of 20 percent of petrol vehicles to LPG	−635	−60	1.0
32	Electrification of paraffin burning households	188	133	1.3

Sensitivity Analysis

Sensitivity analysis was performed on the residential sector measures in order to determine whether changing assumptions regarding the value of a statistical life, productivity, and the discount rate would change the ranking of measures according to their benefit-to-cost ratios. It was found that changes in the discount rate, while naturally affecting the NPVs, did not change the benefit-cost rankings of the interventions, nor did they change the sign on any NPVs.

The ranking of interventions was also insensitive to the valuation of mortality and morbidity benefits. The analysis was rerun using the following assumptions:

1. Value of a statistical life set to zero
2. Value of a statistical life based on WTP measures for very-low-income households
3. Value of a statistical life based on WTP measures for low-income households
4. Value of a statistical life based on the human capital approach and assuming an average income per person of R26,000 (US$3,455.66), resulting in an NPV of earnings of R176,260 (US$23,426.72)
5. Value of a statistical life based on an average between WTP measures and average lifetime income stream

Using these assumptions the value of a statistical life was varied from zero to a maximum of R3,785,906 (US$503,185), which corresponds to the high WTP estimate for a medium-income individual. As table 11.7 indicates, the rankings were unaffected.

Sensitivity to assumptions concerning impacts on productivity was tested by first excluding productivity benefits altogether, and then doubling them (table 11.8).

The conclusion was similar to that for mortality: while useful to know and important to quantify, productivity assumptions, taken in isolation, neither change

TABLE 11.7

Sensitivity to Value of Statistical Life

Value of a Statistical Life											
Set to Zero		WTP–Very Low. Inc.		WTP–Low Inc.		WTP–Med Inc.		Income Stream		Avg. of WTP & Inc.. Str..	
Int. No.	B:C Ratio	Int. No.	B:C Ratio	Int. No.	B:C Ratio	Int. No.	B:C Ratio	Int. No.	B:C Ratio	Int. No.	B:C Ratio
1	164.1	1	168.2	1	172.9	1	189.0	1	166.0	1	177.0
2	112.1	2	114.6	2	117.6	2	127.6	2	113.3	2	120.1
9	15.7	9	15.9	9	16.3	9	17.4	9	15.8	9	16.5
10	15.7	10	15.9	10	16.3	10	17.4	10	15.8	10	16.5
6	7.4	6	7.6	6	7.7	6	8.3	6	7.5	6	7.9
7	7.4	7	7.6	7	7.7	7	8.3	7	7.5	7	7.9
5	5.8	5	5.8	5	5.9	5	6.2	5	5.8	5	6.0
4	5.8	4	5.8	4	5.9	4	6.2	4	5.8	4	6.0
8	1.4	8	1.4	8	1.4	8	1.5	8	1.4	8	1.5
3	0.3	3	0.3	3	0.3	3	0.32	3	0.3	3	0.3

TABLE 11.8
Sensitivity to Labor-Force Productivity

	Productivity						
Productivity as used		No productivity		Half productivity		Double productivity	
Int, No.	B:C Ratio	Int, No.	B:C Ratio	Int. No.	B:C Ratio	Int. No.	B:C Ratio
1	177.0	1	148.3	1	162.7	1	205.6
2	120.1	2	101.9	2	111.0	2	138.4
9	16.5	9	15.2	9	15.9	9	17.8
10	16.5	10	15.2	10	15.9	10	17.8
6	7.9	6	7.1	6	7.5	6	8.6
7	7.9	7	7.1	7	7.5	7	8.6
5	6.0	5	5.4	5	5.7	5	6.5
4	6.0	4	5.4	4	5.7	4	6.5
8	1.5	8	1.4	8	1.4	8	1.5
3	0.3	3	0.2	3	0.3	3	0.4

the ranking of interventions nor their signs. The low sensitivity of these results to productivity suggests that the analysis was robust with respect to assumptions concerning morbidity-related aspects such as the additional number of days off work for inpatients or the ratio of inpatients to outpatients or nonpatients.

Conclusion

In 2004 South Africa introduced a new piece of legislation—of which the country was, quite justifiably, proud. The National Air Quality Act was based on the received theory of externalities and on a known reality: that the bulk of emissions come from industry and electricity generation. Sadly, the skills and financial means required to monitor emissions and enforce regulations remain limited, while corporate inertia with respect to known wastage and economic inefficiency suggests that market-based tools may have little effect. When NEDLAC commissioned a set of studies into the efficacy of alternative interventions, the results were illuminating. The greatest benefit-to-cost ratio was not found in abating industrial emissions, despite their high levels, but in low-cost interventions that help curb the household emissions of those low-income households whose own members are the primary victims of poor air quality.

Acknowledgments

The author would like to thank Antony Boteng for his assistance.

Notes

1. Cost-benefit analysis is used widely in South Africa. The South African National Roads Agency uses it extensively and has its own cost-benefit analysis software package, and the Department of Water Affairs uses cost-benefit analysis as its standard. All significant

new greenfield (and many brownfield) projects in South Africa require an environmental impact analysis, and typically this contains an economic component. In most cases, this is designed around either CBA or multicriteria decision analysis.

2. The Tiebout Effect originally described municipalities that provide varying service levels for households and impose differing taxes on them. The households in turn have varying willingnesses to pay for services, and so locate themselves in the municipality that they believe provides the optimal mix of services and taxes. In the context of this paper, the Tiebout Effect suggests that business firms will respond in a similar fashion to jurisdictional differences: where regulations vary across a region, firms will locate themselves so as to minimize costs.

3. NEDLAC describes itself as "the vehicle by which government, labour, business and community organisations...seek to cooperate, through problem-solving and negotiation, on economic, labor and development issues," in its Founding Declaration. It was launched in February 1995 and based on the National Economic Development and Labour Council Act No. 35 of 1994.

4. It is important to stress that the process of ranking in order of benefit-to-cost ratio does not mean that projects with a high net present value but low positive benefit-to-cost ratio should be ignored, but that high benefit-to-cost projects represent low-hanging fruit, which should be picked first.

Bibliography

Baumol, William J., and Wallace E. Oates. 1988. *The Theory of Environmental Policy.* 2nd ed. New York: Cambridge University Press.

Blackman, Allen, Stephen Newbold, Jhih-Shyang Shih, and Joe Cook. 2000. "The Benefits and Costs of Informal Sector Pollution Control: Mexican Brick Kilns." Discussion Paper 00–46, Resources for the Future.

Burtraw, Dallas, Alan Krupnick, Erin Mansur, David Austin, and Deirdre Farrel. 1997. "The Costs and Benefits of Reducing Acid Rain." Discussion Paper 97–31-REV, Resources for the Future.

Howells, Mark I., and John A. Laitner. 2005. "Industrial Efficiency as an Economic Development Strategy for South Africa." Presented at the 2005 American Council for an Energy-Efficient Economy (ACEEE) Summer Study on Energy Efficiency in Industry, New York, July 19–22, 2005.

Howells, Mark I., Alison G. Hughes, Ajay Trikam, and M. Aberg. 2003. "Energy Efficiency Savings: Projections." Unpublished Report No. 2.2.3–06. Department of Minerals and Energy, Pretoria.

Howells, Mark I., and John A. Laitner. 2003. "A Technical Framework for Industrial Greenhouse Gas Mitigation in Developing Countries." Presented at the 2003 ACEEE Summer Study on Energy Efficiency in Industry, New York, July 29–August 1.

Jones-Lee, Michael W. 1989. *The Economics of Safety and Physical Risk.* Oxford: Basil Blackwell.

Jones-Lee, Michael W., M. Hammerton, and P. R. Phillips. 1985. "The Value of Safety: Results of a National Sample Survey." *Economic Journal* 95 (377): 49–72.

Jones-Lee, Michael W., Graham Loomes, Deirdre O'Reilly, and P. R. Phillips. 1993. *The Value of Preventing Non-fatal Road Injuries: Findings of a Willingness to Pay National*

Sample Survey. Transport Research Laboratory (TRL) Contractor Report No. 330. Crowthorne, Berkshire, UK: TRL.

Krupnick, Alan, Anna Alberini, Maureen Cropper, Nathalie Simon, Bernie O'Brien, Ron Goeree, and Martin Heintzelman. 2000. "Age, Health, and the Willingness to Pay for Mortality Risk Reductions: A Contingent Valuation Survey of Ontario Residents." Discussion Paper 00–37, Resources for the Future.

Mullins, David, Gerhard Gehrig, G. E. Mokaila, David Mosaka, Lindi Mulder, and Evert Van Dijk. 2002. *A Manual for Cost Benefit Analysis in South Africa with Specific Reference to Water Resource Development.* South African Water Research Commission (WRC) Report No. TT 177/02. Pretoria: WRC.

Pearce, David W., and A. Howarth. 2000. *Technical Report on Methodology: Cost Benefit Analysis and Policy Responses.* National Institute for Public Health and the Environment (RIVM) Report No. 481505020. Bilthoven, The Netherlands: RIVM.

Jones-Lee, Michael W., M. Hammerton, and P. R. Phillips. 1985. "The Value of Safety: Results of a National Sample Survey." *Economic Journal* 95 (377): 49–72.

Jones-Lee, Michael W., Graham Loomes, Deirdre O'Reilly, and P. R. Phillips. 1993. *The Value of Preventing Non-fatal Road Injuries: Findings of a Willingness to Pay National Sample Survey.* Transport Research Laboratory (TRL) Contractor Report No. 330. Crowthorne, Berkshire, UK: TRL.

Krupnick, Alan, Anna Alberini, Maureen Cropper, Nathalie Simon, Bernie O'Brien, Ron Goeree, and Martin Heintzelman. 2000. "Age, Health, and the Willingness to Pay for Mortality Risk Reductions: A Contingent Valuation Survey of Ontario Residents." Discussion Paper 00–37, Resources for the Future.

Mullins, David, Gerhard Gehrig, G. E. Mokaila, David Mosaka, Lindi Mulder, and Evert Van Dijk. 2002. *A Manual for Cost Benefit Analysis in South Africa with Specific Reference to Water Resource Development.* South African Water Research Commission (WRC) Report No. TT 177/02. Pretoria: WRC.

Pearce, David W., and A. Howarth. 2000. *Technical Report on Methodology: Cost BenefitAnalysis and Policy Responses.* National Institute for Public Health and the Environment (RIVM) Report No. 481505020. Bilthoven, The Netherlands: RIVM.

U.S. Environmental Protection Agency (EPA). 1999a. *Benefits and Costs of the Clean Air Act, 1990–2010.* Washington, D.C.: EPA.

U.S. Environmental Protection Agency (EPA). 1999b. *OAQPS Economic Analysis Resource Document.* Washington, D.C.: EPA.

U.S. Environmental Protection Agency (EPA). 2002. *Methodologies for the Benefit Analysis of the Clear Skies Initiative: Technical Addendum.* Washington, D.C.: EPA.

12

Economic Costs of Air Pollution in Singapore
Euston Quah and Wai-Mun Chia

Understanding the costs associated with abatement strategies and the benefits that might result from reducing the quantities of pollutants in the atmosphere is crucial to the process of formulating long-term air pollution control strategies. In many economically developed countries, cost-benefit analysis is commonly used to compare the costs and benefits associated with alternative air pollution control strategies.

Before the work of Euston Quah and Tay Liam Boon in 2003, however, no study had thoroughly analyzed the economic costs associated with particulate matter air pollution in Singapore.[1] Therefore, government agencies could, at best, only monitor how far the actual air quality in Singapore diverged from guidelines set by the U.S. Environmental Protection Agency (EPA) or the World Health Organization (WHO). Without monetary valuation of health effects, however, it is impossible to compare the costs of reducing the risk of ill health from air pollution to the benefits on a single scale. This makes comparative analysis of alternative programs extremely difficult, or even impossible.

Motivated by a desire to calculate the economic costs of air pollution in Singapore, Quah and Boon modified a previously conducted "burden of disease analysis"[2] to include social costs. Their method involved a three-step procedure (Quah and Boon 2003). First, they determined the ambient concentrations of the air pollutants. Second, they used a damage function approach using dose-response relationships to estimate health impacts—specifically the increases in mortality and morbidity resulting from air pollution. Third, they calculated the monetary values of mortality and morbidity. However, since neither formal epidemiological nor health valuation studies have been conducted in Singapore, they extrapolated the health effects estimates from other contexts, and adapted and transferred the economic values associated with mortality and morbidity effects from studies in developed countries using the benefit-transfer approach. This method provides for the assessment of benefits in one site (the policy site) using figures obtained from another site (the study site).

This chapter updates Quah and Boon's previous work from 2003, focusing on estimating the health cost of particulate matter (PM_{10}). We assess and evaluate the economic costs of air pollution on public health in 2009 based on the newly revised air quality guidelines by the WHO. Table 12.1 summarizes the EPA standard and the WHO air quality guidelines (WHO-AQGs). These guidelines

TABLE 12.1
Ambient Air Quality Standards for PM10 (µg/m³)

Pollutant	Averaging Time	USEPA Standard	WHO Air Quality Guidelines (AQG)
PM₁₀	Annual Average	50	70—Interim Target 1
			50—Interim Target 2
			30—Interim Target 3
			20—AQG
	24-hour Average	150	150—Interim Target 1
			100—Interim Target 2
			75—Interim Target 3
			50—AQG

are set based on current scientific evidence relating to air pollution and its health impacts. The WHO-AQGs were developed for worldwide use to support actions targeted toward achieving air quality that protects public health. The guidelines were first produced in 1987, then revised in 1997, and subsequently updated in 2005. These current and more stringent guidelines are preferable because they are based on a greater body of evidence, especially with regard to particulate matter. This new evidence indicates that there are risks to health at concentration levels observed in many cities in developed countries. Recent studies, using more refined and improved methods, show that an increasing range of adverse health effects has been linked to air pollution at ever-lower concentrations.

How does Singapore fare in terms of PM_{10} control? Figure 12.1 shows the annual average level of PM_{10} from the period of 1993 to 2009 in Singapore.

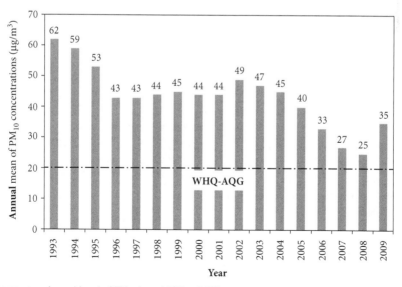

FIGURE 12.1 Annual Level of PM₁₀ from 1993 to 2009

Generally, the annual average level is declining. The annual means of the ambient concentrations of PM_{10} range from the lowest of 25 μg/m³ in 2008 to the highest of 62 μg/m³ in 1993. Figure 12.1 demonstrates that the levels of PM_{10} in the ambient air in Singapore were well below the EPA standard of 50 μg/m³ while well above the WHO-AQGs of 20 μg/m³. The annual level of PM_{10} in 2009 remains higher than the WHO-AQGs by 15 μg/m³.

Estimating and Evaluating the Health Effects and Economic Costs Associated with Changes in Air Pollution

METHODOLOGY FOR ESTIMATING THE HEALTH EFFECTS

To estimate the value of health effects associated with changes in air pollution, this study relies on dose-response coefficients borrowed from the existing literature. A damage function approach using dose-response relationships is used to estimate the health effects of air pollution reduction. This approach is a commonly used methodology in the literature (Ostro et al. 1996; Ostro 1994; Künzli et al. 1999; 2000; see also NEPC 2002). Strengths of this approach include simplicity and ease of interpretation.

In estimating the health effects associated with changes in air pollution, three main factors must first be determined: (1) the dose-response relationships, (2) the population at risk, and (3) the relevant change in air pollution.

The first step is to develop estimates of the effects of air pollution on various health outcomes. Health impacts are estimated using the dose-response functions that link variations in the ambient levels of certain pollutants to health effects. This step involves calculating the partial derivative or slope of the dose-response function to provide an estimate of the change in a given health effect associated with a change in air quality.

The second step involves multiplying this partial derivative or slope of the dose-response function by the population at risk from the air pollutant under consideration. For certain pollution-related health effects, this may include the entire population exposed to air pollution; for other effects, there may be particularly sensitive subgroups, such as children, the elderly, and asthmatics.

The final step in estimating the health effects of air pollution involves the change in air quality under consideration. Usually this is the deviation between the actual ambient levels of air pollutants and the acceptable average concentration of air pollutants. Therefore, the relevant change in air pollution is dependent on both the policy alternative under consideration along with the state of scientific knowledge embedded in existing guidelines. The relevant change in air pollution can be calculated by considering either the change from current air pollution levels to some ambient air quality standard or a given percentage of reduction, such as 10 percent. In this study, since the annual level of PM_{10} in 2009 is 15 μg/m³ higher than the WHO-AQGs of 20 μg/m³, we examine a change of 15 μg/m³. Generally, the estimated health effects can be represented by the following relationship:

$$\Delta H_i = b_i \times POP_i \times \Delta A, \tag{12.1}$$

where ΔH_i is the change in population risk of health effect i, b_i is the slope from the dose-response curve for health impact i, POP_i is the population at risk of health effect i, and ΔA is the change in ambient air pollutant under consideration. In this study, ΔA is 15 μg/m³.

When careful data collection to establish local dose-response functions is costly and time consuming, risk analyses from other policy sites can be used. Though such a transfer of dose-response relationships has its limitations, this method serves to reduce individual study-level uncertainty. While one study that finds a statistically significant association between a health effect and a specific air pollutant does not prove causality, the inference of causation is strengthened. This is particularly true if (1) the epidemiological results are duplicated across other studies, (2) a range of effects is found for a given air pollutant, and (3) the results are supported by other human clinical and/or animal toxicology literature.

This chapter uses the extensive literature linking high concentrations of air pollution to adverse health effects and establishes that the evidence accumulated to date can be used with sufficient confidence. While some uncertainties remain, it is implicitly assumed that the relationship between the levels of air pollution and subsequent health effects in developed countries, where most of these studies have taken place, can be extrapolated to estimate the health impacts in Singapore. Because Singapore's progress is similar to that of many developed countries, there are arguably negligible differences between the foreign and Singaporean populations in baseline health status, access to health care, demographics, and occupational exposure, among other factors. It is therefore likely that the estimates obtained closely reflect the actual health effects in Singapore.

METHODOLOGY FOR EVALUATING THE MORTALITY COST

To complete the estimation for health effects, it is possible to calculate the economic valuation of this effect (V_i). The valuation is developed from estimates of the willingness to pay for reducing risk to attach values to the expected changes in premature mortality, and a modified cost-of-illness (COI) approach to value changes in morbidity. Thus, the change in value (ΔV_i) of the health effects due to the change in air pollution under consideration is the summation of all effects and is represented by

$$\Delta T = \sum V_i \Delta H_i.$$

$$(12.2)$$

However, there is still a great deal of uncertainty about much of the research that forms the basis for these estimates. Recognizing this, upper- and lower-bound estimates are provided to indicate the ranges within which the actual health effects are likely to fall.

Although the valuation of mortality and morbidity is very important to cost-benefit analysis of air pollution programs, relevant studies are more limited in scope than the literature on health effects. The present study estimates the unit values of mortality and morbidity using the benefit-transfer approach, where unit values of mortality and morbidity are transferred from developed countries. It is noted that when the benefit-transfer approach is used, it is assumed that the stated preferences of people in developed countries are similar to that of the people in Singapore. Transfer of values may neglect factors that would cause people to value health differently. Despite these limitations, there are advantages for analysts of the benefit-transfer approach, in terms of time and resources.

For the case of estimating the value of statistical life in Singapore (VSL_{Sing}), we use the value of statistical life in the United States (VSL_{US}). The adjustment to the VSL_{US} is done based on the purchasing power parity (PPP) estimates of the per capita gross domestic product (GDP) of Singapore and the United States. Thus the VSL_{Sing} is computed based on the following expression:

$$VSL_{Sing} = VSL_{US} \times \left(\frac{GDP_{Sing}}{GDP_{US}} \right)^{e}, \qquad (12.3)$$

where VSL_{Sing} is the value of statistical life for Singapore in 2009, VSL_{US} is the value of statistical life for the United States in 2009 prices, GDP_{Sing} is the per capita GDP of Singapore in 2005, GDP_{US} is the per capita GDP of the United States in 2009, and e is the elasticity of willingness to pay with respect to income.

METHODOLOGY FOR EVALUATING THE MORBIDITY COSTS

Similarly, the costs of morbidity are computed based on the unit economic values of morbidity estimated in the United States (Rowe et al. 1995). Adjustments are also made to these transferred-unit economic values for the estimation of morbidity costs for Singapore. The morbidity unit value for Singapore is expressed as follows:

$$MUV_{Sing} = MUV_{US} \times \left(\frac{GDP_{Sing}}{GDP_{US}} \right)^{e}, \qquad (12.4)$$

where MUV_{Sing} is the morbidity unit value for Singapore in 2009, MUV_{US} is the morbidity unit value for the United States in 2009 prices, GDP_{Sing} is the GDP of Singapore in 2009, GDP_{US} is the GDP of the United States in 2009, and e is the elasticity of willingness to pay with respect to income.

Estimating the Health Effects and the Unit Values of Health Effects Associated with Changes in PM$_{10}$

Extensive epidemiological studies have been conducted in attempts to estimate the health effects associated with changes in PM$_{10}$. Evidence suggests that the studies linking particulate matter to mortality generate remarkably consistent results. Ostro (1994) suggests some morbidity coefficients for respiratory hospital admissions (RHA), emergency room visits (ERV), restricted activity days for adults (RAD), lower respiratory illness for children (LRI), asthma attacks, respiratory symptoms, and chronic disease. These are summarized in table 12.2 (see also Khatun 1997).

Following the dose-response function in equation (1), the number of premature mortalities due to PM_{10} can then be expressed as

$$\Delta Mortality = b \times \Delta A \times (1/100) \times CMR \times POP, \qquad (12.5)$$

where b is the mortality coefficient based on some epidemiological studies from the existing literature, and b has its lower, central and upper estimates, CMR is the crude mortality rate in Singapore, POP is the population exposed to risk, and 1/100 converts percentage to absolute numbers.

We use equation (5) to estimate the mortality effect of PM_{10} in Singapore. The population exposed to particulate air pollution is equal to the total population in Singapore. This assumption can be justified by its small geographical area. According to the Singstat Time Series Online, the crude mortality rate is 4.3 per 1,000 and the size of population is 4,987,600 in 2009. The number of children under the age of fifteen is 667,900, and the number of elderly people age sixty-five and above is 330,100. The number of adults between the ages of fifteen and sixty-four is 2,735,900. Total population in 2009 includes both residents and nonresidents. The resident population includes Singapore citizens and noncitizen permanent residents.

Based on this information, the mortality effect of PM_{10} in Singapore can be estimated by the relationship in equation (5). In this case,

$$\Delta \text{Mortality} = 0.096 \times 15 \times (1/100) \times 0.0043 \times 4{,}987{,}600 = 309.$$

Similarly, the upper and lower estimates of the total number of mortalities are determined to be 418 and 199, respectively.

Table 12.3 presents the results of the estimation of the morbidity effects of particulate air pollution in Singapore using equation (1) and the morbidity coefficients in table 12.2. For the estimation of the number of restricted activity days due to PM_{10}, only the adult population is considered because they are the main

TABLE 12.2
Mortality and Morbidity Effects of a 1 µg/m³ Change in PM10 Using Benefit Transfer

Mortality and Morbidity	Lower Estimate	Central Estimate	Upper Estimate
Mortality	0.062	0.096	0.13
RHA/100,000	0.657	1.2	1.73
ERV/100,000	11.6	23.7	35.4
RAD	0.029	0.058	0.078
LRI	0.001	0.0017	0.0024
Asthma attacks	0.033	0.058	0.196
Respiratory symptoms	0.08	0.168	0.256
Chronic bronchitis/100,000	3	6.12	9.3

Source: Ostro (1994); Khatun (1997).

TABLE 12.3

Mortality and Morbidity Effects of a 15 μg/m³ Change in PM10 Using Benefit Transfer

	Lower Estimate (# of cases)	Central Estimate (# of cases)	Upper Estimate (# of cases)
Mortality	199	309	418
Morbidity			
RHA	492	898	1,294
ERV	8,678	17,731	26,484
RAD (thousands)	1,190	2,380	3,201
LRI	10,019	17,031	24,044
Asthma attacks (thousands)	2,469	4,339	14,664
Respiratory symptoms (thousands)	5,985	12,569	19,152
Chronic bronchitis	2,244	4,579	6,958

Source: Author's calculations.

participants in the workforce. Only those under the age of fifteen are considered in the estimation of the incidence of lower respiratory illness in children. All other estimates are computed based on the entire population in Singapore.

In estimating the mortality cost, we propose to transfer the estimates from countries where willingness-to-pay studies have been conducted to Singapore using equation (3). The VSL_{US} in 2009 prices is calculated to be $7.0725 million.[3] This figure is obtained by converting the VSL_{US} in 2008, $6.9 million, to the 2009 prices using an annual inflation rate of 2.5 percent in the United States. In 2009, per capita GDP at PPP was 50,522.72 (in international dollars) and 46,380.91 (in international dollars) for Singapore and the United States, respectively. Hence, the ratio of Singapore GDP per capita to United States GDP per capita is 1.0893. As for the elasticity of willingness to pay with respect to income, e, we assume a value of 0.32 (Quah and Boon 2004). This gives us a VSL_{Sing} of $7.2684 million. Similarly, in estimating the morbidity costs, again we propose to transfer the estimates from countries where morbidity unit values have been computed for Singapore

TABLE 12.4

Unit Values for Morbidity Effects in 2009 Using Benefit Transfer (US$)

	Lower Estimate	Central Estimate	Upper Estimate
Morbidity			
RHA	9,820.9	19,641.6	29,462.5
ERV	370.8	741.5	1,112.3
RAD	NA	69.2	NA
LRI	NA	NA	NA
Asthma attacks	18.0	50.2	80.2
Respiratory symptoms	8.0	14.0	20.1
Chronic bronchitis	NA	193,739.1	NA

using equation (4). In estimating the cost of reduced activity days for adults, it is assumed that 20 percent of reduced activity is realized in lost working days and the remaining 80 percent loss is equal to one-third of the daily average wages. Assuming $1 is equal to 1.4034 Singaporean dollars, the monthly average wage in Singapore during 2009 is about $2,964. Assuming that people work for twenty days in a month, the daily wage rate in 2009 is $148. Thus, the cost of reduced activity days for adults in Singapore is $164.61 million (central estimate). Other unit values of morbidity are calculated and summarized in table 12.4.

Economic Costs Associated with a 15 µg/m³ Change in PM$_{10}$

Based on equation (2), the economic costs associated with changes in PM$_{10}$ can be computed. In calculating the central estimate of the mortality cost, we multiply the number of cases of mortality due to a 15 µg/m³ change in PM$_{10}$ by the VSL calculated for Singapore in 2009 using the benefit-transfer approach. This is calculated as 309 × $7,268,400 = $2.25 billion. Similarly, the estimates of the morbidity costs are summarized in table 12.5.

Table 12.6 presents the total estimates for mortality cost, morbidity cost, and total health damage cost (mortality and morbidity) associated with particulate air pollution in Singapore. The total estimated economic cost of health damage

TABLE 12.5

Costs of Mortality and Morbidity Due to a 15 µg/m³ Change in PM10 in 2009 (US$ millions)

	Lower Estimate	Central Estimate	Upper Estimate
Mortality	1,449.71	2,244.72	3,039.72
Morbidity			
RHA	4.8	17.6	38.1
ERV	3.2	13.1	29.5
RAD	82.3	164.6	221.4
LRI	NA	NA	NA
Asthma attacks	44.5	217.7	1,176.4
Respiratory symptoms	48.1	175.9	384.8
Chronic bronchitis	NA	911.6	NA

TABLE 12.6

Total Costs of Health Effects Due to a 15 µg/m³ Change in PM10 in 2009 (US$ millions)

	Lower Estimate	Central Estimate	Upper Estimate
Mortality	1,449.71	2,244.72	3,039.72
Morbidity	182.93	1,500.54	1,850.22
Total Costs	1,632.64	3,745.26	4,889.94
Ratio of total costs to GDP	0.89	2.04	2.66

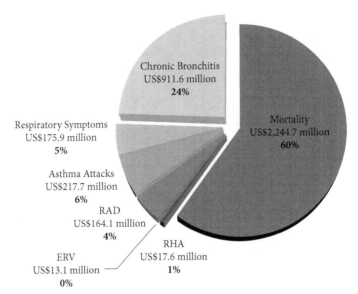

FIGURE 12.2 Composition of the Health Costs Attributable to Air Pollution, by Cause, in 2009

attributable to PM$_{10}$ in Singapore is $3.75 billion (central estimate), which is about 2.04 percent of total GDP of Singapore in 2009.

The health cost estimates appear to be sufficiently robust. Figure 12.2 is based on these estimates and attributes 60 percent of health costs to premature mortality, while various illnesses are responsible for the remaining 40 percent. Chronic bronchitis and asthma attacks are the largest contributors to the morbidity cost.

Conclusion

This chapter quantifies the health costs associated with exposure to air pollution in Singapore. It serves as an important guide for policymakers because the estimates reflect the magnitude of the problem and provide the necessary perspective so that air pollution control may be prioritized relative to other interventions that improve public health. Based on this study, it is found that the current concentrations of PM$_{10}$ in Singapore are above the WHO-AQGs. PM$_{10}$ concentrations in 2009 are below all three WHO interim targets but are above the WHO-AQGs by 15 µg/m^3. The analysis suggests that the health costs associated with a 15 µg/m^3 change in PM$_{10}$ is $3.75 billion (central estimate), which is about 2.04 percent of total GDP of Singapore in 2009. Therefore, the overall health costs associated with PM$_{10}$ are not small compared to the overall GDP. The study suggests that current air quality is not sufficient to protect the public from substantial adverse health costs.

Further control of air pollution through more stringent regulation of emissions is likely to result in health benefits. Such regulations are likely to restrict other economic activities and hence may lead to economic costs. This aspect of analysis is beyond the scope of the present study but must be seriously evaluated in cost-benefit analyses of any air pollution control programs. Ultimately, cost-benefit analysis will favor those interventions that maximize net benefits, a calculation that considers both the economic losses and the public health gains of regulating harmful emissions.

Notes

1. In Singapore, throughout most of the 1980s and 1990s, cost-effectiveness analysis was the most commonly used economic analysis in policymaking. However, the government has become more interested in cost-benefit analysis because of the demand for accountability and the increased pressure on the government budget to pursue the different objectives of various ministries. In recent years, cost-benefit analysis has been more important to determine the allocation of funding.

2. Burden of disease analysis is a comprehensive and comparable assessment of mortality and health complications caused by disease and injury.

3. All monetary figures are in U.S. dollars.

Bibliography

Khatun, Fahmida Akter. 1997. "The Cost of Particulate Air Pollution in Dhaka City." *Bangladesh Development Studies* 25 (1–2): 95–124.

Künzli, Nino, Reinhard Kaiser, Sylvia Medina, Michael J. Studnicka, Olivier Chanel, Paul Filliger, Max Herry, et al. 2000. "Public-Health Impact of Outdoor and Traffic-Related Air Pollution: a European Assessment." *Lancet* 356 (9232): 795–801.

Künzli, Nino, Reinhard Kaiser, Sylvia Medina, Michael J. Studnicka, G. Oberfeld, and Fritz Horak. 1999. "Health Costs Due to Road Traffic-Related Air Pollution: An Impact Assessment Project of Austria, France and Switzerland." Air Pollution Attributable Cases, Technical Report on Epidemiology. Prepared for the WHO Ministerial Conference for Environment and Health, London, June.

National Environment Protection Council (NEPC). 2002. *Exposure Assessment and Risk Characterization for the Development of a PM2.5 Standard.* Canberra: NEPC.

Ostro, Bart D. 1994. "Estimating Health Effects of air Pollutants: A Methodology with an Application to Jakarta." World Bank Policy Research Working Paper No. 1301.

Ostro, Bart D., Jose Miguel Sanchez, Carlos Aranda, and Gunnar S. Eskeland. 1996. "Air Pollution and Mortality: Results from a Study of Santiago, Chile." *Journal of Exposure Analysis and Environmental Epidemiology* 6 (1): 97–114.

Quah, Euston, and Tay Liam Boon. 2003. "The Economic Cost of Particulate Air Pollution on Health in Singapore." *Journal of Asian Economics* 14 (1): 73–90.

Rowe, Robert, Lauraine G. Chestnut, Carolyn Lang, Steve Bernow, and David White. 1995. *New York State Environmental Externalities Cost Study*, vol. 1. Dobbs Ferry, N.Y.: Oceana Publications.

13

The Challenges of Estimating Compliance Costs in Developing Countries

EXPERIENCES FROM BRAZIL

Emilio Lèbre La Rovere, Martha Macedo de Lima Barata, and Amaro Olimpio Pereira Jr.

Estimating the cost of compliance with a public policy goal in the context of developing and emerging economies poses a number of methodological and data estimation challenges. This chapter illustrates the point in the case of environmental policies in Brazil, particularly policies regarding climate change mitigation.

There is growing awareness in the country—within government and academia, as well as broader society—about the need to transition to a green economy and to lower greenhouse gas (GHG) emissions. Initially, proposed reductions in GHG emissions in Brazil were attributable to plans to increase national energy security through the production of ethanol. Legislators launched the National Alcohol Program, called PROALCOOL, in 1975. This program reduced the need to import energy, created local jobs, and reduced GHG emissions: it was thus understood to be a win-win economically, socially, and environmentally. Subsequently, however, as international pressure began to mount about deforestation in the Amazon, and the fear of nontariff barriers for countries without GHG emissions reduction targets augmented, Brazil committed to reducing its emissions even further. The government and representatives of national business sectors supported the Ministry of Environment in its adoption of voluntary targets for reduced GHGs before the Fifteenth Conference of the Parties (COP15) of the United Nations Framework Convention on Climate Change (UNFCCC). This choice of targets put Brazil in a leading position among other participating countries.[1] The targets were established through studies conducted by government agencies in collaboration with the scientific community and under the leadership of the Ministry of Environment.

This chapter begins by discussing the GHG mitigation goals for 2020, as adopted by the Brazilian government. Then it presents an estimate of the costs of complying with the mitigation targets set for the power generation sector. These costs are estimated in the medium to long run (2020–2030), and the results are derived primarily from a previous study carried out by CentroClima.[2] Finally, the chapter delves into a short discussion of the main methodological issues faced in attempting to estimate mitigation costs, including the use of different cost concepts. The mitigation cost estimates calculated for the Brazilian power sector in this chapter provide relevant inputs to the design of policy tools in support of the country's mitigation goals.

Perspectives on the Mitigation of Climate Change: Brazil's Voluntary Goals

The UNFCCC seeks to stabilize the concentration of GHGs in the atmosphere at a safe level that will not compromise food safety and will allow for the natural adaptation of ecosystems. Without such stabilization, higher GHG emissions will lead to global temperature changes that could, in turn, undermine food security by increasing the occurrence of extreme weather and reducing agricultural yield. The extent of the impacts caused by climate change is still uncertain at the regional level, which makes it difficult to define where the safe level of concentration lies. However, most studies (including the Intergovernmental Panel on Climate Change [IPCC] reports and the Stern review) show that the impacts of climate change will grow faster at global average temperatures higher than 2°C to 3°C compared to preindustrial levels (IPCC 2007, 38). Based on these studies, the Copenhagen Declaration released at the end of COP15 established that the UNFCCC should aim to limit global temperature increase to 2°C at the most.[3]

Brazil's Federal Decree No. 7390 regulates the National Climate Change Policy Law and establishes voluntary goals to limit Brazil's GHG emissions, as summarized in table 13.1.[4]

Deforestation of the Amazon is still the largest source of GHG emissions in Brazil; therefore, curbing the country's GHG emissions depends substantially on curtailing deforestation. The National Plan on Climate Change set the ambitious goal of reducing deforestation to 30 percent of the average rate between 1996 and 2005 of 19,500 km² per year by 2014.[5] Results in recent years demonstrate that this

TABLE 13.1

Brazil's GHG Emissions and Mitigation Actions in 2020

Emissions(Mt CO$_2$eq/year)	1990 Inventory data	2005 Inventory data	Variation 1990–2005	2020 Business-as-Usual Scenario	Variation 2005–2020 BAU	Avoided Emissions in 2020
Land use change	746	1,268	70%	1404	11%	
Amazon				948		
Savannahs				323		
Others				133		
Agriculture/husbandry	347	487	41%	730	50%	
Energy	215	362	68%	868	140%	234
Industrial	55	86	39%	234	172%	
TOTAL	1,362	2,203	62%	3,236	47%	1,168 to 1,259

Source: MCT (2010); Federal Decree No. 7390, 2010.

goal is feasible so long as the government takes the necessary measures to regulate land use. Deforestation rose to its height in 2004, when it reached 27,400 km² per annum; however, afterward it began to decline. In 2007 it was 11,500 km² per annum, which accounted for a reduction of approximately 500 MtCO₂ per annum in greenhouse gas emissions between 2005 and 2007. After rising to 12,000 km² in 2008, the downward trend resumed, with 7,500 km² in 2009 and 6,500 km² in 2010—the lowest area of deforestation recorded since record-keeping began twenty-two years ago (La Rovere 2009; INPE 2011).

The goal set for the agricultural sector is very ambitious, considering the recent growth in the country's agribusiness exports. Average annual export value between 1997 and 2010 increased by 11 percent per year, and between 2009 and 2010 it increased by 18 percent (MAPA 2011). These increases could affect the environment because higher demand may require larger areas of production, and higher production may induce higher emissions. Agriculture and livestock are crucial economic activities in Brazil. In 2008 agribusiness accounted for over 23 percent of national GDP, so land use policies are very relevant (CEPEA 2012). That said, Brazil still has much land available for expansion of agricultural production without turning to deforestation.

Economically feasible mitigation alternatives for the agricultural sector already exist and have great potential. These alternatives include the recovery of degraded pasture land; agro-forestry schemes; more intensive cattle-raising activities (given the current low average ratio of 0.5 heads per hectare); and biologic nitrogen fixation and low-tillage techniques, which already cover more than twenty million hectares in the country and are rapidly spreading. These goals set by the government were based upon the results of extensive research undertaken by Embrapa, a research wing of the Ministry of Agriculture, Livestock, and Food Supply in Brazil, whose work is focused on devising innovative techniques that benefit both agriculture (farming, livestock, forestry, and agribusiness) and the environment.[6]

The emissions from industrial processes and waste disposal contribute minimally to the total amount of GHG emissions. The business-as-usual scenario in this sector already shows a low-growth trend, and voluntary commitments already aim to keep GHG emissions roughly constant. There are also feasible mitigation options in these sectors, such as the capture, burning, and energy use of biogas in sanitary landfills.

The case of the energy sector deserves special attention. Emissions attributable to the use of fossil fuels, in the form of oil, natural gas, and coal, have been increasing significantly. These fuels play a basic role in running the modern part of the Brazilian economy, such as industry and transportation, as well as agribusiness and the residential, commercial, and service sectors. Fossil fuels' share in power generation has also been increasing, starting from a low departure level, to one that now complements Brazilian hydropower, which has traditionally been the dominant energy source for electricity generation. Thus, because of the increased burning of fossil fuels, the emissions of GHGs, especially carbon dioxide (CO_2), showed a high growth rate in the period between 1990 and 2005, reaching a level 68 percent higher in 2005 than in 1990. Indeed, economic growth, rising urbanization, and the dominance of road transportation in the country are the driving forces behind increasing fossil energy consumption and associated CO_2 emissions. Unlike in other sectors, the business-as-usual scenario projected by the government shows a significant increase in emissions: a rise of nearly 140 percent by 2020 compared to 2005—that is, 2.5 times the level of 2005 emissions in this sector (see table 13.1).

As far as mitigation is concerned for this sector, target levels of hydroelectric power generation, energy efficiency, and ethanol production were included in the Ten-Year Energy Expansion Plan for 2020.[7] Other mitigation actions included the production and use of biodiesel in a 5 percent blend with diesel oil by 2020 (B5) and the increase in power generation from other renewable sources such as small hydropower plants, biomass (especially sugarcane bagasse), and wind energy. The achievement of the mitigation scenario goals will require the implementation of public policy tools capable of stimulating the substitution of renewable energy sources for the use of fossil fuels. This need will be even more acute in driving the Brazilian economy toward a low-carbon path, as fossil fuels will ultimately become the most significant source of GHG emissions, as they are elsewhere in the industrial world.

Estimates of the Compliance Costs for Mitigating GHG Emissions from the Brazilian Power Sector

The estimated costs of compliance for the Brazilian power sector with a voluntary GHG mitigation target are presented here, according to research carried out by CentroClima/COPPE/UFRJ in the framework of the Cost Assessment of Sustainable Energy Systems (CASES) project.[8] The efficiency of adopting a carbon tax to reach the goal proposed by the Brazilian government is assessed, in addition to its impact on the country's energy tariffs.

The CASES project was supported by the European Commission and jointly developed by various independent and academic research institutions from Europe and the developing world under the coordination of Fondazione Eni Enrico Mattei.[9] It contributed to the assessment of different policies that could be implemented in order to foster greater energy efficiency, using as a reference a consistent and detailed picture of the items that make up the social costs (external costs borne by society) and private costs (costs borne by companies) incurred by electricity power generation.

To make it a useful decision-making tool, one of the project's goals was to contribute to the debate on GHG emissions mitigation options. This debate is naturally premised on the consideration of many factors, including the dynamics of the energy scenario, associated social costs, and various country-specific variables.

The methodological approach of the CASES project included a survey and analysis of data on alternative electric power scenarios up to 2030, and considered an increase in costs owing to the adoption of GHG emissions mitigation options in power generation for each country. The Brazilian contribution to the study consisted of building a scenario for the expansion of power generation capacity with the adoption of a carbon tax. The idea for this approach was that damages caused from energy-intensive activities are not integrated into pricing systems, but policy should aim to ensure that prices reflect total costs. To internalize these costs, a carbon tax must be levied.

The necessary carbon tax level was calculated using the EcoSense computer model. This model is a tool that standardizes calculations of fuel-cycle externalities. It looks at the pathway of emissions to different receptors (humans, animals, plants, crops, etc.) and works according to the aptly named Impact Pathway Approach. This was developed within the framework of the External Costs of Energy and uses a bottom-up, site-specific approach to place a monetary value on diverse negative impacts on global temperature, human health, biodiversity, and other factors.[10] Two emissions scenarios are created in every case: the reference scenario and the case scenario. The model proceeds in the following stages:

1. Definition of the activity to be assessed and the background scenario in which the activity is embedded; definition of important impact categories and externalities
2. Estimation of the impacts or effects of the activity (in physical units). In general, the impacts allocated to the activity are based on the difference between the impacts of the scenario with the activity and without the activity
3. Monetization of the impacts, leading to external costs
4. Assessment of uncertainties; sensitivity analysis
5. Analysis of the results; drawing of conclusions

It should be noted that the calculation of the marginal costs of damage caused by climate change is extremely uncertain, because the impacts of GHG emissions are global, spread over time, and are still not completely known. This makes the cost range of the damage extremely wide. Given these uncertainties, the CASES study adopted a carbon tax value based on the mitigation costs associated with setting the global economy on a low-carbon path (see table 13.2). This global scenario assumed an emissions path in accordance with the emissions reduction targets of the Kyoto Protocol, extended up to 2050 as in the study of the New Energy Externalities Development for Sustainability project.[11]

This tax would increase the variable operation and maintenance costs of power generation plants that emit GHGs. As emissions from hydropower plants are not being considered, the tax on GHG emissions was added to the cost of fossil fuel–firing thermopower plants, according to the different GHG emission factors associated with coal, diesel oil, fuel oil, and natural gas.

TABLE 13.2

Tax Imposed on GHG Emissions of Power Generators in Brazil (euro-2005/ton)

	2010	2015	2020	2025	2030	2040	2050
CO_2	21	21	21	23	30	46	61
CH_4	441	441	441	483	630	966	1281
N_2O	6510	6510	6510	7130	9300	14260	18910

Source: La Rovere, Barata, and Villar (2008).

The reference scenario used in the research was based on the study *Development First: Linking Energy and Emission Policies with Sustainable Development*, also developed by CentroClima/COPPE/UFRJ within the framework of the Development and Climate Project (La Rovere et al. 2007).

The development of scenarios for the Brazilian economy was based on the following assumptions for the 2005 to 2030 period:[12]

- GDP—annual average growth of 4 percent
- Population—average annual growth of 1.09 percent
- Hydropower potential—tapping in on 191 GW of the 230 GW total available
- Nuclear—1.3 GW of the Angra III Nuclear Plant will come onstream in 2014, taking into account the construction schedule approved by the National Energy Policy Council. A further expansion of nuclear power generation through the construction of two more 1 GW nuclear power facilities before 2030 was also included.

This set of assumptions was used to simulate a reference scenario for the Brazilian energy system up to 2030, running the Model for Energy Supply System Alternatives and their General Environmental Impacts, originally developed at the International Institute for Applied System Analysis for the optimization of energy systems (Messner and Strubegger 1995).

The result of the expansion in Brazilian power generation is presented in table 13.3.

GHG emissions were calculated according to the Intergovernmental Panel on Climate Change methodology, using GHG emissions factors customized to Brazilian conditions as in the National Communication to the UNFCCC (MCT 2010). The results are presented in table 13.4.

In the mitigation scenario, a carbon tax is applied from 2010 onwards. As a result, with the increase in power generation costs of thermopower plants induced by the carbon tax, the new optimum solution scenario points to a different mix of primary energy sources of generation, as shown in table 13.5.

In this scenario, hydropower capacity, and, to a lesser extent, nuclear power, will replace fossil sources. It should be emphasized that in the referenced scenario,

TABLE 13.3

Power Generation Capacity in Brazil (GW): Reference Scenario, 2010–2030

Year	Coal	Oil	Natural Gas	Hydropower	Nuclear	Biomass	Wind	Total
2010	2.42	1.43	13.50	78.74	1.97	6.44	0.65	105.15
2015	2.42	1.43	17.50	95.13	1.97	10.44	1.35	130.23
2020	2.42	1.93	18.00	121.60	3.31	13.44	1.85	162.55
2025	3.42	1.93	20.00	150.06	3.31	13.44	2.85	195.01
2030	3.42	2.43	22.00	169.82	3.31	15.44	2.85	219.27

Note: Hydropower also includes small hydropower plants.
Source: La Rovere et al. (2007).

TABLE 13.4

GHG Emissions from Power Generation in Brazil: Reference Scenario, 2010–2030 (MMtCO2eq = million tons of CO2eq)

Year	Coal	Oil	Natural Gas	Total CO_2
2010	16.61	4.46	31.93	53.00
2015	16.61	4.46	41.39	62.46
2020	16.61	6.02	42.57	65.20
2025	23.47	6.02	47.30	76.79
2030	23.47	7.58	52.03	83.09

Source: La Rovere et al. (2007).

TABLE 13.5

Power Generation Capacity in Brazil (GW): Mitigation Scenario, 2010–2030

Year	Coal	Oil	Natural Gas	Hydro power	Nuclear	Biomass	Wind	Total
2010	2.42	1.93	13.50	78.74	1.97	6.44	0.65	105.65
2015	2.42	1.93	15.50	98.13	1.97	10.44	1.35	131.73
2020	2.42	1.93	15.50	126.60	3.31	13.44	1.85	165.05
2025	2.42	1.93	15.50	160.06	3.31	13.44	2.85	199.51
2030	2.42	1.93	16.50	178.38	4.31	15.44	3.85	222.83

Source: La Rovere, Barata, and Villar (2008).

TABLE 13.6

Power Generation Costs and GHG Emissions: Reference and Mitigation Scenarios in Brazil, 2015–2030

Year	Generation (TWh)	Cost (US$ millions–2005)		GHG Emissions (MMtCO$_2$eq)		Change in Mitigation Scenario Compared to Reference Scenario (%)	
		Reference	Mitigation	Reference	Mitigation	Cost	Emissions
2015	648.15	4,293	4,522	62.46	59.29	5,33	−5,09
2020	808.23	5,873	6,074	65.20	59.29	3,42	−5,15
2025	964.19	5,732	6,016	76.79	59.29	4,95	−22,80
2030	1 083.39	4,172	4,358	83.09	61.65	4,46	−25,98

Source: Adapted from La Rovere, Barata, and Villar (2008).

both biomass and small hydropower generation capacity expand until reaching the potential assumed in the study. This shows that, with the exception of wind power plants, renewable power generation sources considered in this study are already competitive in Brazil. In fact, results of recent energy auctions in the country, where the plants that offer the lowest energy production prices are chosen, prove that these sources of renewable energy are already competitive.

The mitigation scenario results show that taxing GHG emissions makes thermopower plants less competitive, with declining shares of power generation during the period. Thus, GHG emissions in 2030 are projected to decline from 83 MMtCO$_2$eq to 62 MMtCO$_2$eq, a reduction of 25 percent. The increase in costs of total power generation is less than 5 percent, as shown in table 13.6.

According to these results, the inclusion of carbon taxes in the generation cost of power may contribute toward achieving Brazil's mitigation goal for 2020, allowing for greater generation from hydropower plants and other low-carbon sources of energy. However, the carbon tax level simulated in this study would induce a minor contribution (5 $MMtCO_2$eq per annum) to the GHG emissions reduction required from the power generation sector in 2020 (around 100 $MMtCO_2$eq per annum; see table 13.1). It should, however, be taken into account that the governmental scenario did not include the number of hydropower plants that are already part of the scenario in our study. Naturally, the baseline assumptions included in our scenario strongly influence the mitigation response to a given carbon tax level. In the case of Brazil, a key assumption is the level of hydropower generation already considered as the baseline. This assumption involves a high level of subjectivity. It is also worth noting that Brazil is endowed with a great variety of primary energy resources, but that their exploitation would require large investments and cause significant environmental impacts (Pereira et al. 2008). In the case of hydropower, Brazil has barely tapped 30 percent of its overall hydropower potential, but the bulk of the untapped potential is located in the highly environmentally sensitive Amazon region.

Based on the results presented above, the additional costs and the GHG emissions reductions induced by a carbon tax can be calculated. Figure 13.1 shows the total cost of avoided emissions: the horizontal axis represents total avoided emissions and the vertical axis represents the additional total cost of this reduction between 2015 and 2030, compared to the reference scenario. Thus, during the 2010 to 2030 period, 46 $MMtCO_2$ could be avoided at a total cost of $1.2 billion, or an average abatement cost of $26/tCO_2$ for this period.

Interestingly, the total reduction cost curve is practically linear. This is explained by the large availability of renewable energy resources (mainly hydropower) along

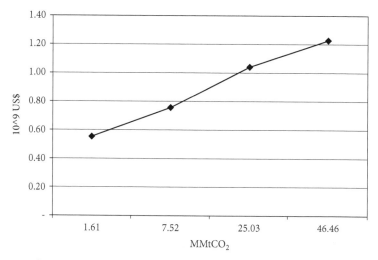

FIGURE 13.1 Total Cost of GHG Emissions Reduction in the Mitigation Scenario

Source: La Rovere, Barata, and Villar 2008

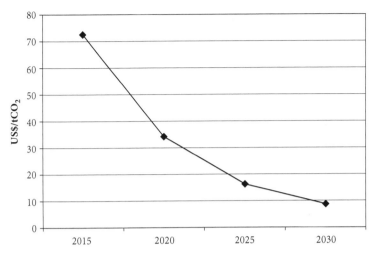

FIGURE 13.2 Marginal Abatement Cost Curve in the Mitigation Scenario
Source: La Rovere, Barata, and Villar 2008

the time horizon considered in the study, implying that there is no upward pressure on energy production costs. This is also indicated by the negative slope of the marginal reduction cost curve, shown in Figure 13.2.

It should be emphasized, however, that in our scenario, hydropower generation already faces progressively higher marginal costs, given its location in environmentally sensitive areas and the long distance from the Amazon region to main consumer centers. Increased production will entail not only the adoption of stricter environmental impact mitigation measures, but also substantial investment in power transmission lines.

The study was complemented by considering the impact of a carbon tax on the cost of new electricity generated. To this end, the total generation cost of new plants in the mitigation scenario was compared with the cost of the other scenario. This analysis provides a proxy for the carbon tax impact on the electricity price for final consumers, assuming that the pricing policy would follow the marginal cost of expansion. Figure 13.3 shows this impact.

It can be seen in figure 13.3 that the impact of a carbon tax may increase costs by almost 9 percent in 2030, because of the higher hydropower expansion costs. The costs are much lower in the first years of the analysis, so this cost increase would not hamper the achievement of Brazilian mitigation goals in 2020. Even if this increase may not look particularly high, the difficulty of introducing additional taxes should not be underestimated, as no matter what the current tax burden is, it tends to be difficult to raise taxes. Additionally, since revenue is not equally distributed, taxes are levied on only a small portion of the population. This will make it politically difficult for the government to pass a law imposing another tax. One possible way to increase social acceptability of a carbon tax would be to recycle its revenues back to the taxpayers, either through government transfers, as proposed by Timilsina and Shrestha (2007), or by channeling

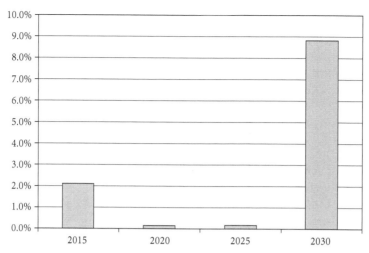

FIGURE 13.3 Carbon Tax Impact on New Electricity Generation Costs (%)

Note: Hydropower also includes small hydropower plants.

Source: La Rovere, Barata, and Villar 2008

revenue to a fund dedicated to making investments in renewable energy sources. In Brazil, however, because of legal restrictions, taxes cannot be earmarked for specific expenditures; thus, it would be difficult to use these funds to foster renewable energy.

Conclusion

This chapter addressed some methodological issues associated with estimating mitigation costs in the Brazilian power sector, within the framework of the voluntary targets for GHG emissions announced by the Brazilian government in 2009.

Some of these issues were initially discussed in the early work of the IPCC (Hourcade et al. 1996), including the distinction between different cost concepts: from the engineering costs estimated at the project level to the macroeconomic costs as a percentage of GDP loss estimated by "top-down" models (Margulis et al. 2009). At an intermediate level, "bottom-up" models can estimate mitigation costs for a given sector, as illustrated in this chapter for the Brazilian power generation case. The costs of GHG emissions mitigation for the energy sector have also been discussed in a number of studies (Halsnaes et al. 1998), including several in Brazil.[13] Key assumptions that strongly influence the final results of these studies tend to include the mitigation options already included in the reference case (baseline scenario), the magnitude of the mitigation goal, the time horizon to reach the mitigation goal, and the order in which mitigation measures are introduced.

In spite of all their uncertainties, these estimations remain relevant for designing the most appropriate policy tools to drive market forces into a low-carbon development path. The primary economic tools applied to this end are carbon taxes and cap-and-trade programs, which both have well-known pros and cons (Krugman 2010).

Economic policy tools can be complemented effectively by command-and-control measures, which are particularly relevant in the context of developing countries. The main challenge for developing countries lies in establishing policies and measures that combine different tools to ensure that voluntary mitigation goals are met in due time, with the least negative economic, social, and environmental impacts. All the while, these policies should induce technological advancement and shift consumption patterns toward a low-carbon economy.

Since energy prices will likely rise in the future, it is important to act now in order to lessen the negative impacts on society in the long run. The Brazilian experience has also shown that tackling climate change can be advantageous for technological innovation, the economy, and the social and environmental balance of the country. Given this history, other countries may also have an interest in carving out a position of leadership by adopting voluntary targets for reductions in GHG emissions, independent of any international influence.

Notes

1. United Nations Framework on Climate Change, Conference of Parties 15th Session (COP15), Dec 7–18, 2009, *Copenhagen Accord*, 2/CP.15, U.N. Doc. FCCC/CP/2009/11/Add.1 (March 30, 2010).

2. Centre for Integrated Studies on Climate Change and the Environment (Centro Clima/COPPE/UFRJ) Energy Planning Program, Institute for Research and Post-Graduate Studies of Engineering, Federal University of Rio de Janeiro, Brazil.

3. COP15, *supra* note 1, at 4.

4. Brazil Federal Decree No. 7390/2010 (December 9, 2010).

5. Institui a Política Nacional sobre Mudança do Clima—PNMC e dá outras Providências, Federal Law No. 12187 (December 2009).

6. Embrapa, Ministério da Agricultura, Pecuária e Abastecimento. 2011.

7. Ministerio de Minas e Energia, 2007, Empresa de Pesquisa Energética, *Plano Nacional de Energia 2030*.

8. European Commission Coordination Action, Cost Assessment for Sustainable Energy Systems (CASES).

9. For more information on the research institutes involved, see European Commission Coordination Action, Cost Assessment for Sustainable Energy Systems (CASES).

10. European Commission, ExternE, *Externalities of Energy: A Research Project Series of the European Commission*.

11. New Energy Externalities Development for Sustainability Consortium, NEEDS Project.

12. The assumptions on GDP and population are consistent with those used by the Brazilian government when establishing the voluntary GHG emissions limitations presented in table 13.1. However, the governmental reference scenario only included hydropower

plants already under construction in 2009, leading to higher thermopower generation and GHG emissions, as will be discussed later.

13. Brazilian studies include La Rovere et al. (1994); La Rovere, Legey, and Miguez (1994); La Rovere et al. (2002); La Rovere et al. (2006); La Rovere et al. (2007); Pereira et al. (2008); McKinsey (2009); de Gouvello (2010).

Bibliography

Centro de Estudos Avançados em Economia Aplicada (CEPEA). 2012. *Produto Interno Bruto (GDP) do Agronegocio Brasileiro 1994-2011.* Saõ Paolo: CEPEA.

de Gouvello, Christophe. 2010. *Estudo de Baixo Carbono para o Brasil.* Washington, D.C.: World Bank.

Halsnaes, Kirsten, Daniel Bouille, Emilio Lèbre La Rovere, Steven Karekezi, Willy Makundi, Vute Wangwarcharakul, and John M. Callaway. 1998. "Sectoral Assessment: The Energy Sector." In *Mitigation and Adaptation Cost Assessment: Concepts, Methods and Appropriate Use,* 65–98. Roskilde: United Nations Environment Programme.

Hourcade, Jean-Charles, R. Richels, J. Robinson, W. Chandler, O. Davidson, J. Edwards, D. Finon, et al. 1996. "Estimating the Costs of Mitigating Greenhouse Gases." In *Climate Change 1995: Economic and Social Dimensions of Climate Change,* 263–96. Cambridge: Cambridge University Press.

Instituto Nacional de Pesquisas Espaciais (INPE). 2011. *Project PRODES Data on Amazon Deforestation.* São Jose dos Campos: INPE.

Intergovernmental Panel on Climate Change (IPCC). 2007. *Climate Change 2007: Synthesis Report.* Geneva: IPCC.

Krugman, Paul. 2010. "Building a Green Economy." *New York Times Magazine,* April 11.

La Rovere, Emilio Lèbre. 2009. "Perspectivas para a Mitigação das Mudanças Climáticas: Ações do Brasil e no Mundo." In *IV Conferência Nacional de Política Externa e Política Internacional (CNPEPI),* 145–58. Rio de Janiero: CNPEPI.

La Rovere, Emilio Lèbre, and Branca Bastos Americano. 2002. "Domestic Actions Contributing to the Mitigation of GHG Emissions from Power Generation in Brazil." *Climate Policy* 2 (2–3): 247–54.

La Rovere, Emilio Lèbre, L. F. L. Legey, and J. D. G. Miguez. 1994. "Alternative Energy Strategies for Abatement of Carbon Emissions in Brazil: A Cost-Benefit Analysis." *Energy Policy* 22 (11): 914–24.

La Rovere, Emilio Lèbre, Amaro Olimpio Pereira Jr., Ana C. Avzaradel, André F. Simões, Carolina B. S. Dubeux, Jacqueline B. Mariano, Jeferson B. Soares, et al. 2006. *Greenhouse Gas Mitigation in Brazil: Scenarios and Opportunities Through 2025.* Washington, D.C.: Center for Clean Air Policy.

La Rovere, Emilio Lèbre, Amaro Olimpio Pereira Jr., André Felipe Simões, André Santos Pereira, Amit Garg, Kirsten Halsnaes, Carolina Burle Schmidt Dubeux, et al. 2007. *Development First: Linking Energy and Emission Policies with Sustainable Development for Brazil.* Roskilde: UNEP Risø Centre.

La Rovere, Emilio Lèbre, M. A. Santos, R. Schectman, L. P. Rosa, and L. F. Legey. 1994. "Case-Study: Brazil." In *UNEP Greenhouse Gas Abatement Costing Studies,* vol. 2, 1–17. Roskilde: UNEP Risø Centre.

Margulis, Sergio, Carolina B. S. Dubeux, and Jacques Marcovitch, eds. 2009. *Economia da Mudança do Clima no Brasil: Custos e Oportunidades.* São Paulo: IBEP Gráfica.

McKinsey & Co. 2009. *Caminhos para uma Economia de Baixo Emissão de Carbono no Brasil.* São Paulo: McKinsey & Co.

Messner, Sabine, and Manfred Strubegger. 1995. *User's Guide for MESSAGE III*, WP-95–69. Laxenburg, Austria: International Institute for Applied Systems Analysis.

Ministério da Agricultura, Pecuária e Abastecimento (MAPA). 2011. *AgroStat Brazil Data on Agribusiness Exportation.* Brasília: MAPA.

Ministerio da Ciencia e Tecnologia do Brasil (MCT). 2010. *Second National Communication to the UNFCCC.* Brasília: MCT.

Pereira, Amaro Olimpio, Jr., Jeferson Borghetti Soares, Ricardo Gorini de Oliveira, and Renato Pinto de Queiroz. 2008. "Energy in Brazil: Toward Sustainable Development?" *Energy Policy* 36 (1): 73–83.

Timilsina, Govinda R., and Ram M. Shrestha. 2007. "Alternative Tax Instruments for CO_2 Emission Reduction and Effects of Revenue Recycling Schemes." *Energy Studies Review* 15 (1): Art. 5.

PART FIVE

Case Studies in Protection of Natural Resources

14

Improving Cost-Benefit Analysis in the Assessment of Infrastructure Projects in the Brazilian Amazon

Marcos Amend, Leonardo Fleck, and John Reid

From the viewpoint of neoclassical economics, public policy interventions are justified only as instruments to correct market failures—situations in which free markets are unable to maximize social welfare. Such failures must be corrected in order to maximize economic and social well-being. Government interventions, such as building a road, providing police forces, or imposing taxes on pollution, can all be seen as strategies for correcting market failures.

When it comes to the environment, market failures such as externalities and incomplete markets can create distortions that lead to inefficient resource allocation, which in turn reduces overall social welfare. An externality occurs when the actions of a market participant, such as a consumer or producer, affect the well-being of a person or entity who was not a party to that transaction and who has not been compensated for those effects. Government interventions are justified in seeking to reduce negative environmental effects to economically efficient levels.

In this context, cost-benefit analysis and cost-effectiveness analysis are important tools to improve the selection of appropriate policies. Cost-benefit analysis compares alternative policy options in terms of their net impacts on social welfare (net costs or net benefits). Cost-effectiveness analysis has a narrower scope and consists of evaluating the costs associated with accomplishing a given nonmonetary goal, such as vaccinating a certain number of people.

Both of these frameworks can incorporate environmental issues in decision making, even though their methods have significant limitations for determining fairness and estimating intangible costs and benefits (Nogueira and Pereira 1999). While some analysts go no further than using cost-benefit analysis to assess economic efficiency, many commentators stress the importance of supplementing a standard cost-benefit analysis with risk analysis (e.g., Belli et al. 2001; Campbell and Brown 2003) and distributional analysis (e.g., Jenkins and Harberger 2000; Belli et al. 2001).

Because a substantial portion of Brazil is covered by the Amazon rain forest, and because of the particular environmental value of that natural resource, environmental decision making in Brazil is closely linked with the Amazon. In particular, projects that seek to expand development within the Amazon will typically carry substantial environmental costs, which should be taken into consideration. The traditional criteria established by neoclassical economics demand that cost-benefit analyses account for the complete range of effects that are anticipated by the decision maker.

Civil society actors in Brazil have played an important role in shaping environmental policymaking, including decisions that involve development in the Amazon. When these actors have had access to more sophisticated tools for policy analysis, including cost-benefit analysis, they have been better positioned to press their arguments in a way that can influence these debates. Expanding the capacity of civil society actors to engage with and use economic arguments is an important challenge for the future of cost-benefit analysis in Brazil.

This chapter canvasses several case studies where researchers from the Conservation Strategy Fund (CSF) examined the costs and benefits of government-backed infrastructure projects with significant impacts on the Amazon. In all of these cases, the analyses that were conducted on behalf of the project were inadequate and failed to take into account a range of important considerations. We close with a discussion of the main shortcomings associated with official cost-benefit analyses of infrastructure projects in the Brazilian Amazon.

Case Studies

RECONSTRUCTION OF THE PORTO VELHO-MANAUS (BR-319)

The Porto Velho-Manaus highway, known as BR-319, was constructed and paved in the 1970s as part of the military government's strategy to occupy the Amazon rain forest. The road received little use and was built to relatively weak specifications. The government neglected to maintain it, and by 1986, the road had become impassable. In 2005, the government announced its intention to rebuild the road in order to link Manaus, the capital city of the state of Amazonas, to the rest of the country by road. Currently the city is only connected to Southern Brazil by airplane or boat (Fleck 2009).

Over the past three decades, the construction and paving of roads in the Amazon has been the subject of intense national and international debate. Roads can be important for regional economic development (Perz et al. 2007), but are among the main factors leading to deforestation and environmental degradation (Pfaff 1999; Kaimowitz and Angelsen 1998; Soares-Filho et al. 2006).

The reconstruction of BR-319 was part of a package of infrastructure projects contained in a set of national policies adopted in 2007 called the Growth Acceleration Program (PAC), which was aimed at speeding Brazil's economic growth. The program had a strong focus on infrastructure investments for the period 2007 to 2010 (Ribeiro 2007).

One critical gap in the plans for BR-319 was the lack of a separate cost-benefit analysis by the project's official executing agency, the National Department of

Transport Infrastructure (DNIT). The agency has since explained that because the project was not new, but rather the restoration of an existing highway, and because projects under the PAC were considered to be such high public priorities that they did not require feasibility or similar analytic studies (a legally contestable claim), no cost-benefit analysis was needed.

A cost-benefit analysis was done, however, as part of the environmental impact assessment process. While the Brazilian Institute of Environment and Renewable Natural Resources (IBAMA), has the power to request that a cost-benefit analysis be done as part of the environmental impact assessment, it typically does not do so, and did not do so in this case. The voluntary inclusion of a cost-benefit analysis by DNIT in the environmental impact assessment was an important step and very unusual.

Nonetheless, the cost-benefit analysis that was conducted contained several rather grave conceptual and methodological flaws that ended up biasing the results in favor of the reconstruction project. For example, the analysis included the use of market prices with no economic price adjustment to reflect externalities, and the analysis did not consider demand relationships (the price elasticity of demand). These flaws contributed to a bias that overestimated the total benefits of the project.

Estimations of project benefits also failed to consider differences between transportation costs for various project alternatives. Normally, road reconstruction projects generate benefits that are estimated by comparing the transportation costs for travel along the road to the transportation costs of making the same trip by air or river. This analysis instead estimated benefits by multiplying the potential price of the bus ticket for a future trip between Manaus and Porto Velho, 877 kilometers away, by the estimated number of people that would use the road. But by failing to take into account alternative transportation methods, wealth transfers in the form of private revenues for bus companies were substituted for social benefits, an approach that is inconsistent with well-accepted methodologies (Belli et al. 2001).

A similar error occurred with estimating benefits for cargo transportation. The analysis assumed that certain commodities—such as grains, wood, and fuels— that are currently transported through the nearby Madeira waterway would be redirected to the highway once it was reconstructed. This assumption was almost certainly mistaken. The Madeira waterway is considered a model for cargo transportation in Brazil, and data suggests it would offer much lower transportation costs for bulk cargo than would be available on the new highway.

Analysts did not use the best available information to estimate demand for the reconstructed road or the deforestation that would result. Rather than using publicly available data from national transportation agencies on current transit in the region, the analysts made assumptions about several key figures. The resulting estimates about future demand were likely overestimates. The number of passengers that were projected to travel the road during its first year of operation was much higher than all of the passengers currently traveling in all available modes between all of the major destinations to be served by the project. In projecting the amount of deforestation that would occur under a business-as-usual scenario, the analysts failed to use the sophisticated model of project-induced deforestation created by Soares-Filho et al. (2006) that was well known at the time (and was even cited in the EIA), but which would have estimated larger impacts from the project.

One of the biggest flaws in the analysis was the treatment of mitigation strategies. Three different scenarios were envisioned: strong governance (avoiding 95 percent of potential deforestation); average governance (avoiding 75 percent of potential deforestation); and weak governance (avoiding 50 percent of potential deforestation). The analysts recommended that the project should only be implemented under the strong governance scenario, which was the only one predicted to achieve economic efficiency. Yet no scenario was based on well-supported deforestation models, and there was no description of the specific government actions required under the strong government scenario to produce such a large effect. The analysis also did not include the costs of avoiding the deforestation under this preferred scenario, although the expense associated with protecting 83,000 km^2 of land in such a remote region would likely be significant.

The controversy over paving a road in one of the most pristine parts of the Amazon mobilized civil society and inspired nongovernmental actors to conduct their own assessments of the project's costs and feasibility. Fleck (2009) conducted an independent cost-benefit analysis that considered two scenarios: the first assessed only the direct costs of the road; the second assessed those costs as well as the costs of externalities associated with deforestation. These externalities included the values for carbon sequestration, the value of biodiversity for pharmaceutical research (Simpson, Sedjo, and Reid 1996) and nonuse, or existence, value (Horton et al. 2002; Seroa de Motta 2002). For all externalities, both domestic and global costs were included. Table 14.1 shows the results of Fleck's first analysis (without externalities). Table 14.2 shows the results of Fleck's second, more comprehensive analysis. For both cases the real discount rate adopted is 12 percent and the time horizon is twenty-five years.

The government decided to pursue a strategy of mitigating the highway's negative environmental impacts by creating a mosaic of protected areas nearby. A working group was created to estimate the costs of creating and implementing twenty-nine protected areas that would stave off deforestation and related economic losses to acceptable levels. According to the group, the cost to protect these

TABLE 14.1

Summary Results of the Scenario without Externalities (US$ millions)

	Costs	Benefits		
	Reconstruction, bridges, and maintenance	Local benefits	Regional benefits	Total
NPV $_{12\%, 25 \text{ years}}$	(240.94)	25.15	53.60	(162.19)
IRR (%)				0.2%
Benefit/cost ratio				0.33

Source: Fleck (2009).

TABLE 14.2
Summary Results of the Scenario with Externalities (US$ millions)

	Costs			Benefits	
	Reconstruction, bridges, and maintenance	Economic and environmental costs	Total	Regional benefits	Total
NPV $_{12\%,\ 25\ years}$	(240.94)	(971.08)	25.15	53.60	(1,133.27)
IRR (%)				<0%	
Benefit/cost ratio				0.065	

Source: Fleck (2009).

areas was $185 million for the first ten years, in present-value terms (ICMBio et al. 2009). Fleck and Amend (2009) conducted an independent analysis, adjusting these costs to reflect the same time period that had been used to calculate the impacts of the reconstruction project (twenty-five years). They found that the total costs of the government's mitigation strategy were $233 million. Thus, even if the developer successfully avoided all environmental costs, the net present value of the project would be negative $395 million, with costs from construction and environmental mitigation totaling $473 million, and benefits of only $78 million. In addition, there would still be environmental damage outside the protected areas.

THE BELO MONTE HYDROELECTRIC DAM

The Belo Monte hydroelectric complex is located on the Xingu River in the Amazon Basin, in an area called Volta Grande. It is a federal government project carried out by private companies under a concession agreement. When the project was proposed in 2002, it was estimated to cost $3.16 billion, although that number has been vigorously debated, with estimates ranging to over $17 billion (Sousa and Reid 2010). The installed electricity generating capacity was projected to be 11,181.3 MW (Eletronorte. 2002). The project's design had also changed substantially from initial proposals put forth in the late 1980s. The most significant change was the shrinking of the reservoir from 1,225 km^2 to 440 km^2, mainly on account of environmental issues. The generating capacity, however, stayed the same despite the reduction in water storage.

The debate over the project's economic feasibility added force to civil society actors that opposed the dam. Some civil society groups have fought the Belo Monte project, citing its negative impacts on the environment, local communities, and indigenous people. The civil society groups raised awareness over the course of several years to call attention to the negative impacts associated with the project.

When the contract was opened to bidders in 2010, interested contractors complained that the government had underestimated necessary investment costs. This prompted the government to enhance bidding incentives by offering additional credit subsidies and tax breaks. Still, only one consortium was interested, which cast further doubt on the project's feasibility.

There was a great deal of uncertainty associated with the costs and timetable for the project. Completing the dam required moving more earth than it took to build the Panama Canal. Given its massive scale, the project raised a wide range of environmental concerns that could bring significant costs and delays.

To help clarify the debate, a group of analysts led by Jose de Sousa conducted an alternative cost-benefit analysis (Sousa et al. 2006). Their analysis used, as a starting point, the official study conducted by Eletronorte, the state-owned company, and evaluated three different scenarios: (1) the baseline scenario that did not consider externalities; (2) a scenario that included the costs of externalities; and (3) a scenario that included the costs of externalities and adopted an alternative model of water flow.[1] The results in each scenario are shown in table 14.3. The discount rate used was 12 percent.

As indicated in the table, including externalities only minimally altered the results of the analysis. This suggests that those particular externalities—which were by no means an exhaustive list—could be readily compensated for using net revenues generated by the project. The alternative water flow model, which resulted in a lower power generation scenario, completely undermines the viability of the venture.

Sousa's team also examined how sensitive its analysis was to underlying assumptions and conducted risk assessments of the project using Monte Carlo simulations. The variables tested were the length of the construction period, the cost of construction, the energy price, and the amount of energy that would be generated. Unsurprisingly, the vast difference in the amount of energy that was anticipated to be generated under the competing water flow models was extremely important for outcomes. For each simulation, the team calculated the probability of the project generating a positive net present value, finding that in the most pessimistic analysis, there was only a 2.28 percent chance of a positive outcome, and only a 39.11 percent chance of a positive outcome in the most optimistic scenario.

Although Eletronorte criticized these findings when they were published, the lack of private interest in the auction for the project seemed to affirm the study's main thrust concerning the sizable risks involved. Even with large government subsidies, only one consortium had submitted a proposal. And given the potential for only thin profit margins for private investors, the partial value calculated for the negative externalities—$189 million—is much more relevant.

PAVING THE CUIABÁ-SANTARÉM (BR-163) HIGHWAY

The project to pave the BR-163 highway, which links Cuiabá, the capital of Mato Grosso, to the city of Santarém in Pará, has the primary goal of reducing the cost

TABLE 14.3

Cost-Benefit Analysis of Viability of Belo Monte

Indicator	Scenario 1	Scenario 2	Scenario 3
NPV (US$)	1,624,880,117	1,436,159,306	−3,558,796,969
IRR	14.86%	14.53%	3.87%

of transporting soybeans grown in central Brazil to the ports of Santarém. The national highway also serves as a connection between the Amazon region and the more populated areas of the country. It was initially built in the 1970s as part of a program to develop lands in the Amazon. Although initial construction finished in 1972, more than half of its total length remains unpaved (956 of 1,756 km).

Current efforts to pave the missing portion are led mainly by soybean producers in the state of Mato Grosso. BR-163 can also be used as an alternative route for transporting goods from the industrial city of Manaus to the important markets of southern and southeastern Brazil. Soy producers also expressed interest in investing privately in the paving project. Alencar et al. (2005) found the private benefits of the paved highway to be $166 million over twenty years of analysis, using a 12 percent discount rate. The results are presented in table 14.4.

Despite its potential to generate cost savings for producers and importers, the project has come under strong criticism due to deforestation that would take place along its route. Indeed, the mere announcement of the project spurred some level of deforestation. A common way to establish ownership of government lands is to occupy it with cattle or agriculture, and the potential for increased land values along the newly paved route spurred some efforts to create a foundation for future claims.

In 2004, an interministerial working group released a Sustainable Development Plan for managing the area likely to be impacted by the project. The plan proposed various government actions in the region to prevent deforestation. Alencar et al. (2005) estimated potential deforestation induced by the highway—borrowing figures from Soares-Filho et al. (2006)—and projected scenarios with and without government intervention. Based on these scenarios, the authors calculated the economic costs of forest loss, which are presented in table 14.5. The actual economic loss could be considerably lower than these estimates, however, because they are based on average costs rather than marginal environmental costs in an area with abundant forests. Nevertheless, they provide a rough approximation of the general size of the externalities.

As the tables show, the costs of externalities outweigh the benefits that would be generated by the project. However, since the lion's share of negative

TABLE 14.4

Privately Commissioned Cost-Benefit Analysis of the BR-163

Present Values	US$ Millions
Transport savings—soybeans	303.8
Transport savings—Manaus goods	128.5
Total benefits	432.3
Construction costs	(206.0)
Maintenance costs	(60.3)
Total costs	(266.3)
Benefits–costs	166.0

Source: Alencar et al. (2005).

TABLE 14.5

Total Costs of Externalities

Scenarios	Present Value for 20 Years (US$ millions)
Without governance	1491.4
Cost of carbon emissions from deforestation	845.1
Loss of hydrological recycling	144.0
Loss of Option Value and Existence Value	485.4
Cost of wildfires	16.9
With governance	608.1
Cost of carbon emissions from deforestation	293.2
Loss of hydrological recycling	70.7
Loss of option value and existence value	238.3
Cost of wildfires	5.9

Source: Adapted from Alencar et al. (2005).

externalities—including carbon emissions, biodiversity existence values, and option values—will accrue to actors outside Brazil, they may have limited persuasive value in national policymaking.

The distribution of costs and benefits from the project was also an issue. The benefits of the highway would be highly concentrated among certain private interests, while the costs would be shared globally among disparate social groups. The authors of the study proposed various strategies for transferring some of the project's private benefits into conservation and regional sustainable development. A "green toll" was proposed that would be collected on each ton of cargo that was transported along the road, thereby diverting some of the cost savings generated by the project to public works projects dedicated to lessening the project's environmental damage.

This scheme has the potential to improve the distributional merit of the project by mitigating some of the externalized costs that are generated by the project. The authors found that a tax on regional transportation of two dollars per ton of cargo would raise revenue with a net present value of $86 million. This equals nearly 40 percent of the private benefits created by the paving project, or 8 percent of the cost of the Plan for Prevention and Control of Deforestation in the Amazon, a substantial interministerial effort to reduce the rate of deforestation throughout the forest, launched in 2004 (Alencar et al. 2005, 17). If the toll were sufficient to fund the governance activities required for the "With Governance" scenario in table 14.5, the reduction of the externalities associated with the project would be worth as much as $883 million. In this case, the green tax would not only help distribute some of the proceeds for the project in a more equitable fashion, but would fund activities that were cost-benefit justified in their own right.

SUMMARY OF CASES

Table 14.6 presents a summary of the shortcomings of cost-benefit analyses conducted for each of the three case studies.

TABLE 14.6

Summary of the Cases Examined

Case	Project Type	Analytical Gap	Finding of the Cost-Benefit Analysis	Potential Consequences of the of Analytical Gap
BR-319	Highway	Lack of official cost-benefit analysis. The cost-benefit analysis that was conducted independently had serious methodological flaws.	Project infeasible	1. Distortions in decision making result in a project with economic losses estimated at about $162 million. 2. With potential negative externalities, damage may reach $1.13 billion. 3. The costs of mitigation of negative externalities are about $233 million. Mitigation costs would be offset by significant reductions in externalities, on the order of $971 million.
Belo Monte	Hydroelectric dam	Lack of risk analysis	Project feasible, but at high risk of infeasibility	1. The risk of a flow lower than officially estimated could make the NPV of the project go from $1.62 billion to negative $3.56 billion. 2. In the risk scenarios analyzed, the probability that the project has positive NPV ranges from 2.28% in the worst case up 39.11% in the more optimistic case.
BR-163	Highway	Lack of distributional analysis and assessment of environmental externalities	Project financially viable, yet economically infeasible without investments in governance	1. Massive external costs due to the inadequate distribution of benefits. 2. The channeling of a portion of net benefits for mitigation, political obstacles notwithstanding, can reduce the environmental costs of the project by an estimated $883.3 million.

Discussion

Infrastructure projects in the Amazon region often stir intense controversy, as governments and private actors seek to justify their investment agendas, often with little clarity or transparency, and environmentalists mobilize opposition, often relying on noneconomic arguments that cannot be readily compared to official claims about a project's impacts.

Although cost-benefit analysis is only one tool for evaluating government policies and projects, it can play an important role in the selection and prioritization of infrastructure projects by adding transparency to the process and by comparing their negative and positive effects. But in the particular case of large public works projects that will have significant environmental impacts, additional effort must be expended to identify externalities and risks and to incorporate assessments of these factors into the final analysis. All feasible alternatives must be evaluated, including both technical and investment alternatives.

Significant gaps compromise the reliability of the cost-benefit analyses conducted in each of the three case studies discussed in this chapter: these gaps misrepresent the costs and benefits of the projects and could lead to decisions that are economically inefficient or inequitable, or both. The lack of rigorous, government-sponsored cost-benefit analysis could, across all three projects, lead to economic losses totaling $5.57 billion that were not examined.

Notwithstanding methodological limitations, especially in the valuation of nonmarket environmental costs, sound cost-benefit analysis can make notable contributions to our understanding of a project's impacts—both the size and the incidence of those impacts. Consideration of costs and benefits should be incorporated into all potentially significant projects. Although cost-benefit analysis is not usually sufficient on its own to guide policymakers in deciding whether to undertake a project (for instance, distributional analysis and moral considerations should also be considered), cost-benefit analysis can tip the scales in favor of certain alternatives, clarify risk factors, and influence thinking about potential mitigation strategies.

Cost-benefit analysis is essential to environmental policymaking in Brazil today. Environmental impact assessment can examine the risks in physical terms, but cost-benefit analysis is needed to place a value on these impacts. When there are additional expenditures needed to mitigate negative externalities from a project—for instance, though command-and-control instruments—these costs should be accounted for as inherent elements of the project rather than as unrelated spending. Combined with risk assessments and distributional analyses, the use of cost-benefit analysis can ensure that infrastructure projects in the Brazilian Amazon generate greater gains in social welfare.

In each of the three case studies discussed herein, cost-benefit analysis influenced decision making. In the case of highway BR-319, the cost-benefit analysis conducted by Conservation Strategy Fund researchers spurred a federal prosecutor to halt the project until the Transportation Ministry presented an official feasibility study on how the government could reduce the project's inefficiencies. In the case of the Belo Monte dam, before an independent cost-benefit analysis was conducted, the dam had been widely considered to be a highly efficient project. The independent risk analysis that was conducted using an alternative hydrological model opened a new round of debate between stakeholders, including civil society groups. Other major project flaws have since been exposed, mainly related to investment costs. In the case of BR-163, cost-benefit analysis showed that the project's negative externalities rendered it economically inefficient. However, since these and other costs would be borne diffusely by various social groups inside and outside of Brazil, it appeared as though the inefficiency would not be enough to turn political tides against the project. Nonetheless, the distributional analysis spurred the creation of a working group tasked with finding alternative ways to distribute the project's benefits and mitigate its negative externalities.

Conclusion

Recent experience in Brazil shows that cost-benefit analysis can play an important role in shaping environmental policy in the context of an emerging economy.

While there are many methodological issues that should be addressed, and political decision-makers are not always completely receptive to analyses that run counter to the interests of powerful and well-organized groups, cost-benefit analysis can add transparency to the decision-making process, force some degree of accountability for the effects of political decisions, and provide an important resource that can be utilized by civil society actors in their efforts to promote a more just and sustainable society.

Notes

1. The Hydrosim model is used to simulate the operation of hydro dams and was applied to calculate Belo Monte's actual generation (Hydrolab 2006).

Bibliography

Alencar, Ane, Laurent Micol, John Reid, Marcos Amend, Marilia Oliveira, Vivian Zeidemann, and Wilson Cabral de Sousa Jr. 2005. *A Pavimentação da BR-163 e os Desafios à Sustentabilidade: Uma Análise Econômica, Social e Ambiental*. Lagoa Santa: Conservation Strategy Fund.

Belli, Pedro, Jock R. Anderson, Howard N. Barnum, John A. Dixon, and Jee-Peng Tan. 2001. *Economic Analysis of Investment Operations: Analytical Tools and Practical Applications*. Washington, D.C.: World Bank.

Campbell, Harry F., and Richard P. C. Brown. 2003. *Benefit-Cost Analysis: Financial and Economic Appraisal Using Spreadsheets*. Cambridge: Cambridge University Press.

Eletronorte. 2002. *Complexo Hidrelétrico Belo Monte: Estudos de Viabilidade—Relatório Final*. Vol. 1. Brasília: Eletrobrás/Eletronorte.

Fleck, Leonardo. 2009. "Eficiência Econômica, Riscos e Custos Ambientais da Reconstrução da Rodovia BR-319." Série Técnica Edição No. 17, CSF, Lagoa Santa.

Fleck, Leonardo, and Marcos Amend. 2009. "Why Rebuild BR-319? Economics of an Amazon Road." Economics of an Amazon Road. Policy Brief, CSF, Lagoa Santa.

Horton, Bruce, Giordano Colarullo, Ian J. Bateman, and Carlos Peres. 2002. "Evaluating Non-users' Willingness to Pay for the Implementation of a Proposed National Parks Program in Amazonia: A UK/Italian Contingent Valuation Study." Working Paper ECM 02–01, Centre for Social and Economic Research on the Global Environment (CSERGE), Norwich, UK.

Hydrolab. 2006. *Hydrolab H2o Operating Manual*. Hydrolab. Hydrolab Documentation. Loveland, Colorado: Hach Hydromet/Hydrolab.

Instituto Chico Mendes de Conservação da Biodiversidade (ICMBio), Secretaria de Estado do Meio Ambiente e Desenvolvimento Sustentável (SDS/AM), (Secretaria de Estado do Desenvolvimento Ambiental (SEDAM/RO), and CSF. 2009. *Grupo de Trabalho BR-319: Subgrupo Proteção e Implementação das Unidades de Conservação da BR-319—Resumo Executivo*. Portaria No. 295 MMA (Brazilian Ministry of the Environment), on September 22, 2008. Brasília: MMA.

Jenkins, Glenn P., and Arnold C. Harberger. 2000. *Cost-Benefit Analysis for Investment Decisions*. Cambridge: Harvard Institute for International Development.

Kaimowitz, David, and Arild Angelsen. 1998. *Economic Models of Tropical Deforestation: A Review.* Bogor, Indonesia: Center for International Forestry Research.

Nogueira, Jorge M., and Romilson R. Pereira. 1999. *Critérios e Análise Econômicos na Escolha de Políticas Ambientais.* Brasília: University of Brasília.

Perz, Stephen G., Marcellus M. Caldas, Eugenio Arima, and Robert J. Walker. 2007. "Unofficial Road-Building in the Amazon: Socioeconomic and Biophysical Explanations." *Development and Change* 38 (3): 529–51.

Pfaff, Alexander S. P. 1999. "What Drives Deforestation in the Brazilian Amazon? Evidence from Satellite and Socioeconomic Data." *Journal of Environmental Economics and Management* 37 (1): 26–43.

Ribeiro, Ana Paula. 2007. "Lula Anuncia Hoje Pacote para Acelerar o Crescimento." *Folha de S. Paulo*, January 22.

Seroa de Motta, Ronaldo. 2002. "Estimativa do Custo Econômico do Desmatamento na Amazônia." Discussion Paper No. 910, IPEA, Rio de Janeiro.

Simpson, R. David, Roger A. Sedjo, and John W. Reid. 1996. "Valuing Biodiversity for Use in Pharmaceutical Research." *Journal of Political Economy* 104 (1): 163–85.

Soares-Filho, Britaldo S., Daniel C. Nepstad, Lisa M. Curran, Gustavo C. Cerqueira, Ricardo A. Garcia, Claudia Azevedo Ramos, Eliane Voll, et al. 2006. "Modelling Conservation in the Amazon Basin." *Nature* 440: 520–23.

Sousa, Wilson Cabral de, Jr., John Reid, and Neidja Cristine Silvestre Leit ão. 2006. *Custos e Benefícios do Complexo Hidrelétrico Belo Monte: Uma Abordagem Econômico-Ambiental.* Série Técnica Edição No.4, CSF, Lagoa Santa. Lagoa Santa, Brasil.

Sousa, Wilson Cabral de, Jr., and John Reid. 2010. "Uncertainties in Amazon Hydropower Development: Risk Scenarios and Environmental Issues around the Belo Monte Dam." *Water Alternatives* 3 (2): 249–68.

15

A Cost-Benefit Analysis of Resettlement Policy in Southeast Asia

Orapan Nabangchang

An increasing number of small-scale farmers in Thailand now occupy ecologically fragile areas in watersheds, national forestry reserves, and protected areas including national parks and wildlife sanctuaries. While these lands are legally protected, the absence of clear physical boundaries and the lack of public resources dedicated to preventing intruders has led to a de facto open access regime for these lands. Notably, settlements within protected areas have grown, resulting in the continued conversion of forested land to human use.[1]

Complications arise when the socioeconomic circumstances of the "encroachers," or "forest occupants," must be balanced with environmental and economic considerations. Policies and measures targeted at addressing forest encroachment and settlement in protected areas focus predominantly on institutional and legal issues, and economic arguments are generally downplayed.

One of the most active debates in the field of conservation is whether local communities should be allowed to live on and use land and forest resources within protected areas. Policymakers are often deadlocked between conservation pressure to resettle local communities and equity considerations that favor allowing them to remain. Such debates are seldom informed by concrete evidence of the costs and benefits associated with resettlement. Because of the absence of thorough analysis, it has been difficult to establish whether society in general stands to gain more from policies that allow communities to remain in protected areas than from options that would resettle them to alternative sites.

This chapter discusses a cost-benefit analysis that was conducted of several policy options related to the resettlement of the village of Ban Pa Kluay, located in Ob Luang National Park in Chiang Mai Province in the Northern Region of Thailand. This village was selected not only because it was located inside a protected area, but because of a history of difficulty that it has with other villages located further downstream.

Background to the Situation in Ban Pa Kluay

The history of Ban Pa Kluay dates back to 1975, when the military officials moved four Hmong households from Chiang Rai Province to resettle in what became known as the village of Ban Pa Kluay. In 1982, additional Hmong households were resettled to the village. Nine years later, in 1991, the resettled area—as well as surrounding lands that were being cultivated by the villagers—was declared part of the Ob Luang National Park. Since then, the population of Ban Pa Kluay has increased substantially, mainly due to the emigration of relatives from the provinces of Chiang Rai and Nan in the Northern Region and the province of Phetchabun in the Northeastern Region.

Conflict arose when downstream communities accused the Hmong settlement of large-scale deforestation. Downstream communities believe that the Hmong of Ban Pa Kluay still practice swidden agriculture (sometimes referred to as "slash-and-burn"), rotating production among many parcels. This method does not involve any measures to conserve the topsoil, and as cultivated land becomes less productive and is abandoned, more forestland must be cleared. Large-scale conversion of land use from poppy farms to commercial crops also tends to leave large areas of topsoil exposed. This creates a high risk of flash-flooding and deposits large amounts of sediment into the water supply, making it nonpotable. The intensive use of chemicals and the cleaning of chemical mixing containers in the stream are also believed to have caused water contamination. However, the major source of discontent for downstream communities is the diversion of surface water by Ban Pa Kluay for irrigation, which is believed to have caused reduced volume of surface water flow. On November 28, 1999, in response to complaints filed by the downstream communities, the national cabinet decided to move Ban Pa Kluay inhabitants down from the watershed area. However, no action was taken, partly because of the concerns of the government about the lack of alternative sites, and partly because officials wanted to maintain a positive relationship with individuals within the Hmong settlement who could potentially provide information on drug trafficking in the area.

The situation in Ban Pa Kluay is indicative of many other cases of enclave settlements in protected areas where there are policy deadlocks caused by conflicting pressures surrounding the resettlement of existing communities. The study discussed below examined the costs and benefits of three policy options. The first option was the status quo, which would have allowed the existing settlement to remain. The second option was a compromise option, where additional investments would be allocated to conserve the forest, and a number of restrictions on land and forest use would be imposed on Ban Pa Kluay in return for the community's right to remain and use certain forest areas. Under the third option, the households in Ban Pa Kluay would be resettled outside the protected area, with investments made to provide adequate social protection and economic livelihood for the community.

The Stakeholders in Protected Areas

THE UPSTREAM COMMUNITY: BAN PA KLUAY

Ban Pa Kluay is located in Ob Luang National Park. The park lies approximately 1,400 meters above sea level and extends over 55,330 hectares within a high-value watershed area. The park is among the most ecologically important areas in Thailand. Ban Pa Kluay is the only village located upstream in the park and includes approximately eighty-six households and a population of approximately 704 people, all from the Hmong ethnic group.

In late 1998, the Ban Pa Kluay settlement covered twenty hectares. Although the settlement is located in Ob Luang National Park, a production area of nearly 140 hectares located in Doi Inthanon National Park is used by residents for farming purposes.[2] This production area land lies within the watersheds of three rivers: the Mae Tia, the Mae Pae, and the Mae Soi. These rivers are major water suppliers for the thirteen downstream villages. Contrary to the expectation that land holdings among the Hmong villagers in protected areas would be relatively small, most of the holdings were between one and three hectares—relatively large holdings compared to the downstream communities. One explanation for this is that because their land was located in a national park, the residents of Ban Pa Kluay did not have the land tenure security enjoyed by villagers downstream, and they acted strategically to clear and cultivate more land as a means of increasing the likelihood that they would be left with sufficient holdings to maintain their livelihood if the state one day reclaimed a portion of their land.

THE DOWNSTREAM COMMUNITIES

Ban Pa Kluay is one of fourteen villages in the Maesoi Subdistrict, within the Chom Thong District of Chiang Mai Province. The predominant ethnicity of the thirteen downstream villages is ethnic Thai. Two of the downstream villages that are in open conflict with Ban Pa Kluay are Ban Huey Ha and Wang Nam Yad. These two villages use water from the Mae Soi River for domestic use as well as for production of longan trees, which provide their main source of income. Downstream communities believe that the deteriorated condition of the water supply and the reduced surface water flow is due to the upstream construction of weirs to divert water to agricultural fields. Between 1983 and 1986, when the water from the Mae Soi had stopped flowing altogether, the downstream communities took several conservationist steps, including replanting sections of the forest and constructing forest fire protection lines. They also erected a fence around watershed areas to discourage further deforestation. This boundary remains controversial and has not been supported by the national government; it serves as a physical reminder of the unresolved conflict in the region.

Management Options for Resolving Upland-Lowland Conflicts and Corresponding Costs and Benefits

MANAGEMENT SCENARIO

As outlined above, the costs and benefits of the three policy options were analyzed to provide information to stakeholders during discussions over resettlement. The three management scenarios that were considered were the Status Quo Option, the Compromise Option, and the Resettlement Option.

The Status Quo Option assumes the business-as-usual approach and provides no additional investments or policy measures. The upstream community inhabitants will continue to utilize the land for cultivation, collect timber forest products (TFPs) and nontimber forest products (NTFPs), and expand the area by continually converting the remaining forests in the protected areas. The public agencies will continue to perform their normal mandates as in the past, responding to situations or problems such as forest fires, the occasional arrests for poaching and cutting trees, and protests for or against resettlement on an ad hoc basis.

Under the Compromise Scenario, upstream community inhabitants will be granted a conditional right to stay and become partners with the Royal Forestry Department (RFD) to patrol and protect the forest. This option will entail a range of supporting institutional and legal adjustments as well as financial outlays to cover administrative and operating expenses for forestry resources monitoring and protection. In return for the recognition of the right to remain on land already converted to agricultural use, communities will enter into agreements with the RFD, acknowledging limits on the size of the population and restrictions on land expansion. Collection of TFPs and NTFPs from protected areas will no longer be permitted, but an area will be set aside for use as community forest. Households will enter into an agreement with the RFD to patrol and protect assigned coverage of forest areas and accept that the land rights of that particular household will be terminated should any damage occur in the assigned area.

In the Resettlement Scenario, the residents of Ban Pa Kluay will be resettled outside the protected area. In addition to the expenses for resettlement, sufficient inputs are needed to ensure that once relocated in the destination settlement, the upstream community will be able to earn an income comparable to the level in their previous settlement. Parallel measures are needed to rehabilitate the degraded forests and to prevent both the return of Ban Pa Kluay residents and encroachment from newcomers.

BASIC ASSUMPTIONS IN THE CALCULATIONS OF COSTS AND BENEFITS

The study followed nine steps in conducting its cost-benefit analysis: (1) defining each affected group; (2) selecting the portfolio of the project being assessed; (3) listing the project's outputs, impacts, and potential impacts; (4) quantifying the outputs and impacts; (5) monetizing the outputs and impacts; (6) calculating the net cost or net benefit, in net present value terms; (7) conducting a distributional analysis of the project's costs and benefits; (8) performing a sensitivity analysis; and (9) making policy recommendations based on the results of the analysis (Laplante 2008).

In conducting the cost-benefit analysis, basic assumptions were made concerning each policy option that affected estimates of costs, as well as the anticipated value of land use and the collection of timber forest and nontimber forest products. These assumptions were developed in consultation with upstream and downstream villagers, foresters in Chiang Mai, local people, and NGOs familiar with the conflict. Benefit-transfer was used to arrive at indirect and nonuse values.

Estimates of the timing of costs and benefits were determined using input from dialogue with stakeholder groups, including the Ban Pa Kluay residents, downstream residents, and other interested groups. Assumptions in the calculation of costs and benefits are as follows.

STATUS QUO COSTS

In the absence of conservation measures or methods of sustainable extraction and as the quality of the resource base declines, Ban Pa Kluay residents are assumed to face rising costs of production: production costs are assumed to rise 10 percent during first through fifth years, with a 30 percent increase in cost per hectare after the fifth year. Likewise, collection costs of TFPs and NTFPs are assumed to increase 10 percent each year because of a rising wage rate as well as the increasing scarcity of timber. The costs to downstream communities and the general public are the monetized value of environmental damages, including the existence value of lost forest resources and the loss of ecological functions.

STATUS QUO BENEFITS

The economic rent of land is indicated in terms of net revenue generated from 0.16 hectares of land (gross revenue minus cost) multiplied by the total cultivated area. In each year, cultivated land is assumed to increase by an area equivalent to the forest area's decline, each at a rate of 2.5 percent per year. The net revenue from TFPs and NTFPs is based on the equivalent market value of the types of TFPs collected, minus the collection and marketing costs. Both values are assumed to increase by 2.5 percent per year through the increase in the number of households, based on population growth in Ban Pa Kluay during the past twenty-year period.

The monetary value of damages avoided were computed based on the costs of the measures that would be required to address negative environmental effects. For instance, soil loss impact is monetized by how much investment it would take to avoid that impact.[3] Carbon storage value was included as a forgone benefit. While substantial uncertainty remains about whether and when carbon storage value will be tradable, assumptions were made based on estimates regarding the likelihood and timeline of future global carbon markets. The value is based on the reduction in carbon sequestration that occurs with the conversion of closed secondary forest to permanent agriculture. This value is multiplied by the accumulative loss of forest cover in each year (Brown and Pearce 1994).

Nonuse values of biodiversity resources were estimated based on benefit-transfers from existence value surveys associated with areas of high ecological importance. Based on field surveys, the increase in area occupied by the Ban Pa Kluay residents is 59.2 hectares within a period of four years, or an average forest loss of 14.88 hectares per year. The existence value is transferred from Thongpan et al. (1990) and Panayotou and Parasuk (1990) and converted to 2002 prices.[4]

COMPROMISE OPTION COSTS

The Compromise Option assumes that an agreement can be reached relatively soon and that preparatory measures will take at least three years; expected benefits are assumed to commence in year 4. Each year of delay means that the expected benefits from avoided ecological harms become opportunities forgone, which are represented as costs.

The costs to the upstream community are forgone revenues from TFPs and NTFPs until the fourth year of the project. The revenues forgone in the successive years of the project period are assumed to increase by 2.5 percent per year, corresponding to the annual loss rate of forest coverage.

Costs to the downstream communities are the costs of implementing the various components of this option:

1. Demarcating the watershed and the production areas by planting buffer forest around the headwaters, the settlement, and production areas that will serve as a physical boundary
2. Recurrent costs for fence maintenance
3. Investment and management costs associated with maintaining forest fire patrols and water distribution canals for fire control
4. Supplementary planting of watershed forests
5. Land for establishment of a community village woodlot to supply domestic firewood and associated expenses
6. Monthly stakeholder meetings
7. Expenses to cover trainings for both upstream and downstream communities in forest protection, agricultural production improvement, and alternative occupations

The Compromise Option includes the monetary loss of the value of ecological functions for a period of three years to reflect the start-up period of the Compromise Option. Items covered are the existence value of forest areas that would have been converted to alternative use, the imputed cost of soil erosion, and the loss of carbon storage value. It adopts the same calculation approach as the one used in the Status Quo Option.

COMPROMISE OPTION BENEFITS

Under the Compromise Option, the benefits to the Ban Pa Kluay residents will be in terms of the economic rent from land that has already been brought under cultivation and net benefits from TFPs and NTFPs during the three years of the start-up phase.

The benefits are measured in terms of existence value of biodiversity resources in areas that would have been cleared, which are calculated from the value per unit area multiplied by the forest areas that would have been converted. The same principle is followed to estimate the damage avoidance of cost of soil erosion and the imputed value of carbon sequestration.

RESETTLEMENT OPTION COSTS

Forgone revenue for Ban Pa Kluay residents is determined by the economic rent of the land after year 10. The compensation payment that is expected to be paid to residents is assumed to cover the difference in net revenue of what upstream residents would have earned in the protected area versus the resettlement area.

To implement the Resettlement Option, a range of costs will be incurred:

1. Compensation cost for the loss of revenue during the relocation period
2. Livelihood provisions for Ban Pa Kluay residents during the first two years in the new settlement area
3. Costs to demarcate the headwaters by planting and maintaining strips of forest buffers
4. Reforestation cost
5. Investment in building and maintaining forest fire lines and operational costs for forest fire protection
6. Annual forest patrol expenses
7. Management and administration costs for validation of land rights
8. The value of the land where the community will be relocated
9. Public hearings and stakeholder meetings

RESETTLEMENT OPTION BENEFITS

All expected benefits of this scenario are shown to commence after year 10, under the assumption that reaching agreements and all preparatory measures will take at least ten years. Each year that the benefits are delayed means that the expected benefits from ecological functions will become opportunities forgone and are therefore been represented as costs. During the ten-year negotiation before resettlement can take place, Ban Pa Kluay inhabitants will continue to benefit from land resources in the protected area.

Recovered value of TFPs that had formerly been harvested are assumed to be 10 percent of the original TFPs' value harvested from the eleventh year onwards, increasing each year thereafter by 10 percent. In the case of the regeneration of NTFPs, it is assumed that 30 percent of the original value of the NTFPs can be recovered from the beginning of the eleventh year, increasing by another 30 percent in year 12. The original market value of the NTFPs is expected to be fully recovered at the end of year 13.

Among the expected environmental benefits of the Resettlement Option is that the threat to biodiversity resources would diminish. Thus society will benefit in terms of the existence value as well as the value of ecological functions of watersheds in areas that would otherwise have been subject to deforestation.

The net present values (NPVs) of the various policy options are estimated based on certain basic assumptions, revenues from land use and forest products, and economic values of the ecological functions of forests borrowed from previous studies. The analysis finds that net welfare gains for society could only be achieved by the Compromise Option, since that was the only policy option that generated a positive NPV.

Distribution of Costs and Benefits and Sensitivity Tests

This section examines the distribution of costs and benefits for each of the three policy options.

STATUS QUO OPTION

Table 15.1 displays the costs and benefits from forest use for the upstream and downstream communities. The costs to Ban Pa Kluay residents are based on the rising input costs associated with deforestation. The cost to downstream communities centers on the imputed value of the negative impacts of deforestation. The benefits to the upstream households are income from crops produced (in technical terms, this income may be referred to as "economic rent" from the land) and revenue from forest products. The present value of the net benefits for the upstream community at a 6 percent discount rate is approximately $640,000.

As anticipated, the downstream communities faced a net loss from the Status Quo Option, even including assumptions of a reduced rate of deforestation and lower values for environmental services provided by the forests. The net cost to downstream communities was significant, totaling $3.7 million. Sensitivity analysis of the NPVs for the Status Quo Option were negative for all variations, except where the rate of deforestation could be substantially controlled.

COMPROMISE OPTION

The Compromise Option allows the upstream community to continue to reap benefits from the land and from nontimber forest products as a supply of

TABLE 15.1
Costs and Benefits of Forest Protection Options (US$ millions)

	Upstream			Downstream		
	Benefit	Cost	Net Impact	Benefit	Cost	Net Impact
Base case: Status Quo	2,372	1,729	643		3,718	(3,718)
Base case: Compromise	1,110	1,019	91	5,747	921	4,826
Base case: Resettlement	1,563	1,184	380	1,248	2,582	(1,334)

Note: Using exchange rate at the time of the study, which was 43 Baht/USD.

firewood. However, given that the source of these products is from the community forest, the sustainability of the supply depends on efforts to protect and maintain the resource. In addition to the community forest, the Ban Pa Kluay residents also obtain use value from the buffer forests planted around the watersheds, the settlement, and the land used for agricultural production. The sustainability of these resources depends on the agreement reached by community members over the rules governing resource use. Despite restrictions on the further expansion of land use, community members are compensated in various other ways, such as through security of tenure and extension services for occupational promotion, which, among other things, maximizes returns from the land and opens channels for alternative off-farm and non-land-based employment opportunities.

In return, beyond agreeing to the area expansion restriction, the upstream community will have to agree to share a number of cost items that have been formerly borne by the downstream communities. Among these are the costs of forest fire protection, forest patrol, replanting, and maintenance of watersheds. The social implication of the cost sharing and mutual benefits of this option will be the integration of members of the upstream community into mainstream Thai society. Naturally, to what extent this social integration can become more than a symbolic change will depend on the sincerity of each stakeholder in abiding by the commitments entailed in this option. With these restrictions, the NPV to the upstream community is $90,000.

The Compromise Option provides the highest NPV for the downstream communities, at $4.8 million. Even excluding the carbon storage value altogether (which would occur if the carbon sequestration benefits cannot be captured by the local community through a trading system), this option still earns downstream communities a net gain of $2.7 million. Moreover, the net loss to downstream communities from deforestation is reduced to $50,000. The NPVs of the Compromise Option are positive in all sensitivity tests.

RESETTLEMENT OPTION

Under the Resettlement Option, the interests of the upstream and downstream communities diverge. Delays work in favor of the upstream community, since they continue to benefit from the use value of the land and forestry resources. The longer the delay in resettlement, the higher the costs to the downstream communities. In addition to the higher administrative costs, there are elements of uncertainty with regards to the suitability of the new location. These concerns center on the community's ability to generate income from the new land. The uncertainty also risks neutralizing the perceived benefits resulting from the security of tenure.

The allocation of costs and benefits is substantially different for this option than under the Compromise Option. For the upstream community, the net benefit is higher in the Resettlement Option ($370,000) than in the Compromise Option ($90,000), assuming a ten-year delay in implementing resettlement. During those years, the upstream community continues to access and use forest resources.

Sensitivity analysis reveals that downstream communities confront net losses under the Resettlement Option. The only exception is where the execution of resettlement is sped up, which provides a net gain to the downstream communities of $2.35 million. Most of this gain is derived from the value of damage cost avoidance and the existence value of the forestry resources.

Contrary to expectations, the upstream community will still reap net gains from the Resettlement Option. This is mainly due to the ability of the upstream people to utilize resources during negotiations, but also because they are provided with compensation for the loss of their livelihood, and because the projected revenue earnings for the resettled area are included in tabulating their benefits. Thus, the longer the delay, the higher the net gain to the upstream community. If, however, resettlement is moved earlier, to year 5, the upstream community will face a net loss of $500,000. This is because of lost revenue from forest products and the shorter window to expand agricultural holdings. A faster implementation of resettlement is the only scenario where the upstream community faces a net loss and the only scenario where the downstream communities reap net gains from resettlement.

Sensitivity analysis reveals that the speed of implementation has a crucial effect on the feasibility of the Resettlement Option. In all but one scenario, the NPVs of resettlement are negative. In sum, it is only feasible to consider resettlement if it is launched by the sixth year. However, since resettlement has been debated in Thailand for more than two decades with no resolution, speeding up the negotiation process is unlikely. This weighs in favor of the Compromise Option and its distribution of costs and benefits among both the direct users of resources and the general public.

SENSITIVITY TESTS

In addition to the three main options, several variations are run to illustrate the sensitivity of the NPVs to several parameters. For each sub-scenario, four discount rates are used in the calculation of the NPV, namely 6 percent, 8 percent, 10 percent, and 12 percent. The parameters for conducting sensitivity analysis for this study include:

1. *Two different rates of deforestation.* One test assumes that the rate will be the same as the average loss per year at 14.88 hectares. The other assumes that deforestation has been more or less contained and that forest conversion will be quite marginal, with a net reduction of forest of 1.6 hectares per year.

The change in the effectiveness in controlling deforestation is a major factor in determining the outcome of each policy option and scenario. Assuming that deforestation can be slowed down, the NPV of the Status Quo becomes positive, at $60,000. Moreover, there is not much difference between the NPVs of the Status Quo and the Compromise options. From a policy perspective, it may be worthwhile to examine how present measures to control deforestation can be made more effective. The main difference under the scenario with lower deforestation rates centers on distribution of gains and losses, which will still differ across options.

2. *Changes in the inclusion of carbon storage value.* For Thailand, the experience with trading carbon credits is limited and mainly restricted to the voluntary markets. It may take a number of years before the carbon credits that are generated from the study area can be traded either through voluntary markets or more robust international exchanges. Several sub-scenarios are therefore run, varying the number of years before the market for carbon trade is assumed to become functional. Timelines of five years, ten years, and fifteen years are estimated, in addition to a scenario where the value of carbon storage is excluded altogether.

3. *The timing of resettlement also has a significant impact on the NPVs.* The only scenario that can render the Resettlement Option feasible occurs when negotiations can be concluded for resettlement within five years. On the other hand, given that resettlement has been a topic of discussion for over two decades, it would appear unlikely that the agreement for resettlement can be concluded within the next five years.

Conclusion

SUMMARY OF FINDINGS

The higher net benefits under the Compromise Option, of course, should not be taken to imply that human settlements in the forest do not have negative effects on the local ecosystem. Costs have already been incurred in terms of the continued loss of forest coverage and the associated ecological functions. Given the past pattern of resource use, more losses are inevitable if nothing is done, as illustrated by the net costs of all variations of the Status Quo Option.

Under the Compromise Option, the upstream community could remain in the forest if tighter conditions of use are implemented and enforced to minimize further losses. These conditions would require a range of investments to protect and conserve the forest, the cost of which could be spread fairly evenly over the project's twenty-year period, not exceeding $230,000 in any year. This steady cost is presented in contrast to the Resettlement Option, which involves high upfront payments in year 1. In addition, the Compromise Option will be more acceptable to the upstream community and those concerned for the rights of ethnic minorities, because it does not involve forced relocation.

Under the Resettlement Option, the costs include not only the cost of land acquisition and administrative expenses for reallocation, but also of ensuring against the return of old settlers and the entry of newcomers. Reaching a consensus over resettlement would be difficult given that opinions in society have become highly polarized. Cost-benefit analysis also suggests that speed is crucial to the viability of the Resettlement Option. Besides the increasing difficulty of executing resettlement as time passes, delays also neutralize the benefits that make this option desirable. A further complication is the lack of alternative settlement sites. With the demand for land among the landless and the near-landless lowland Thais, any news of resettlement and possible relocation sites would result in the targeted land being occupied and claimed. The longer the delay in launching the resettlement process, the greater the net loss to society.

BEYOND COST-BENEFIT ANALYSIS

While the results of the Compromise Option suggest a win-win situation, the option is only feasible if the parties accept the new conditions. One channel through which the option could be translated into action is the Tambon Administration Organization (TAO), which is a local government body authorized by the 1997 constitution to steward natural resources. The TAO could provide a forum where the conditions imposed on the upstream community could be discussed in conjunction with the terms and the commitments required of the downstream community. Representatives of the concerned public agencies should also be present to provide information about the technical aspects of implementation and the financial resources available.

Once a general agreement is reached, the details of the Compromise Option need to be discussed. These include issues such as whether to establish individual or community rights to access and utilize resources; the demarcation of the new settlement boundaries; and how to manage the land previously under production and restore the watersheds and protected areas. An important consideration for a successful outcome, and one of great importance to the downstream communities and the general public, is the need to increase the capacity of the upstream community to use resources sustainably. Finally, restricting the access rights of the upstream community to land and forest resources is only realistic if there are concurrent measures adopted to increase the productivity of the land already under cultivation and to secure alternative sources for the timber and nontimber forest products that were previously collected from the natural forests.

Given that nationwide there are some 180,000 households living within protected areas in situations similar to Ban Pa Kluay, there is much to be gained by applying cost-benefit analysis to support decision making. With clearer analysis of the distribution of costs and benefits under different management options, the debate can be shifted away from emotional appeals.

Whether local communities who have been looking after community forests should be given the rights to manage and benefit from timber and nontimber forest products has been the subject of debate for the past two decades. Policymakers and technocrats have considered an array of administrative and technical solutions. Using aerial photographs and satellite imagery, the government has attempted to prove when settlements occurred—either before or after a public announcement was made about a given site being deemed a protected area. Local communities generally respond to these activities by producing their own local proof, such as the age of planted trees and historical accounts of settlement, which are often verbal. Some ethnic groups also justify their rights on the basis of conservation measures that contribute to the sustainable flow of goods and services and provide both on-site and off-site benefits. The application of cost-benefit analysis could provide a way to move beyond discussion of current rights to land and instead focus on how policymaking can best generate mutual benefits for all relevant stakeholders. Cost-benefit analysis could also be applied to decision making concerning the major drivers of land use change in Thailand, including extraction of mineral resources and conversion of forest land for the production of cash crops. Finally, infrastructure expansions could also benefit from being assessed in a cost-benefit framework.

While there is great potential for the practical application of cost-benefit analysis in Thailand, use of the technique may, unfortunately, in the short term, be restricted to academic settings. This is not due to the complete absence of an enabling policy framework. Both the Thai constitution and the Enhancement and Conservation of National Environment Quality Act (NEQA)—Thailand's most important environmental legislation—recognize the importance of understanding the impacts of policy on environmental quality.[5] The problem is that this framework is not specific enough. The legislation does not go any further than calling for an assessment of the physical aspects of the impacts; there is no requirement to assess a policy's potential economic aspects or social costs.[6] And while the national constitution expressly embraces efficiency and effectiveness in the sustainable allocation of natural resources, such as land and water, it contains no references to economic efficiency, nor does it acknowledge the social costs and benefits or the potential externalities that could arise from the extraction of natural resources. Although perhaps it would be unreasonable to expect the constitution to go into such detail, it is surprising that the country's key piece of environmental legislation, NEQA, lacks any explicit reference to the principle of economic efficiency. Instead, NEQA only mentions the physical aspects of environmental impacts. The absence of any mention of economic impacts or call for economic analysis of environmental projects is striking because the legislature used clear language evoking the government's commitment to pursuing economic efficiency in other areas, such as land purchases and the construction of waste treatment facilities.

In Thailand, practical and ideological constraints have, for a number of reasons, restricted the use of cost-benefit analysis to small groups of environmental economists and activists. To start, practical constraints (such as the time and expertise necessary to conduct a thorough cost-benefit analysis) have prevented its widespread use. In this study, for example, the analysis involved predicting deforestation rates, the collection of forest products, and changes in hydrology, humidity, and precipitation—all of which called for significant expertise. Another difficulty is quantifying and valuating nonmarket goods and services. The expense of carrying out cost-benefit analysis could potentially be lowered if it were undertaken at the same time as the environmental impact assessment. Unfortunately, this does not often occur. Another practical limitation is the limited number of environmental economists trained to conduct cost-benefit analysis. This obstacle may be overcome in the future given the ongoing efforts to build research capacity in the field of environmental economics in Thailand.

Ideological barriers pose an even greater challenge, for three reasons. First, there is general concern about placing monetary values on nature as well as on cultural and traditional ways of life. Advocates of economic growth and private sector investment see this type of valuation as obstructing development. At the same time, local communities and environmental NGOs fear that the valuation techniques used by environmental economists will commoditize nature. Thus, a basic challenge in advocating for the wider utilization of cost-benefit analysis in Thailand is cultivating widespread understanding of the technique itself.

Second, recognition of the difference between the social costs and benefits and the private costs and benefits must be better communicated. Policymakers and the public must be made aware of the need for incentives to internalize the costs of negative externalities, on the one hand, and to stimulate positive externalities on the other hand. At present, there is an inconsistent approach to the issue of externalities, as the constitution embraces the "polluter pays" principle, but Section 6 of NEQA stipulates that the state must budget for negative environmental impacts.

Third, despite the government's stated commitment to principles of efficiency, effectiveness, sustainability, and public consultation, decisions are often driven by political and economic forces. Theoretically, land use planning and zoning initiatives acknowledge the importance of balancing social and economic objectives, and efficiency and equity objectives, in ways that do not compromise environmental quality. In practice, however, land use planning relies heavily on command-and-control measures, and decision making is largely done by those wielding the most political and economic power. When a decision must be made between options that benefit the wealthier segments of society and those that benefit the poor, the balance often tips in favor of the former owing to the potential private gains for those in control of political and administrative organs.

These practical and ideological barriers continue to hinder wider application of cost-benefit analysis in decision-making processes in Thailand. While scholars and activists are likely to continue to look to cost-benefit analysis to improve the quality of policymaking, for it to fulfill its promise, the usefulness of the technique will need to be more broadly recognized by the public and by political actors.

Notes

1. See, for example, Nabangchang (1992).

2. According to the cadastral survey conducted in 1993 by the staff of the Chom Thong's Land Department.

3. Assumption about the function of forests in protecting top soil is based on Ruangpanit (1971); Lal (1983); Takahashi et al. (1983); Tangtham (1991); Kraipanond et al. (1995); LDD (2000), among others.

4. Some parameters used were also drawn from the literature and previously conducted research, such as a recent paper on the works of SCBD (2001) and Hanley (2000).

5. Enhancement and Conservation of National Environment Quality Act, B.E. 2535 (1992) (Thail.).

6. Constitution for the Kingdom of Thailand, B.E. 2550 Ch. VIII (2007).

Bibliography

Brown, Katrina, and David W. Pearce. 1994. "The Economic Value of Non-market Benefits of Tropical Forests: Carbon Storage." In *The Economics of Project Appraisal and the Environmental Economics*, ed. John Weiss, 102–23. Cheltenham: Edward Elgar.

Hanley, Nick. 2000. "Cost-Benefit Analysis." In *Principles of Environmental and Resource Economics*, ed. Henk Folmer, H. Landis Gabel, and Hans Opschoor, 104–29. Cheltenham: Edward Elgar.

Kraipanond, Nawarat, N. Chumyen, S. Tasingha, S. Thanawibunsetr, O. Chantrapol, P. Borisut and P. Yaemchoo. 1995. "The Study of the Environmental Quality in the Basin Area in the Highlands of Tak Province" [in Thai]. *Soil and Water Conservation Journal* 15 (2): 27–39.

Lal, R. 1983. "Soil Erosion in the Humid Tropics with Particular Reference to Agricultural Land Development and Soil Management." In *Hydrology of Humid Tropical Regions*, ed. Reiner Keller, vol. 140, 221–39. Norfolk, UK: International Association of Hydrological Sciences.

Land Development Department (LDD). 2000. *Soil Erosion in Thailand* [in Thai]. ISBN 974-7723-79-4. Bangkok: LDD.

Laplante, Benoit. 2008. "Key Steps of Cost-Benefit Analysis" [in Thai]. In *Cost-Benefit Analysis and the Economic Valuation of Environmental Impacts,* chapter 8, section 8. Nonthaburi, Thailand: Economy and Environment Program for Southeast Asia, Regional Training on Natural Resources and Environmental Economics.

Nabangchang, Orapan. 1992. "The Socio-Economic Impact of Land Reform in Thailand: The Case Study of the Involvement of the Agricultural Land Reform Office, 1975–1989." PhD diss., University of Cambridge.

Nabangchang, Orapan. 2009. "Land Use Changes in Thailand, Strategy and Action Plans" [in Thai]. In *Land Classification for Sustainable Land Use,* 197–378. Report submitted to the Office of Environmental Policy and Planning. Bangkok: Vitoon Printers.

Panayotou, Theodore, and Chartchal Parasuk. 1990. *Land and Forest: Projecting Demand and Managing Encroachment.* Chon Buri: Thailand Development Research Institute.

Ruangpanit, Niwat. 1971. "Effects upon Crown Cover on Surface Runoff and Soil Erosion in Hill Evergreen Forest." MS thesis, Kasetsart University, Thailand.

Secretariat of the Convention on Biological Diversity (SCBD). 2001. *The Value of Forest Ecosystems.* CBD Technical Series No. 4. Montreal: SCBD.

Takahashi, T., K. Nagahori, Charat Mongkolsawat, and Manas Losirikul. 1983. "Runoff and Soil Loss." In *Shifting Cultivation—an Experiment at Nam Phrom, Northeast Thailand and Its Implications for Upland Farming in the Monsoon Tropics*, ed. Kazutake Kyuma and Chaitat Pairintra, 84–109. Bangkok: Ministry of Science, Technology and Energy.

Tangtham, Nipon. 1991. "Erosion Study and Control in Thailand." In *Proceedings of RTPESA 5 Workshop on Soil Erosion and Debris Flow Control,* 126–42. UNDP-Regional Training

Program on Erosion and Sedimentation for Asia. Yogyakarta, Indonesia: Indonesian Institute of Science.

Thongpan, Sopin, Theodore Panayotou, Songpol Jetanavich, Ketty Faichampa, and Charlie Mehl. 1990. *Deforestation and Poverty: Can Commercial and Social Forestry Break the Vicious Circle?* The 1990 Thailand Development Research Institute Research Report No. 2. Chonburi: TDRI.

16

Cost-Benefit Analysis of Water Management Initiatives in China

A CASE OF SMALL, MULTIPURPOSE RESERVOIRS

Shahbaz Mushtaq

China faces many strategic challenges as it copes with its rapid economic growth and the transformation of its economy (Mushtaq et al. 2008). Water scarcity, which is exacerbated by population growth and climate change, will remain a central challenge in the years to come. Escalating water demand and increased water pollution help contribute to a problem that can affect a range of important interests, including food security (Mu et al. 2009). While food security issues are not yet serious in China, an increase in demand or reduction in China's ability to produce food supplies could create substantial risks in international markets, causing food shortfalls in food-importing countries (Mu et al. 2009). If China turns to global markets to make up for a poor harvest, it could outbid developing countries and sharply drive up prices. Therefore, sustained production from irrigated agriculture in China is vital to food security for the Chinese people and the international community.

China is not particularly well endowed with water resources, although water has been used throughout the country as a cheap resource in agricultural production. This has led to water shortages (Mushtaq et al. 2006). China's annual water supply is equivalent to 1,856 cubic meters per capita, or about 25 percent of the world's average. The geographic distribution of water resources within China is also uneven. An estimated 81 percent of water resources are found in the south, while most of China's arable land (64 percent) is in the arid north. Water supplies are particularly low in arid portions of the country, such as the Yellow River Basin (750 cubic meters per capita) and the Hai-Luan basin (355 cubic meters per capita). These average supplies are much lower than the internationally accepted definition of water scarcity of 1,000 cubic meters per capita (Khan et al. 2009).

China hosts one of the world's largest irrigated areas (59.3 million hectares), which encompasses about half of China's cultivated land and produces about 70 percent of the country's grain harvest. While China suffers from water shortages, water efficiency remains low, with GDP per cubic meter of water about one-fourth that of the world's developed countries. Only 45 percent of irrigated water is actually used, which is also very low compared to more economically developed countries

(Zhenyu 2007). Surface and groundwater resources are overexploited in many important food-producing areas, such as the Yellow River Basin. Furthermore, increasing water scarcity and temporally uneven distributions of rainfall (around 70 percent of the precipitation falls in four months) put additional strains on dwindling resources. Ensuring water and food security is a high-priority issue on the Chinese political agenda.

Water Resources Management Initiatives

Researchers have linked China's serious water challenges to the country's dwindling water supply, which also suffers from considerable pollution, booming demand from the country's rapidly growing economy, and a massive population (Khan et al. 2009; Molden et al. 2007; Mu et al. 2009; Mushtaq et al. 2008; see also Gleick et al. 2009; Lohmar et al. 2003; Liao et al. 2008). China's central government has already acknowledged that the prospect of water scarcity is an important problem and has attempted to address this issue at nearly all governmental levels, from the national level down to village and farm levels (Gleick et al. 2009; Lohmar et al. 2003). The government has also been strengthening its top-down approach to policymaking by adopting new water management and water-pricing regulations. These efforts include passing environmental impact assessment (EIA) laws, tightening supervision of polluting industries and waste emissions that affect major drinking water sources, reforming the river basin commissions that are responsible for the management of the country's seven main rivers, and generally emphasizing the importance of water conservation and protection.

The agriculture industry consumes a majority (roughly 65 percent) of the nation's fresh water. So while water conservation is becoming a national strategy across all sectors, conservation within agriculture is of paramount importance, especially given the industry's notoriously low water-use efficiency (Loeve et al. 2007; Mushtaq et al. 2006). In response, the Chinese government has successfully implemented water management initiatives that divert water from the agricultural sector to fulfill the growing demand in the other industrial and urban sectors (Zhang et al. 2009). In addition, water conservation projects have been implemented, buoyed by the introduction of water-saving irrigation practices. Some of these new projects either incentivize farmers to voluntarily reduce their water use or require them to do so (Mushtaq et al. 2006). Affected farmers have generally managed to successfully maintain their agricultural production, despite the considerable decrease in water deliveries, by relying on local sources, such as small reservoirs and ponds, and by adopting new irrigation techniques.

WATER MANAGEMENT AT ZHANGHE IRRIGATION SYSTEM

The Zhanghe Irrigation System (ZIS) is a multitiered irrigation system located in Hubei Province in the Yangtze River basin of China. The ZIS is managed by several institutional actors, including the Hubei Provincial Water Resources Bureau, the

Zhanghe Irrigation Administration Bureau, the canal management authority, as well as local village and farmer groups (Molden et al. 2007). The Zhanghe basin has an area of 7,740 square kilometers, including a catchment area of 2,200 square kilometers, and is designed to irrigate an area of about 160,000 hectares, which is typical of large-size irrigation systems in China. The major water source is the Zhanghe main reservoir. Management of the reservoir requires a delicate balance of supply and demand. The factors that affect the amount of water in the reservoir include the total available storage capacity, rainfall, and irrigation needs (Barker et al. 2001).

A combination of various water management initiatives starting in the late 1980s allowed the ZIS to save a considerable amount of water that otherwise would have gone to agricultural uses. Irrigation water deliveries from the ZIS were reduced by over 60 percent and redirected to meet the increasing demand from industry and municipal users (figure 16.1); all the while, Chinese farmers were able to maintain their crop production. Several factors have allowed the ZIS to reallocate reservoir water to higher-value uses without a significant decline in crop production (Loeve et al. 2007). These factors include research and development investments in irrigation techniques, increases in crop productivity through improved and hybrid rice varieties, lower tax burdens for farmers through tax-for-fee reforms, and the introduction of two-tiered water tariffs. In addition, investments in local, small water reservoirs for rainwater storage have resulted in more reliable and less expensive water supplies (Loeve et al. 2007; Mushtaq et al. 2008).

The successful management of the ZIS demonstrates that policies and strategies designed to deal with water use must address the practices and needs of different actors—farmers, system managers, basin managers, and the broader society—so that water use may become more efficient in multiple sectors simultaneously.

Because these irrigation reforms are revolutionary when compared to traditional water management in China, their potential impact is largely unknown. Additional investment in analysis is necessary for irrigation reforms to be understood and adaptable at the national scale. To this end, more attention should be paid to conducting cost-benefit analysis of irrigation investments (Liao et al. 2008).

A core solution for maintaining agricultural production while reducing water use is investment in small, local, multipurpose reservoirs. Local reservoirs allow

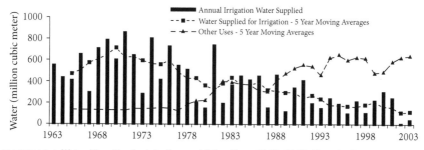

FIGURE 16.1 Water Allocation for Irrigation and Other Uses, 1966–2003, Zhanghe Reservoir, China

farmers in irrigated areas to capture rainfall, store surplus water from irrigation canals, and conserve water from other sources. The multipurpose reservoirs are operationally efficient and allow users to obtain water on-demand and store water within close proximity (Barker et al. 2001). Local reservoirs also reduce floods, recharge groundwater, and provide drainage in high-rainfall periods. Because of these attributes, they can be responsive to consumer needs and minimize mismatch between supply and demand. For example, in Hubei Province, these small, local reservoirs play an important role in agriculture by providing supplemental irrigation. The managerial and administrative issues local reservoirs pose are also comparatively easy to handle (Keller et al. 2000).

Since a considerable amount of investment is required to make irrigation water available through these multipurpose reservoirs, it is important to understand the economic efficiency of the investment, which is in fact a durable asset that can provide a stream of benefits for several years (Pandey 1991).

Benefit-Cost Evaluations of Small, Multipurpose Reservoirs

SMALL RESERVOIR CHARACTERISTICS

Thousands of small, multipurpose reservoirs are located in the ZIS. Besides the main reservoir, there are around 86,000 small, local reservoirs in the area that allow farmers to harvest rainfall, store surplus water from the ZIS, and capture water from other sources. The ZIS obtains one-fourth of its water from these reservoirs, as well as other medium- and large-sized reservoirs, to complement the supply from the main Zhanghe reservoir.

One significant operational benefit of the small storages is their rapid response times (Keller et al. 2000). Like groundwater systems, they can respond to rainfall on fields, thus maximizing effective rainfall and minimizing operational losses. These small reservoirs are ideal from the standpoint of operational efficiency, but generally less effective than groundwater or large dams for water conservation.

Characteristics of the small, multipurpose reservoirs include the following:

- Small, multipurpose reservoirs are categorized on the basis of storage capacity. Small reservoirs have a storage capacity of less than 1,000 cubic meters; medium reservoirs have a storage capacity between 1,000 and 10,000 cubic meters; while large reservoirs have a storage capacity of more than 10,000 cubic meters.
- The main reservoir water, drain water, rainfall, and surface water run-off are major water sources for small reservoirs. When it rains, farmers capture as much water as possible from rainfall and nearby drainage areas, and store it in the reservoirs.
- The small, multipurpose reservoirs are local communal property, and water in reservoirs is collectively owned by agricultural economic organizations. The number of farmers using a given reservoir depends on the topography and the population of the area. Overall, a single

reservoir serves an average of eight farmers. The averages for small, medium, and large reservoirs are five, eight, and eleven farmers, respectively.

- The average area served by a reservoir is about 3.70 hectares. The average areas served by large, medium, and small reservoirs are 6.73, 3.16, and 1.13 hectares, respectively. The maximum areas served by large, medium, and small reservoirs are 16.7, 6.6, and 2.0 hectares, respectively.

COST-BENEFIT ANALYSIS: CONCEPTUAL FRAMEWORK

Economic evaluation of small, multipurpose reservoirs requires a comparison of their costs, including construction costs, with their estimated benefits. As costs and benefits accrue during different points in time, the analysis is based on comparing their net present value, meaning the discounted sum of all future benefits and costs associated with the reservoirs (Pandey and Rajatasereekul 1999). The benefits of small reservoirs are determined based on the bounty of crops with and without reservoirs (Pandey 1991), and are quantified by measuring incremental net returns.

Over time, the water used from the ZIS reservoir for irrigation purposes has declined about 60 percent because of the growing demand for water in commercial industry and cities. Figure 16.2 shows the decline in deliveries from the ZIS reservoir and the increase in water use from small reservoirs. The water supply provided by small reservoirs enables farmers to sustain crop production despite a significant decrease in water deliveries from the ZIS reservoirs. The potential benefits of reservoirs can be measured by comparing areas where there is no reservoir water available to areas with reservoirs. Increases in yield and cropped area are the potential benefits, which are illustrated by the shaded areas in figures 16.3 and 16.4.

COST-BENEFIT ANALYSIS CRITERIA

Two dynamic economic indices, financial net present value (*NPV*) and financial internal rate of return (*IRR*) were used to analyze the costs and benefits arising from small, multipurpose reservoirs. The *NPV* was calculated using equation (16.1):

$$NPV = GB_p - (TC + NB_{RF}),$$

(16.1)

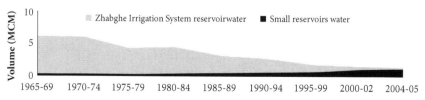

FIGURE 16.2 Changes in Water Delivery from Zhanghe Irrigation System Reservoir and Increase in Small Reservoir Water of Time in Zhanghe Irrigation System, China

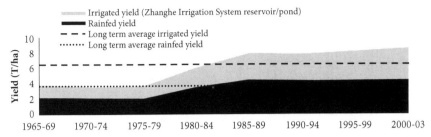

FIGURE 16.3 Changes in Yield over Time and Long-Run Average Rain-Fed and Irrigated Yield of Rice in Zhanghe Irrigation System, China

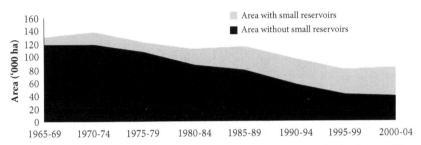

FIGURE 16.4 Area with and without Small Reservoir Situation in Zhanghe Irrigation System, China

where GB_p is the net present value of gross benefits from small reservoirs, TC is the net present value of total costs associated with small reservoirs (including costs of reservoir excavation, construction, and irrigation equipment), and NB_{RF} is the net present value of the net benefit from the rain-fed agriculture. In the absence of rain-fed agriculture, $NB_{RF} = 0$. The internal rate of return (IRR) was computed using equation (16.2):

$$IRR = \sum_{t=1}^{n} \frac{GB_t}{(1+IRR)^t} - \frac{(TC_t + NB_{RF(t)})}{(1+IRR)^t}. \tag{16.2}$$

The IRR is acceptable if it is greater than the minimum expected interest rate.

The cost-benefit analysis relied on data collected from thirty-six village heads, thirty-eight reservoir water managers, and one hundred farmers using reservoir water.

COST-BENEFIT ANALYSIS MODEL CHALLENGES, ASSUMPTIONS, AND PARAMETERS ESTIMATION

The key to cost-benefit analysis is identifying relevant benefits and costs parameters associated with small, multipurpose reservoirs, and then quantifying and valuing these parameters. If all costs and benefits can be measured and monetized in dollar terms, then a cost-benefit analysis can provide rigorous criteria to rank investments in small, multipurpose reservoirs.

The small reservoirs generate tangible and intangible benefits. Tangible benefits include the incremental benefits to crop production—increased cropped area, increased yields, positive changes in cropping patterns, and increased fish production. Intangible benefits include improved groundwater recharge; improved domestic water supply for drinking, household purposes, and livestock; recreational values; and environmental benefits such as reduced flooding.

The key challenge with cost-benefit analysis is that all costs and benefits need to be quantified in monetary terms; any error in monetary valuation can radically change the results. Monetary valuation is especially difficult where environmental benefits are intangible. In some instances, for example, the recreation values of these small, multipurpose reservoirs are not observable because markets do not exist for services provided by the environment. Furthermore, some of these benefits are hard to quantify because of their nonuse values. For example, a pond owner may derive satisfaction from knowing good-quality water exists in her pond. There are techniques available for estimating nonmarket values; however, the process can be complex, costly, and time-consuming. Therefore, considering the time frame and difficulties involved, only tangible benefits were included in this cost-benefit analysis.

The costs of providing water from small, multipurpose reservoirs can be divided into "use" and "opportunity" components. Use costs are those associated with the construction, operation, and maintenance of the reservoirs and conveyance canals, including pump replacements. Opportunity costs are those associated with alternative uses. For example, the ZIS main reservoir water could be used for growing additional crops in the area rather than storing it for future uses. While use costs were easy to determine, opportunity costs were more difficult to calculate because of their nature.

Various assumptions were used in identifying costs and benefits:

- Yield estimate: To evaluate crop yields, water quality in local reservoirs and the ZIS canal was assumed to be similar, as the ZIS canal is one of the main contributors to local reservoir water. This assumption aided in distinguishing between irrigated and rain-fed yields of wheat, rapeseed, and rice. Long-term average yields were then used to estimate both irrigated and rain-fed crop yields. Rice yields were higher than wheat and rapeseed yields (table 16.1). The reservoirs also yielded fish (table 16.2), although only 28 percent of reservoirs are partially used for fish farming. In these reservoirs, the main fish types are silver carp, bighead, grass carp, and common carp. The average annual fish catch was 964 kilograms.

- Profit estimates: The net returns of various crops were calculated as gross returns minus the costs of all variable inputs, including the costs of irrigation, seed, fertilizer, chemicals, and labor. The average household size in the ZIS is about 4.4 members. Considering this relatively small size in conjunction with increasing off-farm employment opportunities in growing urban industries, household labor may

TABLE 16.1
Estimated Yield and Net Returns of Major Crops

Crop	Yield (kg/ha)	Net Return ($/ha)[a]	Net Return ($/ha)[a]
Irrigated			
Rice	6,624	373	515
Wheat	5,850	340	492
Rapeseed	1,980	323	462
Rain-fed			
Rice	3,460	234	299
Wheat	2,048	240	295
Rapeseed	1,287	216	277

[a]Net returns do not account for the imputed cost of family labor.

TABLE 16.2
Estimated Fish Yield and Net Value of Fish Based on Reservoir Size

Size	Fish Harvest (kg/year)	Net Value ($/year)
Small	100	19
Medium	225	27
Large	2,134	399
Overall	964	253

have opportunity costs. Therefore, the imputed cost of family labor is included when calculating net returns from crops. However, net profit was calculated without imputed family labor costs. Rice yielded the highest return ($515), followed by wheat ($492) and rapeseed ($462). Family labor accounted for between almost 19 percent and 28 percent of the total cost (table 16.3).

- Construction costs of local reservoirs: The costs of construction depend on the method of construction and the suitability of a site's topography. Most construction costs are incurred in the excavation of reservoirs. Other major cost items include the construction of terraces, bunds, and canals for water conveyance. The average cost of reservoirs construction was about $1,440, while an additional $805 was required for improving or expanding reservoirs. The expected cost of future improvement and expansion was about $388 (table 16.3).
- Pumps and pumping costs: Pumping is required both for refilling and for releasing water from the reservoirs. Pumping costs depend on the elevation and distance of reservoirs and farms. These costs are calculated by multiplying the number of hours the pump is used in refilling and releasing water from the reservoir with the electricity or diesel unit costs. The average annual pumping cost of large reservoirs was $532, followed by the medium and small reservoirs, which were $266

TABLE 16.3

Estimated Capital and Variable Costs of Irrigation Reservoirs in Zhanghe Irrigation System, China

Parameter	Local Reservoirs Size		
	Small	Medium	Large
Capital cost ($)			
Reservoir construction costs	444	1,037	3,272
Cost of improvement/extension	171	274	1,951
Expected cost of reservoir improvement/extension	396	358	459
Price of pump set	549	732	1,098
Piping, wires, and hose costs	183	244	366
Total capital cost	1,743	2,645	7,146
Variable cost ($)			
Pumping cost	114	266	532
Desiltation	73	62	59
Channel cleaning	33	66	99
Repair & maintenance	28	26	27
Wage of the reservoir manager	31	133	172
Other O&M expenditure	35	27	27
Miscellaneous cost	18	37	55
Cost of ZIS water	23	35	46
Imputed cost of land use for reservoir	22	44	97
Total variable cost	377	696	1,114

and $114, respectively (table 16.3). In general, pumping costs increase as the size of the reservoir increases.

• Desilting, repairing and maintaining reservoirs, and cleaning canals: The costs of desilting, repairing and maintaining reservoirs, and cleaning canals were estimated by multiplying the number of times desilting, repairing, channel maintenance, and channel cleaning were performed in a year by the opportunity costs of labor used to perform these activities. The estimated average costs of desilting for large, medium, and small reservoirs are $59, $61, and $73, respectively. The estimated average costs of repair and maintenance for large, medium, and small reservoirs are $27, $26, and $28, respectively. Similarly, it costs $99 to clean canals associated with large reservoirs, and $68 and $40 to clean canals linked with medium and small reservoirs, respectively (table 16.3).

• Cost of ZIS water: The cost of ZIS water is the amount of money paid to the water management board for receiving canal water, including the water stored in local reservoirs. The cost of canal water is estimated by multiplying the average number of farmers using a given local reservoir with the average farm size, with the cost of irrigation from the canal water, and with the proportion of canal water stored in reservoirs. The estimated opportunity cost for the canal water for large, medium, and small reservoirs is $46, $35, and $23, respectively (table 16.3).

- Opportunity costs of land used for reservoirs: The opportunity costs are derived from the net benefit that might have been earned if the land had not been used for reservoir development. In the absence of suitable land prices due to state ownership, the opportunity costs of land were estimated using the value of forgone agricultural production. The average opportunity cost was about $54, with the estimated opportunity cost of large, medium, and small reservoirs being $97, $44, and $22 per reservoir, respectively (table 16.3).

- Opportunity costs of local reservoir manager and family labor: Some of the large reservoirs hire professional managers with a monthly salary for operation and maintenance. Therefore, for those reservoirs that do not hire a professional manager, the salary of the professional manager is included as the opportunity cost for volunteer managers. Similarly, the daily wage rates for labor in the study area are used as opportunity costs of family labor due to increasing off-farm employment opportunities in nearby cities. Managers of larger reservoirs receive a higher salary ($172/year) than do medium ($133/year) and small ($31/year) reservoir managers (table 16.3).

Other assumptions:

- Time horizon: The time horizon depends on the type of reservoir that is built and its surrounding environment. A ten- to twenty-year horizon is usually sufficient. In the case of local reservoirs, Yuan, Fengmin, and Puhai (2003) used ten years as the service life. Because future benefits are discounted, benefits are greatly diminished beyond ten to twenty years and thus have minimal impact on the decision-making process. The useful life of a reservoir was estimated to be up to twenty years. Beyond twenty years, major rehabilitation work might be required.

- Discount rate: Discount rates are a much-debated issue. Gittinger (1982) holds that the appropriate discount rate is the rate at which an enterprise is able to borrow money. Generally, for cost-benefit analysis, interest rates are considered to be between 5 percent and 15 percent (Kunze 2000; Enters 1992). In the case of local reservoirs, previous analysts have used a 6 percent discount rate (Yuan, Fengmin, and Puhai 2003). A 10 percent discount rate was selected for this study. A sensitivity analysis was performed using 8 percent, 12 percent, and 15 percent discount rates.

Cost-Benefit Analysis

Cost-benefit analysis was performed under two scenarios:

- Scenario 1: Farmers irrigate all crop areas, provided that sufficient water is available from the ZIS reservoir. If the available water is less than the amount required to irrigate the entire crop area, then the irrigated area is proportionately reduced. However, farmers *do not* grow rain-fed crops in the absence of local reservoirs.

- Scenario 2: Farmers irrigate all crop areas, provided that sufficient water is available from the ZIS reservoir. If the available water is less than the amount required to irrigate the entire crop area, then the irrigated area is proportionately reduced. However, farmers *do* grow rain-fed crops in the absence of local reservoirs.

The cost-benefit analysis is given in table 16.4. In Scenario 1, both with and without the imputed cost of family labor, investing in small, medium, and large reservoirs is profitable, which is evidenced by the high IRR, positive NPV, and a cost-benefit ratio (CBR) greater than 1. When the imputed cost of family labor is included in the analysis, the results show a lower but still healthy IRR, positive NPV, and a CBR greater than 1. Larger reservoirs are more profitable than medium and small reservoirs, which is due mainly to economies of scale. Large reservoirs offer relatively larger storage capacity and better opportunities for fish harvesting.

In Scenario 2, investing in medium and large reservoirs is profitable, which can be seen from a reasonably high IRR, positive NPV, and CBR greater than 1. However, small reservoirs barely justify the investment decision as seen by the IRR,

TABLE 16.4

Estimated Internal Rate of Return, Net Present Value, and Benefit-Cost Ratio for Small Multipurpose Local Reservoirs in Zhanghe Irrigation System, China

Local Reservoir Size	Evaluation Indices		
	IRR (%)	NPV ($) (10%)	CBR (10%)
Scenario 1[a]			
Small	77	6,371	2.52
Medium	126	19,184	3.71
Large	127	45,943	5.09
Scenario 1[b]			
Small	13	253	1.06
Medium	35	3,896	1.55
Large	48	14,366	2.28
Scenario 2[a]			
Small	10	35	1.01
Medium	33	3,470	1.47
Large	46	13,618	2.15
Scenario 2[b]			
Small	–	-2,471	0.44
Medium	–	-2,801	0.62
Large	12	642	1.05

[a]Without imputed cost of the family labor.
[b]With imputed cost of the family labor.

TABLE 16.5
Sensitivity Analysis Based on Various Discount Rates

Local Reservoir Size	Net Present Value ($)			
	15%	12%	10%	8%
Scenario 1[a]				
Small	4,386	5,452	6,371	7,521
Medium	13,598	16,597	19,184	22,418
Large	32,550	39,739	45,943	53,694
Scenario 1[b]				
Small	−113	83	253	465
Medium	2,358	3,184	3,896	4,788
Large	9,334	12,035	14,366	17,279
Scenario 2[a]				
Small	−273	−108	35	214
Medium	2,045	2,810	3,470	4,297
Large	8,784	11,379	13,618	16,416
Scenario 2[b]				
Small	−2,115	−2,306	−2,471	−2,676
Medium	−2,570	−2,698	−2,807	−2,943
Large	−756	−5	642	1,453

[a]Without imputed cost of the family labor.
[b]With imputed cost of the family labor.

NPV, and CBR, which hardly go beyond the minimum criteria for project evaluation. When the imputed cost of family labor is included, only large reservoirs justify the investment decision; both small and medium reservoirs are not profitable.

SENSITIVITY ANALYSIS

The robustness of the cost-benefit analysis is tested at different discount rates: 8 percent, 12 percent, and 15 percent. In Scenario 1, net economic benefits remain strong for all sizes of reservoirs, other than in one instance where small reservoirs show a negative NPV at a 15 percent discount rate (table 16.5).

In Scenario 2, without the imputed cost of labor, medium and large reservoirs are still economically viable at the 15 percent discount rate. However, at discount rates of 12 percent and 15 percent, small reservoirs are not economically feasible. When the imputed cost of family labor is incorporated, none of the reservoirs show a positive economic benefit except for large reservoirs, which show positive NPV at the lower discount rates of 8 percent and 10 percent.

Conclusion

Small, multipurpose reservoirs have been used widely in the ZIS for many years because of the numerous economic benefits they generate. These reservoirs have contributed to the transfer of water from irrigation to higher-value uses by capturing rainfall and storing surplus water from other sources. The results of cost-benefit analysis show that reservoirs of all sizes were profitable. This profitability, along with decreasing water supplies from the ZIS, explains why farmers are increasingly investing in reservoirs. Overall, large reservoirs showed higher profits than small and medium ones. This is mainly due to economies of scale, which allow farmers to store relatively large quantities of water and provide ample opportunities for fish harvesting.

There are two main conclusions of this analysis. First, governments and investors should develop relatively large water conservation investment projects, irrigating bigger areas to achieve significant economies of scale, while limiting size so as to minimize the occurrence of serious environmental and social risks. Second, aquifers and small and large reservoirs serve an indispensable role in water storage and have strong comparative advantages in certain circumstances. When it is possible to do so, governments and investors can realize substantial gains by combining large and on-farm reservoirs into an integrated system.

WIDER APPLICATION OF COST-BENEFIT ANALYSIS

China suffers from a range of water availability and quality issues, from overstressed rivers and aquifers in the arid north to flood-prone rivers in the south. The key challenge is to adopt strong water resource management plans that improve water and food security and environmental balance without hampering continuous economic growth. Investments in water resources need to be more strategic and better aligned with climate change adaptation policies. Importantly, investments need to be justified by cost-benefit analysis since they are funded through public monies and, if they can be shown to have high rates of return, could also be structured to attract private capital (Inocencio et al. 2006).

Despite increased investment by the central government and the private sector (mostly from farmers, individually or collectively) in the late 1990s and early 2000s, investment in reservoirs has remained low. One of the key reasons has been the lack of a rigorous cost-benefit analytical framework to facilitate decision making and investment in the water sector, particularly regarding measures of efficiency and water productivity (Pegram 2010). Evidence is emerging that farmers in China will also invest heavily in on-farm water storage (Molden et al. 2007). However, the lack of a robust investment framework currently blurs farmers' investment decisions.

Recently, China has implemented large-scale water projects such as the Three Gorges Dam at Yangtze River and the South-North Water Transfer Project. While cost-benefit analysis is applied regularly to evaluate water resource projects in China—for example in the fields of infrastructural investment, river basin management, and flood risk management—large-scale water projects have not been subjected to rigorous analysis. This is mainly due to complexities in quantifying the favorable and unfavorable consequences and the difficulty of quantifying many of the complex environmental, social, and cultural impacts.

Successful investment in water resources requires a systematic benchmarking approach to rank possible investments according to the economic value they generate. The strength of a cost-benefit analysis framework lies precisely in its ability to value the range of individual impacts associated with a project. These impacts (social, economic, environmental) are determined using clearly delineated valuation and quantification practices; disclosure of these practices also enhances the transparency of the decision-making process. Importantly, they also reveal the trade-offs between alternative policies and demonstrate which options are winners and which losers.

Returns on water sector investments are often understated, and investment preparation must ensure that all benefits are taken into account. The cost-benefit analysis developed in this chapter can help bring rationality and transparency to the decision-making process. Significantly, it provides a framework for consistently providing useful information about small to medium farm-level investments in water resources.

Historically, financing major capital works for water resource development has come from international development banks with varying levels of contribution from national budgets. There have been experiments with financing packages to attract private investment through design, build, and operational contracts and franchises; however, the economic niche for these instruments is limited, and expected financing levels have not been, and are unlikely to be, achieved because of limited opportunities for profit (World Bank 2005). Investment risk is also a widespread concern within the private sector. A rigorous analytical framework may provide a necessary tool for private investment to see the benefits of participating in these types of projects.

China has been extraordinarily successful in attracting foreign direct investment. However, it is unevenly distributed, with nearly 80 percent allocated to coastal areas. Ample opportunities exist in water sector investments, particularly for wastewater treatment systems in central and northern China. The framework developed in this chapter can provide a systematic examination for evaluating the costs and benefits, at micro and macro levels, which may ultimately attract foreign private capital to China's water sector.

Acknowledgments

This chapter relies on Mushtaq et al. (2006), an economic evaluation of small, multipurpose ponds in the Zhanghe Irrigation System, China.

Bibliography

Barker, Randolph, Yuanhua Li, and To Phuc Tuong, eds. 2001. *Water-Saving Irrigation for Rice: Proceedings of an International Workshop Held in Wuhan, China, 23–25 March 2001*. Colombo, Sri Lanka: International Water Management Institute.

Enters, Thomas. 1992. "Land Degradation and Resource Conservation in Highlands of Northern Thailand: The Limit to Economic Evaluation." PhD diss., Australian National University, Canberra.

Gittinger, James Price. 1982. *Economic Analysis of Agricultural Projects.* Baltimore: Johns Hopkins University Press.

Gleick, Peter H., Heather Cooley, Michael J. Cohen, Mari Morikawa, Jason Morrison, Meena Palaniappan, et al. 2009. *The World's Water 2008–2009: The Biennial Report on Freshwater Resources.* Washington, D.C.: Island Press.

Inocencio, Arlene, Masao Kikuchi, Manabu Tonosaki, Atsushi Maruyama, Douglas Merrey, Hilmy Sally, and Ijsbrand de Jong. 2006. *Costs and Performance of Irrigation Projects: A Comparison of Sub-Saharan Africa and Other Developing Regions.* Research Report No. 109. Colombo, Sri Lanka: IWMI.

Keller, Andrew, R. Sakthivadivel, and David Seckler. 2000. *Water Scarcity and the Role of Storage in Development.* Research Report No. 39. Colombo, Sri Lanka: International Water Management Institute.

Khan, Shahbaz, Munir A. Hanjra, and Jianxin Mu. 2009. "Water Management and Crop Production for Food Security in China: A Review." *Agricultural Water Management* 96 (3): 349–60.

Kunze, Dagmar. 2000. "Economic Assessment of Water Harvesting Techniques: A Demonstration of Various Methods." *Quarterly Journal of International Agriculture* 39 (1): 69–91.

Liao, Yongsong, Zhanyi Gao, Ziyun Bao, Qingwen Huang, Guangzhi Feng, Di Xu, Jiabin Cai, et al. 2008. "China's Water Pricing Reforms for Irrigation: Effectiveness and Impact." Discussion Paper No. 6, International Water Management Institute, Colombo, Sri Lanka.

Loeve, Ronald, Bin Dong, Lin Hong, C. D. Chen, S. Zhang, and Randolph Barker. 2007. "Transferring Water From Irrigation to Higher Valued Uses: A Case Study of the Zhanghe Irrigation System in China." *Paddy and Water Environment* 5 (4): 263–69.

Lohmar, Bryan, Jinxia Wang, Scott Rozelle, Jikun Huang, and David Dawe. 2003. "China's Agricultural Water Policy Reforms: Increasing Investment, Resolving Conflicts, and Revising Incentives." Agriculture Information Bulletin No. 782, U.S. Department of Agriculture, Washington, D.C.

Molden, David, Bin Dong, Ronald Loeve, Randolph Barker, and T. P. Tuong. 2007. "Agricultural Water Productivity and Savings: Policy Lessons from Two Diverse Sites in China." *Water Policy* 9 (Supplement 1): 29–44.

Mu, Jianxin, Shahbaz Khan, Munir A. Hanjra, and Hao Wang. 2009. "A Food Security Approach to Analyse Irrigation Efficiency Improvement Demands at the Country Level." *Irrigation and Drainage* 58 (1): 1–16.

Mushtaq, Shahbaz, David Dawe, Hong Lin, and Piedad Moya. 2006. "An Assessment of the Role of Ponds in the Adoption of Water-Saving Irrigation Practices in the Zhanghe Irrigation System, China." *Agricultural Water Management* 83 (1–2): 100–110.

Mushtaq, Shahbaz, Shahbaz Khan, David Dawe, Munir A. Hanjra, Mohsin Hafeez, and Muhammad Nadeem Asghar. 2008. "Evaluating the Impact of Tax-For-Fee Reform (*Fei Gai Shui*) on Water Resources and Agriculture Production in the Zhanghe Irrigation System, China." *Food Policy* 33 (6): 576–86.

Pandey, Sushil. 1991. "The Economics of Water Harvesting and Supplementary Irrigation in the Semi-Arid Tropics of India." *Agricultural Systems* 36 (2): 207–20.

Pandey, Sushil, and S. Rajatasereekul. 1999. "Economics of Plant Breeding: The Value of Shorter Breeding Cycles for Rice in Northeast Thailand." *Field Crops Research* 64 (1–2): 187–97.

Pegram, Guy. 2010. "Global Water Scarcity: Risks and Challenges for Business." Business Briefing. Lloyd's 360 Risk Insight, London.

World Bank. 2005. *World Development Report 2006: Equity and Development.* Washington, D.C.: World Bank.

Yuan, Tian, Li Fengmin, and Liu Puhai. 2003. "Economic Analysis of Rainwater Harvesting and Irrigation Methods, with an Example from China." *Agricultural Water Management* 60 (3): 217–26.

Zhang, Fenghua, Munir A. Hanjra, Yong Hui, and Shahbaz Khan. 2009. "Green Strategies for Enhancing Economic Growth and Ecological Sustainability in Xinjiang Province in China." In *WTO Accession and Socio-economic Development*, ed. Parikshit Basu and Yapa Bandara, 59–78. Cambridge: Chandos Publishing.

Zhenyu, Wang. 2007. "China's Water Management in Rural Areas." Presented at The Pacific Economic Cooperation Council (PECC) Seminar on Water Management in Islands, Coastal, and Isolated Areas, November 13–15, Singapore.

17

Cost-Benefit Analysis of Water Projects in India
Pawan Labhasetwar

In India, the importance of water is always readily apparent. In the dry season, many regions suffer from drought; during the monsoon, flooding is a common occurrence. Population growth, industrial development, and agricultural production contribute to high demand, but India's water resources are relatively limited: India's freshwater availability is only 1,852 cubic meters per capita per year, compared to an average of 9,974 cubic meters per capita per year in the United States (FAO 2012).

Water is important not only to meet basic human needs, but to sustain agriculture and ensure food security. Two-thirds of the Indian population, particularly in rural regions, are employed in agriculture. But while water is essential for agriculture, farming places stress on water resources. Changes in cropping patterns and land use, overexploitation of water storage, and changes in irrigation and drainage negatively affect the hydrological cycle in many climate regions and river basins in India.

Water scarcity has gotten worse over time, a trend that is likely to continue (Jain, Agarwal, and Singh 2007). Surface water availability continues to fall precipitously: from 2,300 cubic meters per person per year in 1991 to 1,900 a decade later. By 2025, this number is expected to fall to 1,400 cubic meters per person per year; by 2050, the per capita yearly surface water availability is projected to be only 1,191 cubic meters—nearly half the amount in 1991 (Kumar, Singh, and Sharma 2005).

Contributing to the problem of scarcity, water sources have also become increasingly contaminated, adding a quality issue to the water scarcity problem. Declining water quality levels result in costs to recreation and amenity use, human health, and overall environmental quality. Rural areas, which often have especially high water needs for agricultural uses, are often most affected by these issues (World Bank 1992).

The solution to the problem of water scarcity in India is highly debated. Government officials and technocrats often believe that the best options involve large-scale water development projects. India has already invested a large amount of money in water resource projects. But these projects can have long gestation periods, massive cost overruns, resettlement issues, costs and benefits that accrue outside the project site, adverse environmental impacts, and the potential for poor planning and execution as well as corruption. All of these factors introduce substantial uncertainty into large-scale water resource development. While the potential negative consequences of these projects are widely recognized and debated, many still argue that dams, irrigation projects, and interbasin transfers are the only viable solutions to the problem of water scarcity in India.

The Sardar Sarovar Dam on the Narmada River in Gujarat State and the Tehri Dam in Uttarakhand State are the most politicized and controversial projects. Opponents of these projects strongly protest their adverse effects on local communities and the environment. Proponents argue that directing fresh water to populations in need will improve public health and alleviate poverty.

Traditional methods of battling water scarcity, such as rooftop rainwater harvesting, check dams, and village recharge ponds, have been offered as alternatives, but critics doubt that these methods can ensure a steady supply of water. Evidence is also lacking that, on the scale that is necessary to fulfill water demand in India, the cumulative environmental and social impacts from these smaller projects would be any less adverse. Many small dams and recharge structures will have their own associated environmental impacts. Distributed storage may require greater surface area than one large reservoir, leading to increased surface evaporation and increased mosquito habitat and malaria prevalence.

To answer questions about what types of water projects are justified, cost-benefit analysis is often used. In the past, large-scale dam projects in particular have been subject to cost-benefit analysis. For smaller-scale projects, the required scientific, engineering, and economic capacity to conduct such studies is sometimes lacking, but as knowledge of the technique grows, application of economic principles to small water projects has become more widespread. The following discussion examines how cost-benefit analysis can be and has been used in the context of water resources in India. From examination of small-scale projects like gray-water recycling at residential schools to analysis of the economic value of avoiding waterborne diseases, cost-benefit analysis can be used to inform decisions about how best to manage this precious commodity.

Cost-Benefit Principles and Water Resource Management

By applying cost-benefit analysis to its water crisis, India can become a powerful case study for the wider adoption of economic analysis in developing countries. Because the methodology of cost-benefit analysis relies on estimating consumer willingness to pay, in certain water scarcity contexts, in which the very basic survival needs of a population have not been met, the analysis may be inappropriate. But generally speaking, a systematic tool to examine the positive and negative effects of a decision can be an important aid to policymakers making choices about future water development.

Because of the difficulty of assigning unambiguous economic values to all water usages, water resources may be implicitly undervalued or overvalued. As population and income levels rise, the likelihood that water use by one agent will interfere with the use by another increases. In economic terms, water now has an opportunity cost with a value equivalent to the willingness to pay of the user who is losing the water. Analysts have developed and propagated a number of ad hoc methods and techniques in order to estimate monetary values for the amenity and environmental services provided by water bodies.

The literature on benefits estimation covers both use and nonuse value components of total economic value (Pearce and Turner 1990). To take just a few selected examples, the recreation value of a lake or river, or "use value," can be estimated via the travel cost method, which utilizes data on the costs of recreation travel as a proxy for consumer willingness to pay to use the resource. The value that individuals might derive from the mere knowledge that pristine mountain lakes still exist and flourish, or "nonuse value," can be estimated by the contingent valuation method, which utilizes survey techniques to generate willingness-to-pay values.

Economists can extend the principle and method of cost-benefit analysis to water resource projects. Cost-benefit analysis suggests that policy or action is preferred if social benefits exceed social costs, taking into account private costs and benefits as well as externalities. For activities like wastewater disposal, which are unavoidable, the most cost-effective solution will lead to efficiency.

Cost-Benefit Analysis of Water Resource Projects in India

Analysts can gauge the merits of water resource projects by examining the ratio of benefits to costs (McKean 1967). If the ratio of benefit to cost is greater than 1 then the project should be allowed to proceed (assuming no mutually exclusive option with higher total net benefits). Major water projects require extensive economic analysis to weigh the benefits of the projects against the costs of implementation and operation (Schoengold and Zilberman 2007). Most water projects funded by international agencies, such as the World Bank, also require such studies as part of an environmental impact assessment (EIA) before approval.

Cost-benefit analysis, if properly undertaken, assists in answering the important question of whether a project should be built or not. The project with the highest net present value (benefits minus costs) should be built (assuming at least one of the alternatives has a positive net present value). The decision makers sometimes go beyond the question of "to build or not to build" and consider the importance of when to build. Arrow and Fisher, and later Dixit and Pindyck, developed models for decision makers to consider delaying optimal project design so that analysts could learn more information (Arrow and Fisher 1974; Dixit and Pindyck 1994). Delaying a project may lead to a loss in potential benefits that would have been realized if the project had been undertaken earlier. However, prolonging the building stage can also generate future gains as more information is learned about efficiencies.

The use of cost-benefit analysis to understand water policy has grown substantially in the developing world over the past several years. Below are a few examples of prominent analyses that have been done in this area.

COST ESTIMATES OF INDUSTRIAL WATER POLLUTION IN RURAL COMMUNITIES

Reddy and Behera (2006) applied a cost-benefit analysis approach and assessed the economic costs of industrial water pollution in India's rural communities in terms of losses to agricultural production, human health, and livestock. The cost estimates were based on detailed, primary household-level data collected from an intensive study of two villages: one a pollution-affected village and another a control, not affected by pollution; both were located in one of the industrial belts in Andhra Pradesh, South India.

The cost estimates revealed that the impact of industrial pollution on rural communities is quite substantial in monetary terms. This is mainly due to its direct impact on human health and livelihood. Sick days and medical treatment resulting from consumption of polluted water are the primary factors creating economic stress. Contaminated drinking water can cause employees to miss work or livestock to be lost, and can have a substantial impact on the agricultural industry.

The net impact of pollution was estimated to be $53[1] per household per annum. Villagers reported 149 cattle deaths owing to drinking polluted water between 1995 and 2000, along with deterioration of the health of the cattle. Villagers found that some cows lost their reproductive ability. These cows then became a liability to their owners. Grazing on contaminated grasses and drinking polluted water resulted in poor quality products. Fearing more cattle deaths, people sold their cows at very low rates, leading to further financial loss. About forty-five hectares of cultivable land had become uncultivable by soil pollution, leading to drastic changes in the livelihood of Kazipalle villagers (Kazipalle is one of the two villages observed). The loss of productive land in Kazipalle was solely attributed to irrigation of polluted water. Besides the decline in agricultural productivity, the polluted water imposed other costs like corrosion of agricultural equipment and damage to pump sets. The amount of land under cultivation declined substantially (88 percent) between the before-pollution time and the after-pollution time because of the increased pollution. The average loss per household per annum to the pollution-affected households in Kazipalle village was about $282.50, with some households in the village suffering few if any pollution-related effects and others suffering greatly.

COST-BENEFIT ANALYSIS OF GRAY-WATER REUSE IN RESIDENTIAL SCHOOLS IN MADHYA PRADESH

The central Indian state of Madhya Pradesh has a population of nearly seventy-three million and spans over three hundred thousand square kilometers. The principle cities in Madhya Pradesh are Indore, Jabalpur, Sagar, Bhopal, Gwalior, and Ujjain (ORGCC 2011), and its per capita GDP is roughly $545 (VMW 2012). The total net groundwater availability of Madhya Pradesh (in 1998) was 31 million hectare meters. About 99 percent of the drinking water needs are fulfilled with groundwater, and 90 percent of the groundwater is being used for irrigation purposes (Khanna and Khanna 2005, 2).

The infrastructure in Madhya Pradesh for ensuring proper wastewater disposal is currently inadequate, and a third of rural households and a quarter of urban households have no wastewater drainage system. Inadequate wastewater disposal can lead to contaminated water percolating into groundwater, making drinking and irrigation water unsafe, and causing many different kinds of waterborne diseases, such as dysentery and cholera (Momba, Osode, and Sibewu 2006).

Several organizations, including the National Environmental Engineering Research Institute (NEERI), examined how implementation of gray-water treatment and reuse systems in residential schools in Madhya Pradesh could provide low-cost solutions to both wastewater disposal and water availability issues. Pilot program locations were identified and used to evaluate the feasibility of a larger roll-out across the region. If successful, these programs would provide a model for a substantial effort to expand gray-water recycling to hundreds of locations.

The gray water to be recycled for this project consisted of the wastewater emanating from showers and basins, but not from kitchen or toilet uses (NEERI 2007). Gray-water reuse can reduce freshwater demand as well as the strain on wastewater treatment plants and energy production. It can also encourage plant growth from nutrients that may otherwise have been wasted (Godfrey et al. 2009).

The most detailed analysis of the costs and benefits of the gray-water recycling initiative was based on one girls' boarding school in Madhya Pradesh. The school housed three hundred children from the months of July through April. The economic feasibility for gray-water reuse systems constructed in this school was calculated using standard economic methodologies (Hernández et al. 2006).

Cost-benefit analysis was undertaken for gray-water reuse by considering the full range of costs and benefits (Godfrey et al. 2009). These include the costs of constructing, operating, and maintaining the gray-water reuse system. The construction costs (material and labor costs) totaled roughly $1,000, and operation and maintenance costs were about $115 per year.

While estimating benefits due to the gray-water reuse system, Godfrey et al. collected data to quantify benefits such as time saved because water and sanitation facilities were in the school. Teachers and children were asked about where they went for water whenever sources available in the school were dry. Godfrey et al. visited the sources, measured the distance to the sources, and time required to fetch water. This was significant in determining the benefits that accrued due to gray-water reuse system in school.

The project accrued a range of benefits. Health benefits were the largest category, with over $15,500 in annual benefits. The largest category of health benefit was time savings due to the greater availability of on-site water and sanitation facilities. Using an estimated value for the students' time based on government education expenditures of $2 per student per day (and assuming a twenty-four-hour school day), the value of the time saved by students by virtue of easier access to water and sanitation facilities totaled over $9,000 per year. The time saved by virtue of easier access to water and sanitation facilities was one and a half hours per day for each student. By also reducing water purchase requirements, the gray-water recycling system saved roughly another $1,000 per year. The bulk of the other health benefits were caused by or related to averted diarrhea cases, including decreased hospitalization, lost school days avoided, and caregiver workdays avoided. Together, these figures clearly justify the relatively modest investment in construction and maintenance of these systems.

Considering the findings of the cost-benefit analysis, the government of Madhya Pradesh has allocated funds for construction of 412 gray-water reuse systems. Out of these, about two hundred systems have already been built in schools in Madhya Pradesh, India.

COST-EFFECTIVENESS OF WATER QUALITY INTERVENTIONS FOR PREVENTING DIARRHEAL DISEASE

As part of a recent series on the costs and effectiveness of interventions to achieve the United Nations Millennium Development Goals, the World Health Organization's (WHO) Choosing Interventions that are Cost Effective (CHOICE) team used cost-effectiveness analysis to examine strategies to combat malaria and HIV/AIDS, control tuberculosis, improve child health, and promote maternal and neonatal health (Evans et al. 2005). This method compares the various interventions being considered, including no intervention, or the "null" scenario, on a sector-wide basis for a group of populations with comparable health systems and epidemiological profiles (Tan-Torres Edejer et al. 2003).

CHOICE's process for conducting its generalized cost-effectiveness analysis consisted of five basic steps: (1) defining the interventions to be investigated, as well as the counterfactual or baseline state; (2) estimating the costs associated with the interventions; (3) estimating the effectiveness of the interventions; (4) modeling the study population based on demographic, exposure, and risk data; and (5) using the effectiveness data to determine the disability-adjusted life-years (DALYs) averted by each intervention compared to the counterfactual and calculating the cost per DALY averted.

CHOICE evaluated five interventions to improve water quality to prevent diarrhea. Using effectiveness data from a recent systematic review, cost data from program implementers, and WHO databases, it conducted cost-effectiveness analysis to compare non-piped-in source-based interventions from dug wells, boreholes, and communal stand posts, as well as household-based interventions using chlorination, filtration, solar disinfection, and flocculation/disinfection to improve the microbial quality of water for preventing diarrheal disease. CHOICE reported results for two WHO epidemiological subregions, Afr-E (sub-Saharan African countries with very high adult and child mortality) and Sear-D (Southeast Asian countries, including India, with high adult and child mortality) at 50 percent intervention coverage. Measured against international benchmarks, source- and household-based interventions were generally cost effective or highly cost effective even before the estimated savings in health costs were taken into account. Household-based chlorination was the most cost effective where resources were limited, while household filtration yielded additional health gains at higher budget levels. All other interventions strongly dominated flocculation/disinfection, and chlorination weakly dominated solar disinfection. In addition to cost effectiveness, Clasen et al. (2007) found that choices among water quality interventions must be guided by local conditions, user preferences, potential for cost recovery from beneficiaries, and other factors.

COST-BENEFIT ANALYSIS OF CLEANING THE GANGES

Attempts to estimate the social benefits of cleaning the Ganges River highlight some of the emerging environmental and development issues in river-cleaning programs. Markandya and Murty (2004) estimated the benefits of river cleaning by using the market and nonmarket values of environmental goods and including the use and nonuse benefits, health benefits to the poor households living along the Ganges, and agricultural benefits to farmers. However, the benefits from fisheries, which are significant, could not be quantified in their study. Factoring in only those quantifiable benefits, the Ganges cleanup program has positive net present social benefits at a 10 percent discount rate and a 15 percent internal rate of return (Markandya and Murty 2004).

When the study was completed, $153 million had been spent during the first phase of the cleanup program, and $9.6 million had been spent during the second phase (Markandya and Murty 2004, 75). An attempt was made at comparing benefits from the action plan to these costs. An indicator calculated the different biochemical oxygen demand concentrations at different points on the Ganges to summarize the quality level. A first assessment of benefits was done through valuation of use and nonuse benefits associated with different levels of river quality: (1) the initial level of water quality before the implementation of the cleanup plan; (2) the actual level of water quality at the time of the study; and (3) the targeted final level of river quality that would allow for safe use for bathing.

The survey on nonuse value estimated an average willingness to pay for higher water quality in the Ganges for 8.7 million households within the urban literate population in twenty-three cities with a population over one million. The willingness to pay measured by the survey varied between $2.03 per annum per household for the past quality to $11.16 per annum per household for bathing quality.

The survey of use benefits was targeted at households living within one kilometer of the riverbanks. The average willingness to pay measured by the survey varied between $1.87 per annum per household for the past quality and $11.63 per annum per household for bathing quality. The fact that the nonuse value estimation is similar to the use value may be accounted for by the greater level of wealth of the urban population compared to those households that lived closer to the riverbanks.

The positive health impacts from the cleanup program were calculated based on the results of a study carried out by the All India Institute of Hygiene and Public Health (AIIHPH) about the improvements to users' income due to reduction in lost working days, and the additional costs to treat water for public supply in the

TABLE 17.1
Health Benefits from Reduced Loss of Working Days

Town	Average No. of Working Days Saved Yearly per Family	Regular Users of Ganges in Town (no. of families)	Individual Daily Income (US$)	Total Value (US$)
Hardwar	6.09	41,300	1.25	313,619.25
Kanpur	3.42	15,560	0.69	36,458.24
Patna	6.58	22,480	1.72	254,031.60
Chandan nagar	6.44	5,690	0.74	26,853.65
Nabadwip	7.37	4,760	1.27	44,690.74
Titagarh	2.61	4,920	0.61	7,644.47

Source: AIIH and PH (1997).

absence of a cleanup program (Markandya and Murty 2004). According to the survey carried out by the AIIHPH, the health benefits in table 17.1 were inferred in six cities on the Ganges' banks (Markandya and Murty 2004).

COST OF ENVIRONMENTAL DEGRADATION

Two experts from the World Bank undertook a study in 1995 to analyze the cost of environmental degradation in India (Brandon and Hommann 1995). Their aim was not to provide precise figures but rather comprehensive gross estimates of the different economic burdens caused by environmental degradation, which are provided in figure 17.1.

It is noteworthy that the only quantified cost of water pollution was the health burden due to domestic pollution. Brandon and Hommann calculated this cost as the achievable reduction of infectious and viral water-related diseases assuming full water supply and sanitation coverage. The significant costs that they did not

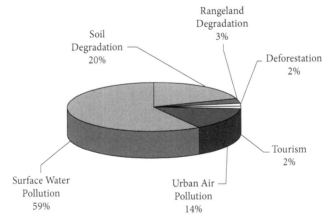

FIGURE 17.1 Contribution of Water Pollution in the Overall Burden of Environmental Degradation in India
Source: Brandon and Homman (1995).

TABLE 17.2

Summary of Major Annual Environment Costs in India

Problem	Impacts on Health and/ or Production	Low Estimate (US$ millions)	High Estimate (US$ millions)
Urban air pollution	Urban health impacts	517	2102
Water pollution (health impacts)	Urban and rural health impacts, esp. diarrheal diseases	3,076	8,344
Water pollution (production impacts)	Higher incremental costs for clean water supply	Not estimated	Not estimated
Industrial hazardous waste	Long-term health impacts, esp. cancer	Not estimated	Not estimated
Soil Degradation	Loss of agricultural output	1,516	2,368
Rangeland degradation	Loss of livestock carrying capacity	238	417
Deforestation	Loss of sustainable timber supply	183	244
Coastal and marine resources	Unsustainable harvesting of marine resources	Not estimated	Not estimated
Loss of biodiversity	Loss of use, option, and exis-tence values	Not estimated	Not estimated
Tourism	Decline in tourism revenues	142	283
Total costs of environmental degradation		5,672	13,758
Total cost as % of GDP		2.64%	6.41%
Average total cost		9.715	
Average total cost as % of GDP		4.53%	

Source: Brandon and Hommann (1995).

quantify were the health cost of chemical pollution, the higher cost of municipal water supply, the cost of treatment for industries, and the loss of agricultural productivity due to bad water quality. These results are summarized in table 17.2.

MEASURING BENEFITS FROM INDUSTRIAL WATER POLLUTION ABATEMENT: USE OF CONTINGENT VALUATION METHOD IN NANDESARI INDUSTRIAL AREA

This study was carried out to assess the potential benefits from pollution abatement in the Nandesari Industrial Estate in the state of Gujarat (Maria 2003). Two separate questionnaires were used to assess the willingness to pay for environmental protection from urban and rural populations. Both use and nonuse values were assessed.

The urban survey covered 386 households for use value and 366 households for nonuse value. The estimated average willingness to pay was $1.48 per capita per annum for use value and $1.14 for nonuse value (Maria 2003).

The rural survey covered six villages having a population of 7,890 households; 405 households were covered for use value, giving an average estimate of the willingness to accept equivalent to $54.18 per capita per annum (Maria 2003).

The disparity in the willingness to pay between the urban and rural household reveals how rural households are more directly exposed to the adverse effects of environmental degradation. While the urban disutility of water pollution is linked to a hypothetical increased risk of contaminated drinking water, the rural disutility caused by the same degradation can be expressed in terms of revenue loss due to a decrease in agricultural productivity, as well as a direct increase in the health risks associated with contaminated water.

It also is possible that the urban survey respondents did not take into account the additional cost of water supply they have to bear. If this is the case, then the results obtained do not give the full extent of the potential benefits from pollution abatement (Maria 2003).

Conclusion

The demand for water in India is increasing exponentially, stressing the available water sources, which in turn has led to conflict between India's states. Climate change, receding water availability, and the inability to harness water during flooding compound the problem of meeting demand. Therefore, developing water resources is paramount. Cost-benefit analysis of various water resource projects provides India with information about project prioritization and fund allocation. Indian agencies must use due care in their analyses, however, to avoid misusing this tool by overestimating benefits and underestimating costs.

Unfortunately, the Ministry of Environment and Forests prefers the voluntary application of cost-benefit analysis in evaluating water development projects instead of relying on cost-benefit analysis as a default starting point for decision making. While cost-benefit analysis has been used in the Environmental Impact Assessment Guidelines of Water Resources Projects issued by the ministry, there is no evidence that cost-benefit analysis is used by government organizations in practice. Many of the analyses that have been conducted by the government remain confined to these agencies, and the conclusions of these studies are not published. There should be efforts to identify such studies, and participating organizations should be encouraged to publish findings of cost-benefit analysis to spread the broad application of this useful tool to a wide range of important environmental questions.

Notes

1. An exchange rate of 1 U.S. dollar to 50 Indian rupees is used throughout this chapter.

Bibliography

Arrow, Kenneth J., and Anthony C. Fisher. 1974. "Environmental Preservation, Uncertainty, and Irreversibility." *Quarterly Journal of Economics* 88 (2): 312–19.

Brandon, Carter, and Kirsten Hommann. 1995. "The Cost of Inaction: Valuing the Economy-Wide Cost of Environmental Degradation in India." Paper presented at the United Nations University Conference on the Sustainable Future of the Global System, Tokyo, Japan, October 16–18.

Clasen, Thomas, Laurence Haller, Damian Walker, Jamie Bartram, and Sandy Cairncross. 2007. "Cost-Effectiveness of Water Quality Interventions for Preventing Diarrhoeal Disease in Developing Countries." *Journal of Water and Health* 5 (4): 599–608.

Dixit, Avinash K., and Robert S. Pindyck. 1994. *Investment under Uncertainty*. Princeton: Princeton University Press.

Evans, David B., Tessa Tan-Torres Edejer, Taghreed Adam, and Stephen S. Lim. 2005. "Methods to Assess the Costs and Health Effects of Interventions for Improving Health in Developing Countries." *British Medical Journal* 331 (7525): 1137–40.

Food and Agriculture Organization of the United Nations (FAO). 2012. "Water Resources: Total Renewable Per Capita (Actual) (m3/inhab/yr)." From *The Aquastat Database*, updated 2012. Rome: FAO.

Godfrey, Sam, Pawan Labhasetwar, and Satish Wate. 2009. "Greywater Reuse in Residential Schools in Madhya Pradesh, India: A Case Study of Cost-Benefit Analysis." *Resources, Conservation and Recycling* 53 (3): 287–93.

Hernández, F., A. Urkiaga, L. De las Fuentes, B. Bis, E. Chiru, B. Balazs, and T. Wintgens. 2006. "Feasibility Studies for Water Reuse Projects: An Economical Approach." *Desalination* 187 (1–3): 253–61.

Jain, Sharad K., Pushpendra K. Agarwal, and Vijay P. Singh. 2007. *Hydrology and Water Resources of India*. Dordrecht: Springer.

Khanna, Amod, and Chitra Khanna. 2005. *Water and Sanitation in Madhya Pradesh: A Profile of the State, Institutions, and Policy Environment*. New Delhi: WaterAid India.

Kumar, Rakesh, R. D. Singh, and K. D. Sharma. 2005. "Water Resources of India." *Current Science* 89 (5): 794–811.

Maria, Augustin. 2003. *The Costs of Water Pollution in India*. Paris: Center of Industrial Economics.

Markandya, A., and M. Narsimha Murty. 2004. "Cost-Benefit Analysis of Cleaning the Ganges: Some Emerging Environment and Development Issues." *Environment and Development Economics* 9 (1): 61–81.

McKean, Roland N. 1967. *Efficiency in Government through Systems Analysis*. New York: John Wiley and Sons.

Momba, M. N. B., A. N. Osode, and M. Sibewu. 2006. "The Impact of Inadequate Wastewater Treatment on the Receiving Water Bodies—Case Study: Buffalo City and Nkokonbe Municipalities of the Eastern Cape Province." *Water SA* 32 (5): 687–92.

National Environmental Engineering Research Institute (NEERI). 2007. *Greywater Reuse in Rural Schools: Guidance Manual*. Madhya Pradesh, India: UNICEF.

Office of the Registrar General and Census Commissioner, India (ORGCC). 2011. *Census of India 2011: Provisional Population Totals—Madhya Pradesh*. Bhopal, Madhya Pradesh, India: Directorate of Census Operations.

Pearce, David W., and R. Kerry Turner. 1990. *Economics of Natural Resources and the Environment*. Baltimore: Johns Hopkins University Press.

Reddy, Ratna V., and Bhagirath Behera. 2006. "Impact of Water Pollution on Rural Communities: An Economic Analysis." *Ecological Economics* 58 (3): 520–37.

Schoengold, Karina, and David Zilberman. 2007. "The Economics of Water, Irrigation, and Development." *Handbook of Agricultural Economics*, ed. Robert E. Evenson and Prabhu Pingali, vol. 3: 2,940–85.

Tan-Torres Edejer, Tessa, R. Baltussen, T. Adam, R. Hutbessy, A. Acharya, D. B. Evans, and C. J. L. Murray, eds. 2003. *WHO Guide to Cost-Effectiveness Analysis.* Geneva : World Health Organization.

VMW Analytical Services (VMW). 2012. "GDP of Indian States & Union Territories for FY2011—The Federal States of India—Financial Year 2011." *VMW Analytical Services.* Last modified June 2, 2012. http://unidow.com/india%20home%20eng/statewise_gdp.html.

World Bank. 1992. *The World Development Report 1992: Development and the Environment.* Washington, D.C.: World Bank.

18

The Role of Distributional Analysis in Cost-Benefit Analysis

A CASE STUDY OF HYDROELECTRIC PROJECTS IN PANAMA

Sarah Cordero

Most economists are concerned with the equity of market outcomes, because even a perfectly efficient market outcome could leave some individuals with poverty levels that are too great to be acceptable to society as a whole. The tension between equity and efficiency has provided a frequently cited rationale for justifying government intervention in economic affairs.

This chapter examines the importance of distributional analysis in understanding the equity consequences of government decisions, using as a case study the cost-benefit analyses of four hydroelectric projects contemplated by the Panamanian government in 2006. What makes those analyses unusual is that they were not conducted as part of a mandatory regulatory process but rather by a nongovernmental organization (NGO). The NGO's specific goal was to apply rigorous cost-benefit analysis methodology to development projects being considered by the government and how those projects might impact environmental and social conditions. In fact, cost-benefit analysis is not part of the regulatory process in Panama. The only requisite for the approval of an energy project is an environmental impact assessment (EIA), which must be presented to the Autoridad Nacional del Ambiente (ANAM).

The team in charge of conducting the cost-benefit analyses calculated the net cash flow from a financial and economic point of view and then discounted the cash flows to obtain net present values. A positive economic net present value indicates that the results are efficient, thus generating a positive absolute change in wealth, but says nothing about the fairness of the results for affected groups.

The team conducted two types of cost-benefit analysis of the proposed hydroelectric projects. First, the team conducted a *financial* analysis to determine the fiscal feasibility of each project. The results revealed that all four projects appeared attractive to potential investors and lenders. If the projects could be built and financed at the cost estimates used in the study, it is highly probable that the net present value of the financial return would be in excess of $68 million.[1]

Next, the team conducted an *economic* cost-benefit analysis to determine the attractiveness of the four projects from the point of view of Panamanian society. **279**

Given the assumptions, the projects stood to make a substantial contribution to the national economy. The net present value of the net economic benefits (in 2006 dollars) that would accrue to society amounted to approximately $62 million. Thus, the net benefits of the hydroelectric projects would exceed their costs.

Although the results obtained from both analyses were positive—in the sense that they suggested that both private investors and Panamanian society stood to realize positive net gains—the findings pertaining to society deserved greater parsing. They demonstrated that society as a whole would realize a net benefit but failed to account for the specific impacts that would be felt by particular stakeholders or segments of society.

Because of the different impacts felt by different populations, there was a need for a *distributional analysis*, also known as an *analysis of stakeholders*. The distributional analysis conducted after the cost-benefit analysis showed that there would be "losers" and "winners" from the construction and operation of the four hydroelectric projects. The main beneficiaries of the hydroelectric projects would be the financing bank (which would receive a return on investment amounting to $193 million), the government (which would benefit $86 million), and the concessionaires undertaking the projects ($68 million). The "losers" would be the inhabitants of the projects' surrounding areas: inhabitants of the Changuinola and Bonyic river valleys would bear a cost of more than $56 million and see a negative environmental impact amounting to $26 million in present values.[2]

This is a clear case of an investment that may well be economically efficient, but that is also inequitable. The distributional analysis showed that an energy company (AES Corporation), banks, and the government stood to reap the benefits of the project, while the costs would fall disproportionately on particular indigenous communities and surrounding natural ecosystems. Although it is clear that there is room for negotiation, where the winners could agree to compensate the losers and still realize a net gain from the projects, the Panamanian government did not take this approach. Rather than undertaking or endorsing the use of compensation measures, the government ignored the distributional impacts of the projects and gave its approval for them to move forward. In addition, although the energy company promised to compensate inhabitants that would have to be relocated, as of April 2011, compensation was not forthcoming (CBD 2011).

Background

After having financed projects that created huge negative environmental and social effects, such as the Three Gorges Dam in China, most development banks changed their policies for becoming involved in and financing water and energy projects (WCD 2000). The use of recognized assessment techniques, such as strategic environmental and social assessments, for project proposals has become a mandatory part of the selection and justification process for projects that receive most of their funding from international financial institutions, such as the World Bank and the International Finance Corporation; from regional banks like the African, Asian, and Inter-American Development Banks; and from other donor agencies.

Cost-benefit analysis is a methodology that generates information that improves decision making at all levels. It usually includes both a financial and economic analysis of a policy or project, and is becoming increasingly important as a method for choosing between alternative projects in circumstances where resources are limited.

A traditional financial cost-benefit analysis examines the financial feasibility of a project from the owners' point of view (including debt capitalization) and the total investment point of view (the cost of the project without outside financing). When the cost-benefit analysis shows a positive net present value for these stakeholders' financial interests, this indicates a positive expected change in their wealth. By comparison, an economic analysis evaluates the feasibility of a policy or project from the point of view of the whole country's economy; this includes an assessment of any social and environmental externalities. A positive economic net present value implies a positive change in the wealth of the country. Both financial and economic analyses can be disaggregated to determine how various impacts are allocated to affected parties (Harberger and Jenkins 2002).

For example, a policy that acts as a price ceiling will have economic effects that are different from financial effects. Financially, the reduction in price simply lowers total revenue, but from an economic perspective it generates a gain in consumers' surplus as well as a loss in producers' surplus. (Of course, that does not mean that an economic analysis would favor such a policy.) The differences between the financial and economic values of inputs and outputs also may arise through a variety of market distortions including taxes and subsidies, externalities, or any other reason for which the item is sold to consumers at a price different from the marginal economic cost of additional supply.

In addition to conducting financial and economic cost-benefit analysis, a distributional analysis can also be conducted to expand the information that will form the basis of policy decisions. In essence, a distributional analysis seeks to allocate the net benefit or net losses generated by a project. Such analysis allows decision makers to estimate the impact of a particular policy or project on discrete segments of society, and to predict which groups or communities will be net beneficiaries, and which groups will be net losers.

The distributional analysis of a project asks the following questions:

1. Who will benefit from the project, and by how much?
2. Who will pay for the project, and how much will they have to pay?

Local Stakeholders

In 2006, given that the government was not showing signs of conducting a participatory process for the evaluation of these projects, the Conservation Strategy Fund (CSF)—an NGO whose mission is to work with environmental organizations to facilitate their use of economics to promote conservation—assembled a team of professionals to conduct cost-benefit analyses of some of the seventy hydroelectric projects then being considered by the Panamanian government. In performing the study, the team used data obtained from the National Public Services Authority (ASEP).

Ultimately, the team analyzed four hydroelectric projects in Panama's Bocas del Toro Province, located in the Changuinola-Teribe watershed, within the limits of the Bosque Protector Palo Seco. Three of the projects would be built on the Changuinola River, and the fourth was proposed to be built on the Bonyic Stream, which is part of the Teribe River. The projects were named, respectively, Chan 75, Chan 140, Chan 220, and Bonyic. Notably, both the Changuinola and Teribe rivers have their headwaters within the Amistad International Park (PILA), which is both a UNESCO World Heritage Site and a core area of the Amistad Biosphere Reserve. According to ASEP, the dams' combined installed capacity would be 446 megawatts, equivalent to 30 percent of Panama's total capacity at the end of 2004.

The team's cost-benefit analyses of the projects suggested that they would most likely be both economically and financially feasible. The team estimated the cash flows using project data obtained from ASEP and from cost estimations based on the energy industries of Panama and Costa Rica. Specific tables were prepared for investment cost, electricity production cost, maintenance cost, electricity sales, inflation, administrative costs, and so on. At the same time, the projects would cause environmental damage in an area of global conservation interest and impose serious hardship on indigenous communities living along these rivers. For example, PILA—a global center of biological diversity and endemism—would be more exposed to deforestation due to new access roads. Aquatic biodiversity would be affected in over 704 kilometers of rivers, with some migratory fish species likely to fade. The total area within which aquatic species could be lost would be approximately 1,493 square kilometers. If the PILA ecosystem were affected, the impacts would most likely stretch beyond its boundaries because it serves as a biological corridor between North and South America.

CSF had to adjust the economic cost-benefit analysis to correct for distortions such as taxes and subsidies, since these are considered transfer payments. It used "shadow prices" to adjust for any distortion. Finally, it included the economic value of some externalities (costs and benefits neither paid for nor received by the company but which would be caused by these projects). Because of time and financial resources constraints, not all externalities were included in this study. With adjustments, the CSF team concluded that the projects would generate an economic benefit of $62 million.

The population located in the impacted area is largely indigenous and lives in the communities of Ngöbe (along the Changuinola River) and Naso (along the Teribe River). According to information provided by the most recent national census, conducted in 2000, the total population of the affected communities is 2,480 persons (DEC 2000). However, according to an even more recent 2005 survey that was conducted for the purposes of performing the distributional analysis, the true number is more than 5,000 people: about 4,000 from the Ngöbe ethnic group and 1,000 from the Naso.

Agriculture is the main livelihood in both territories, followed by fishing and hunting; herding livestock is an emerging business. Agricultural production is intended primarily (90 percent) for household consumption, and the main crops include rice, corn, pixbae, plantains, oranges, root vegetables, beans, avocado, coffee, cocoa, and coconut. The difficulty and cost of transportation is the main obstacle to bringing products to market. To date, however, problems of scale also render the commercialization of products unprofitable. Given the circumstances, the flow of money into these communities is minimal, especially for those farthest away from urban centers. Most trade occurs through barter, except in isolated and rare cases in which inhabitants will use revenues from products sold to acquire goods that are not produced locally or to cover medical expenses.

In these communities, there is no electricity, and water supply systems are rudimentary. Some communities have primary schools and health care facilities; however, their proper functioning is often at risk through lack of skilled personnel and necessary resources. When people need additional services, such as educational programs or medical care, they often move to the nearby cities of Changuinola or Almirante.

The abundance of timber in the area allows people to live in homes that are structurally solid and capable of harboring large families, sometimes more than fifteen people. In some cases, families have two houses: one near the center of the town to facilitate the school attendance by children and participation in religious services, and another house closer to farming areas.

Indigenous communities living in the area do not have property rights because Panama lacks adequate legal mechanisms for indigenous people to obtain title to their land—notwithstanding the constitutional recognition of indigenous peoples' rights to their traditional lands—and because indigenous people have not gained sufficient influence in Panama's administrative processes. Thus, the government possesses title to the land in the area, and the vast majority of indigenous peoples have only limited land use rights. The Ngöbe area (Changuinola River) is considered an annexed territory to the Ngöbe-Buglé's *comarca*, their legally recognized reservation of land; however, it does not have the same legal status as a *comarca*. The Naso, meanwhile, have spent decades fighting for the creation of their own *comarca*. The matter is currently under discussion in the National Assembly, which is considering a bill to create such an autonomous district.[3]

In response to growing concerns about the effects of the hydroelectric projects on indigenous communities, the United Nations Human Rights Council sent a special rapporteur to investigate the matter. In a follow-up report, the special rapporteur stated, among his main conclusions, that "the Chan 75 hydroelectric project has got under way, and has made a significant impact on the indigenous communities in the surrounding area, without the consultation process required by international standards on free, prior and informed consultation with indigenous peoples. Their insecurity as regards land tenure and natural resources contributes to the vulnerability of the communities affected by the project" (Anaya 2009, 2).

The Projects

Due to its geographic position, Panama has been a zone of transit and cultural exchange since colonial times. From a biodiversity perspective, two highly biodiverse zones converge in a relatively small territory, producing high levels of biological diversity.

The Province of Bocas del Toro has a territory of 8,917 square kilometers, and approximately 68 percent of it is covered by forest. It is located in the Caribbean region of Panama and is a key area for the conservation of migratory species from the neotropical rain forest. The tropical forests of this region form a rain forest corridor that connects South America with Costa Rica, Nicaragua, and Honduras.

According to the ASEP, as of year 2009, the installed electricity generating capacity in Panama was 1789 MW. In April 2009, fifteen hydroelectric projects were under construction in Panama, and it is expected that they will start operations no later than 2013. Those projects would increase the installed capacity by 600 MW and would cost $1.353 billion. Most of the projects are located in Chiriqui and Bocas del Toro. The most important one is Chan 75, with a capacity of 223 MW and an investment of $502 million. The Chan 75 project had not begun operating as of March 2012.

THE CHANGUINOLA RIVER

The large and rich Changuinola River rises in the Cordillera de Talamanca at an altitude of 2,000 meters above sea level, and it winds along the north region about 100 km before emptying into the Caribbean Sea, just south of the Panama–Costa Rica border.

The Changuinola River is located in one of the wettest areas of the country, with a short dry season and abundant precipitation throughout the year. Under these climatic conditions, typical vegetation is known as tropical wet forest. The average annual rainfall in the area of Changuinola (middle basin) is 4,600 mm (average in Washington, D.C., is 1,050 mm) and the temperature fluctuates throughout the year between eighteen and twenty-seven degrees Celsius (sixty-four to eighty-one degrees Fahrenheit).

In its course, the Changuinola River receives numerous tributaries, among which are Tararia, Teribe (as plenteous as the principal), Risco, Sursuba, San San, and Culubre. At its source, course, and mouth, the Changuinola River crosses territories under different management categories. The top of the basin lies within the boundaries of La Amistad International Park (PILA), the middle along the Bosque Protector Palo Seco (BPPS), while the lower part of the watershed goes through private land with extensive crops and the San San Pond Sak wetland that was declared a wetland of international importance under the Ramsar Convention on Wetlands.

These protected areas along with others located in the Costa Rican territory are part of the La Amistad Biosphere Reserve. These nature reserves, characterized by an annual rainfall of around 5,000 mm, were created to protect watersheds with hydroelectric potential and all life zones in the region, from the lowlands of the Atlantic slope to the Cordillera de Talamanca. In this regard, the rules for the creation of PILA and the BPPS explicitly highlight the need to preserve this watershed because of its potential for hydroelectric development.

THE PRIVATE INVESTOR

AES Changuinola S.A. conducts the development, construction, and operation and management of the Changuinola I generation power unit, where the Chan 75 project, also known as *el Gavilan*, is located.[4] A group of international companies that specialize in the development of large-scale infrastructure projects is in charge of the design, engineering, and construction of the civil works. They work as a consortium under the name of Changuinola Civil Works Joint Venture, Inc.

In September 2008, AES Changuinola presented an inventory of flora and fauna in the middle watershed of the Changuinola River. AES hired Montgomery Watson Harza (MWH),[5] a well-known international company, to perform all the environmental studies, and in turn, MWH contracted the Smithsonian Tropical Research Institute (STRI) to carry out the inventory. This is the area of two of the projects—Chan 75 and Chan 140.

The biological inventory took place between December 2006 and February 2008 on a stretch of twenty kilometers from the middle basin of the Changuinola River in the riverbed and surrounding area. The inventory included a large number of scientists associated with the STRI, specialists in flora and fauna, who used multiple and complementary sampling techniques that comprehensively registered the biodiversity of the area. This information was not available at the time that the cost-benefit analysis was conducted; hence, it was not included in either the EIAs or the cost-benefit analysis.

The Study

FINANCIAL ANALYSIS

The financial cost benefit analysis used market prices to calculate the cash flow and potential investment returns from the energy company's point of view.

The team calculated receipts by multiplying energy generated times energy price (per KWh). The loan/equity ratio assumed was 70/30. Given the assumptions made, the analysis shows that the project is financially feasible if not very attractive, since the investor will realize a return of close to $68 million, as shown in table 18.1.

TABLE 18.1

Financial Cost-Benefit Analysis from the Investors' Point of View (US$ millions)

	2006	2007	2008	2009	2010	2011	2012	2013	...	2031
Receipts										
Energy sales				7.3	47.9	83.7	124.2	128.0		188.4
Loan disbursement	18.8	38.7	108.4	135.6	45.5	30.4	0.4	0.0		0.0
Liquidation values										136.7
Total receipts	18.8	38.7	108.4	143.0	93.4	114.1	124.6	128.0		325.2
Expenditures										
Investments	26.8	55.3	154.9	193.8	64.9	43.4	0.6			
Energy generation										
Generation costs				2.2	14.2	24.1	34.7	35.2		46.1
Administrative costs				0.3	1.7	2.9	4.3	4.5		6.6
Financial expenses										
Interest payment					17.3	44.1	44.7	43.0		
Principal repayment					5.6	–5.2	16.7	18.3		
Taxes							4.3	5.1		37.4
Total expenditures	26.8	55.3	154.9	196.3	103.7	109.3	105.3	106.2		90.1
Financial net benefit	–8.0	–16.6	–46.5	–53.3	–10.3	4.7	19.3	21.9		235.1

Owner's nominal net present value: $68

ECONOMIC ANALYSIS

This analysis looked at the costs and benefits of the hydroelectric projects from the point of view of Panamanian society. Calculations showed that the projects would generate a net benefit of $62 million, meaning that the projects would indeed be efficient from a national perspective. This figure differs from the result of the financial cost-benefit analysis, because the economic cost-benefit analysis used economic prices, rather than market prices, and took account of environmental and social costs of the projects. In addition, the economic values were discounted at the economic opportunity cost of capital, which is different from the financial discount rate.

Table 18.2 shows the projects' economic cost-benefit analysis, including the projects' externalities.

Both changes to the natural environment and human environment (living conditions) were considered as externalities in the analysis. Natural environment externalities included forest coverage elimination, aquatic fauna modifications, and fragile zones that were threatened.

A discussion of forest coverage elimination provides an example of how the team approached the task of valuing externalities. To begin, information about the amount of forest removed was obtained from the EIA, which examined areas that would be constructed on or flooded as part of the hydroelectric projects. The EIA estimated that altogether, the four projects would deforest approximately 2,527 hectares. It is likely, however, that the ultimate area will be larger in order to accommodate the construction of new roads and indirect deforestation that will result from the projects.

TABLE 18.2

Economic Cost-Benefit Analysis (US$ millions)

	Conversion Factor	2006	2007	2008	2009	2010	2011	2012	2013	...	2031
Benefits											
Energy sales	1.038	0	0	0	7.2	46.2	79.4	116.1	117.9	0.0	132.8
Loan disbursements	0.000	0	0	0	0	0	0	0	0	0	0
Liquidation values	1.000	0	0	0	0	0	0	0	0	0	92.9
Total benefits		0	0	0	7.2	46.2	79.4	116.1	117.9	0.0	225.7
Costs											
Investments		27.0	54.3	150.1	185.2	61.1	40.3	0.5	0.0	0.0	0.0
Energy generation											
Generation costs	1.056	0	0	0	2.2	13.9	23.2	33.0	33.0	0	33.0
Administrative costs	1.035	0	0	0	0.2	1.6	2.8	4.1	4.1	0	4.6
Taxes	0	0	0	0	0	0	0	0	0	0	0
Externalities											
Natural environment											
Forest elimination		0	10.6	6.2	13.4	0	0	0	0	0	0
Aquatic fauna		0.2	0.1	0.1	0.1	0.2	0.1	0.1	0.1	0.0	0.1
Fragile zones		0	0	0	0	0	0	0	0	0	0
Human environment											
Living conditions		4.6	4.7	4.8	5.0	5.1	5.2	5.3	5.4	0.0	8.4
Total costs		31.8	69.7	161.3	206.1	81.8	71.6	43.0	42.7	0.0	46.1
Economic net benefit		-31.8	-69.7	-161.3	-199.0	-35.7	7.8	73.1	75.2	0.0	179.5

Economic net present value: $62 million at the economic opportunity cost of capital

To assign a monetary value to the cleared forest, the team used a "change in productivity" method. For the valuation element, the team used the transfer of carbon dioxide into the atmosphere due to deforestation. The team assumed the following:

1. One hectare of tropical forest has 175 tons of carbon.
2. One ton of carbon is equivalent to 3.7 tons of CO_2.

Both assumptions were based on Roper and Roberts (2000). The price of carbon dioxide used was $18.52 per ton, which was a weighted average of several international carbon prices at the time that the analysis was conducted.

Although the team expected that the projects would generate other negative externalities, especially regarding the region's ecological biodiversity, a monetary estimate of those biodiversity values was beyond the scope of the analysis. Nor did the team estimate the added costs of protecting the BPPS and PILA from being impacted by the projects. The analysis did, however, consider the effects of the projects on greenhouse gas emissions and migratory fish. Regarding the former, the team estimated the gross value of the greenhouse gases that would be emitted. Regarding the latter, the team estimated the costs of preventing migratory fish from fading; this figure was calculated as the cost of having to transport fish around the dams. The cost of losing the migratory fish due to the projects was estimated at $25 million, whereas the fish rescue effort would, in theory, cost around $1 million. Ultimately, however, the team believed that transporting the fish around the dams would be very unlikely to work because of a lack of expertise in controlling external factors such as water temperature and levels of oxygen in the water. Therefore, this figure should be considered only as a proxy for losses that would almost inevitably occur, rather than a mitigation expense actually incurred by the company undertaking the projects.

The most significant "human environment" externality that would arise as a result of the hydroelectric projects was the relocation of people living in the area and their changed living conditions. To arrive at these values, the team used the "replacement cost method" and calculated the value of the residents' productivity and the value of expenses they would have to incur as a result of no longer having access to free natural resources. Thus, the figure arrived at represents only a calculation for purposes of analyzing the cost of residents' basic needs and should not be viewed as suggested compensation for their having to relocate. The figure does not take into account additional losses the residents may sustain as a result of having to relocate, such as costs to their recreation, autonomy, and legacy.

To obtain the sought-after value, and to be able to better understand the impacts of the projects, the team conducted a field survey. The purpose of the survey was to obtain information on the composition, characteristics, income, and consumption and production patterns of households in the area.

In quantifying the changes in affected communities' living conditions, the team looked at the value of production and expenses that would *not* be incurred annually for a twenty-five-year period, as a result of the projects. This value came to $56.2 million. Further analysis demonstrated that 16 percent of the loss would be suffered by the Naso communities and 84 percent by the Ngöbe, the reason for the discrepancy being that the Ngöbe community is four times larger than the Naso and is located closer to where the flooding is projected to occur. These figures also reflect a projected 2.4 percent rate of population growth per year (DEC 2005).

STAKEHOLDER ANALYSIS

The purpose of this component of the cost-benefit analysis was to bring the other analyses together, to assess the viability and inherent risks of the projects, in conjunction with their expected impacts on investors, society generally, the environment, and local communities. The analysis draws attention to the "winners" and "losers" within society who have different stakes and interests in the projects. This analysis identified the following five major stakeholders:

1. The government
2. The inhabitants of Changuinola and Bonyic
3. The natural environment
4. The shareholders of the companies involved in working on the projects
5. The bank financing the projects

Table 18.3 shows that if the hydroelectric projects are undertaken, on one hand, the big winner will be the financing bank, which stands to recover a net gain of $193 million; the government and private investors will also see net gains of $86 million and $68.5 million, respectively. On the other hand, indigenous communities currently inhabiting the land stand to lose significantly because of costs that

TABLE 18.3

Distribution of Project's Profits and Losses among the Participants (US$ thousands)

	Government	Chan-Bon Inhabitants	Natural Environment	Company	Bank
Energy sales	27,736				
Construction taxes on investment	307				
Generation costs	−10,479				
Sales and administrative costs	−906				
Taxes	69,580				
Natural environment					
Forest coverage elimination			−24,896		
Aquatic fauna modifications			−1,068		
Fragile zones (biodiversity,etc.)			Nonquantified		
Human environment					
Changes in living conditions		−56,202			
Changes in indigenous culture		Nonquantified			
Total per sector	$86,238	−$56,202	−$25,964	$68,488	$193,187

will be imposed upon them. In addition, the projects will impose net costs on the natural environment, largely due to the elimination of forest coverage and modifications to fauna ecology. The total expected losses equal $82 million.

Again, many sociocultural impacts are already befalling the Naso and Ngöbe indigenous communities as a result of the hydroelectric projects. Their traditions, cultures, and attachments to the land are complex, and this chapter does not presume to include a study of how these factors should be included in policymakers' analyses of the projects. Field expeditions did permit the team to observe, however, that both riverside communities have largely self-sufficient subsistence economies, and have thus far enjoyed autonomy as a result of their relative geographic isolation. The hydroelectric projects will change all of that. The projects will render their subsistence economies more tenuous, since outside competition for resources will necessarily increase. And while it is impossible to reduce a people's culture and shared history to a monetary figure, the team was able to quantify the potential losses arising out of the communities' newly compromised access to resources, as well as their additional costs of day-to-day living, should they have to relocate. These losses would total approximately $56 million in present-day dollars.

Conclusion

In theory, an unfair distribution of costs and benefits can be corrected when those who benefit from a project compensate those who are impacted negatively by the project. In practice, however, compensation and environmental mitigation measures for large infrastructure projects have been inadequate and poorly implemented. Unfortunately, the environmental impact assessments conducted for the Changuinola and Bonyic dams give no indication that the amount of resources that will be spent on minimizing social and ecosystem losses will come anywhere close to our monetary estimates of these damages. Nevertheless, between the company's profits of $68 million and government tax revenues of around $86 million, there should be a substantial pool of funds with which to pay additional compensation and mitigation packages.

In general, the sustainability of a large-scale development project is heavily determined by which stakeholders stand to gain or lose from the project. If a politically influential group is projected to bear the brunt of the costs, then it might be difficult to achieve the regulatory approval necessary to carry out the project. By contrast, if the group that will be impacted the most negatively does not have political clout, then it is more likely they will not be adequately compensated for their losses. All too often, indigenous populations fall in the latter category; they lack political influence and are often not considered in the decision-making process. As a complement to cost-benefit analysis, distributional analysis is very useful, both because it helps identify the winners and losers of a policy or project and because it can help guide more political decisions about possible compensation mechanisms. In the case of Panama's hydroelectric projects, it is up to the Panamanian public, whose voice is heard through their democratically elected representatives, to decide whether the benefits of new energy production are worth the costs that will be imposed on the environment and on indigenous people.

Although Panama is not currently using cost-benefit analysis as an analytical tool in government decision making, the information provided by such analyses could be instrumental in helping officials identify projects and policies that maximize social welfare and improve upon those projects that are selected. For example, if the Changuinola projects are approved and the government accepts the $26 million cost to environmental conditions, it could also choose to mitigate these costs by creating an environmental fund with an initial endowment equal to those costs and use it to preserve the environment in another area of the country.

Notes

1. All monetary figures in U.S. dollars.

2. All calculations are in present-value terms. These "net present value" figures are the sum of yearly profits, discounted with an interest rate that is a weighted average of returns on alternative investments and the lending rate for similar projects. If the net present value of a project is positive, it is generally considered feasible.

3. In Panama, indigenous peoples are ruled by their own customs and traditions, as well as by specific laws. The *comarca* is legally recognized as indigenous peoples' land. Panama has five *comarcas*: Ngöbe-Buglé, Kuna Yala, Emberá-Wounaan, Kuna de Madungandí, and Kuna de Wargandí. The *comarca* of Naso Teribe is currently under review by the Assembly of Representatives as well as within Naso's own congress. Both the indigenous reserve and the *comarca* are concepts included in the country's legislation and recognized in the sociopolitical realm, each having its own judicial tradition and relatively distinct functions.

4. AES Changuinola, S.A. is part of the Latin American operations of Virginia-based AES Corporation, one of the largest energy enterprises in the world. In Panama, AES Corporation owns AES Panama, a power generation company that, since 1999, has operated the Bayano hydroelectric plants in the provinces of Panama and La Estrella, and Los Valles in the Chiriquí province.

5. MWH is a U.S. firm in the business of energy and environmental engineering, and construction and management of water resources. It was created in 2001 as a result of the merger between Montgomery Watson and HARZA Engineering Company.

Bibliography

Anaya, James. 2009. "Addendum: Observaciones Sobre la Situación de la Comunidad Charco la Pava y Otras Comunidades Afectadas por el Proyecto Hidroeléctrico Chan 75 (Panamá)." In *Report of the Special Rapporteur on the Situation of Human Rights and Fundamental Freedoms of Indigenous People*. UN Report No. A/HRC/12/34/Add.5. Geneva: United Nations Humans Right Council.

Center for Biological Diversity (CBD). 2011. "Activists Confront AES over Damage Dam Project, Broken Promises in Panama." Press release, April 29. http://www.biologicaldiversity.org/news/press_releases/2011/aes-04-29-2011.html.

Dirección de Estadística y Censo (DEC). 2005. *Estimaciones y Proyecciones de la Población en la República de Panamá, Por Provincia, Comarca Indígena y Distrito, Según Sexo y Edad: Años 2000–2015 y 2020*. Bulletin No. 9. Panama City: DEC.

Harberger, Arnold C., and Glenn J. Jenkins. 2002. *Cost-Benefit Analysis for Investment Decisions*. Kingston, Ontario, Canada: Queen's University.

Roper, John, and Ralph W. Roberts. 2000. *Forestry Issues: Tropical Forests and Climate Change*. Quebec: CIDA Forestry Advisers Network.

World Commission on Dams (WCD). 2000. *Dams and Development: A New Framework for Decision Making*. London: Earthscan Publications.

19

Assessing Potential Carbon Revenues from Reduced Forest Cover Loss in Liberia

Jessica Donovan, Keith Lawrence, Christopher Neyor, Eduard Niesten, and Eric Werker

After fourteen years of conflict that led to a collapsed economy, destroyed infra-structure, and the displacement of hundreds of thousands of people, Liberia is rapidly restructuring its government institutions and developing a platform for strong and sustainable economic development. Following a 2003 peace agree-ment, economic growth quickly rebounded to an estimated 9.5 percent in 2007 and 7.1 percent in 2008 (CIA 2010). However, continued recovery must over-come difficult challenges, with over half of all Liberians living in poverty, high unemployment, few functioning schools and hospitals, limited potable water, and a lack of electricity infrastructure outside of Monrovia.

One consequence of the civil conflict was relatively low deforestation rates, as much of the population was forced by safety considerations to leave the countryside and migrate to the capital and other major cities. Exports of timber and agricultural products, like every other industry in the coun-try, drastically slowed (although they picked up substantially toward the end of the civil war under the regime of Charles Taylor).[1] The net result is that Liberia currently hosts nearly 40 percent of all remaining forests within the Upper Guinean Forests, a region stretching from Guinea to Togo (Poorter et al. 2004). This is a natural asset that Liberia can choose to manage in various different ways. Depending on how international markets for carbon evolve, one option is to implement policies that reduce deforestation rates and sell the carbon credits that these policies generate, providing a much-needed source of revenue for the nation.

Global efforts to limit global warming by reducing the quantity of carbon emitted into the atmosphere are likely to yield significant market opportuni-ties. Reducing emissions through policies to avoid deforestation or regenerate forest in developing countries like Liberia may generate carbon credits much more cost-effectively than through emissions reductions in industrialized coun-tries. These credits may be sold through bilateral agreements like the one signed between Norway and Guyana in 2009;[2] through voluntary transactions between private parties; or through a market framework such as the Reduced Emissions from Deforestation and Degradation (REDD+) mechanism proposed within global negotiations currently taking place under the United Nations Framework Convention on Climate Change (UNFCCC). Under REDD+ transactions, the amount of compensation would be linked to performance based on monitored and verified reductions in carbon emissions relative to a business-as-usual baseline.

Today, several driving factors place Liberia's forests at risk. The predominant form of cultivation, slash-and-burn agriculture, threatens new areas of forest each year. This source of pressure will intensify as war-displaced populations leave the cities and return to rural areas and establish farms for local production. Expansion of the road network will open previously untouched tracts near or within forest areas and further contribute to deforestation rates. Illegal pit sawing, mining activities, and the collection of fuelwood and charcoal are eating away at Liberia's forests. Without adequate planning, expansion of plantations and concessions for rubber, oil palm, timber, and other products will also accelerate deforestation.

The agriculture and timber sectors make significant contributions to Liberia's economy, as do development programs such as road building. However, the associated forest loss also causes a range of negative impacts that impose real costs on the people of Liberia and globally. Deforestation leads to soil erosion and impoverishment, reduction in the quantity and quality of freshwater supplies, habitat loss and accompanying declines in availability of wild foods, increased risk of fires, and more. Forest loss also produces carbon emissions that contribute to global climate change. Understanding the trade-offs between policy options—in terms of opportunity costs, land requirements, the distribution of benefits and impacts on local communities—is essential to making policy choices, including any possible move toward a low-carbon economy.

Positive steps toward a low-carbon economy are already visible. Liberia has initiated a forest sector reform process to evaluate these trade-offs and rationalize forest use. The resulting National Forest Management Strategy centers on the "3C approach," seeking an optimal allocation of the nation's forest resources between Communities, Commerce, and Conservation. This strategy positions the forestry sector to create jobs, drive economic growth, and generate revenues from the global market for carbon credits. Guidelines in the new forest reform law provide the legal framework for sustainable forest management and establish oversight for an industry that once helped fuel the country's conflict.

To pursue a low-carbon economy, Liberia will have to implement activities that limit deforestation within its current development strategy, even though these activities will generate costs in addition to benefits. Liberian policymakers must carefully consider the decision to depart from a trajectory of aggressive forest exploitation and conversion to commercial plantations and agriculture. A coalition of civil society groups has been seeking support for a deal with a major bilateral donor that restricts activities linked to deforestation and compensates Liberia for the opportunity cost of these steps. Because of the importance of these decisions for the country's future, the Liberian Cabinet decided that a formal cost-benefit analysis would assist them in weighing the merits of a low-carbon policy.

To inform policy deliberations, Conservation International and the government of Liberia—including some of the authors of this chapter—conducted an analysis that explores the merits of a low-carbon development strategy for Liberia. The government assessed the costs involved, the potential value of carbon credits that could be generated, and potential sources of funding. The study focused on deforestation and degradation rather than other sources of carbon emissions such as energy and transportation.

Although formal cost-benefit analysis has not historically been part of the lawmaking process in Liberia, the country's policymakers are prudent and often risk-averse, and will demand further studies before committing to a change in policy direction. In the past, the government has used quantitative analysis to evaluate policies and agreements governing its natural resource sector, including the largest investments in Liberia: the iron ore and tree crop sectors. Through quantitative analysis, the government has sought to identify the most practicable tax instruments to maximize revenue while continuing to attract investors.

Estimating Costs and Benefits

To ensure broad acceptance of the results, we engaged relevant audiences in Liberia early on to agree on a methodological approach that was rigorous enough to yield meaningful conclusions but straightforward enough to permit easy communication of results. We proposed a simple approach that models the costs and benefits of land placed under different uses. Policy scenarios then determine the amount of land under each land use and the implications for costs, benefits, and carbon emissions. Before proceeding with the analysis, this approach was vetted through a carbon working group in Liberia that convened key government agencies as well as civil society representatives. This group was made up of a broad spectrum of interested stakeholders in climate change mitigation and REDD+ issues; it was initially formed prior to COP 13, the Bali Climate Change Conference, to help coordinate Liberia's participation. It is cochaired by the Forestry Development Authority and the Environmental Protection Agency and includes members such as the Ministry of Gender, Ministry of Agriculture, University of Liberia, Conservation International, Fauna and Flora International, International Union for Conservation of Nature, and civil society groups in Liberia. Since then, the group, now renamed the REDD technical working group, has been providing technical guidance to government agencies in relation to REDD+ and other climate change mitigation opportunities. This has included reviewing the prospects for carbon trading and developing the national document for the Forest Carbon Partnership Facility. The group agreed on a three-step approach to identify potential policies to reduce emissions from deforestation and forest degradation, and to perform cost-benefit analyses of these policies.

STEP 1: IDENTIFY CANDIDATE POLICIES WITH POTENTIAL TO REDUCE CARBON EMISSIONS

The analysis team consulted policymakers in a wide range of sectors during a series of visits to Liberia, including representatives from forestry, agriculture, planning, lands, mines and energy, infrastructure, public works, finance, the governance commission, internal affairs, and the Liberia Institute of Statistics and Geo-Information Services, as well as representatives from the private sector, international organizations, civil society, and academia. We sought to elicit suggestions for possible low-carbon alternatives to the business-as-usual policy scenario. These proposals were complemented by a literature review and ideas drawn from best practices in other countries to generate a set of candidate policies to assess. Alternative policies that were evaluated included only those deemed plausible for implementation in Liberia, at some scale, with a clear and quantifiable reduction in deforestation and degradation or increase in forest regrowth.

STEP 2: ECONOMIC MODELING OF THE COSTS, BENEFITS, AND CARBON IMPACTS OF EACH PROPOSED POLICY

Economic costs—including opportunity costs and, when possible, employment impacts—and benefits were estimated for each individual potential carbon emissions reduction measure with assumptions developed from published sources (e.g., Barbosa Filho and Yamada 2002; Duflo, Kremer et al. 2008; Openshaw 1974; Persson 1974; Pinard and Putz 1996; Pretty 1999; Ullah et al. 2009); particular attention was given to projecting the costs per tons of carbon emissions potentially avoided. Different modeling techniques were required for each proposed measure, depending on the nature of the policy (for example, whether it changes the area under a given land use or changes the practices of the land use) and the availability of different types of data sources. Other types of benefits, such as biodiversity gains or impacts on water supply, were excluded and noted qualitatively. We did not discount future values (hence we ignored the effect of any differences between the timing of the costs and the timing of the carbon savings), but capped all analyses to a twenty-five-year time horizon. In addition, we did not model beneficial multiplier effects from environmental sustainability or job creation.

STEP 3: ASSESS THE POTENTIAL FOR CARBON REVENUES

As noted earlier, carbon transactions can take several forms—bilateral arrangements, voluntary deals, and, eventually, sales in a global market for carbon credits—which will determine the actual carbon revenue from Liberia's forests. Given prices seen in existing forest carbon projects (with an average around $7 per ton of carbon dioxide in Madagascar, and $5 per ton in the bilateral agreement between Norway and Guyana), and the potential prices under a post-2012 REDD+ finance mechanism (which could be higher), Liberia may expect to obtain between $5 and $15 per ton of carbon dioxide. Our analysis compared the costs of emissions-reduction measures to potential revenues assuming a price of $5 per ton of carbon dioxide in order to provide a conservative assessment of those policies that would create a net benefit for Liberia.

Perhaps the most challenging methodological issue was the definition of an appropriate baseline or business-as-usual scenario. First, the long period of recent civil conflict in Liberia does not permit simple extrapolation of existing trends, as there have not been any well-defined trends in the Liberian economy since the 1970s (Werker and Beganovic 2011). Second, ambitious existing policy frameworks with respect to forestry, agriculture, mining, and road development, for example, might have well-defined goals, but gaps between policy goals and implementation capacity mean that these frameworks do not necessarily represent a likely business-as-usual scenario without qualification. However, defining something else as business-as-usual would contradict stated government policy, leaving the analysis in somewhat of a bind. This ultimately was resolved through careful use of language and terminology, and a general agreement that many key features of likely scenarios remain in flux. We based our projections on the best available data, including trends observed in geographically and economically similar countries.

Results

The results of the analysis (Lawrence et al. 2009) suggest that several low-carbon policy options could be economically beneficial for Liberia. Together, these could comprise the potential foundations of a "low-carbon development strategy" for Liberia. This strategy would include the elements summarized below.

1. Moving to a more efficient agricultural system can be an extremely cost-effective way to generate carbon credits. By replacing shifting cultivation with either conservation agriculture or irrigated lowland rice cultivation, or by subsidizing fertilizer inputs, Liberia can reduce the amount of forest lost to slash-and-burn practices each year. Under these systems there would be enough land available to both produce Liberia's food needs and assign large areas to regenerate the natural forest cover. Although these policies require significant setup costs, they would be profitable, and sometimes even self-financing, for farmers on an ongoing basis, even without carbon credits. Carbon finance could certainly help to fund the setup costs; at a price of $5 per ton of carbon dioxide, these policies would all be profitable for Liberia. However, the challenges in changing the dominant mode of agriculture should not be understated: land tenure is often insecure; access to capital, knowledge, and appropriate land is often absent; and mind-sets are difficult to change.

2. There is already legislation in place to create 1.5 million hectares of protected areas. The government of Liberia included this commitment in the redrafting of forestry laws, demonstrating its commitment to sound forest management practices under the 3C approach of harmonizing

Commercial, Conservation, and Community uses. The commitment to the proposed protected area network is outlined within the Forestry Reform Law of 2006. Accelerating the establishment of these areas would further reduce carbon emissions, as well as protect the cultural and natural assets they contain. Carbon revenues could help fund the setup costs involved; at $5 per ton of carbon dioxide, this acceleration would be profitable for Liberia.

3. Ensuring that tree crop plantations are located on degraded land rather than forest areas can generate significant carbon credits at virtually zero cost. Essentially, all that would be required is a policy decision not to allow foreign-invested plantations to be located on primary or secondary forests; there is more than enough degraded land for this purpose, as the significant current tree crop base represents less than one-tenth of degraded land. The zero-cost assumption assumes that plantations are equally beneficial to the Liberian economy on degraded land as on forests, and that other economic activities that might have occurred on the degraded land are not displaced.

4. Timber sales contracts (TSCs) are small concessions that permit total clearing and conversion. Reducing the number of TSCs issued, and instead placing these areas into carbon concessions, would save large amounts of carbon at an estimated cost of $3.75 per ton of carbon dioxide, due to the intense nature of the logging of these areas. The agricultural land opened by clearing under TSCs would not be needed if the above-mentioned agricultural policies are also implemented.

5. Introducing energy-efficient stoves for charcoal and fuelwood would reduce pressure on the forests. This policy would be profitable for Liberia if $5 per ton of carbon dioxide was received for them.

Together, this twenty-five-year low-carbon development strategy would provide substantial benefits for Liberia:

- Carbon revenues of $58.7 million per year, assuming a price of $5 per ton is received, and an ambitious but nonetheless gradual adoption of modern agricultural techniques (revenues could increase to three times this amount if prices of carbon credits continue to rise)
- More efficient, higher-yielding agriculture
- Increased protection of natural and cultural heritage within protected areas
- A reduction of 11.7 million tons of carbon dioxide emissions per year, equivalent to around one-half of Liberia's annual deforestation
- Status as a regional leader in climate change mitigation, creating green jobs

Setup costs, management costs, and lost timber revenues are estimated to average around $22 million per year, plus an additional $5 million per year for national coordinating and monitoring institutions (which could also coordinate climate-change adaptation policy). However, these costs would not be spread evenly over the twenty-five years. Costs would be significantly higher in the early years as programs are initiated and setup costs are incurred. Liberia could look for opportunities to partner with organizations prepared to fund these setup costs.

Other policies could also be attractive, depending on factors such as the price of carbon that is achieved. Replacing some commercial timber with carbon concessions could be financially beneficial if the price of carbon credits rises relative to timber, or if Liberian forests are found to contain less timber than is currently estimated. This result depends on the financial performance of forest management contracts (FMCs—large concessions for sustainable commercial timber harvest) and whether the profits generated stay within Liberia. Under our baseline assumptions,[3] a carbon credit price of at least $13.50 per ton of carbon dioxide would be required before this policy becomes beneficial to Liberia. If the FMCs are less productive than currently anticipated, then the alternative use of the land for carbon concessions could be justified at a carbon credit price of as little as $7.25 per ton of carbon dioxide. These same considerations also influence the decision over whether community forest areas should be managed for sustainable forestry or as carbon concessions. Table 19.1 summarizes the key results by policy.

To realize these carbon revenues, Liberia could choose to participate in different types of carbon finance arrangements. This includes signing a bilateral deal

TABLE 19.1

Key Results by Policy, Including Potential Carbon Revenues

Policy	Average CO2 Saved per Year over 25 Years (million tons)	Cost of Carbon Saved ($/tCO2)	@$5/Ton: Carbon Revenues per Year ($ millions)	@$5/Ton: Net Benefit per Year ($ millions)
100,000 ha of plantations are located on degraded land rather than forest areas	2.1	Very low	10.6	10.6
Fertilizer subsidies to increase efficiency of shifting agriculture	1.8	< 2	8.8	7.1
Lowland rice promoted in place of shifting agriculture	1.6	< 2	8.2	6.3
Conservation agriculture promoted in place of shifting agriculture	1.7	< 2	8.6	6.1
Accelerated creation of Protected Area Network	0.2[a]	< 2	0.8	0.5
Increased efficiency of charcoal production and use	1.1	2.67–3.20	5.7	2.1
No further TSCs	3.2	3.75	16.0	4.0
Subtotal for potential low-carbon development strategy	*11.7*		*58.7*	*36.7*
Restrict FMCs to 1.6 million ha	1.8	7.25–13.50	9.2	−4.1 to −15.6

[a]0.8 for five years, then zero.

similar to the agreement between Norway and Guyana, engaging in the current voluntary carbon markets and the Clean Development Mechanism (CDM), or participating in a global carbon market.

The low-carbon economic analysis yielded several policy approaches that could reduce Liberia's deforestation rate and create opportunities to generate credits from Liberia's vast forest estates. These proposed policies would be challenging to implement for a number of reasons. Changes in agricultural practices require better definition of property rights, capacity building among farmers and extension agents, coordination across communities and landowners, and drastic reshaping of subsistence farmer perspectives. Securing broad-based buy-in for reorienting the forestry sector faces political and practical hurdles. Finally, generating carbon revenue requires sophisticated national and legal policy and regulatory support, and enhanced (or outsourced) governance capacity.

The benefits of a low-carbon economy extend beyond revenue generation. Implementing a low-carbon development strategy and producing carbon credits can provide new opportunities for entrepreneurs and create green jobs that help address unemployment. Successful carbon transactions also offer distributional benefits. Since carbon revenue depends on performance, community decisions and actions will be critical in determining the level of revenues received. Communities must derive tangible benefits from these deals. Thus, appropriately structured carbon deals will advance Liberia's poverty reduction strategy, which emphasizes equitable distribution of benefits as an essential element of poverty reduction.

Effective implementation of a low-carbon economic strategy requires strengthened governance structures at all levels, from local communities to national bodies. Indeed, preparing for REDD+ carbon market opportunities can catalyze improved governance structures that will help reduce the potential for conflict in rural areas and can subsequently be applied to other needs, such as climate change adaptation and protecting watershed services provided by forests.

FROM COST-BENEFIT ANALYSIS TO POLICY

The cost-benefit study on its own is still a long way from constituting a set of concrete Liberian policy proposals. Moreover, as described in the subsequent section, putting forward a low-carbon economic development plan is not something the government could do in isolation, because it stands on the premise that developed countries will finance carbon sequestration efforts. With that in mind, we sought to embed the study in a larger Liberian-run initiative.

As a first step, the results of the study were presented at a workshop in Monrovia attended by many members of the sustainable development community in Liberia. Such workshops form an important part of the process by which policies are presented and legitimized in the Liberian context. The adviser to President Johnson Sirleaf on energy, environment, and climate convened the workshop and invited high-level decision-makers from a variety of ministries and agencies, as well as from the donor community and civil society. The workshop proceeded in two parts. First, the president's energy and climate czar proposed the creation of a National Climate Change Steering Committee (NCCSC), which would be supported by a Climate Change Secretariat and housed in the Office of the President, to coordinate national climate change policy. Second, the technical authors of the cost-benefit analysis presented the findings of the study.

This two-part process reflected a deliberate strategy. Although external technical authors could research the areas in which Liberian development could be made less carbon intensive and quantify the trade-offs involved, they would be less suitable for developing and balancing the actual policies. For the latter, a high-capacity yet streamlined body within the government would need to take the initiative, coordinating engagement across the various ministries and agencies that oversee economic activity in Liberia. Thus, the cost-benefit analysis itself was only intended as the first step in an iterative process between a small climate change team in the Office of the President and the various actors who would need to actually formulate an externally funded low-carbon development plan. The cost-benefit analysis was generally well received, with minimal controversy, aided by the technocratic and nonpolitical nature of the findings. But this does not imply that the findings will be quickly adopted. The ultimate take-up of the policies will no doubt follow a more political process.

Once the proposed Climate Change Secretariat is set up, its technicians can take the lead in investigating how, and if, each carbon-saving measure examined in the cost-benefit analysis can be implemented in Liberia. Coordinating with governmental ministries and agencies, development partners, and civil society organizations, the secretariat will create a comprehensive proposal. The proposal would spell out a series of specific interventions, as well as implementation costs, timelines, and the amount of carbon emissions avoided. The secretariat may need to cultivate buy-in from other government actors to pursue these policies. This would be conditional on there being sufficient financing to see them through.

The secretariat would next submit the proposal for a low-carbon development strategy to its advisory body, the NCCSC, and other domestic stakeholders. Once validated, it can be "shopped around" by the government to potential carbon buyers. Buyers will most likely include the government of Norway, a World Bank facility, or another bilateral partner if present trends continue. Taking into account credit constraints in the Liberian public and private sectors, the proposal will include a combination of traditional up-front development funding for activities like agricultural extension, as well as performance-linked incentives tied to observed emission reductions based on an appropriate monitoring, reporting, and verification system.

At the time of this writing, the proposal to establish the NCCSC and its Climate Change Secretariat had just been approved by the Liberian Cabinet. Initial groundwork to flesh out the potential components in a national low-carbon economic development strategy has been undertaken. With organization of and capacity building in the Climate Change Secretariat now under way, the broader task of costing out the strategy and integrating it into national policy can now begin. It promises to be an exciting journey.

Implementation Risks

We have discussed the complexities of progressing from the technical cost-benefit report that describes low-carbon options to specific government policies. As in any political process, there are inherent risks in using the cost-benefit study to endorse and to implement these national policies.

First, there is the risk that the study will not draw the necessary understanding and response from the relevant government functionaries. In a postconflict country like Liberia, where senior policymakers are preoccupied principally with short-term results, adopting a long-term policy position at the expense of short-term gains is unappealing no matter the value of long-term benefits. For instance, employment is an urgent priority. Timber extraction and forest conversion to oil palm plantations are seen as two of the most promising avenues for job creation, though in direct conflict with low-carbon ambitions. This is where funding commitments from the donor community (Annex I parties, in UNFCCC jargon) can make an important difference.

However, securing donor commitment also introduces uncertainties. The funding risks are of two types. The first type of risk involves funding for the secretariat and other national institutions that are required to make the most efficient use of Liberian forest cover. Senior policymakers in developing countries are leery of the slow pace that typically characterizes significant commitments and disbursements by donors. They are also apprehensive about the possibility that new money will not be committed or released until after considerable time and resources have been spent shifting to low-carbon policies. This interplay poses a risk to the transition from cost-benefit study to policy, in a chicken-and-egg situation where policymakers are reluctant to commit scarce time and budget until they see donor commitments, and donors do not want to commit funds until they see policy change.

The second risk with donor funds concerns the very creation of a market for REDD+ carbon credits more generally. Of all the modes of carbon emission mitigation, REDD+ in tropical countries may be the most difficult to verify as having actually reduced emissions. As a result, tropical REDD+ credits are among the least likely to become part of compliance markets anytime soon—even though they may be among the cheapest credits to produce, assuming they could be measured accurately. Donors recognized this dilemma, and in the discussions in Copenhagen in December 2009, six nations pledged $3.5 billion to jump-start REDD+ projects (Morales and Penny 2009). This is by far the largest potential market for REDD+ carbon credits today, yet there is still no certainty that it will be realized in such a quantity and in an institutional form that may feed into a national program in Liberia.

Once the funding and market challenges have been overcome, and proper low-carbon policies are in place, there will be risks associated with implementation. Among these is the risk that human capacity and available technology are inadequate for ensuring effective implementation, for instance with respect to monitoring and verification provisions that meet international standards. In addition, since any eventual policy is likely to rely on incentives to individual actors though a market-like approach, there remains a risk that the analysis in the cost-benefit study does not accurately reflect the decisions people may make in the future. At the end of the day, policies can only set the incentives, and it will be farmers, communities, and firms that will determine how to use or not use the forest. The prices of timber and cocoa and the unemployment rate in urban Liberia will all affect that equilibrium. Political risk may discourage private carbon concessionaires from making long-term investments. This means that the amount of carbon revenue that actually materializes may not meet expectations.

In ongoing climate change negotiations, the UNFCCC has been working to address these cross-cutting risks in a new legally binding climate change treaty. The outcome of these negotiations will have a critical impact on prospects for addressing climate change, on the fate of forests throughout the developing world, and on economic opportunities for highly forested countries like Liberia. Given that Liberia has signaled a willingness to entertain the possibility of a low-carbon development strategy that protects forests, we strongly hope that the emerging climate change treaty includes provisions that accommodate trade in carbon credits generated through REDD+ activities. Although overall progress on such a treaty has been extremely disappointing, with no resolution appearing imminent at the time of this writing, there have been positive developments on the acceptance and inclusion of REDD+ specifically. In the meantime, a bilateral deal appears to be the most promising route to Liberia receiving revenues from generating carbon credits.

Conclusion

This chapter describes both our cost-benefit analysis initiative and a plausible policy process for Liberia. A "low-carbon development strategy" for Liberia would include a number of cost-beneficial policies, the most obvious being a transition to more efficient agriculture. Other beneficial policies include accelerating the establishment of protected areas; ensuring that tree crop plantations are located on degraded land rather than forest areas; and introducing energy-efficient stoves for charcoal and fuelwood. The net benefits of changes to forestry policies are less clear: reducing the number of timber sales contracts would be cost-beneficial, but replacing commercial timber with carbon concessions is more marginal.

It can be difficult to communicate the concept of generating revenue through *not* emitting carbon dioxide. It is hard to understand how to produce an emissions reduction, and harder still to evaluate and communicate to a lay audience the costs and benefits of a national policy to engage in this market—especially when that market is yet to be created. These challenges are multiplied when working in a capacity-constrained environment like postconflict Liberia. Nevertheless, we believe a committed effort to achieve this would be worthwhile, for our results highlight the tremendous potential for this emerging market to contribute to Liberia's development and suggest a path to move it forward.

Notes

1. See International Tropical Timber Council, Achieving the ITTO Objective 2000 and Sustainable Forest Management in Liberia (2005).

2. See Memorandum of Understanding Between the Government of the Cooperative Republic of Guyana and the Government of the Kingdom of Norway Regarding Cooperation on Issues Related to the Fight Against Climate Change, the Protection of Biodiversity and the Enhancement of Sustainable Development, Guy.-Nor. (November 9, 2009).

3. Our baseline assumptions for the forestry sector are 8 m^3 of timber achieved per harvested hectare on a sustainable basis with export prices of $230/$m^3$.

Bibliography

Barbosa Filho, M. P., and T. Yamada. 2002. "Upland Rice Production in Brazil." *Better Crops International* 16 (Special Supplement): 43–46.

Central Intelligence Agency (CIA). 2010. *World Fact Book: Liberia*. Washington, D.C.: CIA.

Duflo, Esther, Michael Kremer, and Jonathan Robinson. 2008. "How High Are Rates of Return to Fertilizer? Evidence from Field Experiments in Kenya." *American Economic Review* 98 (2): 482–88.

Lawrence, Keith, Eduard Niesten, and Eric Werker. 2009. *Economic Analysis of a Low Carbon Economy for Liberia*. Arlington, Va.: Conservation International.

Morales, Alex, and Thomas Penny. 2009. "U.S. Pledges $1 Billion toward $3.5 Billion Deforestation Fund." *Bloomberg News*, December 16.

Openshaw, Keith. 1974. "Wood Fuels the Developing World." *New Scientist* 61: 271–72.

Persson, R. 1974. *World Forest Resources: Review of the World's Forest Resources in the Early 1970's*. Department of Forest Survey, Reports and Dissertations No. 17. Stockholm: Royal College of Forestry.

Pinard, Michelle A., and Francis E. Putz. 1996. "Retaining Forest Biomass by Reducing Logging Damage." *Biotropica* 28 (3): 278–95.

Poorter, Lourens, Frans Bongers, François N'Guessan Kouam é, and William D. Hawthorne, eds. 2004. *Biodiversity of West African Forests: An Ecological Atlas of Woody Plant Species*. Singapore: CABI Publishing.

Pretty, Jules. 1999. "Can Sustainable Agriculture Feed Africa? New Evidence on Progress, Processes and Impacts." *Environment, Development and Sustainability* 1 (3–4): 253–74.

Ullah, Ehsan, Atique-ur-Rehman, Qaisar Arshad, and S. Shamshad Hussain Shah. 2009. "Yield Response of Fine Rice to NP Fertilizer and Weed Management Practices." *Pakistan Journal of Botany* 41 (3): 1351–57.

Werker, Eric D., and Jasmina Beganovic. 2011. "Liberia." Harvard Business School Case 712-011. Cambridge, Mass.: Harvard Business School.

PART FOUR

Paths Forward

Challenges and Opportunities
Michael A. Livermore

Cost-benefit analysis of environmental decision making is a global phenomenon. The future of cost-benefit analysis presents many challenges, from building the capacity to conduct sophisticated assessments of complex environmental policy to updating the methodology of cost-benefit analysis to reflect the reality of developing and emerging countries. But these challenges must be addressed because, as governments take on more sophisticated regulatory tasks, the need to estimate the effects of their decisions and weigh the positive against the negative will only grow. This volume helps document how governments and intergovernmental institutions, academics, and civil society actors have responded to that need and addressed those challenges through analyses that have helped inform decision making on a range of pressing environmental questions around the world.

Perhaps the most important theme throughout this book is that cost-benefit analyses of environmental policy are happening in developing and emerging countries; that the challenges associated with conducting rigorous analysis have not overwhelmed the ingenuity and persistence of committed analysts around the world. While the analyses collected here are imperfect and incomplete, so are the most well-funded and methodologically complex cost-benefit analyses in the developed world. Because cost-benefit analysis is an exercise in predicting the future, errors and limitations are inherent to the process. But in an uncertain world, it is not enough for policymakers to throw up their hands in despair and forsake reasoned analysis. Governments have a responsibility of rationality, and that means doing the best they can to foresee the effects of their decisions and make choices that will maximize their goals with the fewest negative effects. In a variety of different political contexts, facing a range of difficult challenges, and addressing a diverse set of environmental issues, the analyses described in the previous chapters demonstrate that cost-benefit analysis of environmental decision making is possible, even in difficult and resource-constrained circumstances.

But while cost-benefit analysis is happening, there is much that can be done to make it easier, more accurate, and more useful for developing and emerging countries. Several of these issues are discussed in detail in the cross-cutting chapters in Parts II and III of this volume. This chapter builds on those discussions, as well as on the case study chapters in Parts IV and V, to propose three broad programs for institutional innovation and methodological research that can help expand the opportunity to use cost-benefit analysis to improve environmental decision-making: increasing capacity, conducting valuation research, and incorporating development issues. Each of these proposals responds directly to some of the largest and most important barriers that interfere with widespread adoption of balanced, well-conducted cost-benefit analysis. By moving forward on these paths, the challenges currently facing analysts and decision makers can be transformed into opportunities to improve how cost-benefit analysis is done.

Capacity

Even where there is broad support for cost-benefit analysis, finding the resources to implement it on a widespread basis continues to pose a challenge. The analytic requirements are large, developing countries have fewer resources to work with, and in smaller economies, the effects of policy are smaller, justifying less expenditure on analysis. Outlined below are two important steps that can be taken to help overcome the capacity challenges faced by developing and emerging countries: first, supporting an international community of scholars and decision makers interested in cost-benefit analysis; second, developing simplifying tools so that cost-benefit analysis can be deployed at lower cost.

THE COSTS OF COST-BENEFIT ANALYSIS

Developed countries have devoted significant resources to conducting cost-benefit analysis. In the United States, for example, administrative agencies have hired a substantial number of personnel with expertise in economics, risk analysis, and related disciplines. The U.S. Environmental Protection Agency (EPA) in particular has devoted time, money, and staff to conducting cost-benefit analysis, with a National Center for Environmental Economics (NCEE) that employs dozens of economists, an Environmental Economics Advisory Committee composed of economists and other experts from academia, and extensive guidelines for conducting economic analysis (EPA 2010). In addition to the capacity within administrative agencies at the federal level, there is also a centralized body, the Office of Information and Regulatory Affairs (OIRA) within the Office of Management and Budget (OMB), that has its own complement of several dozen professional staff who have developed significant expertise in the practice of cost-benefit analysis and regulatory review.

Beyond direct government spending, there is also a complement of academics and independent organizations that provide a great deal of data and analysis that augments government efforts. The fields of risk analysis, cost-benefit analysis, and environmental and public health economics are well developed, with faculty at top institutions of higher education devoted to teaching new professionals and enhancing and expanding the field through scholarship. Significant literatures—on topics as diverse as risk-exposure and technological responses to regulations—help support government cost-benefit analysis. In addition, there are a number of civil society actors with the capacity to evaluate the cost-benefit analyses conducted by government and hold officials to account if they depart from sound practices.

In the developed world, it has made economic sense to devote resources to regulatory analysis. Even where regulations have relatively small impacts as a percentage of the economy, the overall size of their economies means that they have large impacts in absolute terms. The threshold for subjecting national regulations to full cost-benefit analysis in the United States is $100 million (USD) annual impact: regulations that have less of an impact are subjected to less analysis. Similarly, the European Union guidelines limit full impact analysis to "significant" policies and recommend proportionally less analysis for those policies with less impact (European Commission 2009). Even within developed countries, however, smaller governmental units sometimes have difficulty mustering the analytic resources to carry out cost-benefit analysis, in part because the economic stakes are lower (Schwartz 2010; Hahn 1998).

For countries with relatively small economies, subjecting regulation to expensive cost-benefit analysis generally will not be efficient. Formal cost-benefit analysis requires significant resources—the decision whether to use cost-benefit analysis should itself be subject to cost-benefit criteria. For many types of decisions, the benefits (in terms of more efficient policies) may not be worth the budgetary expenditures to conduct the analysis. If there will be relatively few policy moves that have sufficient economic impact to justify lengthy and resource-intensive cost-benefit analysis, the start-up costs necessary to develop sufficient capacity to conduct sophisticated analysis may be prohibitive.

BUILDING THE GLOBAL COMMUNITY

An important step to help reduce capacity costs associated with conducting cost-benefit analysis, and one that has already begun, involves building a global network of analysts and decision makers. To the extent that countries share common problems, steps like pooling analytic resources among countries or conducting analysis of similar policies across a number of countries can reduce redundancies and allow developing countries to take advantage of returns to scale. A global community can also facilitate training and the sharing of knowledge across borders.

Progress has already begun on this front. Regional collaboration networks and professional associations facilitate the exchange of ideas among analysts in different countries. International institutions have also provided a supporting role, building on existing programs to support regulatory impact analysis, by facilitating regional networks and collecting and disseminating best practices (OECD 2008).

But more can be done. Communications technology can be leveraged to create robust and sustained relationships among far-flung actors. Academic institutions can share resources and join in educational collaboration to encourage the global spread of knowledge. A global clearinghouse that collects and disseminates best practices and recent research could make information broadly available at low costs to governments, nongovernmental organizations, and scholars.

There are a host of concrete steps that could be taken, but there are three factors that will undergird any serious effort to generate a truly robust global network oriented toward the practice of global cost-benefit analysis. First, there must be demand for a global community that arises from the local needs of domestic actors. Without tangible and consistent demand for international relationships and cross-border interaction, a global community cannot be sustained. The chapters in this volume powerfully make the case that this demand exists. Across the globe, analysts and policymakers care about cost-benefit analysis, they are carrying it out already with important effect, they can benefit enormously through interactions with their peers, and they have much to contribute.

Second, interconnections must be made among important, but disparate, efforts that are already being undertaken by transnational networks and institutions. A diversity of institutions and networks can generate positive results by fostering creativity and offering a variety of ways for parties to interact and connect. But unless these efforts are linked in some way, redundancy, isolation, and wasted effort will result.

Finally, a global community cannot be sustained without the commitment of sufficient resources. Donor organizations and governments in developed countries must recognize the utility of cost-benefit analysis for environmental decision making in developing and emerging countries and use their resources to fund educational and professional training programs, collaborative projects, and research. Countries that have already built substantial expertise in the field of cost-benefit analysis—most notably the United States—can share resources and help facilitate knowledge transfer. Again, these efforts are already occurring—the Environmental Protection Agency, for example, has engaged in joint research examining the economic impacts of air quality controls in China in collaboration with analysts from the Chinese government (US-China Joint Economic Research Group 2007), and the work of nongovernmental organizations to incorporate cost-benefit analysis into their advocacy has been funded by charitable sources. But a consistent stream of funds and other resources targeted at expanding the opportunity to use cost-benefit analysis to inform environmental policy in developing and emerging countries could play an extremely important role in facilitating and sustaining a global community around these issues.

SIMPLIFYING ANALYSIS

As cost-benefit analysis spreads, it will also need to be leaner, simplified, and easier to use. Countries facing extreme limits on analytic capacity will not be able to devote substantial resources to regulatory evaluation—the most useful forms of cost-benefit analysis will be those that are easiest to carry out.

Where default values can be generated on the basis of existing literature, they can greatly simplify the analytic task. A great deal of scientific research has been done to estimate the various parameters concerning risk and health endpoints, but these values may not always be universally applicable. For example, environmental risks with very long latencies, or which primarily affect the elderly, may have less of an impact in developing countries where life expectancies are far shorter, as was noted by Rojas-Bracho and colleagues in this volume.

Research to translate epidemiological studies to different public health contexts can help generate defensible default values for impacts associated with environmental pollutants. Research on certain economic questions can also be used to develop default values for parameters like rates of technological growth, productivity returns to increased health, or industry responses to increased compliance costs, so long as there is sufficient sensitivity to how local conditions can affect those parameters. These economic variables are distinct from nonmarket valuation studies (which are discussed below) and instead relate to standard market variables that can be more easily subjected to empirical study and may have more cross-border applicability.

Checklists and other off-the-shelf evaluation tools could also prove extremely helpful. In the United States, there are several sets of guidelines for conducting economic analysis of environmental policies that have been developed by the EPA, OIRA, and the Council on Environmental Quality at the national level, as well as by some states. Standardized methodological approaches that are appropriate for developing and emerging countries can be developed and disseminated. Variants on cost-benefit analysis that require fewer resources—such as cost-effectiveness analysis or the establishment of "break-even" values (OMB 2009, 17)—can be tailored to meet the needs of developing countries.

Conducting cost-benefit analysis is not easy, and it is a signal of how useful the technique can be that it is already in use in such different contexts around the world. But there are many steps that can be taken to increase capacity, from knowledge transfer programs to research efforts to provide default values, so that cost-benefit analysis can be deployed more easily by decision makers facing tight budget constraints. Expanding the capacity to conduct this type of analysis will help empower governments around the world to engage in more transparent, well-informed, and rational decision making.

Valuation Research

Valuation is a necessary component of cost-benefit analysis. Not only must the positive and negative effects of a decision be estimated, but those effects must be compared on a common scale. As discussed in Part I of this volume, valuation raises a number of important and thorny issues for developing and emerging countries. Discussed below are two steps that can be taken to both facilitate accurate valuation and counter potential criticism of cost-benefit analysis. First, research to establish region specific valuation of mortality risk should be undertaken so that, eventually, the benefits-transfer methodology becomes less of a central tool. Second, greater research into valuation of natural resources, especially domestic valuation, should be conducted because of the special importance that natural resources play for environmental policy in developing and emerging countries.

GLOBAL COMPARISON AND REGION-SPECIFIC VALUES

Because risk preferences tend to be highly correlated with wealth, it can be expected that rich countries will be willing to pay more to reduce environmental, public health, and safety risk than countries in earlier stages of development. From a purely economic standpoint, regional differences in risk preferences are neither surprising nor troubling (Hammitt and Zhou 2006).

This correlation between valuations and wealth is the foundation of the benefit-transfer methodology, which uses studies that were carried out in developed countries and then translates them to take account of income differentials between countries. Many of the case studies discussed in this volume relied to some extent or another on benefit-transfer to conduct valuation of nonmarket goods.

At the same time, differing preferences for risk, especially when those preferences are closely associated with levels of development, highlight inequalities between countries. One consequence of differing risk preferences is that lower levels of environmental protection will be justified in developing countries because they are willing to spend less to reduce mortality risks than developed countries: the trade-off between economic growth and environmental protection is simply different in countries that have different levels of economic development. To some, this result seems unfair because populations in developing countries face higher degrees of environmental risk (Boyle 2007). As cost-benefit analysis becomes more widespread, the problem of international comparison will grow. The reality of global inequities means that risk valuations will differ by country, meaning that public health and environmental protection will be "worth more" in some countries than in others.

Solving this problem will not be easy. Two solutions that could be proposed are laundering preferences and using a single global value. Preference laundering in this context refers to the rejection of risk valuations that are determined to be too low. There are potential justifications for such laundering: risks may be misunderstood or populations could be subject to information-processing disadvantages or flawed heuristic mechanisms (Adler and Posner 2006). But there are strong arguments against laundering preferences purely on the basis of income. Most clearly, it creates the possibility that a policy will make the poorest members of society less well-off, according to their own estimation, by costing them more than they would be willing to pay.

A second option would be to use a single average global value for mortality risk reduction. The U.S. EPA, for example, does not create differing risk valuations for differing populations—it uses an average value for the entire U.S. population. The use of an average value avoids troubling fairness problems, and, so long as regulatory costs are not focused toward the lower side of the income distribution, results in mild redistribution downward as poor people receive slightly more protection than they would be willing to pay for, but regulatory costs are mostly carried by wealthier portions of the population.

Demographic clustering around wealth and income at the global scale, however, undercuts the assumption that regulatory costs would track wealth. If a relatively poor country would bear all of the costs of a policy—which would often be the case—then use of a global average value would lock it into adopting regulations that would not maximize domestic net benefits. This result, which would make the poorest countries less well-off from their own perspective, again seems perverse.

Developing region-specific valuations for mortality risk may be a more promising path forward. Some of the negative political connotation associated with benefits transfer could be avoided if valuations were based on studies that were carried out in the region where the policy impact will be felt. With region-specific values, the disparity between local and global valuation levels will be based on data gathered on the local population, not on assumptions made about countries on the basis of income differences.

Benefits transfer is used because it is the easiest tool at hand, and in many circumstances, when analysts face severe time and budget pressures, it is the best that can be done. But, with the support of academic institutions, professional societies, developed countries, and international institutions, research can be supported to build more robust data on risk preferences around the world. With that information, cost-benefit analysis can become more accurate in reflecting local conditions in a variety of different contexts, and an important political barrier to cost-benefit analysis can be mitigated.

NATURAL RESOURCES

As noted by Euston Quah in this volume, given developing countries' relative wealth of natural resources, especially living resources like forest land, some of their most important environmental measures will be targeted at preserving and managing these resources. Cost-benefit analysis, however, has traditionally been best applied to public-health-oriented environmental regulations, where parameters to value regulatory benefits can be set through risk preferences. While techniques do exist for setting values for non-health-related environmental protection policies, these techniques are less accurate and less complete than those used to measure the benefits of environmental health regulations.

The concept of "ecosystems services" has been used to describe the wide range of positive benefits that are generated by healthy and well-functioning ecosystems. The Millennium Ecosystem Assessment has defined ecosystem services to include "*provisioning services* such as food, water, timber, and fiber; *regulating services* that affect climate, floods, disease, wastes, and water quality; *cultural services* that provide recreational, aesthetic, and spiritual benefits; and *supporting services* such as soil formation, photosynthesis, and nutrient cycling" (MEA 2005, v).

In general, the category of ecosystem services that involve the use of a natural resource—as opposed to nonuse values—are easier to value. The recreational value of natural parks has been estimated by tracking the amount of time and money that people are willing to spend to visit those areas (Gürlük and Rehber 2008). The value of fisheries or lands for timber harvest can be estimated through the aggregate commercial rents that are generated by the resource. Dollars generated by the tourism industry can be used to provide valuations for certain environmental benefits. Water filtration services can be valued by the capital costs necessary for infrastructure built to replace them;[1] the value of pollination services can be based on the agricultural industry they support (Ricketts et al. 2004).

Other types of services, such as supporting cultural or religious values, are much harder to monetize. Where indigenous cultures have specific knowledge that can be used for broader social benefit—and ecosystems support maintenance of that knowledge—the value of that benefit could conceivably be monetized (Zimmerman 2005). The concept of existence value is sometimes used to capture "nonuse" value. Because existence value is expressly nonmarket, however, there are significant measurement problems (Arrow et al. 1993). Existence value has also been the subject of persistent conceptual criticism (Aldred 1994). Even countries with highly advanced systems of environmental regulation and strong familiarity with cost-benefit analysis, like the United States, have difficulty capturing the full range of value associated with protecting natural resources.

Research that focuses on natural resource valuation, and especially ecosystem services that accrue to local populations, can help cost-benefit analysis better inform decision making in developing and emerging nations. This can and should be an area of increasing research for both natural scientists and economists. All societies depend on natural systems to support basic economic functions as well as more advanced economic activity. It is often much cheaper to protect land in a watershed than it is to build a water filtration system for a city; maintaining a healthy habitat for pollinating insects and birds is less costly than risking large-scale agricultural losses. These are real benefits that should be recognized in cost-benefit analysis. Research to better understand the connections between natural systems and human activities and preferences for healthy ecosystems can be especially useful for developing and emerging countries.

As noted by Alberto Alemanno in this volume, one question that analysts must ask is whether global externalities should be considered in domestic cost-benefit analysis. Natural resource protection often raises this issue because reduction of forest losses can have important climate benefits, which accrue to the entire global population, and because certain high-profile resources, like the Amazon rain forest, raise sufficient global interest to generate existence value at an international scale. But while global valuations may be useful to know for a neutral social decision maker, and could help attract support from international coalitions or donors, political actors in most countries are likely to focus primarily on domestic concerns. Where global benefits can be monetized by local actors, as would occur under a global carbon market, incentives would be created for domestic actors to protect global public goods. But in the absence of those types of markets, it seems improbable that the global effects of environmental decisions will be foremost on policymakers' minds. Much can be done, however, purely on the basis of the domestic value of natural resources.

Development Economics

Many of the regulatory effects of most concern to policymakers in developing countries, such as how an environmental rule might affect foreign direct investment, are often ignored by traditional cost-benefit analysis. While policymakers in developed countries are also interested in the effect of regulation on employment and economic growth (OMB 2011), in developing countries, these issues are more even pressing.

The field of development economics, which focuses on identifying policies associated with long-range economic growth, can potentially help make cost-benefit analysis more relevant for developing and emerging countries.

Environmental regulation can have effects on several variables that are important for capital accumulation, which is at the foundation of economic growth. Countries with low levels of capital have less productive workers and fewer opportunities to participate in the global economy through trade, and these countries rely to a greater extent on agricultural production and raw materials for wealth—subjecting them to climate risks and highly variable global prices. Accumulating the wide range of assets classified as capital—from factories to technological know-how—lies at the heart of industrialization and development.

There are a variety of positive and negative impacts that environmental regulation can have on physical capital. From the ecosystem services perspective, natural capital can be extremely important for long-term development. These capital assets are often ignored, meaning that conversion of valuable natural capital to low-value uses will show a positive gain to GDP. According to the Millennium Ecosystem Assessment, this problem is so severe that "[w]hen estimates of the economic losses associated with the depletion of natural assets are factored into measurements of the total wealth of nations, they significantly change the balance sheet," taking some countries from positive to negative growth (MEA 2005, 9). If countries are engaged in practices that shift capital to less valuable uses—for example, by converting intact wetland to intensive farming, or converting intact mangroves to shrimp farming—they are engaged in a practice of capital destruction.

Influence on foreign direct investment is another important consideration for development. If environmental regulations increase production costs, they could lead to a decrease in foreign investment—an important consideration for a developing country to take into account. There are many confounding factors that make the study of the relationship between investment and environmental regulation difficult (Fullerton 2006). The relationship between environmental protection and foreign investment may not always be negative. Higher environmental standards may also increase investment, by making it easier for firms to attract highly skilled labor, or by increasing returns to tourism.

Technological development and human capital are also key development variables. Gains in worker productivity brought about by technological development are vital to economic growth (Maddison 2001). Development theory in particular has focused on the role of technical knowledge and worker capacity play in facilitating development (Romer 1990; Blakemore and Herrendorf 2009; Nelson and Phelps 1966). Human capital accumulation takes the form not only of formal education but also learning-by-doing and on-the-job training.

Environmental regulation has spurred technological development in the past (Ellerman et al. 2000) and has even been argued to have the potential to increase net productivity (Porter and van der Linde 1995). If, in the process of complying with environmental regulations, firms expose their workers and researchers to new technologies, that may generate positive externalities for development by facilitating the diffusion of other technological developments in the future.

Alternatively, some environmental regulations can reduce technological development by increasing the price of inputs or diverting natural resources to other uses. They may also influence the direction of technological development rather than its overall pace. If resources that would have been used to develop low-cost food production or water purification techniques are diverted to research that results in a less carbon-intensive manufacturing process, for example, the results for improving a country's capacity for technological development and diffusion are ambiguous. And if high-cost environmental standards cause overall funds available for research and development to decline, that can have negative effects on development over the long term.

There are other pathways through which environmental regulation can affect human capital. Experience implementing environmental control technology can be easily transferred to other situations where technological upgrades can improve worker productivity. Better environmental amenities can help firms attract and retain high-quality workers. Environmental regulation can also contribute more directly to human capital accumulation by reducing exposure to pollution that has harmful effects on health. Long-term and acute conditions can interfere with productivity at school or at work, and some pollutants, including neurotoxins like lead and mercury, can have long-range effects on intellectual capacity.

Some environmental regulation could also threaten human capital accumulation. The distributional effects of environmental policy may be particularly important in this respect. Even in systems where public education is widespread, for example, private actors are called on to make important contributions to human capital accumulation, including giving children proper nutrition and attention, paying for school supplies, and allowing children to remain free from overbearing work commitments during childhood and adolescence. To the extent that an environmental regulation has negative distributional consequences, especially for the lowest income sectors of society, it may have the effect of reducing expenditures for human capital accumulation, undercutting social efforts at development.

Environmental regulation can also affect other important development issues, such as dual-economy problems. One of the persistent challenges of many developing countries is the clustering of positive economic progress, while large portions of the population remain poor (World Bank 2007). Often, large productivity in many sectors is hampered by a lack of legal institutions, including strong property rights (Soto 2000). If certain regulations create a barrier to entering the legal economy—for example, by creating burdensome record-keeping requirements or subjecting small business owners to arbitrary and/or unreviewable action by bureaucrats—it may exacerbate a dual-economy problem. Environmental policy can also help to reduce dual-economy problems: for example, preservation programs can be designed to incorporate the participation of local groups and help spur local economic development outside of the urban core.

Overall, environmental policy can influence development through natural, built, and human capital accumulation, technological development, and other issues like dual-economy and rural development. But, to date, cost-benefit analysis has not focused on these issues, which can limit the utility of this analysis for policymakers in developing countries. When analysts cannot provide sound answers to questions, for example, about the impact of a rule of foreign investment, decision makers are forced to rely on intuitions and instinct rather than evidence-based models and estimates.

Expansion of cost-benefit analysis to provide a clearer picture of the effects of policy choices on development outcomes is likely to make the tool more useful for decision makers operating in a number of different governance contexts around the globe. For this need to be addressed, analysts and researchers will have to devote resources to examine in greater detail the effects of environmental protection on development factors, even in the face of (sometimes substantial) research obstacles.

Final Thoughts

Throughout the world, cost-benefit analysis of environmental policy is taking hold. When making environmental policy, governments face hard choices. Inaction, which allows environmental threats to fester, imposes large costs on the public. When selecting the stringency and form of environmental protections, governments must trade off the value of increased public health and natural resource preservation against a range of other social priorities. There is no easy way to make these choices. But cost-benefit analysis can present decision makers with extremely important information about how public policy will affect society, and how affected communities value those changes—both positive and negative. With that information in hand, decision makers are better equipped to make sound choices that maximize social well-being.

Cost-benefit analysis is likely to evolve as it spreads to new decision-making contexts and is used to examine new problems. The challenges posed during this process, if answered properly, can help forge the methodology into a more robust, inclusive, and accurate tool. Through research and innovation, cost-benefit analysis can be improved to better inform the next generation of policy choices.

For governments shouldering the burden of making responsible decisions for current and future generations, cost-benefit analysis poses both an opportunity and a challenge to do better. By increasing transparency and participation in the regulatory process, governments can ensure they have access to the best possible information. By subjecting choices to rigorous analysis, they can improve the consistency, coherence, and rationality of their decisions. By committing to maximize net benefits for society, they can give equal weight and value to the interests of all affected groups. These are the challenges that cost-benefit analysis poses to decision makers. If governments take advantage of the opportunities and take up the challenges presented by the global spread of cost-benefit analysis, people around the world, now and in the future, have much to gain.

Notes

1. U.S. Environmental Protection Agency, New York City Filtration Avoidance Determination (2007).

Bibliography

Adler, Matthew D., and Eric A. Posner. 2006. *New Foundations of Cost-Benefit Analysis.* Cambridge: Harvard University Press.

Aldred, Jonathan. 1994. "Existence Value, Welfare, and Altruism." *Environmental Values* 3 (4): 381–402.

Arrow, Kenneth J., Robert M. Solow, Paul R. Portney, Edward E. Leamer, Roy Radner, and Howard Schuman. 1993. "Report of the NOAA Panel on Contingent Valuation." *Federal Register* 58 (10): 4602–14.

Blakemore, Arthur, and Berthold Herrendorf. 2009. *Economic Growth: The Importance of Education and Technological Development.* Tempe: Arizona State University.

Boyle, Alan. 2007. "Human Rights or Environmental Rights? A Reassessment." *Fordham Environmental Law Review* 18 (3): 471–511.

Ellerman, A. Denny, Paul L. Joskow, Richard Schmalensee, Juan-Pablo Montero, and Elizabeth M. Bailey. 2000. *Markets for Clean Air: The U.S. Acid Rain Program.* Cambridge: Cambridge University Press.

European Commission. 2009. *Impact Assessment Guidelines.* SEC (2009) 92. Brussels: European Commission.

Fullerton, Don. 2006. *The Economics of Pollution Havens.* Cheltenham: Edward Elgar.

Gürlük, Serkan, and Erkan Rehber. 2008. "A Travel Cost Study to Estimate Recreational Value for a Bird Refuge at Lake Manyas, Turkey." *Journal of Environmental Management* 88: 1350–60.

Hahn, Robert W. 1998. "State and Federal Regulatory Reform: A Comparative Analysis." Working Paper No. 98–03, AEI-Brookings Joint Center for Regulatory Studies, Washington, D.C.

Hammitt, James K., and Ying Zhou. 2006. "The Economic Value of Air-Pollution-Related Health Risks in China: A Contingent Valuation Study." *Environmental & Resource Economics* 33 (3): 399–423.

Maddison, Angus. 2001. *The World Economy: A Millennial Perspective*. Paris: OECD.

Millennium Ecosystem Assessment (MEA). 2005. *Ecosystems and Human Well-being: Synthesis*. Washington, D.C.: Island Press.

Nelson, Richard R., and Edmund S. Phelps. 1966. "Investment in Humans, Technological Diffusion, and Economic Growth." *American Economic Review* 56 (1–2): 69–75.

Organisation for Economic Co-operation and Development (OECD). 2008. *Building an Institutional Framework for Regulatory Impact Analysis: Guidance for Policy Makers*. Paris: OECD.

Porter, Michel E., and Class van der Linde. 1995. "Toward a New Conception of the Environment-Competitiveness Relationship." *Journal of Economic Perspectives* 9 (4): 97–118.

Ricketts, Taylor H., Gretchen C. Daily, Paul R. Ehrlich, and Charles D. Michener. 2004. "Economic Value of Tropical Forest to Coffee Production." *Proceedings of the National Academy of Sciences of the United States of America* 101 (34): 12579–82.

Romer, Paul M. 1990. "Endogenous Technological Change." *Journal of Political Economy* 98 (5): S71–S102.

Schwartz, Jason A. 2010. *52 Experiments with Regulatory Review: The Political and Economic Inputs into State Rulemaking*. Institute for Policy Integrity Report No. 6. New York: IPI.

Soto, Hernando de. 2000. *The Mystery Of Capital: Why Capitalism Triumphs in the West and Fails Everywhere Else*. New York: Basic Books.

US-China Joint Economic Research Group. 2007. *US-China Joint Economic Study: Economic Analyses of Energy Saving and Pollution Abatement Policies for the Electric Power Sectors of China and the United States*. Washington, D.C.: EPA.

U.S. Environmental Protection Agency (EPA). 2010. *Guidelines for Preparing Economic Analyses*. Report EPA 240-R-10–001. Washington, D.C.: EPA.

U.S. Office of Management and Budget (OMB). 2009. *Report to Congress on the Benefits and Costs of Federal Regulations and Unfunded Mandates on State, Local, and Tribal Entities*. Washington, D.C.: OMB.

U.S. Office of Management and Budget (OMB). 2011. *Report to Congress on the Benefits and Costs of Federal Regulations and Unfunded Mandates on State, Local, and Tribal Entities*. Washington, D.C.: OMB.

World Bank. 2007. *World Development Report 2008: Agriculture for Development*. Washington, D.C.: World Bank.

Zimmerman, Erika M. 2005. "Valuing Traditional Ecological Knowledge: Incorporating the Experiences of Indigenous People into Global Climate Change Policies." *New York University Environmental Law Journal* 13: 803–47.

INDEX

3C (communities, commerce, conservation) approach, 294

ability to pay *vs.* willingness to pay, 26
academia's global community of scholars, capacity-building for complex environmental policy assessments, 309, 310
accountability. *See* transparency and accountability in decision making
acid rain in South Africa, 180, 182
Administrative Burdens Board (Netherlands), 126, 127
Administrative Evaluation Bureau (Japan), 126, 127
Administrative Procedure Act of 1946, 130
AES Changuinola S.A., 280, 285
Africa
    air pollution in Liberia. *See* Liberia
    air pollution in South Africa. *See* South Africa
    Middle East and North Africa (MENA), 142–158
    valuing health risks in sub-Saharan Africa, 35–46
agriculture, 21, 22, 315
    cattle, environmental effects on, 210, 229, 270
    in Brazil, 210
    in China, 251–261, 263, 264
    in India, 267, 270, 273
    in Liberia, 294, 297, 298, 300, 303
    in Panama, 283
    in Taiwan, 94
    in Thailand's ecologically fragile areas. *See* Thailand
    and need for irrigation, 236, 237, 251–261, 263, 264
    non-land-based employment opportunities, 243, 257, 260
    slash-and-burn agriculture, 236, 294, 297
air pollution, 7, 10, 31, 42, 77
    asthma, 200, 203, 206
    benefit-transfer framework to estimate value of reducing mortality risks, 35–46
    Brazil's greenhouse gas emissions reduction. *See* Brazil
    goods related to transportation, 61
    Mexico, air pollution in. *See* Mexico

    Singapore, air pollution in. *See* Singapore
    South Africa, air pollution in. *See* South Africa
    WHO-AQGs (WHO air quality guidelines), 198, 199
Almirante, Panama, 283
Amazon region, 20
    See also Brazil
Amistad Biosphere Reserve, 282
Amistad International Park (PILA), 282, 284
ANAM (Autoridad Nacional del Ambiente), 279
Arab countries, 9, 142, 143
    See also Middle East and North Africa
ASEP (National Public Services Authority), 282
asthma, 200, 203, 206
audience, simplicity of communications for, 8, 93, 98, 100
auditors, regulatory oversight by, 124
Australia, 58, 59, 108, 111, 126, 127
authoritarian states, 78, 88, 90, 94, 100, 102, 142
Autoridad Nacional del Ambiente (Panama), 279
averted/avoided costs, 32, 34

Ban Huey Ha, 237
Ban Pa Kluay, 236, 237
Basa Njengo Magogo project, 185, 186
Belo Monte hydroelectric complex, 227, 228
benefits transfer, 31–46, 312, 313
    abatement of health hazards, 31–46
    air pollution mortality risks, 35–46
    averted costs, 32
    avoided costs, 34
    "break-even" VSL, 40
    changing relationship between extrapolated VSL and estimates of future income and consumption, 40
    disability-adjusted life-years (DALYs), 32–34
    explained, 31
    health-adjusted life-years, 32–34
    health risk reductions in low-income countries, 35–46
    human capital approach, 32, 34
    illness, cost of, 34
    income elasticity, 38–41
    income in exchange for risk reduction, 31–46
    joy and satisfaction of living, value of, 39
    lifetime income and consumption, 39, 40

Printed in the USA/Agawam, MA
December 13, 2013

583052.067